Advances in
Psychotherapy
of the
Borderline
Patient

Advances in Psychotherapy of the Borderline Patient

edited by
Joseph LeBoit
and
Attilio Capponi, Ph.D.

New York • Jason Aronson • London

Preface

The borderline syndrome is an area of psychoanalysis fraught with controversy concerning its definition and extent, the theory of its origin and development, and, most particularly, the methods of treatment of the syndrome. Within this area the entire subject of the validity and nature of modifications in technique comes into question.

This book presents recent advances in thinking on psychoanalytic theory and treatment technique concerning the borderline and narcissistic conditions, and aims to go beyond the already existing familiar and substantial literature on these subjects. Distinguished psychoanalysis from America and abroad, whose names are associated with innovative work on the psychoanalysis of borderline, narcissistic, and schizophrenic patients are represented by papers in this book. Some of the papers were presented at the New York Conference on the Borderline Disorders sponsored by the Advanced Institute for Analytic Psychotherapy.

We wish to give special thanks to Mollie LeBoit, M.S.W., for her valuable editorial suggestions, to Joan Langs, M.S.W., for her perceptive and critical judgment in the execution of this endeavor, and to John Simmons for his sensitive editing of the manuscript.

Joseph LeBoit
Attilio Capponi, Ph.D.

Contents

Part I

Concept of the

Borderline Patient

Chapter 1

The Technical Problem with the Borderline Patient

Joseph LeBoit

The Ubiquitous Borderline Patient

The borderline individual has performed a valuable service for psychoanalysis in compelling a reassessment of classical analytic technique. The frequent appearance of this difficult patient has repeatedly demonstrated the inadequacy of the standard procedure, originally designed for the cure of neurosis, as a vehicle for the treatment of the borderline condition. The challenge thus presented to the technical process itself, together with an inquiry as to what can be done for the borderline individual and how it is to be done, has stimulated a polemical consideration of these problems within psychoanalysis.

The views of psychoanalysts regarding borderline pathology remain divergent, as do the approaches to technique derived from them. This chapter, a positional statement, in addition to offering a particular viewpoint on the subject, also presents observations on selected writings of the authors in this book relevant to the technical problem. In this regard, I will indicate what I consider some of the strengths and limitations of traditional technique, and the directions being pursued by innovative psychoanalysts whose techniques with the borderline are breaking new ground. The methods they employ, their theoretical justification, and the implications these methods have for psychoanalysis are vividly described by the authors themselves.

Prior to 1950 a small number of courageous men and women in the United States were working intensively in psychoanalysis with borderline and schizophrenic patients, even though others at the time tended to declare such individuals unsuitable for psycho-analysis. Borderline patients were also being treated by psycho-therapies which followed psychoanalytic principles but lacked the rigorous procedural discipline of psychoanalysis. In England and elsewhere analysts were treating borderline patients using or adapting Melanie Klein's concepts. It came about that those using the standard procedure, those deviating from it, as well as those following a divergent theoretical orientation were all achieving some therapeutic success with borderline patients. This paradox—positive results with borderline patients obtained by a number of different approaches—presented a formidable prob-lem for psychoanalysis.

With the widening scope of psychoanalysis the analytic treat-ment of the borderline condition has become more common-place. Currently, many clinicians who work intensively with borderline patients are soon convinced that modifications in technique are required, because a large number of borderline individuals seem incapable of tolerating the deprivation required by the classical method.

Description of the Borderline

An air of mystery surrounds the concept and definition of the borderline condition, which remains no less incomprehensible when the indefinite origins of the concept and the varied and imprecise attempts at definition are considered. The mistiness arises because, in actuality, the term "borderline" is not a clear diagnostic entity, but a descriptive title for a rather broad category of individuals with arrest in psychic development. The diagnosis of borderline is not made from a clear and defined set of symptoms, as with a phobia or hysteria, but in some cases only after a period of treatment during which mental phenomena such as splitting and denial make themselves felt in the transference. If, at one end of the spectrum, the distinction between the character disorder and the borderline condition is difficult, the distinction between the borderline condition and schizophrenia at the other end is at times even more difficult.

The borderline condition lies on a continuum between neurosis and psychosis, and encompasses conditions which range from the more severe character disorders through latent schizophrenia. The class of patients termed borderline are nonpsychotic character disorders who suffer from serious developmental failure, and who possess the potential for slipping into and out of psychosis. The ego of the neurotic can be said to be wrestling with the problems presented by the id, and the ego of the psychotic as one that has broken with reality and has been overwhelmed by the id. The ego of the borderline can be said to be occupied primarily with problems of a preoedipal nature centering around symbiosis and object relatedness. In his contribution to this book (chapter 5) Spotnitz suggests that the dichotomy of neurosis/psychosis is currently evolving into the trichotomy of neurosis/borderline/psychosis.

The borderline individual is one who in earliest childhood lived in a pathological symbiosis with a parent or surrogate, and repetitiously carries the effect of that early experience into his present-day object relations. Searles (1965c) characterizes the borderline individual by his ambivalence over the unremitting

choice between symbiosis and object relatedness. He considers
the borderline patient as one "who literally lives on the borderline
between autism and symbiosis on the one hand, and object
relatedness on the other. It is as if he were trying to have
gratifications of both modes of relatedness, without relinquiqi
mode . . . " (p. 640).

Agreement prevails among clinicians that both schizophrenia
and the borderline illness have their origins in the first years
of life, pre-dating the period of oedipal development with the
disease entities generally crystallizing in late adolescence or adult-
hood. The proposition that an illness with onset during infancy
flowers only decades later seems so familiar as not to appear
startling, until looked at afresh. In order to maintain this proposition a particulwithout lar assumption needs to be made, namely,
that following the pathological childhood symbiosis, the pathological relationship with one or both parents continues, so that
early developmental arrest is given little chance to be healed or
undone. A reinforcement process has to occur for the mental
representation of the parent to become solidified as a toxic
introject, as otherwise the early pathological introject would be
tempered or supplanted by a healthier one.

It could be argued that the borderline adult has carried a
schizophrenic or borderline schizophrenic illness within himself
all the years between infancy and adult life, and merely requires a
triggering mental event to allow the condition to blossom, regardless of whether reinforcement occurred outside of infancy. Such a
mental event, derived from what is objectively perceived as a
trauma, would in most cases be merely a dramatic precipitate of
the person's ongoing relationship and the manner in which he
conducts himself. In the parent-child interaction, it is the parent
who wields the decisive influence that affects the child's emotional life and psychic structure. The alternative of continuous or
reinforced psychic trauma explains the greater number of phe-

nomena and includes the possibility that allows for therapeutic change.

A facet of the borderline concept, indispensable for its comprehension, is the unequal development of parts of the ego in mental life, paralleling the unequal development of diverse aspects of behavior—intellectual, emotional, sexual, and social. It is this nature of the unequal development of different parts or aspects of the ego that produces a wide variety of character types in the borderline personality. For example, the borderline individual may be a schizoid, paranoid, narcissistic, inadequate, or impulse ridden character. Most times he exists not as a pure nosological entity, but as a mixed type with a selection from a kaleidoscope of symptoms, the content of which is often insufficient to account for either the intensity of the anxiety or the degree of impairment.

The unequal development of parts of the ego allows some borderline individuals to function at a good intellectual level and yet be close to emotional breakdown, and for some to function sexually and at the same time have the utmost difficulty in relation to love objects. If, descriptively, psychic disturbance is seen as rooted in fixations and regressions of the ego, the borderline condition can be described as one in which part of the mental life may have reached the sexual or oedipal level, with the major portion fixated at the level of narcissism or symbiosis.

Modifications Required for the Borderline

With the borderline patient, the question is no longer whether he is to be treated by the standard technique, but rather what modifications of this procedure hasten and insure the curative process. The technical problem then is to determine which variations are of general psychoanalytic use.

The standard technique requires the patient to associate freely and enforces a transference regression culminating in the development of a transference neurosis, which is then resolved by interpretation alone. According to the classical viewpoint, for treatment to be considered psychoanalysis it must be carried out by the standard procedure without modification if possible. If a variation in technique or "parameter" is to be used, it needs to be analyzed and the analyst to return as soon as possible to the standard procedure (Eissler 1953).

This viewpoint gives a shading to Freud's rule of abstinence which perhaps was not intended by him, namely, that the analytic situation should be bereft of gratification for the patient. Modifications in technique are disapproved of because, in using them, the analyst supposedly is not adhering to the rule of abstinence. He is gratifying the patient rather than providing him with insight and, in this way, is furthering the curative process by love rather than by understanding. Freud (1915) was more generous in this matter, indicating that close consideration needs to be given to defining the limits of application of the principle of carrying through the treatment in a state of renunciation. He stated: "The treatment must be carried out in abstinence. By this I do not mean physical abstinence alone, nor yet the deprivation of everything that the patient desires, for perhaps no sick person could tolerate this . . . " (p. 165).

On the issue of whether the use of a procedural modification in and of itself converts psychoanalysis into psychotherapy, Freud (1914) indicated that it may not be necessary to abandon psychoanalysis in adopting suitable modifications. He said:

It may thus be said that the theory of psycho-analysis is an attempt to account for two striking and unexpected facts of observation . . . the facts of transference and resistance. Any line of investigation which recognizes these two facts and takes them as a starting-point of its work has a right to call itself psycho-analysis . . . [p. 16].

Accordingly, the use of a modification in itself does not necessarily convert psychoanalysis into psychotherapy. If, by using a variation in technique, the analyst brings about inner structural change by resolving resistances and dealing with the issues of the transference, then he can be said to be employing psychoanalysis.

Although a number of institutionalized differences between psychoanalysis and psychotherapy exist, such as the use or nonuse of the couch, daily visits or visits of lesser frequency, these technical differences are not the critical ones. There is little doubt that more frequent sessions and use of the couch are often desirable. Nevertheless, the crucial difference between the two procedures lies not in analytic rituals but becomes manifest in the process itself. In psychotherapy, actual events reported by the patient are looked upon by the analyst as realities and treated that way. In psychoanalysis, the content and structure of the patient's verbal productions in the analytic session are considered to be derivatives of the unconscious, similar to the manifest contents of a dream, and are treated that way (Tarachow 1962).

As psychoanalysts began to employ modifications in the treatment of borderline conditions, it became customary for them to label their efforts analytic psychotherapy, inadvertently promoting the attendant belief that most borderline patients, as well as a high proportion of others, need to be treated by psychotherapy rather than by psychoanalysis.

The Curative Process

Since Freud was primarily concerned with discovering the lawful operation of mental processes, he gave preference to psychoanalysis as a scientific investigative procedure over psychoanalysis as a method of cure. Subordinated to his concern with the theory of intrapsychic mental life, the study of the process of cure was, nonetheless, closely linked to it. In practice, the process of cure behaved otherwise, seeming at times to break the linkage to lead an unpredictable and independent life. Perhaps it was this elusive quality of the process of cure in contrast to the orderliness of scientific thought that among other reasons prompted Freud (1937) to declare that

> In this field the interest of analysts seems to me to be quite wrongly directed. Instead of an enquiry into how a cure by analysis comes about (a matter which has been sufficiently elucidated) the question should be asked of what are the obstacles that stand in the way of such a cure [p. 221].

There is an irresistible logic that if in theory the obstacles to cure could be identified, and in practice these same obstacles removed, the problem of what constitutes the process of cure would be less troublesome. But the obstacles are not so obliging. Even though we are able to identify them in the spectacularly varied resistances, we are often left with the problem of how to resolve them, because interpretation at times proves to be an unsatisfactory vehicle for that purpose with the borderline patient, particularly in the initial phase of treatment.

Aware of the dialectical interplay between psychoanalytic theory and practice, and of the contradictory nature of a science of the process of cure with attendant failures in practice, Freud (1937) deemed it necessary to explain this contradiction. He stated that

> we may say that analysis, in claiming to cure neuroses by ensuring control over instinct, is always right in theory but not always right in practice. And this is because it does not always succeed in ensuring to a sufficient degree the foundations on which a control of instinct is based [p. 229].

In general, lack of success in the treatment of neuroses was attributed to two fundamental causes, namely, to a greater strength of the instincts as opposed to a lesser strength of the ego, and to the personal characteristics of the analyst. In the first instance, an inability to split off and maintain a steady and dependable observing ego renders a working alliance inoperable. In the latter instance, countertransference problems in the analyst vitiate the treatment.

In work with the borderline patient, two additional significant causes for failure can be offered: incomplete theoretical understanding of borderline dynamics, and a resistance to departing from the standard procedure. To a degree, in emphasizing the oedipal family triangle psychoanalysis was less focused on family relations of the preoedipal period, so important in understanding the pathology of the borderline character, which has its roots in the years antedating the oedipal struggle.

History of Procedural Change

The practice of psychoanalysis today is not the same as it was fifty years ago, nor will it be the same fifty years from now. In its formative years, each advance in psychoanalysis occasioned a corresponding advance in procedural technique, as the mutual relation between theory and practice dictates. Yet, institutional psychoanalysis since Freud has tended to be slow in absorbing theoretical and procedural change in spite of a prior history of such change. During his lifetime, Freud did not hesitate to introduce changes in technique to parallel changes in theory, with the new techniques enriching the psychoanalytic arsenal. These procedural changes roughly followed four periods of psycho-analytic development, identified with the seriate studies of the id, the ego, the superego, and the analytic frame.

Interpretation, the Fundamental
Psychoanalytic Technique

In the inaugural period of psychoanalysis, as it evolved from the application of the hypnotic method to hysteria, the curative process employed free association (the patient says everything that comes to mind), abreaction (catharsis through releasing anxiety), and interpretation (making the unconscious conscious), strategies which became the building blocks of the standard technique. At first, analytic procedure would have the patient recall the memories of the repressed sexual conflicts in order to enable the analyst to interpret the connections between the repressed and the sexual origin of the symptoms.

With the development of the structural theory, attention shifted from the study of the drives to the barriers against them, that is, to the characteristic defense functions and resistances of the ego with a corresponding change in the content of interpretation. Resistance interpretation became the order of the day. This change was soon followed by a further refinement in the technique of interpretation which limits the analyst's interventions as far as possible to interpretation of the transference. These are considered "mutative," effective in overcoming resistance to change since they are applied at the point of urgency in the here and now and rendered emotionally immediate.

With regard to the stress often placed on the interpretation of resistances, Strachey (1969) indicates that they arise in relation to the analyst and, therefore, the interpretation of a resistance will almost inevitably be, or lead to, a transference interpretation and could be phrased as one. Although attributing special qualities to the transference interpretation, Strachey does not maintain that no others should be made. On the contrary, he considers extra-transference interpretations important in a practical sense because they act as feeders paving the way for the "mutative" transference interpretation.

Although not adopted by all psychoanalysts, Strachey's recommendation reflected a dramatic shift in interest from the functions of the other mental agencies to those of the superego. The awakened interest in the functions of the superego as the repository of the parental introjects grew out of several simultaneous developments: Melanie Klein's child analysis (1932), the work of the object relations theorists Fairbairn, Guntrip, Winnicott, and others of the British school. The emergence of Kleinian technique in which all communications by the patient and his behavior in treatment are conceptualized and interpreted as transference of infantile feelings represented a further procedural change.

Originally psychoanalysis divided the neuroses into transference neuroses and narcissistic neuroses, creating a distinction congruent with the usual one between neurosis and psychosis. The theoretical assumptions posited then were neat but imperfect from the vantage point of today's understanding. The neuroses were considered analyzable by the standard technique because with them an object transference could be established, and the psychoses not analyzable because an object transference was supposedly not possible. Theoretically, the classicist considers that, while in the transference neuroses the warded-off impulses related to objects seek expression in the transference, in the narcissistic neuroses (psychoses) the potential for object transference is eliminated because of the regression of psychotics to a phase supposedly prior to a connection with objects. This distinction cannot be said to be absolute for either group. With neurotic character disorders and borderline individuals there can theoretically exist a psychotic core. Although proclivities of each in that direction differ, some have the potential for psychotic breakdown. On the other hand, with psychotics, object representations, however distorted, do exist, together with an ambivalent longing for their fuller reestablishment.

he borderline individual is neither neurotic nor psychotic, but something in between, with fixations and repressions linked to both object oriented and preobject (narcissistically) oriented phases of psychic development. In the past fifty years our knowledge of the structure of the ego has been enriched so that we now believe the more severe defects in ego development occur during the preoedipal and preverbal periods. We are also more attentive to how important a part the parental introjects, good and bad, play in ego and superego formation. New developments in technique adapted to these changes in knowledge now allow for greater mastery of the ego over those areas in which it suffered defeat in the first months of life.

The Frame or Analytic Setting

One of the significant current concerns is with the frame or analytic setting, and the role of the analyst within it, an interest which arose as a result of the extension of psychoanalysis to new classes of patients such as the borderline personality. Included within the frame, in addition to the role of the analyst, is the atmosphere of the setting, the analytic contract, the ground rules, time and money arrangements, and other constants of the technique.

One of the strongest exponents of the need for maintaining a steady frame, Langs (1976) has demonstrated that breaks in the frame lead to changes of a negative character in the patient's unconscious, evidenced in pathological regression and increased resistance. For Langs the analytic situation is an interactional process within a bipersonal field, with the roles of projective and introjective identification as significant factors. The management of the ground rules constitutes a crucial dimension of the analytic situation, as their mismanagement gives rise to the patient's introjective identification of the analyst's pathological projective identifications. What is most primitive (the nondifferentiation) repeats itself in the frame. Bleger (1967) regards the function of the frame as the fusion of the ego, the body, and the external world, upon whose immobility depend the formation and differentiation of ego, object, and world.

There appears to be little doubt that what is primitive is evoked by the frame, and if it is not grossly violated, the frame elicits a reproduction of the early symbiotic relation of mother and child. Out of this analytic symbiosis the patient's ego develops in a similar way to that in which the ego of the child was built in the original symbiosis with the mother.

The borderline patient brings his own frame in opposition to that of the analyst. Often an "actor outer," the borderline patient will try, under the impetus of the repetition compulsion, to install his frame over that of the analyst, which is his way of establishing a repetition of his prior symbiotic tie to his mother's ego. Bleger says that the analyst must not hinder, but rather help to establish a similar symbiosis, in order to change it. The analyst accepts the frame the patient brings but does not abandon his own. On an emotional level, this paradigm replicates the physical process of weaning.

In confining the patient's behavior to its institutional requirements, the frame operates in setting the limits of the patient's body image, and helps define his ego and his identity. The frame functions in defining identity because within it the analyst sets controls over the other's "acting in" behavior. It functions as the embodiment of the limit-setting of the "good" parent, helping to define the patient's ego boundaries. Maintaining the frame reverses the treatment the borderline individual received in early childhood when he was the victim of inadequate boundary setting in which parental controls were pathologically inconsistent, grossly ineffectual, or missing.

The borderline patient is one who usually experienced a mother-child or father-child relationship in early life in which his sense of identity became impaired by the parent's inability to allow him to establish his own ego boundaries and sense of self. Too loving, too protective, too volatile, or otherwise too intrusive, the parent continually injected himself or herself into the child's ego, interfering with the natural development of autonomy. From such faulty rearing, the patient develops identifications with pathological parental introjects which manifest themselves in an inability to perceive the healthy limits of his own as well as other people's activities. As a consequence, he intrudes into the ego activity of others and allows and indirectly encourages intrusion into his own (Hoedemaker 1960).

The Treatment Paradox

We now arrive at a core treatment problem. How is it possible to have a modification in technique and to maintain a steady frame at the same time? If the assumption is made that the frame must at all times remain fixed for all analysts and all patients, then it is not possible to bring about agreement between the two opposing notions of a steady frame and the use of modifications.

Winnicott (1960) has called our attention to the importance of a secure "hold" in the analytic situation in its similitude to the hold of the infant by the good parent. The psychic hold on the infant can vary and still remain secure in the sense that the physical holds of the pediatrician, nurse, mother, and father are not the same. As a baby grows, the mother's own hold relaxes and the infant, with his adaptive capacity, accommodates to the changing hold so long as it remains secure.

With the borderline patient, the attainment of a steady frame is a developmental process, so that a deviation utilized by the analyst at the outset of treatment may not be employed later on, except during a period of radical regression. The steady frame is an ideal, maintained as a conscious goal toward which the analyst strives. The modification is the strategy adopted in order to bring the borderline patient into the analytic situation to which he otherwise might be immune or from which he might flee. During the course of analysis, the relation of the analyst to the borderline patient is not fixed but undergoes change. At the outset of treatment the analyst allows the symbiosis to develop. With the borderline patient this step may require the analyst to forgo his customary use of interpretation and prompt him to find other ways of relating to the patient both verbally and nonverbally. Later, with the symbiosis established, the analyst can offer occasional interpretations, although he may be talking less than previously and making more use of silences.

In speaking of a modification, the concern is not with the type of break in the frame that results from the analyst's inexperience or from his countertransference difficulties, but rather with a deliberate psychoanalytic strategy. The relation of such a modification to the frame is a dialectical one, with the frame and the necessary modification as opposites, from the unity of which emerges a fitting analytic strategy for the treatment of the borderline patient.

Qualities of a Modification

Irrespective of the methods adopted in the early stages of an analysis, the later ones are destined to be occupied with interpretation as it becomes the instrument through which insight is facilitated. Interpretive statements can be introduced early to good effect at times with the borderline patient. However, interpretations offered in the early stages tend to emphasize the separateness of the analyst's identity and to establish him as a person different from the patient, interfering with the unfolding of the analytic symbiosis. For many patients, interpretations at that stage will do neither much good nor too much harm, as the poorly developed ego of the borderline patient, the intensity of his anxiety, and his increased defensiveness render it difficult for him to take in what is said.

The first criterion for the use of a modification is the failure of interpretation. Under special conditions and employed in particular ways with the borderline patient, interpretation may work and can be the method of choice. When interpretation proves ineffective or injurious to the process of cure, something else is needed. It is then that the use of a tested modification rather than established procedure becomes justified as a therapeutic instrument. A procedural variation of value possesses certain intrinsic qualities of structure, transferability, and theoretical soundness. A desirable modification is not fortuitous, and is generally planned. It needs to be transferable and capable of use by others than its originator, possessing the potential for theoretical justification within the general framework of psychoanalysis.

Procedural changes are either of a limited character, designed to work best with a particular aspect of personality or personality type, or are of a broader nature designed to be generally applicable to the borderline patient. An example of the former is the method employed by Annie Reich (1958) with the impulse-ridden personality, and examples of the latter are the use of induced countertransference feelings by Searles (1965b) to inform the patient of what the analyst experiences in the interaction, and the joining techniques employed by Spotnitz in resolving resistance. These departures from the standard technique extend the range of analytic technique, and in so doing, exercise a profound effect upon the conduct of psychoanalysis.

Analysis of the Introject

An example of a special variation of technique of limited nature is the one employed by A. Reich (1958) which had for its purpose bolstering the weak ego of an impulse-ridden, acting-out hysterical borderline character. With such borderline person- alities, the acting out and acting in threatens the treatment. The ego disturbance, a secondary effect of a relentless superego, results in outbursts of libidinal and aggressive impulses, followed by anxiety and guilt. These borderline characters seem to be casting the analyst in the role of a primitive persecutory superego. This pathology is rooted in the soil of premature demands made by an overstrict and forbidding parent, either mother or father, who assists in producing an introject in the form of a faulty persecutory superego in the child, which interferes, then and later, with instinctual strivings and object relations.

Annie Reich describes a borderline woman whose dominating, overstrict, and quietly intrusive mother imposed herself upon the patient as a saint. The patient, an inadequate and hysterical woman unable to do much on her own, looked to her parental figures—husband, mother, and analyst—whom she endowed with omniscience, to tell her what to do and what to say. To carry the analysis foreword, Reich felt it necessary to "demask" the mother's omnipotence and saintliness by putting together for the patient fragments of information she had about the mother and articulating value judgments about her. As a result, the patient was able and less afraid to see her mother more clearly and take a step towards individuation.

In cases of this type, characterized by an intolerant but insuffi- ciently internalized superego, a careful and judicious attack upon the superego pathology is often helpful. Dismantling a patholog- ical superego, however, cannot be undertaken prematurely, as the attack upon the introject shakes the central column supporting the borderline's emotional edifice. The patient can tolerate criti- cism of the symbiotic parent only when, as a result of the transference, he is fully ready to accept the analyst as a new object of identification. Taking a stand against the borderline's pathological introject, as described above, puts the analyst on the side of reality, and at the same time introduces a parameter. In the open expression of his values the analyst is departing from the requirement of constant adherence to the concept of neutrality.

In practice, so many gross violations of neutrality occur that the need for a maximum endeavor to maintain neutrality is advisable. Total neutrality, however, also remains only an ideal. An analyst is inwardly not neutral with regard to the psychological health of the patient. He is on the side of the healthy part of the ego, against excesses of the id, and against pathology of the superego. In the use of interpretation, these values are couched in neutral terms but are nonetheless communicated to the patient.

With the borderline patient, the issue of neutrality is rather one of how much neutrality the analyst maintains. Inwardly the analyst is also not neutral about whether the patient adheres to the rules of the analytic setting, nor about the patient's acting-in behavior. The question arises as to whether interpretation and further interpretation of the patient's acting in should be the farthest extent of the therapist's verbalizations when the series of interpretations proves futile, as well may happen with a negativistic and rebellious borderline character. At times, clear and simple insistence that the patient follow the rules and stop his acting-in behavior can be the limit-setting required to help secure the inner structural boundaries which the borderline character lacks.

Harold Searles and Therapeutic Symbiosis

Many now who treat borderline patients consider that an initial period of symbiosis is wanted as a prerequisite to uncovering the repressed narcissistic fantasies. Searles (1965a), whose research has prompted creative and highly original contributions to analytic theory and technique, twenty years ago introduced the term "therapeutic symbiosis." He credited Balint, Benedek, and

Mahler with championing childhood symbiotic relatedness as natural and necessary to early infancy, and declared that similarly "such a relatedness constitutes a necessary phase in psychoanalysis or psychotherapy with either neurotic or psychotic patients respectively . . . " (p. 308).

In the therapeutic symbiosis, the patient obtains gratification of his dependency needs indirectly on a symbolic level, and through that process regains missing parts of himself. The key to this therapeutic strategy is the handling of the frustration-gratification continuum. As far as possible, direct gratification of dependency needs is avoided as the analyst rather helps the patient express the needs as fully as he can. Because of the vestiges of his own early symbiotic ties, a constant force acts upon the analyst to gratify the patient's dependency needs. This tendency interferes with the exploration and understanding of the dependency needs and accounts for a goodly number of countertransference errors as well. Searles indicates that the unconscious gratification that the analyst receives in the symbiosis also makes him reluctant to relinquish it despite the knowledge that its resolution has to be achieved for separation and individuation to occur.

Sharing Induced Feelings

Not least among the many contributions that Searles made to psychoanalytic technique, which modify and add to it, is his use of countertransference as a therapeutic tool. He views fluctuation in the sense of identity within the analyst as the most important source of information about the patient. Paula Heimann, among others, emphasizes how much the analyst can learn about the patient from discerning his own feelings in the analytic relationship. Searles demonstrates the therapeutic importance of openly allowing the patient to see such feelings. Sharing information about the analyst's feelings in the therapeutic interaction with the patient is a transaction which reaches the patient on a primitive emotional level. By contrast, interpretations of the patient's verbal productions, primarily based on cognitive understanding, infrequently provide the impact obtained by the sharing of information on the analyst's induced countertransference feelings.

In chapter 8 of this book, "The Countertransference With the Borderline Patient," Searles confirms that much of the borderline patient's ego functioning is at a symbiotic, preindividuation level. Through access to his own unconscious the analyst becomes familiar with and conceptualizes the patient's unconscious, preverbal conflicts, and they become known to the patient in turn through the "liquidly symbiotic transference."

Transference reactions of the borderline have roots in a developmental stage prior to the interpersonal experience of whole objects. In the borderline transference Searles indicates that the analyst is cast in roles strangely different from those he encounters in working with neurotics. For example, he is not only seen as the symbiotic mother of the patient, but may even be seen as the symbiotic infant, with the odd result that the adaptive analyst accustoms himself to experiencing symbiotic dependency feelings toward the mother-patient. These strange experiences of the transference roles can be unsettling to the analyst's sense of reality and to his sense of personal identity.

A characteristic of the borderline patient is the frequent presence of intense and contradictory affects such as intense love and intense hate. Searles indicates that powerful affects of this nature can pervade an introject structure and be encapsulated within it, producing an introject with an identity of its own. As an example, domineeringness experienced in the parent will exist in the patient in a split-off, dissociated state as a largely unintegrated introject. In projecting this mental representation on the analyst, the patient comes to regard him as being an individual with a newly revealed domineeringness, or may replace him in the transference with the intimidating and domineering father.

In his paper on "Jealousy Involving an Internal Object" (chapter 9) Searles states that the analyst is accustomed to working with jealousy phenomena involving three people. By contrast, he finds that phenomena other than derivatives of the oedipal triangle constitute the more frequent jealousy phenomena with the borderline, namely, those involving merely two individuals and an internal object in one of them. Jealousy related to an internal object in the two-person situation, at the heart of much severe pathology, is considered responsible for both resistance and counter-resistance. Searles sees jealousy phenomena derived from early infant-mother relationships comprising "a more powerful source of severe psychopathology than those jealousy phenomena referable to the oedipal phase of development." Ego fragmentation, depersonalization, castration anxiety, as well as the negative therapeutic reaction are all visible in the analytic situation after prolonged work as determinants of primitive two-person jealousy phenomena.

Searles considers that an analysis of these phenomena promotes "a degree of emotional significance between analyst and patient equivalent to that which the internal object has for its possessor." Whenever appropriate occasion arises the analyst reports his own inner jealousy experiences to the patient who generally finds this response illuminating and helpful. Searles credits Melanie Klein's concept of the infant's primary envy of the mother's breast with relevance for his own formulations about jealousy of an internal object in the analytic situation. At the same time, he notes that her writings report little of what she as an analyst feels, or of instances of her becoming more aware of experiencing jealousy during a session with a patient.

Introjection of the Good Object—Lever to Recovery

A number of authors now hold the position that the process of cure with the borderline patient comes about through the introjection of a healthier object, replacing the pathological parental object. As the patient will not surrender his internal bad objects until the analyst becomes a sufficiently good ob ct for him, the success or failure of the treatment hinges upon this transposition. The introjection of the analyst as a good object, instituted in the therapeutic symbiosis, becomes the lever to reco ery. Within the analytic setting the therapeutic symbiosis provi es a corrective experience for the borderline individual, as an alternative to the pathological symbiosis of infancy and childhood. The analyst serves therein not only as a transference object, but also as a new parental model for the patient to identify with and to internalize.

I would further like to suggest that in the therapeutic symbiosis the borderline patient is cognitively aware of the existence of the analyst as a person separate from himself, although on an emotional level this distinction is absent much of the time. Unless the analyst insists on repeated interpretations to the patient which emphasize their separateness, an interchange of feeling states between analyst and patient takes place, and a narcissisticlike identification with the analyst emerges in the movement toward symbiosis.

Interpretation—A Many-Splendored Thing

The interpretive process in general, and the interpretation of the transference in particular, have long been considered cornerstones of the analytic method and the primary instruments available to effect cure. On this basic proposition most psychoanalysts agree. On the detailed aspects of interpretation with the borderline and narcissistic patient, however, as to exactly what, how much, and when to interpret, considerable divergence exists.

The psychic make-up of the borderline character contains distinct paranoid trends which in some individuals are quite strong. The borderline patient with grandiose fantasies, conveying deprecatory feelings about the self, will react adversely to interpretations in the beginning phase of the analysis and remain sensitive to them for some time. It is characteristic of this patient that when the analyst talks about his unconscious motivations he makes the inference that the analyst knows something about him which he himself does not, and the interpretation is experienced as a narcissistic blow. The borderline patient may look upon an interpretation as a criticism, a reproach, or an effort on the part of the analyst to make him feel smaller and more inadequate. To many a patient an interpretation, at best, is a deprivation which robs him of some gratifying fantasy. Interpretations concerning his behavior, gestures, and actions are often seen as value judgments, and the borderline individual reacts to them as if the analyst were telling him that he is bad, or that the analyst considers him bad.

The negative reaction to the interpretation of anxiety and rage arises from the borderline patient's identification of the analyst with his persecutory superego. He responds at those times to interpretive statements with remarks like, "Why are you attacking me?" or "I guess that you don't like me if you think that about me," or he may withdraw into a brooding silence. The more paranoid the borderline individual, the more likely is the prospect that he will perceive an interpretation as an attack, since his persecutory anxieties are quite pronounced. In recognition of the wariness, negativism, and feelings of rejection with which the borderline individual receives an interpretation, it has been recommended by some that, to be better received, an interpretation include the patient's positive effort, as well as the part which he might construe as critical.

Interpretations as Unconscious Communications

The interpretive process, basically a communication system, can be as powerful an instrument in the treatment of the borderline as it is with other patients, provided his negativism and need for symbiosis are taken into account. As a form of communication between analyst and borderline patient, interpretation is not a perfect vehicle. An interpretation, in general, does not communicate insight. Insight is the result of an internal mental restructuring that has to be arrived at as an "Aha" experience by the patient. The analyst needs to formulate consciously what his unconscious observes, and convey it to the patient at the right time and in the right dosages. What is hoped for is that with the accretion of bits of knowledge about his transference manifestations, the patient will be able to fill in gaps in his understanding.

An interpretation is composed of two distinct parts: its formulation and its communication to the patient. To formulate the interpretation the analyst attunes his unconscious to the patient's, and from this resonance and the conscious part of his ego, the analyst formulates the interpretation. He then communicates it to the patient's conscious mind from which it needs to be transmitted to his unconscious. Interpretations registering at the interface between the conscious and unconscious can be seen as exerting an influence upon repressed memories of the verbal period. It remains problematical as to how verbal interpretations influence preverbal memories in the unconscious, which were never experienced in words, and which are only remembered and repeated in action.

For an interpretation to reach the unconscious, the patient needs to be ready to receive it. For most borderline patients this readiness will not be there until a therapeutic symbiosis has been effected, operative for a time, and the individuation process begun. The analyst making an interpretation to a borderline individual cannot at all times be immediately certain what has been communicated. In addition to transference distortions of the analyst's statements, the tone in which an interpretation is given, or the emotional response induced, will often have greater significance to the patient than its cognitive content.

Divergence Concerning Transference Interpretations

When talking about interpreting the transference, not all analysts mean the same thing. Explanations offering the borderline individual suggestions about the origins of his pathology which center in the oedipal triangle and its manifestations in the transference will at best be incomplete without fastidious attention to the separation-individuation phenomena.

According to his personality and his particular school, an analyst will select different manifestations of the transference to interpret. What a classical Freudian would consider to be correct interpretation with a borderline patient might be considered less correct by a modern Freudian or Kleinian, or vice versa, making it difficult to speak of correct or incorrect interpretations but, more readily, good or poor interpretations.

Wide divergencies also exist as to frequency with which analysts make interpretations with borderline patients. At one extreme are some of the British school who interpret as frequently as possible, carrying on a steady dialogue with the patient concerning the meaning of all his verbal productions and bits of behavior. At the other extreme are those analysts who maintain silence and restrict their interventions to but one or two significant transference interpretations each session, based upon what Langs terms the "adaptive context," or upon the theme of the session.

For some analysts the unconscious content of the transference resides almost exclusively in the patient's verbal productions, and it is in the patient's words that the analyst searches for derivatives of the transference. For others, not only the patient's verbalizations but his behavior, gestures, mood, acting out and acting in become significant, seen in the therapeutic interaction as transferential reenactments of his preverbal life.

With the borderline patient it is necessary to consider the unsettling possibility that until the late phase of treatment, transference interpretations do not play the exclusive or primary curative role that they do with the neurotic. Likewise, we cannot be certain that the patient bombarded with "deep" interpretations is reacting favorably as a primary result of incorporating the cognitive content. He may respond well because he is intrigued with all these new and interesting ideas about sex and bodily functions or perhaps because he derives gratification from the analyst's activity which he views as intense interest in him. In the latter instance the act of interpreting and emotional impact of the interpretation, rather than verbal content, become the promoters of the relationship between analyst and borderline patient.

Narcissistic Transference and Symbiosis

An interesting and original contributor to the theory of treatment of the borderline character is Hyman Spotnitz, whose method is outlined in his paper, chapter 5, entitled "Psychoanalytic Technique With the Borderline Patient." His constructions have their roots in Freud's concept of narcissism, an intermediary stage in the passage from autoeroticism to object love, in which the ego takes itself as an object. The borderline individual's fixations reach into the early period when self was not yet differentiated from nonself. Spotnitz avers the continued presence in the borderline adult of that very early ego state, and of its contemporary equivalent, the capacity for narcissistic transference. Thus two modes of transference are posited—narcissistic transference, when the object is experienced as part of the self, and object transference, when the object is seen as an entity distinct from the self. Both modes of transference are manifested simultaneously or in fluid oscillation by the borderline individual.

At the outset of treatment the tilt is toward the narcissistic transference which the analyst tries not to disturb. As the narcissistic transference unfolds, the analyst allows himself to become like the patient, or become one with the patient, as did his mother in the patient's infant mind. Although it rests on a somewhat different theoretical underpinning, the result of this strategy is nonetheless akin to that which allows for the development of the therapeutic symbiosis.

Were the proponents of the therapeutic symbiosis and those of the narcissistic transference to emphasize their differences, one could still consider their aims predominantly similar. Each views the borderline individual's transference regression to a primitive developmental stage as an attempt at a fresh adaptation, with the highly differentiated ego organization of the borderline adult requiring reduction to a less differentiated stage from which a new beginning can be made.

The Negative Narcissistic Transference

Characteristic of the borderline individual are both the vast amount of repression of negative feelings and the unconscious communication of these feelings in oblique ways. Of the many hidden ways that the ego selects to deal with frustration-aggression, the most damaging and self-destructive is the one Spotnitz (1976) terms the narcissistic defense, a readily observable phenomenon in which the borderline individual turns his aggression toward the self instead of toward the parental object. To protect the love object against the discharge of aggression the ego employs the narcissistic defense of turning this hatred upon itself. To protect itself from these murderous feelings the ego takes flight into nonfeeling states or preoccupations. Avoidance and denial of the negative feelings lead to an elimination of feelings and a split in the ego of the borderline.

Sooner or later, as the narcissistic transference blossoms, the negative aspect may come to the fore in libidinal or aggressive manifestations. With the borderline patient who shows either a negativistic, belligerent, or paranoid bent, the negative transference will emerge at the outset of treatment. In the case where the negative transference is not manifest, it needs to be made so, as it has to be dealt with early. Analysts who adhere closely to the psychoanalytic model in treating the borderline patient may make it their first order of business to interpret the negative transference. The early interpretation of the negative transference is a procedure to be recommended as superior to avoiding it, yet care has to be exercised; not at all times does the early interpretation of the negative transference have good results. In some instances it leads to discouraging further expression of such feelings, confusion, or increased negativism.

Spotnitz encourages the expression of the negative transference, and deals with it neither by ignoring it, nor too often by interpreting it, but more often by employing joining techniques. Negative narcissistic transference manifestations such as primitive rage, negativism, withdrawal, and other character resistances which interfere with the patient's ability to communicate, are joined or psychologically reflected. The analyst agrees with the patient, mirrors him, and otherwise functions as far as possible as an egosyntonic object within the bounds of authenticity. These techniques require interaction between patient and therapist on an emotional level, encourage the externalization of aggression, and help the patient accept his angry feelings without acting them out.

Based on an estimation of the patient's need, a choice is made as to which resistances are to be joined. Joining techniques may be of an ego-syntonic nature, for example, when the analyst associates himself with the patient's negative view of a family member, or of an ego-dystonic nature, for example, when the analyst agrees with the patient's attack on himself. Ego-dystonic joining has as its aim the development and accentuation of the negative transference where it might otherwise remain hidden.

The Contact Function as Resistance

The negative transference resistance is fundamental to the analyst's work with the borderline patient and urges attention to his nuclear problem. Spotnitz (1969) alludes to another frequent resistance within the transference, namely, the patient's attempts to contact the analyst during sessions. These "contact functions" are studied as resistance prototypes. When the patient stops associating, asks a question of the analyst or turns to him, he is providing clues to antecedents of his resistance pattern, its origin and history, and is suggesting what techniques might be effective. Spotnitz indicates that the analyst can respond in various ways, with his choice of response determining the intensity of the narcissistic transference. Remaining silent, replying to a question with a question, joining the resistance, or interpreting the attempt at contact will all result in different intensities of the transference.

Resolution of the Narcissistic Defense

In fulfilling the analytic task of removing the obstacles to the discharge of aggression, the analyst as the patient's projected internal object will become the target for the patient's attacks over a period of time. By presenting himself as a willing target for the borderline patient's aggressive feelings, the analyst implicitly sanctions the expression of such feelings. He needs to be able to endure the repeated aggression, negativism, and verbal abuse that will come his way if the analysis is proceeding satisfactorily. Spotnitz insists that at the same time, however, limits have to be set upon unbridled raging, as repeated and unlimited raging is not helpful to the patient, and he needs to be so informed. He draws a line between therapeutically desirable verbal expressions of aggression, and utterances that merely yield sadistic gratification.

In a complementary manner, Spotnitz indicates that the analyst does not have to inhibit the expression of his own feelings, provided they do not arise from his own unconscious. The analyst must constantly endeavor to separate out the feelings objectively induced by the patient from those subjectively arising from his own unconscious. Feelings which are recognized as realistically the effect of the patient's words or behavior are not only an aid in understanding the patient, but provide the basis for communication of an emotional nature.

Ultimately, the narcissistic defense is resolved. The narcissistic transference is reduced and it becomes secondary to the object transference. Analytic treatment then proceeds as it does with a neurotic or milder character disorder.

The Narcissistic Personality

Lately, there has developed within psychoanalysis a trend to more sharply differentiate the narcissistic personality from other borderline characters, who themselves are considered by some to have their own share of narcissistic fixation or regression.

Internally, the difference between the two personality types is seen by Kernberg (1975) as one of psychic organization, for in the narcissistic personality "there is an integrated, although highly pathological, grandiose self. . . ," an organized structure not present in other borderline personalities. The grandiose self screens a hungry, infantile character with exaggerated dependency needs, considerable oral rage and envy.

In his transactions with others the narcissistic personality is characterized by a manic pursuit of gratification, an intense ambition, and a craving for recognition and applause. He strives for power and its handmaidens, wealth, omniscience, and beauty, attributes which he seeks to exploit in the service of power and acclaim. With an ability to contrive a surface social adjustment, the narcissistic individual can achieve in fields such as theatre, politics, or business, where an inflated self-concept and charismatic veneer are not detriments.

The Glass Bubble of the Narcissistic Patient

An interesting contribution to the literature on this personality type is "The 'Glass Bubble' of the Narcissistic Patient" (chapter 10) in which Vamik Volkan comments on the analysis of a handsome and highly narcissistic woman. His graphic narrative of a beautiful lady, dreams, horses, and midnight adventure is like a tale out of the Arabian Nights.

The narcissistic analysand reported upon by Volkan possessed a typical inflated, grandiose self-concept and a set of defenses consonant with primitive, internalized object relations. In discussing the object relations of preoedipal patients, Volkan (1970) threads his way through varied meanings and disparate views of narcissism. His starting point is not the classical concept of narcissism as the libidinal cathexis of the ego, but rather the psychoanalytic object relations view of narcissism as the cathexis of the self, of one's own person.

In his experience with the analysis of patients with narcissistic personality organization, Volkan often discovers an ongoing fantasy of their living in a bubble or cocoon, alone and self-sufficient. He says that when such a patient comes to analysis the fantasy is "actualized" as he places the bubble over the couch and settles back within it. Utilizing the bubble fantasy to establish psychological distance, the patient interposes a wall between himself and the analyst, and denies the analyst his customary interpretative approach.

The "Cocoon Transference"

Whereas Spotnitz divides the treatment of the borderline personality into two major phases, the first being the establishment and resolution of the narcissistic transference, and the second being the emergence and resolution of the transference neurosis, Volkan divides the analytic process of the narcissistic patient into three phases. He finds the period of the narcissistic transference itself to be composed of two distinct parts, beginning with a "cocoon" phase during which the patient acts as if encased in an impenetrable, transparent bubble, inviting the analyst to care for him without his active participation. The "cocoon" phase roughly corresponds to Kohut's (1971) "idealizing" transference in which the analyst is the "all good" mother or father-mother. For the duration of this initial phase, interpretations reaching the patient are regarded by him as intrusive and scornfully dismissed, while others fail to reach him altogether as the patient appears not to be relating emotionally to the analyst. The "cocoon" phase is followed by a symbiotic phase of the narcissistic transference which roughly corresponds to Kohut's mirror transference in which patient and analyst are alike. During this latter phase Volkan begins systematic interpretation, beginning with analysis of the patient's fantasy of living in a glass bubble which protects the grandiose self from what lies outside, and then follows with the analysis of the contents of the grandiose self.

Volkan believes that the clinical picture of the narcissistic personality centers around his failure to integrate the two aspects of his superego, namely, the good ego ideal and the persecutory superego. Contributing to this failure is the splitting of the "all good" and "all bad" self and object images. Volkan agrees with Kernberg that once the primitive splitting is mended and the resolution of the narcissistic transference is under way, a classical transference neurosis may develop. Elements of the transference neurosis may have coexisted all along with the narcissistic transference, but the transference neurosis for the most part is not analyzable until the resolution of the narcissistic transference is sufficiently advanced.

One can venture that whatever other qualities the parents of an individual with a narcissistic personality possessed, of these we can be fairly certain: a difficulty in setting limits together with a tendency to overprotect the child and to encourage the belief in him that he is someone special. It is around this feeling of "specialness" that Volkan states the grandiose self of the narcissist is constructed.

Giovacchini's Borderline Patient

In his paper, "The Many Sides of Helplessness: The Borderline Patient" (chapter 6), Giovacchini presents another type of borderline character. He offers a vivid clinical report of his analysis of a helpless, underdeveloped woman with borderline adaptation as a scaffolding for many rich theoretical ideas. For Giovacchini two characteristics define the borderline patient: (1) the ability to decompensate fairly easily into a psychotic state from which he quickly reintegrates to regain his former equilibrium, and (2) a minimal adjustment to the external world due to his lack of adaptive techniques for dealing with the complexities of reality.

In indicating the ease with which the borderline patient can slip into psychosis, Giovacchini is in agreement with most authors. However, he distinguishes the borderline individual further, as belonging to a group of patients who suffer from a specific ego defect, namely, the lack of memory traces of gratifying experiences. This structural defect is the outgrowth of not having experienced gratification in early childhood. Without adequate experience of either deprivation or satisfaction, memory traces of gratifying events are so minimal as to be virtually missing, with the result that adaptive techniques are poorly developed, and responses different from others whose infancy included frustrating and satisfying experiences.

Giovacchini concerns himself with a different group of patients dwelling in the wide borderland between neurosis and psychosis than does Kernberg (1975), who describes the borderline patient as having a stable ego organization marked, however, by the use of splitting, denial, projection, projective and introjective identification as primary mechanisms of defense, and with narcissistic elements and a tendency to act out.

The patient Giovacchini discusses was unaware of which inner needs were responsible for her enormous discomfort, and therefore unable to make them clearly known to him. At the outset of the analysis she openly displayed her neediness and helplessness, manifesting an urgent and clinging demand that the analyst do something about her sorry state. This infantile and undirected demandingness if not understood, creates a tense, disruptive atmosphere and induces a feeling of helplessness in the analyst.

The attentiveness to the meaning of the patient's words and actions, as well as to his own reactions, which Giovacchini displays in arriving at an understanding of how the patient induces the feeling of helplessness in him, is impressive. Understanding the patient through the analyst's countertransference reactions, as well as searching out and communicating the adaptive aspects of the patient's behavior to him, helps create a secure setting for a patient otherwise fearful of disintegration.

Modifications—Extra-Analytic or Not

Giovacchini (1972a) is a significant figure among the growing number of analysts who treat borderline patients primarily by interpretive means. Although he maintains an interpretive stance, he recognizes that there are occasions when special features and modifications may be required, but regards them not as variations of the analytic procedure but as necessary facets of the analytic process. Giovacchini believes that there is no need for extra-analytic factors and that much that is considered extra-analytic can be achieved by adherence to analytic principles. If in the treatment of the borderline patient one employs such cardinal psychoanalytic tenets as psychic determinism, the dynamic unconscious, developmental and genetic factors, and the resolution of the transference as the basic therapeutic instrument, then in Giovacchini's view one is employing psychoanalysis. To regard the maneuvers relevant to the treatment of the borderline not as a temporary abandonment of psychoanalytic technique but as a stronger adherence to it, as Giovacchini does, is a pragmatic verdict growing out of his experience.

Technical Contributions

In his extensive writings on the borderline personality, Giovacchini deals with many pertinent issues such as the analytic setting and the role of the analyst in an open and refreshing way, offering his conclusions nondogmatically, allowing for their further development or for disagreement with them. One of Giovacchini's (1975) technical contributions in the area of countertransference is its identification and use in the treatment process. The borderline patient will arouse in the analyst countertransference feelings of incompetence, helplessness, and rage, often accompanied by a sense of therapeutic impasse. These unwelcome feelings result from the patient's need to paralyze the analyst. Patients with paranoid trends, who blame the external world for their difficulties, will identify the analyst with it and make him the object of their vengeful attack. As they mount this attack against their pathological introjects, these patients project aspects of their self-hatred and degraded self-representations onto the analyst, impugning his competence, belittling him, and creating within the analyst feelings of helplessness and vulnerability.

Giovacchini regards this process not solely as regressive, but as an attempt at adaptation as well, and stresses its adaptational aspects. The flowering of the negative transference and the parallel feelings induced in the analyst are seen as necessary steps in the treatment of many preoedipal and borderline characters. The identification of his own uncomfortable feelings as induced countertransference feelings, enables the analyst to deal with them instead of surrendering to the spectre of impasse.

Autonomy—An Analytic Imperative

In noting the need to preserve the autonomy of the schizo-phrenic patient, Giovacchini (1972b) indicates that the patient tries to influence the analyst to intrude upon him. Parental intrusion into the ego of the child echoes in the analytic situation. Employing a variety of defenses for the purpose, the patient invites the analyst to intrude as his parents once did. Giovacchini affirms that although the patient found intrusion into his child-hood ego painful, he nevertheless seeks to repeat this grievous situation in the transference as a way of maintaining an adapta-tion to a painful reality with which his ego is familiar.

It is my view that many analytic techniques and principles, whose usefulness have been substantiated in the treatment of schizophrenic patients, are also directly applicable to a broad range of borderline conditions. Experience has confirmed, for example, that with such patients there is a greater need for the analyst's activity than with the neurotic individual. Yet a tendency persists for many analysts to adopt a passive stance at all times because of their concern that activity interferes with the atmosphere of abstinence, and also leads to intrusion upon the patient's autonomy. Activity and intrusion are not synonymous. Intrusion implies encroachment upon the will of another, and many ways exist in which the analyst can be active without imposing his will upon that of the patient or otherwise violating his autonomy.

Aloneness in the Borderline Patient

A pervasive feeling of isolation of greater or lesser intensity is the hallmark of the schizoid personality, and the subject of chapter 11 by Adler and Buie on "Aloneness in the Borderline Patient." The sense of aloneness and the fear of abandonment, growing out of a pathological symbiosis in which mother-infant caring is incomplete, are feelings strengthened in further interaction with primary objects and perpetuated throughout life in subsequent relationships. The sense of aloneness makes its reappearance in the analytic situation, where it may occasionally approach panic, in the desperate feeling that no one is there in reality to offer a positive and sustaining relationship.

Adler and Buie indicate that because of primitive idealizations of the object, the borderline patient is destined to suffer disappointments; experiencing them in the analytic situation, he becomes increasingly angry with the analyst. This anger may be evidenced by generalized and undirected upset, a feeling of increasing worthlessness with the patient attacking himself, or as rage against the analyst. The evocation of anger activates the borderline patient's vulnerability, his sense of aloneness in which he is unable to maintain images of positive experiences with significant objects, including the analyst. The authors indicate that this regression carries with it an unconscious appeal to the analyst to care for and nurture the patient. During the regression issues of basic trust, good enough mothering, and separation-individuation come to the fore, making it essential for the analyst to establish a proper hold, while gradually allowing the rage to emerge without catering to the patient's expressed or implicit demands.

Adler and Buie suggest that in order to deal effectively with the emergence of the negative transference, the therapist needs to evaluate the patient's capacity to acknowledge and tolerate his anger. Most borderline patients are afraid of their anger which they regard as murderous and capable of destroying the object. The authors believe that it may be possible to have these patients acknowledge relatively early that anger is a problem for them and frightens them. By having a label placed on the disturbing feeling, the patient gains distance from it, thus interposing some ego structure between the impulse and its expression.

The Use of Confrontation

Adler and Buie (1972) make considerable use of the technique of confrontation, particularly in countering the borderline patient's feeling of abandonment and his denial of the therapist's existence. They construe confrontation in a particular way, not as a means of trapping the patient into admitting that he is wrong and humiliating him, nor to force changes in the patient's attitudes, decisions, or conduct. They define confrontation as a supportive-analytic technique designed to gain a patient's attention to inner experiences, or to perceptions of outer reality. Confrontation is also used to counter denial and other resistances to recognizing what is available to awareness.

These authors view the borderline patient as relying on defenses of avoidance, particularly denial, distortion, and projection, and place special emphasis on his use of the mechanism of avoidance through taking action. Since acting out can be self-destructive, the authors regard confrontation as urgently required at those times when the patient feels overwhelmed or puts himself in real danger. Adler and Buie regard the psychopathology of the borderline individual to be founded on the fundamental belief that he is, or will be, abandoned. To build the patient's confidence that he will not be abandoned by the analyst requires at times the use of confrontation, an intervention designed to remove resistances to a working alliance, and to bring the patient face to face with a temporarily forgotten or ignored aspect of reality.

The "Good Enough" Therapist

Gerald Adler (1975), adapting Winnicott's concept of the "good enough" mother to the therapist of the borderline patient, indicates that the therapist needs to be empathically in touch with the patient in a way that offers him the opportunity to repair the damage done by his early experiences of inadequate mothering. The "good enough" therapist is one endowed with sufficient understanding to help the patient grow optimally, even under conditions when the patient induces in him feelings of helplessness and anger.

As a consequence of the borderline patient's overwhelming needs and his minimal capacity to modulate the intensity of demands for their fulfillment, he feels readily deprived, misunderstood, and angered. His ensuing rage produces inner disorganization and a feeling of abandonment, from which a conviction emerges that he has destroyed the image of the analyst as a good nurturing figure, and that the outside world has once again become malevolent. The "good enough" therapist is seen by

Adler as one who provides a proper "hold" to contain the patient's disturbed feelings, and whose activity goes beyond interpretation, in the form of questions, clarifications, confrontations, and definitions of therapeutic work to be done. The "good enough" therapist tries to avoid experiences for the patient which he can interpret as rejection, and allows the patient to verbalize fully his inner experiences of abandonment and rage. The borderline patient's provocations, attacks upon and devaluation of the therapist require him to possess sufficient mastery over his own sadism so that his responses are growth-producing and not retaliatory.

Adler believes that for the borderline patient therapeutic growth is dependent upon a corrective emotional experience with a consistent, nonretaliatory object whom he cannot destroy, and upon understanding his pathological processes, which prepares the way for working through higher level, preoedipal and oedipal conflicts.

The Schizoid Mode of Being

In chapter 12, "Schizoid Phenomena in the Borderline," J. H. Rey focuses on the schizoid character as the key organization of the borderline. Rey sees the central attribute of the schizoid character to be his inability to maintain warm and friendly relationships, except those of an intensely dependent nature. In his desire to penetrate into the object and fuse with it, he makes a rapid identification with the object, which evokes anxiety in the threat to the sense of identity and the integrity of the ego.

Following Melanie Klein's theoretical ideas, Rey views the schizoid personality as possessing, along with neurotic fixations and regressions, others derived from the first year of life which determine his basic ego structure. The schizoid personality is characterized by his more frequent use of the defense mechanisms of the earliest period. For Rey the crucial ones are those of projection, splitting, and denial. Projection and splitting are defenses stemming from the paranoid-schizoid period of the first three months of life before there is a relation to whole objects, and denial from the depressive period lasting from then until the end of the first year during which that relationship is being established.

Projection and Projective Identification

One may make the assumption that in the infant's drive toward symbiosis with the mother, the primitive ego evolves projective and introjective mechanisms to counter and ward off anxieties of abandonment and annihilation. In the adult schizoid's desire for symbiosis, the presence of the same projective process is implied. In the movement toward psychic fusion there is the implication that one person is, or readily can be, like another, and the perception of identity is projected. In projective identification parts of the self and internal objects are split off and projected into the external object in order to observe how the object deals with them or to possess and control the object. For example, projective identification may be directed towards a bad object to control the source of danger, as well as towards a good object to achieve symbiosis with it.

Rey indicates that the matter of identity is a major problem for the schizoid individual as it is precariously dependent on an unassimilated or split-off internal object, vulnerable to the varying state of the object. Likewise the schizoid patient projects good parts of himself into the analyst, and will become frantic at the prospect of losing him, for that loss portends the loss of elements of the self and of the good objects, and also threatens his sense of identity.

Splitting

According to Rey and the Kleinian theorists, splitting begins in the paranoid-schizoid period, the inaugural phase of the oral stage when the ego's powers of integration are still weak, as an adaptive measure which allows the budding ego to order its experiences. The infant's earliest perceptions are of part objects, a breast, a face, or a hand. Splitting then takes place between the good and bad breast, that is, at first between the good and bad part object, and only later between the good and bad whole object and the good and bad self. Splitting thus involves both the ego and the object. Depending on the direction that development takes, the process of splitting can produce either stable or pathological mental structures. In healthy development the early part objects are integrated to form a whole object as a stable structure.

Rey indicates that the schizoid individual is preambivalent, because he leads a regressive, part-object kind of life. At times one part of the object is equal to the whole, at other times, another, with neither integration nor ambivalence yet achieved. Only when two or more different characteristics of the object can be appreciated simultaneously, or two or more impulses in the subject, does ambivalence appear.

Since Freud it has been thought that splitting is a function which the ego can use either constructively to expand the scope of its activity, or pathologically as a defensive measure. The ego's constructive use of splitting is seen in the analytic situation in the simultaneous presence of observing and participating egos, and in dreams where the dreamer is both inside and outside the dream scenario projecting aspects of himself into various characters at the same time. Pathological splitting of the ego into contradictory ego states and split-off objects is a primary characteristic of the schizoid patient.

Rey indicates that the schizoid individual uses splitting intensively and repetitiously to get rid of bad parts of himself. One object, the mother, may be the good or ideal object, and the father the bad object, or the other way around, or either object may be good and bad at different times without an integration of the opposing qualities. The analyst comes to stand for the patient's internal objects as the patient projects his good and bad objects onto him. Alert to the shifts in the transference, the analyst is encouraged to make frequent transference interpretations. The Kleinian analyst, attuned to the interaction, interprets what the patient attributes to him and how the patient internalizes him. Segal states that the Kleinian analyst follows the effect of the interpretations on the patient's further material, and is generally more concerned with the to and fro of the interchange than is the case in purely classical technique.

Denial and the Manic Defense

Denial (a form of splitting) is a mechanism in which the actual affect is disavowed and a contrary one insisted upon and bulwarked. The manic defense directed against depressive anxieties functions as a denial of psychic reality.

Rey sees the role of the manic state as a defense against the anxieties of disintegration and schizoid persecution as well as against the pain of the depressive state. He elaborates on the Kleinian concepts of reparation and the manic defense. Melanie Klein defined the period during which these processes develop as the depressive position, lasting from about the fourth month to the end of the first year of life. During this time awareness of whole objects emerges, giving rise to anxiety with regard to dependence upon the object, to threat of object loss, to fear of injuring the object, to mourning, and to guilt. Against these anxieties which arise from the child's discovery of the mother's value and his dependence upon her, the manic defense is organized.

Otto Kernberg and the Borderline

Kernberg presents his method of treatment of the borderline
patient and the frame of reference for it in his paper in chapter 7.
His experience leads him to conclude that some borderline
patients respond to a nonmodified psychoanalytic procedure,
while most respond best to psychoanalytic psychotherapy carried
out on a solid basis of psychoanalytic theory and technique. His
approach is essentially an interpretive one which includes interpretation of the transference and other resistances, and in which
he maintains a position of neutrality or persistent movement
towards it.

Among the main characteristics of the "modified psychoanalytic procedure" suggested by Kernberg (1975) are: systematic
elaboration of the negative transference, followed by its "deflection" from the therapeutic interaction through its examination in
the patient's relations with others; the interpretation of the
characteristic pathological defensive operations in the negative
transference; limit-setting to block nonverbal acting out in the
transference; and a focus on those areas in the transference and
the patient's life which illustrate the expression of pathological
defensive operations as they induce ego weakening.

Where some analysts emphasize the ego defect in the borderline patient, Kernberg places his emphasis on the powerful
defensive role of what generally is considered ego weakness or ego
defect. What first appears as ego weakness Kernberg indicates is
often an inability to establish object relations, reflected in an
active defense against the emergence of intense, threatening
primitive object representations in the transference. The patient
reactivates dissociated self and object images which he projects
upon the analyst in the establishment of a primitive transference.
Kernberg sees these projected object representations as unrealistic and not a repetition of real infantile or childhood experiences,

making the analyst's tasks the detection and resolution of these primitive transference paradigms, and the eventual integration of the dissociated transference aspects into "more realistic childhood experiences."

Inasmuch as the primitive transference manifestations of the borderline patient are unreal internal relations of dissociated aspects of the self with part objects, and not a repetition of prior real experiences, Kernberg recommends that the analyst not engage in genetic reconstructions until later in the analysis when more realistic childhood experiences are reactivated in the transference.

Acting Out in the Transference

Kernberg (1975) indicates that acting out in the transference is one of the things that makes treatment of the borderline patient difficult. The transference regression of the neurotic usually can be resolved by interpretation alone. In the case of the borderline patient, however, Kernberg finds interpretation by itself insufficient to halt the acting out, particularly when that acting out is linked to an incipient transference psychosis which invariably is accompanied by a loss of ego boundaries and of the observing ego in the transference regression. The transference acting out is also highly resistant to interpretation for the reason that it gratifies the patient's instinctual needs, and Kernberg sees this gratification as the major transference resistance. To counter and help resolve this resistance and to control the acting out, he recommends the introduction of a parameter.

Splitting

The mechanism of "splitting" is considered by Kernberg (1975) as central to the psychic organization of the borderline personality. He uses the term "splitting" in a restricted sense, limiting its meaning to the active mental process of keeping apart introjections and identifications of opposite quality. Splitting, a primitive dissociation, is defined as the categoric separation of "good" and "bad" internal object representations, resulting in early life from lack of integrative capacity of the infantile ego. Later this separation is actively utilized by the ego to defend itself from anxiety. The ego's need to preserve the good self- and object images in the presence of the "all bad" self- and object images leads to subsidiary defensive operations. Together with splitting they constitute the body of defense mechanisms which Kernberg regards as characteristic of the "borderline personality organization."

Kernberg sees the treatment of the borderline syndrome therefore as directed to (1) diagnosing the areas of ego weakness; (2) evaluating the ego-weakening effect of the primitive defensive operations and of the dissociated internal object relations; and (3) fostering ego growth by essentially interpretive means.

Herbert Rosenfeld and the Borderline

Herbert Rosenfeld, an innovative proponent of Melanie Klein's theoretical position, treated psychotic and borderline patients over his lifetime, deviating as little as possible from what he terms the usual technique of psychoanalysis, that is, making detailed interpretations of the negative and positive transference from the very beginning of an analysis. When confronted with an impasse he always attempts to understand the blocking problem analytically, utilizing further transference interpretations as the sole means of prevailing over it. Rosenfeld's paper, "Difficulties in the Psychoanalytic Treatment of the Borderline Patient" (chapter 4), provides a useful classification of borderline characters and borderline states based on personality dynamics and structure rather than on symptom formation. It offers indications for technique and expectations regarding treatment development which might otherwise remain obscure.

The five groups distinguished by Rosenfeld are: (1) borderline personalities with psychotic character structures who employ psychotic mechanisms (a group with which he is very familiar); (2) the group of borderline patients described by Kernberg as having stable pathological personality organization; (3) the "as if" personalities described in detail by Helene Deutsch and Grinker; (4) borderline characters who in infancy suffered insufficient mothering and drawnout separations; and (5) borderline characters with narcissistic modes of functioning who intermix an intense need for objects with an overpowering withdrawal reaction.

In the analysis of the borderline patient, I see Rosenfeld's concern as centering about three fundamental treatment issues: pathological narcissism, the negative therapeutic reaction, and the transference psychosis. The groups defined above are delineated by varying combinations of these elements, by the quantity of pathological narcissism as well as by the strength of the tendencies toward the negative therapeutic reaction and transference psychosis.

Narcissistic Object Relations

Freud believed that the narcissistic patient, taking his own ego as an object, had no capacity for transference and was therefore not treatable by psychoanalysis. Allying himself with those authors who disagreed with that pessimistic view, Rosenfeld (1964) investigates the dynamics of the narcissistic transference and narcissistic object relations. He indicates that much confusion could be avoided if it were recognized that many clinical conditions resembling primary narcissism are in fact primitive object relations. In narcissistic object relations, omnipotence, identificaion through projection and introjection, and defense against the recognition of separateness between self and object play important parts, and such narcissistic object relations are generally experienced by the patient as ideal and desirable.

The ideal, ego-syntonic self-image of the narcissistic patient is a pathological mental structure based on his omnipotence and denial of reality and leads to a powerful resistance. Rosenfeld suggests that to the degree that the patient clings to the ideal self-image, progress in the analysis is blocked, as insight and psychic reality are experienced as dangers. In order to bring about improvement in the patient, his omnipotent narcissism and all facets of it have to be laid bare in detail.

Narcissism and Aggression

In tracing the relationship between narcissism and aggression, Rosenfeld (1971) concludes that certain omnipotent, narcissistic states are dominated by violent, destructive processes, with the result that the libidinal self can be completely submerged and appear absent or lost. These omnipotent, destructive parts of the self at times remain disguised or split off, but exercise a forceful effect in preventing adequate libidinal object relations. Clinically, Rosenfeld regards it essential to find access to the libidinal, dependent self, in order to mitigate the effect of the destructive impulses, so that a basis can be erected for a more normal symbiosis of self and object.

In general, when the narcissistic patient experiences someone separate from him and superior to him, aggressive feelings hidden by the omnipotent posture emerge. Under such conditions, envy, hidden behind the narcissistic omnipotence, comes to the surface in the transference in the form of aggression. Rosenfeld's therapeutic method includes dealing actively with the negative transference, maintaining particular alertness to the emergence of the negative therapeutic reaction.

Negative Therapeutic Reaction

The fundamental role that narcissism plays in the negative therapeutic reaction, a reaction in which the patient seemingly gets worse at a time when he should be getting better, was investigated by Rosenfeld. In agreement with Melanie Klein, he perceives envy as responsible for producing chronic negative attitudes in analysis. He believes that the negative therapeutic reaction is caused by the destructive element in mania represented by envy. Envy drives the patient to devalue the analyst in the effort to maniacally triumph over him, allowing the patient to maintain feelings of superiority and omnipotence. Ironically, when such a patient recognizes benefits from the analysis, he gives himself credit for it, for through projective identification the patient feels that he controls the analyst and attributes the analyst's creativity and understanding to himself. When envy remains hidden, powerful negative reactions may occur due to the defenses against envy, such as splitting, idealization, confusion, attacks upon the self, and devaluation of the analyst. Rosenfeld indicates that the analysis of envy to its roots in infancy is an important element in breaking through the negative therapeutic reaction, and regards the detailed analysis of envy and aggression in the transference relationship as the direct means by which the negative therapeutic reaction is made accessible to resolution.

Rosenfeld's explanation above is consonant with the view that the negative therapeutic reaction emanates from the dominance of aggressive over libidinal elements in the borderline personality and makes its appearance in the transference. The negative reaction illuminates the nuclear character resistance of the borderline patient, and is in some way parallel to the more clearly ambivalent transference neurosis in the analysis of the neurotic patient. The negative therapeutic reaction is the hallmark of the borderline patient and an essential ingredient in the treatment of many lower level borderline patients, without which the analysis remains incomplete. When this reaction does not occur at all in either a telling or more subtle form, the analysis may suffer in that a heavily defended, pathological sector of the personality, with the unconscious collusion of the analyst, has been left essentially unmodified.

There is a strong desire in the borderline patient to draw the analyst into some type of collusive relationship where he may act out with the patient without being aware of it. The extent to which the analyst colludes with the patient through mutual projective identification varies. Rosenfeld asserts that to the degree that collusion takes place, the analysis become more difficult. To counter this regressive influence, he recommends that all evidence of entanglements and collusion which attach themselves to the transference be continually exposed.

Transference Psychosis

Critical for the treatment of the borderline patient is the handling of the negative therapeutic reaction and of the transference psychosis. The causes and means of dealing with the former have been briefly indicated. As to the latter, during his analysis of psychotic and schizophrenic patients, Rosenfeld (1952) became aware of the phenomenon of the transference psychosis in schizophrenics which he described in this way: "I have found that if we avoid producing any positive transference by reassurance or expressions of love, and simply interpret any positive and negative transference manifestations of the psychotic patient, a transference psychosis develops" (p.10).

From my own experience I have found that, unlike the psychotic, the borderline patient does not immediately form a transference psychosis, but if permitted to do so without interference, will rather form a fluidly symbiotic or narcissistic transference. In the more paranoid or more narcissistic borderline character, during the course of treatment a transference psychosis may develop as a sudden eruption of psychotic phenomena takes place, attaching itself to the transference and including the analyst in the delusional misrepresentations.

Rosenfeld uses the term "transient psychosis" for transference psychosis in the borderline to clarify the distinction between the transference of the borderline from that of the psychotic patient. An interesting sidelight is that when the analyst first encounters this phenomenon, he is startled to discover that the transference psychosis present in the analysis interferes little with the patient's life outside. In chapter 13, "Transference Psychosis in the Borderline Patient," Rosenfeld deals with the questions of whether a transference psychosis may not be inevitable with some borderline patients, and, when it does arise, whether it is a barrier or an aid to the analysis. He indicates that it is generally difficult to trace the origin of a transference psychosis, but like the negative therapeutic reaction, it may arise from a mistake or misunderstanding centering around an interpretation or action of the analyst. Where the analyst is able to identify the error or misinterpretation he is in a better position to help clarify it and mitigate its effect. Paradoxically, although it arises from an error or misunderstanding, the transference psychosis provides the basis for interpretive work in the same manner as does the transference neurosis with the neurotic patient, and it appears not to hinder but to further the analytic work. Rosenfeld indicates that even when the patient seems overwhelmed, a nonpsychotic part of the personality generally remains quite accessible.

The uneven way in which the transference psychosis develops in different borderline patients is indicated in Rosenfeld's earlier (1952) paper. The borderline character with a developmental defect, for example, is apt to develop a transference psychosis of a paranoid nature, whereas the one who combines an intense need

for objects with overpowering withdrawal reactions is instead
given to acting out in the transference with frequent negative
therapeutic reactions.

It is noteworthy that Searles (1965d) describes various forms of
relatedness and nonrelatedness within the psychotic transference
in the schizophrenic patient which have relevance to the transient
transference psychosis of the borderline. He asserts that a patient
may be apt to show different forms of relatedness at one time or
another during the course of treatment. As if to indicate the
presence of both narcissistic transference and object transference,
as well as the possibility for transference neurosis and transference psychosis in the same individual, Searles states that

> of the forms in which transference psychosis is manifested, it
> should be noted that just as all these various forms may be
> shown by any one patient, at one time or another in the course
> of his psychotherapy, so it is impossible to demarcate clearly
> between transference psychosis in general, on the one hand,
> and transference neurosis on the other [p. 694].

Grotstein's Approach

There exists a need for a single overall theoretical scheme to
explain the phenomena of neurosis, borderline disorder, and
psychosis. In chapter 3 J. S. Grotstein sets himself the task of
providing an integrated theory of mental events for the better
understanding of these disorders, bringing together classical
psychoanalysis, Kleinian object relations theory, contemporary
ego psychology, and the contributions of a number of psychoanalytic investigators identified with the field of borderline and
narcissistic personality disorders, such as Kernberg, Kohut, and
Rosenfeld.

The central idea of Grotstein's theoretical approach is that within each of us, irrespective of the degree of our pathology or normality, there exists or once existed a split, evidenced in the presence of a psychotic and a normal personality. Consistent with this idea Grotstein offers the following propositions: In the psychotic patient, the normal personality is hostage to its psychotic twin, whereas in the normal person the psychotic twin is well contained as the normal personality successfully keeps it in repression.

In the borderline personality organization the containing function of the normal twin has been marred in varying degrees during its early development by the need for excessive use of schizoid and manic defenses. What distinguishes the borderline personality organization according to Grotstein is

at best, the capacity of the normal aspects of the personality to contain the psychotic twin and, at worst, the tendency by the manic and/or schizoid personality organizations to be traduced into a pathological symbiosis with a psychotic personality organization so as to create an amalgamated personality which behaves 'rationally irrational' . . . .

Bion's concept of twin personalities, with its roots in the work of Melanie Klein, is interestingly elaborated by Grotstein. He postulates an infantile psychosis which develops in the paranoid schizoid period, and an infantile neurosis which has its onset in the depressive period when psychotic mechanisms are forsworn in favor of a more neurotic relationship to the object. According to Grotstein the particular character of the borderline personality organization would then depend on the relative strengths and relationships among three forces: (1) the psychotic organization from the infantile psychosis, (2) the normal personality from the infantile neurosis, and (3) the manic and schizoid defenses against the integration of the infantile neurosis. Grotstein indicates that whereas a healthy personality may successfully repress its psychotic twin, a manic or schizoid personality organization colludes with it to achieve "a diabolical amalgam."

In his experience with treatment of the borderline patient by interpretive means, Grotstein discovers a seeming paradox. The normal portion of the personality understands the interpretations but a negative therapeutic reaction immediately sets in. This strange reaction is attributed to the psychotic twin's envy of its more successful normal twin. Grotstein sees one of the characteristic features of psychoanalytic treatment of the borderline disorder as a growing split between the two personalities. Seemingly, the abnormal part of the personality does not understand interpretations nor benefit from them, as does the normal part, thereby widening the split between the two.

Summary and Conclusion

The diversity of approaches to treatment procedure in psychoanalysis of the borderline patient clusters about two basic approaches. In one approach the analyst follows the standard technique in as invariant a manner as possible. In the other the analyst, also recognizing that no systematic method has yet been developed to supersede classical procedure, utilizes it when it is practicable, and employs suitable modifications when it is not, regarding these calculated departures as strengthening and expanding psychoanalytic technique. It is too early to determine the superiority of one method over the other, as in the hands of skilled practitioners both methods bring positive results. However, a common element identifiable in the work of many analysts treating the borderline patient is the utilization or adaptation of Kleinian thought, particularly the concepts of the formation of early object representation, splitting, and projective and introjective identification.

The borderline patient in the past created a problem for psychoanalytic treatment because he was deemed unable to form an object transference, thought by some to be due to developmental arrest at the stage of narcissism, or by others to an ego defect which he carried with him throughout life. Currently, the borderline individual is not expected to form the usual object transference in the initial phase of treatment, and is allowed to form the transference of which he is capable, usually a predominantly narcissistic transference which develops into symbiosis. In the narcissistic transference the patient omnipotently attributes to the analyst feelings and perceptions which belong to himself, so that in his own mind he becomes identified or seemingly confused with the analyst. In the initial stage of treatment a period of therapeutic symbiosis in which the relatedness is dominated by the narcissistic transference over elements of the object transference is either necessary or at least desirable. This symbiosis parallels a good mother-child relatedness and provides the atmosphere for the analyst to become internalized as the good internal object. Supplanting the pathological introject with a healthier one initiates the process of recovery.

The activity of the analyst during the symbiosis may include interventions other than interpretation, particularly those which indicate agreement of thought and feeling between analyst and patient, and those which reflect acceptance of the patient's unconscious wishes and understanding of his maturational needs. Particularly in the initial phase, some borderline patients find themselves unable to utilize interpretation and respond better to other interventions such as information concerning induced countertransference feelings, paradigmatic or joining techniques, neutral responses, and the like. With many patients, transference interpretations dealing with the unconscious content of the patient's manifest productions may be the primary, or at times the only, therapeutic interventions required, and within this range often the most useful are the interpretations of interactions between patient and analyst on both verbal and nonverbal levels. Since technical parameters by their nature employ modifications of the frame, a special demand is placed on the analyst to always be aware of the frame, not to relinquish the analytic attitude, and to continually move toward maximum neutrality.

Profoundly influencing the course of treatment are the particular factors of narcissism and aggression. As all borderline individuals have some amount of narcissism and a weakened ability to handle their own aggression, it is not surprising to encounter expressions of grandiosity along with paranoid defenses against threats to the grandiose self, tendencies to act out or to withdraw, to raging, and to extreme negativism. Treatment procedure has to take these factors into account, as well as the pathological mental structures derived from them, since the borderline patient needs to be able to express his rage against the analyst, and the analyst must be able to accept, understand, and deal with it.

The borderline's negativism and aggression which find expression in the negative transference can intensify during the middle phase of treatment and undergo quantitative and qualitative change, becoming visible in the form of a continued or reappearing negative therapeutic reaction, either by itself or alternating with acting out and other manifestations of aggression. At various times during the therapeutic regression, the analyst's effectiveness may threaten the patient's narcissism, including his need to be flawless, to do the analysis by himself, and to maintain a fantasied superiority over the analyst. Feeling belittled by the analyst's interpretive superiority, the patient, with an unconscious desire to seek revenge, retaliates by trying to humiliate the analyst in an envious attack upon him, or he attains this result in a more oblique, passive, self-punitive form so that he appears worse at a time when he should be getting better. Thus, envy and the defense against it play important roles in the negative therapeutic reaction.

An additional manifestation of the negative transference in the middle phase is the transient transference psychosis, brought on most frequently by a rapid intensification of the patient's unexpressed angry feelings in his identification or confusion of the analyst with a toxic introject. Where the analyst relies exclusively upon interpretation, the question arises as to whether the risk of transference psychosis is not increased with some borderline patients, since interpretations viewed as critical offer the narcissistic and paranoid patient greater opportunity to place the analyst in the role of persecutor, against whom the borderline patient has difficulty defending himself.

The transference psychosis of the borderline patient parallels the transference neurosis of the neurotic patient in one way by offering fresh opportunity for interpretation leading toward the resolution of nuclear character resistances. In another way the two are very different. While the transference neurosis is welcomed as an essential phase in the treatment process, the clinician constantly remains on guard against the development of the transference psychosis. In the concluding phase of treatment the major negative transference manifestations are reduced, the narcissistic transference is resolved, the object transference becomes dominant and analysis can proceed in a more classical vein.

References

Adler, G. (1975). The usefulness of the "borderline" concept in psychotherapy. In *Borderline States in Psychiatry,* ed. J.E. Mack, pp. 29–40. New York: Grune and Stratton.

Adler, G. and Buie, D. (1972). The uses of confrontation with borderline patients. *International Journal of Psychoanalytic Psychotherapy* 1(3):90–108.

Bleger, J. (1967). Psycho-analysis of the psycho-analytic frame. *International Journal of Psycho-Analysis* 48:511–519.

Eissler, K.R. (1953). The effect of the structure of the ego on psychoanalytic technique. *Journal of American Psycho-analytic Association* 1:104-143.

Freud, S. (1914). On the history of the psycho-analytic movement. *Standard Edition* 14:7-66.

———(1915). Observations on transference love (Further recommendations on the techniques of psycho-analysis III). *Standard Edition* 12:159-171.

———(1937). Analysis terminable and interminable. *Standard Edition* 23:216-253.

Giovacchini, P.L. (1972a). The treatment of characterological disorders. In *Tactics and Techniques in Psychoanalytic Therapy,* vol. 1, ed. P. Giovacchini, pp. 236-253. New York: Jason Aronson.

———(1972b). Various aspects of the analytic process. In *Tactics and Techniques in Psychoanalytic Therapy,* vol. 2, ed. P. Giovacchini, pp. 6-91. New York: Jason Aronson.

———(1975). *Psychoanalysis of Character Disorders.* New York: Jason Aronson.

Hoedemaker, E.D. (1960). Psychoanalytic technique and ego modifications. *International Journal of Psycho-Analysis* 41:34-46.

Kernberg, O. (1975). *Borderline Conditions and Pathological Narcissism.* New York: Jason Aronson.

Klein, M. (1932). *The Psycho-Analysis of Children.* London: Hogarth Press.

Kohut, H. (1971). *The Analysis of the Self.* New York: International Universities Press.

Langs, R. (1976). *The Bipersonal Field.* New York: Jason Aronson.

Reich, A. (1958). A special variation of technique. *International Journal of Psycho-Analysis* 39:230-234.

Rosenfeld, H.A. (1952). Notes on the psychoanalysis of the superego conflict in an acute schizophrenic patient. In H.A.

Rosenfeld, *Psychotic States,* pp. 63–103. New York: International Universities Press.

———(1964). On the psychopathology of narcissism: a clinical approach. In *Psychotic States,* pp. 169–179. New York: International Universities Press.

———(1971). A clinical approach to the psycho-analytic theory of the life and death instincts: an investigation into the aggressive aspects of narcissism. *International Journal of Psycho-Analysis* 52:169.

———(1975). Negative therapeutic reaction. In *Tactics and Techniques in Psychoanalytic Therapy,* vol. 2, ed. P. Giovacchini, pp. 218–228. New York: Jason Aronson.

Searles, H.F. (1965a). Integration and differentiation in schizophrenia. In *Collected Papers on Schizophrenia and Related Subjects,* pp. 304–348. New York: International Universities Press.

———(1965b). Oedipal love in the countertransference. In Searles op. cit., pp. 284–303.

———(1965c). The place of neutral therapist responses in psychotherapy with the schizophrenic patient. In Searles op. cit., pp. 626–653.

———(1965d). Transference psychosis in the psychotherapy of chronic schizophrenia. In Searles op. cit., pp. 654–716.

Spotnitz, H. (1969a). Interventions: range and sequence. In *Modern Psychoanalysis of the Schizophrenic Patient,* pp. 178–207. New York: Grune and Stratton.

———(1969b). Recognition and understanding of resistance. In Spotnitz op. cit., pp. 93–109.

———(1976). The narcissistic defense. In *Psychotherapy of Preoedipal Conditions,* pp. 101–116. New York: Jason Aronson.

Strachey, J. (1969). The nature of the therapeutic action of psycho-analysis. *International Journal of Psycho-Analysis* 50:275–291.

Tarachow, S. (1962). Interpretation and reality in psychotherapy. *International Journal of Psycho-Analysis* 43:377–387

Volkan, V.D. (1970). *Primitive Internalized Object Relations.* New York: International Universities Press.

Winnicott, D.W. (1960). The theory of the parent-infant relationship. *International Journal of Psycho-Analysis* 41:585–595

Chapter 2

Origin and Evolution of the
Borderline Concept

Attilio Capponi, Ph.D.

The task for this chapter is to draw a historical background which shows where the concept of the borderline and its various components fit in relationship to other areas of clinical knowledge and theoretical sophistication. Within this general frame a more limited goal is to show the progressive steps in the acquisition of this understanding as the result of accumulated psychoanalytic concepts and theories. In working out this last goal it was thought possible to find the early origins of the borderline concept in the clinical activities of prepsychoanalytic psychiatry.

This proved to be exhilarating work as apparently untapped sources became available. The scholarly historical studies of John Mack (1975) and Parkin (1966) had prepared the ground by mapping the larger directions of the various trends. Valuable clinical studies were found which, although known, had not received the attention they deserved. As the detailed richness of the explicit as well as unacknowledged clinical descriptions of borderline syndromes were gathered, recurrent common features began to appear. The consistency of these elements in the clinical picture was unmistakable, and confirmed the vision of those clinicians who early had recognized the singularity and distinctness of the borderline organization. Yet, within the spread of symptomatology certain modal clusters seemed to exist as well, and some authors, like Rosenfeld (see chapter 13), and Grinberg (1977), are beginning to develop classifications of borderline subgroups.

When enough data and alternative theoretical systems of thought are brought together, another trend may be observed, namely, the complementarity of some of the systems. Recourse to the repertoire of mental mechanisms and developmental conceptions of the British school has made it possible to extend the reach of ego psychology so as to organize the clinical data on the borderline disorders into a coherent whole. Doubtless, drawing explanatory concepts from different theoretical systems involves the risk of introducing implicit inconsistencies; however, psychoanalysis is a single body of ideas and deals with only one realm of data. Whether the implicit divergences make the unified general theory untenable is yet to be seen.

Laplanche and Pontalis (1967) state that the borderline concept refers to a form of "latent schizophrenia presenting an apparently neurotic set of symptoms." They go on to describe what they consider is generally understood to be *borderline pathology,* a term that "has no strict nosographical definition. The variations in its use reflect the real uncertainty concerning the area to which it is applied. Different writers, according to their diverse approaches, have extended the category to psychopathic, perverted and delinquent personalities, and to severe cases of character neurosis. Current usage is apparently tending to reserve the term for cases of schizophrenia whose symptoms have a neurotic aspect" (p. 54).

It is certainly true that there are authors who are still reluctant to accept the borderline concept as a distinct mental disorder, but this attitude is no longer as prominent as it was during the 1940s and 1950s. Since 1953, when Robert Knight brought together a number of observations from the clinical experience of analysts and psychiatrists working with patients who presented this mixed symptomatic picture, and particularly since the work of Kernberg, from the late 1960s on the consensus of opinion has shifted toward considering the borderline disorder a specific form of pathology with specific symptom patterns, retaining stability even though shifts toward overt psychotic manifestations do occur. However, these psychotic episodes do not alter the general stability of the syndrome since the symptoms are limited and they are fully reversible. The concept of latent schizophrenia, furthermore, represents a model of psychopathology based on the concept of an underlying disease entity which implies that there must be a mental equivalent of an organ system dysfunction based on some anatomical defect, an invading organism, or some internal equilibrium deficit. Although we do speak of ego defects, ego distortions, malformations, etc., and are not always as explicit as we ought to be that we are using these terms metaphorically since they still seem to carry the implicit language of concrete body organs, we do mean something different in the sense that we signify a pattern of activity which is a reflection of the total personality.

The inclusion of psychopathic, perverted, and delinquent personalities is of historical importance; these were the first diagnostic groups to be considered borderline because they did not fit into the categories of neurosis and psychosis. In the only instance where Freud used the term borderline, the preface to Aichorn's book, *Wayward Youth* (1925), he was referring to delinquent adolescents. However, it has been said that many of Freud's patients may have been borderline, but in those days the term was not used for cases who could work with the analytic situation. Other groups have been included also, such as the schizoid (Fairbairn 1940) which is a more inclusive category that encompasses those already mentioned. The "as if" personality (Deutsch 1942) has been traditionally considered to be the first clinical description of borderline patients. It may have been Wilhelm Reich, however, who first reported a study of borderline cases, in his book *The Impulsive Character* (1925).

Strictly, in a historical sense, Pierce L. Clark (1921) was the first psychoanalyst to write on the treatment problems of the borderline patient, including a brief reference to the clinical features. His work represents an early and heroic effort to deal with a very complex clinical task without the necessary conceptual tools. After all, his work preceded the fundamental writings of Freud on the structure of the mental apparatus and the papers on neurosis, psychosis, and splitting of the ego.

Pierce referred to the borderline patient's difficulties in dealing with the adult life tasks and properly recognized, in a general way, that this was due to the immaturity of their mental development. His attempts to do psychoanalysis with them did not bring the results that one could expect from neurotic patients and he thought it was necessary to introduce modifications in technique. He preceded the more classical psychoanalytic treatment with a period of supportive work and thus originated a point of view that still has many adherents today.

Others who have described borderline pathology in specific clinical pictures are Bychowski (1953) with his paper on latent psychosis; Gitelson (1958) described a case of "ego distortion"; Frosch (1959, 1964, 1970) wrote about the "psychotic character"; and Giovacchini (1967) who has used such designations as "frozen introject" to indicate borderline pathology.

Laplanche and Pontalis (1967) point out: "The spread of psycho-analysis has had a good deal to do with the coming to prominence of the so-called borderline case" (p. 54). In fact, psychoanalysis has contributed a set of essential concepts which make it possible to propose coherent formulations of borderline pathology and its origin. From observations derived mostly from the transference relationship, the manifestations of the disorder may be viewed as severe functional disturbances that followed from exposure to too great stress in the mother-infant relationship at critical periods of development when the mental processes were at an incipient stage of formation.

The borderline concept lacks the antiquity and distant lineage that distinguishes depression (Beck 1967), and, until recently, also the systematic clinical descriptions of schizophrenia. Some authors believe that the types of clinical pictures change in the course of time, in correspondence with changes in social conditions, and it may follow that this form of pathology is a new development of contemporary society. Fenichel (1945) thought that character pathology, of which borderline is one form, was being seen with increasing frequency as a consequence of modern societies embracing new orders of morality and values and overthrowing the old ones. But it seems more likely that individuals with borderline disorders may have been among us from time immemorial.

Not long ago John Mack (1975) referred to an 1873 text by the English psychiatrist James Cowles Prichard, who described a mental disorder that in some essential details is very consistent with our picture of borderline pathology. Prichard reported his observations about a form of "insanity" that differed from the others found in asylums. This form of madness consisted "in a morbid perversion of the natural feelings, affections, inclinations, temper, habits, moral disposition, and natural impulses, without any remarkable disorder or defect of the intellect or knowing and reasoning faculties, and particularly without any insane illusions or hallucination" (p. 2). Prichard called this disorder "moral insanity," which eventually led to the diagnostic category of psychopathic personality.

The long period of obscurity which preceded the recent outburst of activity over borderline phenomena easily leads us to ask what the reasons might have been that delayed interest or awareness. It is all speculation, of course, but the various answers might fall into several categories as follows: (1) The clinical features span the whole spectrum of psychopathology and do not easily, at first, form well defined clusters of symptoms, and many are not even ego alien, which would make them more easily differentiated as is the case with the more dramatic manifestations of manic-depression, schizophrenia, and hysterical and obsessive compulsive disorders. (2) This very difficulty of differentiating clusters of clinical features as a separate syndrome different from the other preexisting and familiar ones may, on the one hand be due to the scientific preference for parsimony, and on the other, to the more widespread human tendency for perceiving the world with already familiar and available categories, in other words, to cast the new material into old molds. So some pattern of clinical features may at first, and for a long time, seem to be "nothing but" neurotic or psychotic before it would be seen to require a new concept. (3) Still a third reason may be that the prevailing theoretical models, introduced early in the history of psychiatry, led eventually to conceptual dead ends. This may have been the case with the medical model according to which a symptom complex represents the manifestations of an underlying disease entity which, in order to diagnose, one would have to identify specific etiology, onset, course, and outcome.

Kahlbaum (1828–1899) attempted a systematization of the concept of disease entities in psychiatry when he set out to

> build up disease pictures clinically so that as far as possible all phenomena manifested by the individual patient can be used to arrive at a diagnosis, and the total course of the illness is taken into account. The groups of disease patterns which thus emerge from study of the most commonly concurring symptoms, or

from empirical delineations ... were not only ... easy to describe, they also led to a diagnostic approach which enabled one, far better than earlier classifications, to reconstruct very accurately the previous course of the illness from the present state and also to predict its further development with a high degree of probability not only in general terms ... but also in detail with respect to various phases of the symptomatic picture [quoted by Parkin 1966, p. 211].

Kahlbaum failed to support the validity of his model because he was never able to provide such a clinical description of a case that followed the criteria of disease process that he postulated.

The model persisted and could be found in the work of Kraepelin and also in Bleuler, who advanced the concept of "latent schizophrenia." However, dissenting opinion began to appear as early as 1921 when Thomas Verner Moore expressed his dissatisfaction with the requirement that all cases of war neurosis had to receive a diagnosis according to the then current clinical entities of psychiatry.

This led to the peculiar situation of having to change the diagnosis according to the set of symptoms on which one focused; and as patients changed wards different physicians would give different diagnoses. The doctor's predicament would become even worse when a patient's symptoms would spontaneously clear and he would have to change the diagnosis. Moore (1921) argued that this anomaly was due to

an altogether undue importance laid upon the diagnosis of mental diseases. The reason for this is to be sought in the fact that psychiatrists are more dependent than they think on the ideals of clinicians, or that clinicians demand of psychiatry a certain conformity to their ideals and standards. Psychiatry, however, should run its own course, for the relative importance

of diagnosis and treatment in psychiatry are just the opposite of
what they are in medicine. In medicine the matter of prime
importance is a diagnosis. . . . In psychiatry, however, with the
exception of a few exogenous psychoses, the matter of diagnosis is secondary. The diagnosis does not determine the
treatment, on the contrary we often wait the results of treatment before making our final diagnosis [p. 254].

With a clear understanding of the nature of the problem of
characterizing mental disorders according to the unique nature of
psychopathological phenomena, he said:

The analysis of the patient's behavior in the presence of their
difficulties will show us that he is reacting to the situation in a
manner characterisitc of his personality. His behavior, in fact,
can always be analysed into a few characteristic modes of
reactions. These modes of reaction are clear and evident. They
may be treated without ever raising the question as to whether
or not this *tout ensemble* fits into the disease picture of this or
that clinical entity of psychiatry [p. 255].

Moore then took the matter into his own hands and set out to
devise a new diagnostic classification and discuss its criteria. He
proposed the label "borderline mental states" under the more
general headings of "psychotaxes" and "parataxes" and stated:
"These types of reactions exist and fade over by imperceptible
degrees from a normal grappling with the difficulties of life to the
bizarre forms of the major psychoses . . . . " (p. 257).

His classification scheme and labels did not have any impact
and apparently received no attention.

Besides putting too many eggs in the basket of the medical
model, psychiatry at the turn of the century suffered from a
poverty of theoretical conceptions with good enough fit to the

data of observation. Whatever concepts were available, for example, neurosis and psychosis, lacked precision such that their usefulness for organizing the clinical features was limited. Also lacking were theoretical constructs about underlying dynamic processes that could serve as explanatory concepts for clinical observations.

In this theoretical climate, a great deal of difficulty in the diagnostic recognition of borderline pathology seems to have been due to the lack of psychic variables that differentiated between neurosis and psychosis. How were psychiatrists then to characterize borderline symptomatology when in fact it presented a juxtaposition of clinical phenomena of both categories of disorders?

Freud had a great interest in this problem of differentiating neurosis from psychosis, and at first he accepted the current division of functional disorders into neurosis and psychosis as representing two rather exclusive categories of psychopathology (Laplanche and Pontalis 1967). But he took up the task of finding criteria for diffentiating between them and reported his thinking in several papers, including the posthumously published *An Outline of Psycho-Analysis* (1940b).

By the end of the nineteenth century, when Freud began his practice, psychiatry had made enormous progress mapping the field of psychopathology and producing a set of concepts which provided, if not yet understanding, at least some measure of orientation for the study of mental disorders. Many of the concepts it had achieved such as "neurosis" (Cullen 1784), "hallucination" (Esquirol 1817), "psychosis" (Feuchtersleben 1845), "obsessions" (Morel 1861), "symptom complex" (Kahlbaum 1874) would soon be incorporated into psychoanalysis and through this influence some would undergo changes in meaning.

Freud started to practice clinical psychiatry without specialty training, which gave him the advantage of entering the field without preconceived notions or ready-made attitudes toward his clinical material. In fact, as has been pointed out, it was while thinking over someone else's clinical material that he originated a totally new conception of mental phenomena, both pathological and normal. It was the progressive achievements of psychoanalysis, including the observational windfall of the analytic setting, which turned out to be a new human interactional situation, that permitted the gradual emergence of the clinical picture and the concepts with which to meaningfully organize those observations.

Freud's basic idea consisted in regarding mental disorders as the consequences of an internal, psychic conflict between socially unacceptable instinctual wishes and defensive efforts instituted to check the expression of those wishes. As Freud later put it, the ego had to reconcile opposing demands from the id and from reality. As the ego checked the expression of the instinctual energies of the wish, these pressed on and forced the ego to a compromise with reality considerations. Even if the wish was held back, it still surfaced in disguise in symptomatic behavior, that is, in symbolic form.

The varieties of mental disorders resulted from the relative strengths of the competing forces, the varieties of symbolic expressions of the different instincts, and the manifestations of defensive operations. With this model Freud evolved a therapy aimed at the removal of symptoms. This could be done by recovering lost memories of the events that precipitated the original conflict situation so that the adult ego, with a different perspective on reality, may seek more normal solutions to the psychic conflict.

This model proved to be a valuable heuristic tool but its limitations became evident and Freud was quite ready to follow the leads indicated by his clinical material. For instance, in the study of character, the model did not allow much more that an explanation of character formation in terms of the persistence of the infantile instinctual energies into the traits of the adult personality. In an important sense, the implicit assumption of a united adult ego would be proven to be misleading, as it failed to accord with new observations gained from analytic treatment. The first turning point which indicated the need for modifications in theory and technique was the discovery by Freud of the ubiquitous resistance.

By the time he recognized the role of resistance in character formation Freud had elaborated the concept of psychic conflict, the related concepts of the unconscious, the libido theory, the psychosexual stages, narcissism, the early model of the instincts, defenses such as repression and regression, the facts of fixation, symptom formation as compromises between instinct and reality, and character traits as manifestations of the persistence of instinctual energies. In the future, with the development of the structural theory, he would work out the notions of differences between neurosis and psychosis, ego modifications, the defense of disavowal or denial and the related defense of splitting of the ego, all of which would be necessary to elucidate the psychopathology of borderline phenomena.

Returning to the topic of recognizing borderline patients as forming a separate group we may consider as a final reason the disturbing impact these patients have on the consultant or the analyst. These patients' capacity for causing havoc and destroying the analytic setting or for creating cataclysmic countertransference has become one of the indicators pathognomonic of borderline pathology. These reactions in the analyst tend to cloud his understanding at the moment and incline him to a diagnosis of psychosis. It may well have been this type of patient whom Freud meant when he said: "I do not like these patients . . . I am annoyed with them . . . I feel them to be so far distant from me and from everything human. A curious sort of intolerance, which surely makes me unfit to be a psychiatrist" (quoted by Roazen 1975, p. 141).

The Clinical Picture

The clinical description of the borderline patient has become progressively more detailed as clinical studies accumulated, including some which did not declare an overt interest in borderline phenomena but are without doubt quite relevant.

I have already mentioned Prichard, the English psychiatrist who coined the term "moral insanity." It may be a matter of opinion whether his description applies to borderline disorders, but it is to be noted that his concept led to the development of a new diagnostic designation related to the borderline concept. Morel, a follower of Prichard, who had introduced the term *demence précoce* proposed a very influential view of mental disorders as degenerations due to hereditary weaknesses (Parkin 1966, p. 208), a view that was still important to Bleuler in 1923 (Mack 1975). These notions became entangled in the cultural and religious crosscurrents of the late nineteenth and early twentieth century and, as they acquired pejorative connotations, they gained enormous currency for labeling marginal and antisocial "enemies of society" (Mack 1975). A consequence of these developments was the introduction of the terms "psychopathic personality" and "constitutional psychopathic inferiority" which were applied to antisocial and criminal individuals, to alcoholic, addictive, and perverse personalities, and also to severe psychoneurotics.

By the turn of the century the term borderline was beginning to be used as a diagnostic label referring to these disorders, with the particular connotation that they were cases of severe pathology that sometimes took on psychotic manifestations, but somehow different from the known insanities, and difficult to classify otherwise. Kraepelin could not pigeonhole these groups and referred to them as "those psychopathic conditions which develop on a morbid constitutional basis" and "include an extensive borderland between pronounced morbid states and mere personality eccentricities which are wont to be regarded as normal" (Mack 1975).

This line of observation was moving now into the area of character structure, which around 1916 was beginning to turn in a a new direction that would soon lead to the growth of ego psychology. Fenichel (1945) attributes the origin of ego psychology to two factors. One was Freud's discovery of resistance and the other was the growing number of patients coming for treatment with a new form of pathology unlike the classical neurotic whose "well integrated personality" was suddenly disturbed by inappropriate actions and impulses. By contrast, the personality of the new type of patient appeared to be "patently torn and malformed, or at any rate so involved in the illness that there is no borderline between 'personality' and 'symptom'." Fenichel added: "The formula, 'in a neurosis that which has been warded off breaks through in an ego-alien form,' is no longer valid, since the form often is not ego alien, the elaboration of the defense sometimes being more manifest than its failure" (p. 464). Fenichel was referring to the character disorders, not directly to the borderline patients, although the description is consistent for those borderline cases whose pathology is closer to the neurotic than the psychotic end.

Fenichel's first factor was the one mentioned by Freud in "Some Character Types Met with in Psycho-analytic Work" (1916) when he said:

When a doctor carries out the psycho-analytic treatment of a neurotic, his interest is by no means directed in the first instance to the patient's character. He would much rather know what the symptoms mean, what instinctual impulses are concealed behind them and are satisfied by them, and what course was followed by the mysterious path that has led from the instinctual wishes to the symptoms. But the technique which he is obliged to follow soon compels him to direct his immediate curiosity toward other objectives. He observes that his investigation is threatened by resistances set up against him by the patient, and these resistances he may justly count as part of the latter's character. This now acquires the first claim of his interest [p. 311].

As Freud had pointed out, resistance forced psychoanalysis to abandon the technique of treatment for the removal of symptoms in favor of the treatment of character. This became the area of interest and study for Wilhelm Reich, who set out to follow Freud's recommendation and to investigate the manifestations of resistances in treatment as a function of the patient's character structure, that is, of the ego (Fenichel), its origin in the formation of the ego, and the technical means that might be effective for removing them so that the treatment could again proceed.

Wilhelm Reich

Reich was the first analyst to expand the study of character formation and its pathological development from the linear tracing of the continuity of instinctual energies in the character traits to an investigation of the acquisition and operation of defense mechanisms. Freud has provided the basic concepts for the study of the ego in *The Ego and the Id* (1923) and Reich quickly recognized its importance and credited Freud for providing "the groundwork for a psychoanalytically based theory of character." In addition he acknowledged that "the process of identification holds the key to the characterological interpretation of personality," (pp. 3–4). Identification had been proposed by Freud as the basic process by which the ego acquired structure: "we have come to understand that this kind of substitution has a great share in determining the form taken on by the ego and that it contributes materially toward building what is called 'character'" (1923, p. 28). And further on " . . . the character of the ego is a precipitate of abandoned object cathexes . . . . " (p. 29).

At about this same time another line of research was in progress, the work of Melanie Klein, that would yield knowledge about another process of ego growth, projective identification, which, however, would not be accepted within the body of classical theory because it conflicted with some of Freud's basic postulates.

It was already clear to Freud that the same processes that constituted the normal development and functioning of the ego might become involved in pathology. Specifically, of identifications he said, "If they obtain the upper hand and become too numerous, unduly powerful and incompatible with one another, a pathological outcome will not be far off. It may come to a disruption of the ego in consequence of the different identifications becoming cut off from one another by resistances; perhaps the secret of the cases of what is described as 'multiple personality' is that the different identifications seize hold of consciousness in turn" (pp. 30–31). Multiple personality is now regarded as one of the phenomena of borderline organization. Another way in which the concept of identification is important for the study of borderline disorders is that when it fails to occur normally the ego grows impoverished and defective as in the case of "as if" personalities and in the type of case discussed by Giovacchini (1967) whose ego seems to lack certain functions, particularly those for a full range of authentic object relations.

The Impulsive Character (1925) in which Reich reported the findings of his work with patients at the Vienna Psychoanalytic Clinic, conducted within a framework of investigating how the operation of resistance determined the nature of character disturbances and of innovations in technique that this required, was in many ways a sign at the frontier of early psychoanalysis. In this work he established that resistance, as is also true of symptoms, expresses the combined effect of two sets of forces, one containing the repressed material "relating to the specific analytic situation" as well as the repressing mechanism itself. In addition, he said, "every resistance takes its specific character from the total personality structure, so to speak. . . . If we go beyond thinking in terms of mere symptom analysis, we realize the following: the most important consideration is not the removal of symptoms but the substrate of the neurotic reactions—that is, the neurotic character structure itself" (p. 2).

Reich's clinical observations of the impulsive character may be regarded as the first psychoanalytic description and dynamic elaboration of borderline patients, or, more accurately, of one subgroup of the borderline range of phenomena.

The pathology of his patients in its entire scope from the transference to their everyday life and their history, with its juxtaposition of neurotic and psychotic features, led Reich to discuss the question of diagnosis from the very beginning and he said in this regard: "Such patients are not lacking in common neurotic symptoms, but they have an extra something which simple neurotics lack. This 'plus' not only separates them from the conversion hysterias, the anxiety neuroses, and the compulsive neuroses, but also brings a goodly number of them very close to schizophrenia. . . . Later I shall illustrate with case material *how difficult it is even after months of analytic treatment to differentiate diagnostically between schizophrenia and transference neurosis"* (p. 8, italics mine). There are many references to borderline pathology and the criteria for thinking in terms of borderline rather than schizophrenia: "We lay no particular stress on the viewpoint we take here that the impulsive character is a borderline case between symptom neurosis and psychosis on the basis of his particular defense mechanism" (p. 7). And further on,

"The question of borderline cases warrants considerable discussion, since most patients with this clinical picture show not only various schizophrenic symptoms but also an oscillation of their libidinal structure back and forth between autism and object cathexis," (p. 45). For Reich, Freud's criterion of the loss of reality testing resulting from regression to narcissistic libido was the decisive criterion with which he was able to rule out schizophrenia in his impulsive characters whose narcissistic withdrawal was more like the simple neurotic in that the patient retained his object cathexes at the fantasy level. Whereas, "the schizophrenic, or the neurotic with schizophrenic mechanisms . . . deflects the withdrawn libido into the ego and even renounces cathexis of the fantasy" (p. 48). In an earlier passage he had noted that "reality testing and ego boundaries remained intact even if obscured by affect" (p. 14). However, it is possible for these patients to experience a *"transient clouding of reality testing* [italics mine] . . . which enables the patient to experience delusionally the content of his or her experience" (p. 48).

The Relation to Reality

Reich's focus on certain issues, such as the role of defense in character structure, of pregenital conflicts, and the diagnostic problems of his impulsive patients, highlighted important areas of borderline psychopathology which would reappear time and again in the future and require much work to clarify.

The issue of contact with reality in neurosis and psychosis is a case in point. Freud had considered it a most important area to investigate the ego's reaction to conflict and the emergence of the factors that determined whether the outcome would be one or the other. Reich found Freud's early work (1924a, 1924b) helpful to the degree of leaving no doubt in his mind that he was dealing with a form of pathology different from schizophrenia. Freud went on, however, to develop further refinements in the theory, which the controversies of the 1940s and 1950s proved were necessary.

Freud's centering on the relationship to reality inspired others, for example, Frosch and Bion, to continue elucidating the mechanisms involved. In Table 1, below, (and Table 2, later on) the progress of Freud's thought is chronicled as the foundation of the later works.

At first, for Freud the differentiating characteristic was the capacity to maintain proper contact with reality. In neurosis the ego was strong and unitary and opted for repression of the instinct in deference to reality. In psychosis the ego turned away from reality, withdrawing its cathexes from objects and even the internal representations of the external world. Freud adumbrated yet another possibility which is regarded as the first statement of a view of what happens to the ego in character disorders: "And further, it is always possible for the ego to avoid a rupture in any of its relations by deforming itself, submitting to forfeit something of its unity, or in the long run even to being gashed and rent. Thus the illogicalities, eccentricities and follies of mankind would fall into a category similar to their sexual perversions, for by accepting them they spare themselves repressions" (1924a). Later, in the same year, Freud would record his recognition that in neurosis there was also a degree of alienation from reality as well as attempts at reconstruction, as is the case in psychosis.

As we read through the clinical description of impulsive characters and Reich's theoretical conceptualizations we begin to get a view of borderline phenomena. He writes: "Grotesquesness is the hallmark of the impulsive character's symptoms. We may describe them as sick caricatures of the 'stolid bourgeois' symptoms. ... But, in addition to the impulsivity (which they mostly do not perceive as illness), the overwhelming majority of impulsives show all manner of symptoms, such as phobic and compulsive behavior, compulsive rituals and ruminations, and, particularly in female character neurotics, all the familiar forms of conversion symptoms may occur" (p. 8). Some of the other manifestations observed by Reich were "deep-seated states of depersonalization, which none of my pertinent cases failed to show. Also, feelings of alienation, whether from one's own body or the outside world," and, "ideas of reference are not uncommon"; they "coincide with a propensity for feeling slighted and are characteristic of the simple transference neurosis. In an impulsive character, the feelings may snowball into a delusional belligerence." Reich also stated: "Consistent with the defect in repression, undisguised perversions are the rule in the case of the impulsive character. They are mainly from the sadomasochistic area. This special affinity to the realm of Freud's destructive drives we will come to recognize as a disturbance in superego development . . . . " (p. 14).

Reich's theoretical formulations of his clinical material are now an integral part of the conceptualizations of borderline pathology. He was one of the first analysts to emphasize the importance of pregenital experiences in the formation of the personality. He said: "What happens to a person in the first two years of life is more decisive that what happens later on. The child enters the highly critical oedipal phase with attitudes preformed, at least in broad outline, if not in their final detail. The Oedipus complex may be likened to a lens through which the rays of the impulses are refracted. They give this phase its special imprint and undergo far-reaching modifications through the experiences of this phase" (p. 33).

The residuals of this period of development show a mixture of concurrent fixations from all psychosexual levels, "a more or less equal juxtaposition of all known partial impulses in combinations and permutations which most of the time cannot be sorted out. We get the impression—to use a drastic metaphor—of a bull unleashed in the china shop of infantile development" (p. 43–44). Reich gives importance the developmental factor that at this

TABLE 1

FREUD'S DIFFERENTIATION BETWEEN NEUROSIS AND PSYCHOSIS

DISORDER	CAUSE	EFFECT	RESPONSE	DEFENSE MECHANISM	OUTCOME
Neurosis	Intolerable frustration	Psychic conflict: ego vs. id	Renounce instinct	Repression	Motor expression of wish is blocked, object of the wish is disputed (i.e., Oedipal conflict). Symptom is formed, expressing the wish symbolically.
Psychosis	Intolerable frustration	Psychic conflict: ego vs reality	Turns against reality	To be determined in the future.	Contact with reality is lost: Cathexes of external world withdrawn. Outer world no longer perceived. If perception does occur there is no affect. The inner world, once a reflection of the outer world, is also lost.
"Illogicalities, eccentricities, follies of mankind; (i.e. character disorders); perversions.	Intolerable frustration	Psychic conflict	Avoids rupture in any of its relations (id or external world)	Not mentioned	Ego deforms itself, forfeits some of its unity, even becomes gashed and rent (i.e. splits).

(1924a)

Neurosis		Both: checks instinct but also loosening relation to reality.	Repression	Two step reaction to conflict: (1) loosening the relation to reality, (2) repression, i.e., checking the instinct. Second step miscarries as ego tries to reestablish relation to reality at expense of id and also compensate the id for damage done to it. Reality is both avoided and obeyed by an attempt at flight. The instinct cannot create a satisfactory substitute (symptom); reality can't be denied, only ignored. Instinct forces a remodeling of reality in accordance with its desires, in fantasy from memories of external world.
Psychosis	Dread of reality	Tears the ego away from reality	Denial	Two step reaction to conflict: (1) tear away from reality, i.e., denies reality. (2) Attempts to create a new reality which is no longer open to objections like the one that has been forsaken. Denies reality and tries to substitute something else for it, i.e., a fantastic outer world in place of reality. The first step miscarries, the flight at the beginning is followed by active reconstruction.

Both neurosis and psychosis are expressions of rebellion of the id against the outer world; because of the pain involved, the id is unwilling or incapable of adapting itself to reality.

Normality		Combines features of both neurosis and psychosis: Denies reality as little as neurosis and like psychosis is concerned with effecting a change in it.		Leads to an active achievement in the outer world; i.e., is alloplastic.

(1924b)

period of libidinal structure an infant will form its first attach-
ments to body parts of the nurturing person which give gratification and pleasure before it is able to cathect the whole person.
And, since ego boundaries are not yet completed, these pleasure-
giving parts of the object are at first experienced as part of the
ego.

The overcathected tone of the pregenital period lends prominence to the narcissistic position which thus acquires undue
importance in impulsive characters and casts an apparently
schizophrenic quality to their withdrawal. At the slightest disappointment or frustration they move into an acute state of withdrawal with narcissistic regression, but Reich is clear on this
point, that "there are neurotics who could never be called schizophrenic, yet who show a narcissistic position matching in intensity that of the schizophrenic" (p.46).

Ambivalence, of course, is inevitable, and normal, but again, it
may acquire pathological aspects and this is a characteristic
feature of impulsive characters. Reich sought to understand what
set of conditions heightens the pathological elements of ambivalence. He took as a starting point Graber's assertion that
ambivalence develops from the juxtaposition of impulse gratification and denial. Reich pointed out that pathological ambivalence would follow also from the manner of denial, the stage
of gratification of the impulse when the denial is instituted, and
from the quality of the object relation with the person who
enforced the prohibition. The conjunction of these factors determined the persistence of chronic conflict with the nurturing
person, and eventually with the analyst in the transference. Thus
the relationship would be dominated by hate and fear; the
unrestrained impulsivity would become reinforced by stubborn-
ness; yet, at other times "an intense unsatisfied longing for love is
again opposed by a hatred of the same intensity" (p. 36). Those
familiar with contemporary literature of borderline personality

will readily recognize in this sketch the typical transference of these conditions.

In impulsive characters repression is not a reliable mechanism of defense and Reich tried to explain why sometimes it fails to operate. He thought this failure was due to defects in the development of the superego and ego-ideal resulting from identifications with inconsistent objects, now indulgent then punitive. The failure of repression could be recognized from the prevalence of conscious sadistic and masochistic fantasies and tendencies. Reich apparently did not have available two concepts which would later become useful in the understanding of borderline phenomena: *denial,* as a more primitive mechanism than repression (Freud had begun writing on disavowal or denial in 1924), and also *splitting* of the ego (also mentioned by Freud in 1924 but not elaborated until his *Outline of Psycho-Analysis* in 1940), but some of his statements indicate that he observed these phenomena in his patients such as, for instance, "in the sharp separation between sadistic impulse and guilt feelings, we see one of the typical mechanisms of the impulsive character."

Narcissism

The concept of narcissism and its clinical referents is another issue regarded as important by Reich which is a central element of the clinical picture, and which, even today, needs much clarification. It arises in the context of the importance of pregenital conflicts in the formation of personality and psychopathology. The concept of narcissism is frequently used as an organizer of many different clinical phenomena without sufficient attention to the implications of its theoretical roots in the libido theory and the prestructural model of the mind.

Pulver (1970) has taken the first step in filling the need for clarification of the conceptual status of the concept of narcissism and the implications for clinical formulations. He indicates that in spite of its wide use in psychoanalysis it has not been brought up to date in consonance with the advancements of ego psychology, an attention accorded to many other concepts. Pulver ordered the clinical phenomena regarded as narcissistic into four categories as follows: (1) a sexual perversion in which one's own body becomes the loved object, (this use is outmoded and has been abandoned); (2) as a developmental stage characterized by lack of object cathexes and primitive modes of thought, such as magical thinking, belief in animism, and in the omnipotence of thought, and some feeling states such as the "oceaning feeling," "nirvana," etc.; (3) as a mode of object relations, in two different ways, *(a)* a type of object choice in which the self plays a greater role than the real aspects of the object and *(b)* as a mode of relating to others characterized by a lack of genuine involvement that makes the object only useful as a gratifier of one's needs; and (4) the whole range of phenomena related to the regulation of self-esteem.

Many of the clinical features of borderline patients fit into these categories by virtue of trauma, conflict, and fixations experienced when these behaviors were in their incipient stage of development. Lumping them together under one designation obscures the unique properties of the strands that make up the fabric of psychopathology.

Adolf Stern

The next author to be reviewed is Adolf Stern, who was the first to write specifically about borderline patients. Apparently, when he published his first paper on this subject in 1938, he had considerable experience attempting classical psychoanalytic technique with this group of patients and seemed to have been discouraged with their inability to benefit from treatment. But as more patients with this form of disorder came for help, he modified his classical technique and limited his goals. He also focused his investigation to determine what aspects of the clinical picture remained unaffected by treatment methods that were successful in the usual run of psychoneurotics.

As the clinical picture unfolds it readily becomes apparent that Stern's private analytic patients from New York differed in various ways from those clinic patients treated by Reich in Vienna. There are also similarities. Stern found the now characteristic combination of neurotic and psychotic features tending to cluster closer to the psychotic end of the range. Stern had no doubt that this form of pathology was a specific disorder with specific symptomatology although it would be another thirty years before Kernberg, with a comprehensive series of papers on borderline personality organization, would establish this as an accepted notion.

We often take certain facts of our everyday work for granted, and lose perspective of their special significance; the phenomenon of transference is a case in point. Universal as this phenomenon is, psychoanalysis systematized it into an instrument of observation, among other things, which permitted the observation of events not available for study otherwise. In the study of psychological phenomena we come time and again to the realization that important discoveries have been made through the transference. It was on the basis of their transference features that Stern was able to draw a list of characteristics differentiating borderline patients from the classical neurotic. Specifically, borderlines developed exaggerated idealizations and overvaluations of the analyst, they were clinging and dependent, and dangerously vulnerable to extreme negative therapeutic reactions if the analyst was in the slightest degree less than gentle in wording his interventions. These reactions were not unfamiliar to Stern from his treatment of psychoneurotics, but the latter never demonstrated such intense responses or suffered such wide ranging effects.

Stern's delineation of the borderline syndrome consisted of several definite clinical features which functioned in the personality as defense mechanisms to protect the ego from easily inflicted narcissistic damage. When these defenses were inadequate, the patients suffered overwhelming anxiety, depression, and even total collapse.

The central clinical feature was the prominence of narcissism from which all other symptoms derived. In their infancy these patients had suffered sustained affect deprivation, a condition which Stern described variously as "affect hunger," borrowing a phrase from David Levy, and affective (narcissistic) malnutrition. They had been deprived of the security that comes from feeling loved. The dominance of this feature led Stern to raise the possibility, often repeated in discussions of borderline pathology, of constitutional factors as determinants of this sense of insecurity. However, one recurrent observation from the history of these patients is that the infantile trauma they seemed to have been exposed to was, not like that sustained by the psychoneurotic, intense and sporadic. These patients seemed to have experienced the continuous low grade traumatic situations which Khan has called "cumulative trauma."

Stern's borderline patients manifested a reaction pattern that he called "psychic bleeding," consisting of a tendency to collapse totally, to fall into immobility, lethargy, and paralysis in response to stress or traumatic exposure. Stern regarded this response as a recuperative retreat to heal the narcissistic wound.

The personality of these borderline patients had developed an early warning system which Stern called "hypersensitivity" and served to detect any kind of narcissistic danger, insult, or injury which, if not stopped, would precipitate unbearable anxiety. It also functioned as a factor in the next clinical feature, "the rigid personality," which consisted in a defensive stiffening of psychic attitudes which included postural defensive reactions as well, and it was triggered off quickly and automatically.

The "negative therapeutic reaction" already mentioned required an extreme alertness, tactfulness, and sensitivity on the part of the analyst who thus had to function in the capacity of the "protective shield" (Khan) for the patient. A particularly difficult problem appeared in the patient's inability to accept "insight" to which he might respond with depression, anxiety, and hostile withdrawal.

The "feelings of insecurity" were already mentioned. Stern saw this tendency having the power to distort the patient's self evaluation to the point of negating objective achievements and regarding these distortions as rational and justified.

One of the most malignant clinical manifestations was the patient's "masochism," for it operated to perpetuate itself. The patient showed a proclivity for self-commiseration and self-pity, and collecting long lists of grievances and misfortunes.

In addition to the feelings of insecurity Stern singled out another reaction pattern, "organic insecurity," which consisted of a deep-seated and recalcitrant lack of self-confidence and self-assurance that was impervious to the reality of actual achievements attained by the patient.

The feature that brought the borderline patients toward psychosis was their tendency to use "projective mechanisms." Stern reasoned that this could only occur if the patient, from some defect of judgment, would distort his perception of reality. It served as a mechanism of denial of their intrapsychic difficulties which could then be blamed on external circumstances.

Stern was particularly impressed by the patients' overvaluation of the analyst in the transference. Patients cast him in the image of an omnipotent agent with power to heal, to comfort, and to sustain, but equally powerful and capable of dire punishment if he were displeased. Because of the fear of the monster they created it was important for such patients to ingratiate themselves and be ever cautious and careful to please. The vulnerable position they experienced vis-à-vis the analyst made it impossible for these patients to experience and work through their well contained hostility and anger. They opted instead for clinging and dependence.

W.R.D. Fairbairn

Working in Edinburgh, at a distance from other centers of psychoanalytic activity, Fairbairn created an independent set of postulates based on the concept of a basic primary object seeking instinct that set him in opposition to classical theory and may have been responsible for his not being included in mainstream theory.

Very early he was impressed by the regularity with which neurotic difficulties seemed to be related to an underlying incapacity to make satisfying human relationships. It all seemed to go back to incompatible clusters of experiences in the intimate first relationship of the infant with his mother. Fairbairn first presented these views in 1940 in his paper on "Schizoid Factors in the Personality" which does not mention borderline phenomena, although today the schizoid group is regarded as a component of the borderline disorders.

The schizoid factors of the personality are a combination of clinical features determined by an intrapsychic core of tendencies derived from the relationship between mother and infant in the early oral stage of development. This core consists of three prominent features that have a powerful determining influence upon other behavior traits. These are (a) an attitude of omnipotence, (b) an attitude of isolation and detachment, and (c) preoccupation with inner reality. From their inception these tendencies undergo vicissitudes in the course of development so that their reflection in the personality is never linear and direct.

The other characteristics of the schizoid personality include (1) full-fledged depersonalization and derealization; (2) relatively minor or transient disturbances of the reality sense, such as feelings of "artificiality" (whether referred to the self or to the environment), experiences such as "the plate-glass feeling," feelings of unfamiliarity with familiar persons or environmental setting, and feelings of familiarity with the unfamiliar *(déjà-vu);* (3) dissociative phenomena such as somnambulism, the fugue, dual and multiple personality.

These phenomena of schizoid pathology may be found in a great variety of individuals who rarely come for treatment, such as fanatics, criminals, agitators, and revolutionaries. Some of these personality characteristics may also energize socially useful capacities in better integrated personalities, for instance, the type of adjustment based on overvaluation of thought processes and detachment which would be an asset to one engaged in scientific research. Fairbairn found schizoid phenomena very common in patients who seek treatment for problems of social inhibitions, difficulties concentrating on and finishing their work, and particularly in those patients presenting mixed symptomatology, character disorders and sexual perversions which are difficult to fit in any of the current diagnostic classifications.

Fairbairn anticipated the criticism that his definition of schizoid phenomena covered so much ground that it practically involved everybody, whether normal or pathological. He did not disagree with this conclusion and explained that this is so because schizoid phenomena are caused by the splitting of the ego which is a universal and normal mode of defense of the early oral stage. "In my opinion, at any rate, some measure of splitting of the ego is invariably present at the deepest mental level—or (to express the same thing in terms borrowed from Melanie Klein) *the basic position in the psyche is invariably a schizoid position"* (p. 8, italics the author's). In addition, as the earliest developmental stage, this is the time of origin of object relations and feeding

experiences, and, therefore, whether these experiences are gratifying, pleasant, orderly, and serene, they will have an effect on the
kinds of fixations that are developed. In fact, Fairbairn shows
how the characteristic attitudes of the early oral stage are later
expressed in and influence adult behavior.

Splitting of the ego is a primitive but normal process of defense
during the first year of life. It has the opposite effect of integration, so that when it persists at the time when integrative and
synthetic processes come into ascendancy, the tendency for splitting of the ego will disrupt the integration of ego functions.
Among these will be those involved in the relationship with
reality, the discrimination of inner and outer reality, the integration of perceptions of reality, and also the integration of behavior
tendencies. If one assumes that lack of integration extends along
a continuum from a theoretical ideal of perfect integration to the
complete lack of it, and assigns schizophrenic disorganization to
this latter extreme, schizoid characters would fall closer to this
end.

Fairbairn found support for his views in Jung's concept of the
"introverted type," which is closely associated with schizophrenia. The variable of introversion and preoccupation with
inner reality are also related, which suggests a relationship between schizoid characters and schizophrenia. To Fairbairn this
was supporting evidence from an independent source lending
validity to his clinical group.

Fairbairn develops a cogent conceptualization showing that
the clinical manifestations and personality attributes of schizoid
individuals derive their distinguishing characteristics from fixations of the libidinal attitudes of the oral stage brought about by
trauma that cause the ego to split. In the same year that Freud was
discussing the role of splitting of the ego in the neuroses, psychoses, and in fetishism, Fairbairn (1940) said, "In my opinion,
problems involved in splitting of the ego deserve much more
attention that they have so far received" (p. 10).

From these interactions the following consequences may be observed in schizoid individuals: First, since the first libidinal object is a part object, the breast, schizoid persons tend to relate to others as if they were part objects for the gratification of their own needs and not as having an intrinsic worth as persons. Likewise and second, since the activity of feeding implies a greater element of "taking" rather than giving, the attitude toward objects is dominated by consequences of overvaluation of "taking." The schizoid individual overvalues the contents of his body as well as of his psyche in a sense that imparts to "giving" the meaning of losing and becoming depleted and impoverished. They treat their affects this way and tend to repress them as if to keep them inside, and appear to be detached, aloof, and remote. Under the effect of this dynamic schizoid individuals develop means to compensate for the missing affects and experiences by adopting substitute behaviors such as taking roles like actors playing on a stage. Another aspect of the libidinal attitude of "taking" is a third consequence, the attitude of incorporating and internalizing which contributes further to valuing inner contents over those of the external world. For these individuals that which is of value in life is contained internally and the external objects acquire meaning from these internal values. In extreme cases such as in schizophrenia the distinction between inner and outer is largely lost. In other cases the anxiety over losing these valued contents affect the capacity for productivity, creativity, and work since these are experienced as depleting and depriving them of their inner contents. One of the most important aspects of the dynamic of overvaluing inner contents is the attitude of omnipotence or superiority which remains largely unconscious. It is an aspect of narcissistic inflation based on the secret possession of, and identification with, internalized libidinal objects, for instance, the maternal breast or the paternal penis.

The fourth and final dynamic deriving from the incorporative mode is based on the persistence of the unconscious fantasy that the infant is assumed to have when deprived and hungry. The fantasy is that the breast and the mother are not present because in his state of greediness and deprivation the infant has devoured and made them disappear. In schizoid adults, the sense of being unloved, alone, needy, and deprived reactivates the unconscious fantasy of having destroyed his libidinal objects. Likewise, one's love is bad and destructive, otherwise the love object would be present and accept one's love. These unconscious fantasies, derived from deprivation states at the oral stage, make interpersonal and affectional relationships very difficult for these patients. They seem to act in object relationships so as to actively drive others away with their hate and quarrelsomeness. Fairbairn remarks that they do "all of this in order to keep . . . libidinal objects at a distance" (p. 26), so to safeguard them from their destructiveness.

This summary does not do justice to the rich, nicely flowing style, and depth of human understanding in Fairbairn's paper, but it intends to convey the breadth of clinical observation and theoretical integration of such a diverse variety of clinical phenomena under a few basic principles that one finds in this paper. Until the work of Mahler (see Mahler, Pine, and Bergman 1975), Kernberg and Bion, no other author had worked out, in such carefully developed detail, the intrapsychic events at the origin of schizoid pathology. He also seemed to have attracted patients from another segment of the borderline range than the ones treated by Reich and Stern, but with certain similar features described by others that followed him.

Helene Deutsch

Deutsch's famous paper (1942) "Some Forms of Emotional Disturbance and Their Relationship to Schizophrenia" is an expanded version of her 1934 German article in which she first introduced the "as if" concept. The English publication is the one most often quoted, making it apparent that the earlier paper was not well known in America.

The "as if" concept refers to a personality mode of functioning in social relationships characterized by mock normality but lacking in any genuine emotional experience of relatedness; the person moves through life *as if* he were normally involved. In all outward appearances he seems perfectly normal. "There is nothing to suggest any kind of disorder, behavior is not unusual, intellectual abilities appear unimpaired, emotional expressions are well ordered and appropriate," writes Deutsch. But there is an ominous quality, a "something intangible and indefinable that obtrudes between the person and his fellows and invariably gives rise to the question 'What is wrong?' " (p. 302).

The history of these patients suggests that they were exposed to chronic emotional deprivation and inconsistency in their primary relationships at the time preceding the ascendancy of the oedipus complex. This left them without the necessary cathectic energy to internalize and integrate the various fragments of identifications which go to form a unified superego. Deutsch explains that in their pregenital development these patients devalued the objects that could have served them as models for personality development, and thus failed to attain a sense of personal identity.

In the conceptual idiom of psychoanalysis of the 1930s Deutsch thought of the developmental failure as one of sublimation and as limited to the affects and moral tendencies while the intellectual functions were left undisturbed. Reality testing also was to some extent impaired, but not to the degree of a loss of reality, and Deutsch clearly ruled out the possibility of psychosis. She also emphasized that the kinds of impairments she had observed implied a developmental failure, or arrested development and not regression.

The outstanding characteristic of the clinical picture is a tendency for primary identification, that is, they hide their lack of their own identity by an uncanny ability to pick up cues from others and imitate their behavior, attitudes, speech, and mannerisms. But their actual experience is totally empty of emotional relatedness. A second characteristic of "as if" personalities is their suggestibility, a remarkable plasticity based on a passive yielding to external influences. It is very much unlike the suggestibility of hysterics which is based on affectively charged object cathexes. Finally, a third characteristic is covert aggressiveness. It is rather marked by passivity so that they convey a feeling of negative goodness, but are readily influenced to join in antisocial activities if they are in that kind of group.

At a panel on the "as if" characters reported by Weiss (1966), Samuel Atkins, the Chairman, summarized Deutsch's contribution in a manner that makes clear the similarity of the "as if" dynamics to those of borderline patients:

> (a) the primitive stage of object relations without object constancy; (b) the poor development of the superego with objective anxiety still predominant; (c) the prevalence of the primary identification process; (d) the lack of sense of identity; (e) the emotional superficiality and general poverty of affect, of which these patients are unaware; and (f) the lack of insight. This lack of insight . . . is one aspect of the narcissistic state of these patients.

Gustav Bychowski

In reviewing the clinical delineation of Bychowski's concept of "latent psychosis," which he worked out from the basis of Bleuler's notion of latent schizophrenia, it might be useful to examine the ancestry of these concepts. Psychosis is a term first introduced by Feuchtersleben (1806–1849) to indicate the end state of progressive pathological conditions (hypochondriasis in men and hysteria in women were some of the intermediate states). "The term psychosis was adapted to its present day usage, as was the term neurosis [by Kraepelin], implicit in which was the concept of the well-known disease entity." (Parkin 1966a). Kraepelin included under this term among other disease processes the whole deteriorating group he called dementia praecox (Morel 1857). Parkin points out that in later editions of his textbook Kraepelin modified his position, abandoning the invariability of the terminal dementia and the precocious onset. When Bleuler changed the name of the condition to schizophrenia, acknowledging Kraepelin's change of viewpoint, he nevertheless retained the concept of disease entity and made a careful distinction between symptom, symptom-complex, and disease entity.

Bleuler first introduced the term latent schizophrenia in 1911 and in the following years he modified its meaning to the point of being in conflict with his own conception of schizophrenia. In 1911, he said that latent schizophrenia was the most prevalent form of the disease and many who suffered from it never came for treatment. This form manifested in an incipient state all the symptoms and combinations of symptoms that are found in the manifest types. "Irritable, odd, moody, withdrawn or exaggeratedly punctual people arouse, among other things, the suspicion of being schizophrenic." (quoted by Parkin 1966a, p. 222). In 1916 he applied the term latent schizophrenia to cases of simple schizophrenia, a form that has a slow insidious onset which may or may not become manifest. But he also said at a later time: "At all events, the name latent schizophrenia will always make one think of a morbid psychopathic state, in which the schizoid peculiarities are within normal limits." Parkin finally comments: "Here the specific designation of any morbid psychopathic state, other than schizophrenia itself, would place Bleuler in the untenable position of admitting the possibility of states which are potentially transitional to schizophrenia. The torturous attempt to avoid such an admission, which would be a damaging blow to the disease-process concept, is characterized by the struggle with the contradictions in, and the effort to legitimize, the term latent schizophrenia" (p. 223).

The explication of the term latent schizophrenia, upon which Bychowski based his concept of latent psychosis reveals that the reluctance to recognize borderline disorders as separate modes of psychopathology may be related to an implicit resistance to give up the point of view of disease process and disease entity in psychiatry. The same burden is carried by those other attempts to introduce the notion of a classificatory group that would still imply a relationship to schizophrenia, such as Zilboorg's ambulatory schizophrenia (1941), Polatin's pseudoneurotic schizophrenia (1948), Gaw, Reichard, and Tillman's nonpsychotic schizophrenia (1953), and Meares's prepsychotic schizophrenia (1959) among others.

In his concept of latent psychosis Bychowski (1953) included the following manifestation of pathology: (a) character neurotic difficulties which, at an appropriate provocation, may burst into psychosis; (b) neurotic symptomatology with the same outcome; (c) deviant behavior, for instance delinquency, perversion, addiction; (d) an arrested psychosis, posing as psychopathy, and, like other groups, likely to reveal someday its true nature; and (e) psychosis provoked by therapeutic or didactic psychoanalysis.

Cases of latent psychosis could be differentiated with the aid of observations in the analytic situation where the latent psychosis might be inferred from such manifestations as: (1) evidence of primary process predominating the patient's productions, with displacement, condensations, and magical thinking; (2) indications of ego weakness, manifested by (i) vulnerability to the slightest frustration, and (ii) being easily disappointed and readily depressed, particularly by the analyst's "cold and unfeeling" attitude; (3) evidence of narcissistic hypercathexis, as shown by the persistence of primitive megalomania with its characteristic irritability, impatience, and the primitive defense mechanism of blocking, withdrawal, and detachment; (4) associated with all the above, there is primitive nonneutralized aggression which bursts out into reactions of rage at the slightest provocation; and (5) consistent with the above one also finds ideas of reference, massive projections and paranoid reactions coloring the transference.

Bychowski points out that all these clinical manifestations arise from split-off primitive ego states persisting within a context of an actual ego that has, in all other ways, advanced developmentally to states of more mature organization and functioning. He then goes on to present the psychoanalytic view of the psychogenesis of these pathological dynamics:

In the course of early development the splitting mechanism comes into action, so that early ego states remain untouched under the cover of later ego formations. Accordingly, archaic constellations remain fixated and preserved, as it were, for future reference. They form then the psychotic germs which, under the impact of various dynamic and environmental factors, can cause the psychotic breakdown of ego defenses and sever whatever reality contact and testing have been built up in the course of later development [Bychowski 1953, p. 491].

Bychowski illustrated the primary process dynamics to which he had referred in his paper with clinical material from the treatment of a case which, in remarkable fashion, offered confirmation for some of the dynamics which Melanie Klein, in England, had recently (1952) formulated from data provided by the unconscious fantasies of her much younger patients. Bychowski commented that one of his patients, since he realized that he could not possess his mother would, instead, "give the thrill" to himself in being both the mother and the sexually aggressive father. In this way he would no longer need his parents as sexual objects." Later on, "In the course of analytic work the introjected love-hate objects may become extrajected and assume the role of persecutors" (p. 496). And further on, "The patient had felt that his mother had usurped all the power by having at times the father's penis inside her; in his fantasy he would bear her by keeping it inside his stomach permanently" (p. 97). In her theoretical formulations Melanie Klein would postulate an infantile developmental position, the paranoid-schizoid position, during which the baby would be terrified by psychotic anxieties of being destroyed by his own internal destructive drives and by external objects rendered persecutory by the projection of his own destructiveness on them. Against these psychotic anxieties the infant would defend himself by means of psychotic defenses which included splitting of the ego, omnipotent fantasy, and excessive projective identification, among others.

John Frosch

In a series of papers, beginning in 1959, Frosch set out to describe the psychopathology and dynamics of a clinical picture he calls "the psychotic character." The consistency with which the combination of symptoms, the potential for psychotic episodes under conditions of stress, as well as the specificity and reversibility of these breaks with reality occur, justify setting up the concept of "psychotic character" as a group differentiated from the larger area of borderline conditions.

Its differentiating characteristic is the tendency for psychotic loss of reality testing in such situations as for instance, classical analysis, under drugs or alcohol, and fatigue and other forms of stress. This potentially sets this group apart from the psycho-neuroses and, because the patient recovers fully in a short time, also from the actual psychotic groups.

Many of these patients are able to function adaptively and productively for the entire course of their lives, but if one were to scrutinize the details of their life patterns, one would readily discover a marked rigidity of personality, and a need for a high level of external structure in living and working conditions. In fact, adjustment appears to be an all or nothing affair predicated on stable routine.

The psychotic character differs from actual psychosis in that *(a)* the loss of reality during the regressive episode is limited to the duration of the precipitating stress. Removal of the stress brings about complete recovery; and *(b)* during the psychotic free periods the patient functions at various levels of pathology and normality at the same time and under the same conditions.

The term "psychotic character" was chosen to correspond with "neurotic character" to explicitly borrow from the older term the notion of a vulnerable pathological structure free of symptoms under conditions that are also free of stress. In order to identify the nature of pathology in the psychotic character Frosch developed a differential analysis of the concepts of neurosis and psychosis based on three variables: (1) the nature of the psychic conflict, that is, the nature of danger to the ego; (2) the character of the ego defenses mobilized by the conflict; and (3) what, if any, is the nature of ego impairments precipitated by the conflict.

Frosch builds his analysis from a foundation of the classical psychoanalytic view of psychopathology as the vicissitudes of the psychic conflict in early infancy. Beginning with his 1964 paper, however, he also recognizes the validity of some of Melanie Klein's concepts of primitive defenses such as projective identification, and in 1970 he acknowledges the work of Otto Kernberg

in clarifying the operation of these primitive defenses in borderline patients.

(1) *The nature of the danger to the ego.* Psychotic structure of
the personality, and the dynamics that operate within, originates
at the earliest stage of development that precedes the establishment of stable ego boundaries, the emergence of self- and object
differentiation (primary narcissism), and is initiated by a trauma
of such devastating proportions that the actual psychic survival
of the individual is at stake. This danger to the ego can be
actualized in either of two directions, (i) through the actions of its
own destructive drives, or (ii) by the dissolution of the self
through engulfment by the object.

(2) *Defenses.* The result is all-pervasive anxiety, and what
appears to be desperate and disorganized defensive efforts as
shown by the pan-neurotic symptomatology that develops as a
first line of defense against the dissolution of the ego. At this early
development stage only the most primitive defenses operate,
namely, regressive dedifferentiation of whatever self-object separation may have been achieved, fragmentation, introjective-
projective techniques such as projective identification, splitting of
the ego, massive denial, and somatization.

(3) *Ego impairments.* The psychotic character typically presents altered ego states, due to loss of ego boundaries, particularly
twilight, dreamlike, and confused states, feelings of unreality, and
depersonalization, all of which are temporary and reversible.
Frosch ascribes a basic role to these ego defects in determining the
clinical phenomena.

Frosch singles out the capacity for reality testing for special
theoretical elaboration, thus increasing its usefulness for specify-
ing the nature of loss of reality in the psychotic character and
borderline pathology in general. Frosch based his conception of
the function of contact with reality on Freud's work. We see that
as Freud returned to refine his understanding of the processes

differentiating neurosis from psychosis he saw that more was required than the statement regarding the loss and reconstruction of reality. His discovery that in fetishism the mechanism operating to resolve the psychic conflict was splitting, and that this was done in a novel way that both denied and affirmed the perceptions of reality that seemed at first to offer a third alternative. In this case the ego was less unified than in neurosis but more integrated and effective than in psychosis. In his last effort (1940b) Freud came to the conclusion that splitting also occurred in neurosis and psychosis, and even in normal functioning such as in dreams and the observing ego function, thus blurring all clear cut lines of cleavage. Finally, he stated that given the concurrence of all three methods of dealing with a threatening reality which allowed for the persistence of two contrary and independent attitudes towards reality simultaneously, the outcome, whether neurosis, psychosis, or normality depended on an energy factor (the stronger attitude that determined the outcome). However, rather than a solution, this seems to be only another way station along the way to fuller understanding.

Frosch took up the task where Freud left off and made a significant advance with his analysis of the ego function of contact with reality as the processes of relationship to reality, the sense of reality, and reality testing. This added a considerable measure of precision to the evaluation of reality contact and permitted the differentiation of the psychotic character from neurosis and psychosis.

It will be shown later that a great leap in the capacity to account for many of the manifestations of disturbance in the reality function which result from a patient's attempts to cope with intrapsychic tensions is represented by the conceptualizations of Bion of intermediate psychic processes mediating the relationship to reality.

Table 2 presents Freud's formulations in summary fashion for comparison with his earlier papers and the work of Frosch.

TABLE 2

FREUD'S SECOND DIFFERENTIATION BETWEEN NEUROSIS AND PSYCHOSIS

DISORDER	CAUSE	EFFECT	RESPONSE	DEFENSE MECHANISM	OUTCOME
Neurosis	Psychic trauma	Psychic conflict	Renounce instinct	Repression	
Psychosis	Psychic trauma	Psychic conflict	Disavows reality	Denial disavowal	
Fetishism	Psychic trauma	Psychic conflict	Does both at the same time	Splitting of the ego.	Holds simultaneously two contradictory attitudes: one in accord with reality, the other in accord with fantasy.

(1940a)

| Neuroses, states like neuroses | | | | Repression, disavowal, splitting | There are present in the subject's mental life, . . . , two different attitudes, contrary to each other and independent of each other . . . one of these attitudes belongs to the ego and the contrary one, which is repressed, belongs to the id. |

(1940b)

Psychosis	(1) Reality becomes intolerably painful, or (2) an instinct becomes extraordinarily intense.	1) Detach from reality but not completely, and (2) at the same time retain contact with reality.	Psychical split	Two psychical attitudes are formed instead of a single one—one, the normal one which takes account of reality and another which under the influence of instincts detaches the ego from reality. "Even in a state so far removed from reality of the external world as one of hallucinatory confusion, one learns from patients after their recovery that at the same time in some corner of their mind (as they put it) there was a normal person hidden, who, like a detached spectator, watched the hubbub of illness go past him" (p. 59 see also Bion).
Fetishism	(1) Disavows his own sense perception that perception that genitals lack a penis and (2) holds fast to the contrary conviction		Splitting of the ego.	The two attitudes persist side by side throughout their lives without influencing each other.

One may subdivide the interactions of the ego with its environment and with objects into three component functions: (1) the relationship with reality proper; (2) the sense of reality, or feelings of reality; and (3) the capacity for reality testing.

(1) Ego impairments in the relationship with reality are indicated by perceptual distortions, phenomena relating to lack of boundaries, hallucinations and delusions. They would also be revealed in bizarre deviations from cultural attitudes, and ordinary social amenities. The loss of ego boundaries refers to such experiences as confusion and difficulties in experiencing one's separateness from the nonhuman environment.

(2) Disturbances in the feelings of reality are manifested by the perception of internal conditions with a distorted quality of concreteness, such as feelings of unreality and depersonalization.

(3) The capacity for testing reality, finally, is based on the preceding functions and involves the ability to arrive at logical conclusions based on the self-observation of these phenomena. The criterion of psychotic functioning refers to the loss of this capacity for reality testing. The milder clinical manifestations of the psychotic character involve, conversely, disturbances in the relationship to reality and in the sense of reality within a context of correct and objective reality testing. To repeat, the psychotic character's regressive malfunctioning in these areas is fully reversible to nonpsychotic levels.

The most important area of ego impairments, rich in signs of psychotic character functioning, is the area of behavior in relationships with objects. In the psychotic maturation has been impaired from the level that follows pre-object differentiation, that is, fixation has occurred at the point of cosmic identity, autistic and symbiotic modes of relating. In the psychotic character, on the other hand, maturation has progressed to the level of recognition of the object, but only as a need-gratifying object, and not as a person that has a separate existence. This is one of the areas of behavior where modes of relatedness appropriate to various levels of maturation and regression may be observed in the psychotic character.

Frosch takes up another ego variable because of its relevancy to a specification of psychotic manifestations, namely, the ego relationships with other personality structures. Psychosis is characterized by a lack of harmony and dovetailing among the various personality systems. The most readily observable consequence of this failure to keep proper boundaries within the psyche is the prevalence of infiltration of secondary process by primary process. The manifestations of predominance of primary process may be observed in the deneutralization of instinctual drives, in thoughts, feelings, and behavior. And, as it was said of the other dysfunctions, this overflowing of primary process is also reversible in the psychotic character.

A final psychic structure analyzed by Frosch for its utility in differentiating psychosis from the psychotic character and from neurosis is the level of integration and internalization of the superego. The disturbed early object relations which laid down impairments in the formation of the ego, likewise affected the development of the superego as a subsystem differentiating from the ego. The pathological superego may be identified by its lack of depersonification (a system of abstract values and norms has not evolved); by the presence of lacunae, a feature that is revealed by episodes of impulsivity and acting out; and by persistent tendencies to projection and externalization. With inconsistency and temporary instability typical in the psychotic character, one would expect to find attitudes of harsh self-criticism accompanied by episodic outbursts of guilt and depression. The lack of stable defenses and the fear of losing control of his impulses is behind the appearance of severe rigidities and inhibitions which have evolved as long-term, chronic defensive postures.

In his 1970 paper, in the section on treatment, Frosch adds a new focus that has now become typical of borderline pathology. In analysis, these patients are exposed within to an enormous intensity of rage and aggressiveness. These experiences are accompanied by equivalent levels of anxiety and defensive reactions attuned to the dangers which his destructive impulses exposes the ego. Patients fear destruction from retaliation by the analyst, on the one hand, but at the same time they fear destroying the analyst, and because of temporary dedifferentiation and the confusion of the self with the object, they fear their own annihilation and psychic death.

Frosch's view of the psychotic character, which is also applicable to borderline personalities, is a stable and specific disorder, not as a transition stage from neurosis to psychosis, as some other authors believed at another time. His well reasoned and systematic argument contributes a very helpful analysis of variables, adding considerable organization to the often confusing array of borderline manifestations.

Melanie Klein

The work of Melanie Klein has opened up new areas of theoretical understanding of normal and pathological mental function. It has served as a foundation and inspiration to many profound psychoanalytic thinkers like Rosenfeld, Bion, Searles, Grotstein, Kernberg, and Langs, among others. Her conceptions of early psychic development offer the possibility of understanding many phenomena of borderline pathology as the operation of anachronistic mental processes whose persistence and misapplication in adult mental functioning underlies the activation of the clinical manifestations.

The following, extremely condensed presentation of some basic Kleinian concepts may be helpful in following the creative contributions of Kernberg and Bion in later sections of this chapter.

Basic Postulates

Melanie Klein's work with children led her to assume that "sufficient ego exists at birth to experience anxiety, use defense mechanisms and form primitive object relations in phantasy and reality" (Segal 1964, p. 24). She postulated two early developmental positions: the first, the paranoid-schizoid lasting up to the first four months of life is followed by the second, depressive position. The concept of position is chosen rather than that of a developmental stage because it implies a set of anxieties and associated defense mechanisms that predominates at some time early in development, later recedes as more mature constellations of anxieties and defenses take ascendancy, but is never fully outgrown. The particular combinations of experiences and reactions remain as potentialities and under given conditions take ascendancy again, determining behavior manifestations in adult life.

The paranoid-schizoid position is characterized by persecutory anxieties, fragmentation, differentiation, splitting, and other primitive defense mechanism, whereas the depressive position is one of depressive anxiety (loss and separation), of consolidation, cohesion, and synthesis.

The infant's first experience of anxiety is aroused by the operation of aggression, a drive derivative of the death instinct. The infant experiences the danger of destruction by the death instinct and the only mechanism of defense available to him, or her, is to expell the intolerable feelings into the external world. Such is the operation of projective identification by which the infant evacuates a split-off part of the death instinct into an external object, the maternal object, who now is experienced as an external persecutor. Splitting serves the ego to separate unwanted parts of the mind and keep them apart within the psyche, or to evacuate them into an external object. What sets off the mechanisms of defense is the discomfort of frustration. As long as it remains within limits, the operation of projective identification proceeds in tune with an incipient capacity for reality testing. When frustration exceeds tolerable limits, "omnipotent phantasy" intervenes and produces what Klein called "excessive" projective identification which operates with disregard for reality, leading to irrational expectations from the object.

When the maternal object does what the baby requires to be gratified, comforted, and calmed, the theory states that the object has detoxified the death instinct projected into her and makes it available for reintrojection as a "good" object, or the "ideal object." This then becomes the core of the growing ego. At first the "good" object is assumed to be a "part object," such as the mother's breast. Repeated experiences with the quality of gratification, love, and security go to provide many more "part objects," that is, various qualities of positive experience associated with different good aspects of the object. The assumption of a "part object" explains theoretically immature forms of object relations as seen in borderline patients for whom the object is treated solely as a need-gratifying object and without entitlement to a separate existence.

When the mothering object fails to attend to the infant's needs and frustration, discomfort, and anxiety persists, the theory states that the object, by failing to provide relief, has become an external persecutor. It is as if the continuing suffering is now produced by an external agent. The continuation of intolerable frustration amounts to a reintrojection of the death instinct who now becomes, in a new way, an internal persecutor. These developments describe the introjection of a "bad" part object. A parallel development leads to the acquisition of "good" and "bad" part objects, thus setting up an internal world of object relations.

The "good" part objects and the "bad" part objects now coexist, but it is possible for frustration, and anxiety, to become stronger or to occur more frequently than the experiences of pleasure and well-being. These conditions trigger off more anxiety on account of the danger that the "bad" part object may contaminate, spoil, damage, or even destroy the "good" object. This may explain theoretically the toddler's reaction of rejection of the mother when she returns after a prolonged separation. During her absence the object-image of the mother has been transformed into a "bad" object by association with the pain and suffering of separation and loss. Upon her return the mother, who is now a "bad" object, is feared as a persecutor who threatens to damage the "good" object, and is to be avoided.

The need to preserve the "good" part object sets into operation the defense of splitting which keeps the "bad" part object segregated from the "good" part object. Denial, omnipotent fantasy, and idealization are also defenses of this period.

The depressive position is initiated by the coalescence and synthesis of the "good" part objects with the "bad" part objects, and of "good" and "bad" part self-representations, as with growing maturity of the perceptual capacities and of memory the infant becomes capable of relating these contrary aspects to the same object. The integration of the part objects eventually leads to the establishment within the psyche of a "whole" object with good and bad aspects. A similar process of integration leads to the establishment of a "whole" self-representation.

As the depressive position gets under way, the anxieties and defenses of the paranoid-schizoid position do not at once decline, and splitting and fragmentation continue to occur. However, there begins a see-saw movement back and forth between the depressive and the paranoid-schizoid positions, an oscillation between processes of integration and fragmentation, which under normal conditions proceed to progressively integrated functioning. As the ego becomes better organized with the firmer establishment of the ideal object, projections slow down, splitting is not needed as often, and repression takes over.

The attainment of the "whole" object now permits in the infant the awareness of a separate person with an independent existence and interests that do not always include him. As his perceptual and memory apparatuses mature and the "whole" representations become more stable, the infant begins to experience his own helplessness and dependence, and with these, the feelings that the object that is hated is also needed, and, further, that it is also loved. This is the origin of ambivalence and of efforts to regain the lost object, to restore, repair, or recreate it. These events also mark the beginning of concern for the object, remorse and guilt.

The awareness of his own dependence and helplessness and the new experiences of ambivalence contribute to the growing awareness of psychic reality. The distinction between fantasy and external reality begins and is accompanied by parallel acquisition of the differentiation between psychic reality and external reality. A related occurrence is the toning down of omnipotence based on the capacity to bear frustration and the awareness of dependence on others who will not always allow themselves to be controlled.

Symbol Formation

Symbolism has its inception at this time arising from the need and the efforts to regain, restore, and repair the lost love object. All these events take place during the oral phase of psychosexual development, during which introjective processes are in the ascendancy and primitive projective mechanisms decline. Basing her theoretical thinking on Freud's statement that sublimation is the outcome of the successful renunciation of a lost object, Melanie Klein postulates that the object that is given up is also internalized, set up as an internal object in the ego through a process of internal restoration. This assimilated object constitutes the first symbol. Sublimation involves also giving up of instinctual aims and displacement of cathexes to new nonsexual aims. Thus, as the infant gives up the breast he sets up a pattern of renunciation and creation of new aims and new objects which will be repeated many times in life as he develops sublimations and creates symbols.

The Consolidation of Mental Functioning

In the depressive position some paranoid and depressive anxieties continue but, as a result of the integration of the ego and the consolidation of secure object relations, the original intensities of early anxiety and conflicts become considerably toned down. Melanie Klein has sometimes been misunderstood to say that the infant goes through a developmental position during which he is psychotic, whereas in fact, she stated that due to the immaturity of the reality testing (which does exist in incipient form at birth), and the nature of anxiety of the death instinct as well as the nature of primitive defense mechanisms, the infant experiences psychotic distortions of reality only as aspects of infantile psychic experience. With the consolidations gained through the depressive position these psychotic mechanisms are gradually replaced by neurotic mechanisms. Melanie Klein stated in regard to infantile neurosis what Freud had said about adult neurosis, namely, that neurosis sometimes represents the first line of defense against the underlying psychotic anxieties.

Coexistence of Psychotic and Neurotic Modes

A theoretical conception which has imparted order and meaning to otherwise confusing phenomena concerns the coexistence, under various phases of defensive operations, of both psychotic and neurotic processes in normal persons, in analysands, as well as those suffereing from various degrees of pathology. The coexistence of neurotic and psychotic processes in the clinical manifestations of borderline patients seems to call for such formulation.

This view takes many forms. The above mentioned reference to Freud's statement, which reads as follows, is one: "Often enough, when one sees a case of neurosis with hysterical or obsessional symptoms, mild in character and of short duration (just the type of case, that is, which one would regard as suitable for treatment), a doubt which must not be overlooked arises whether the case may not be one of incipient dementia praecox, so called (schizophrenia according to Bleuler; paraphrenia, as I prefer to call it), and may not sooner or later develop well marked signs of this disease" (Freud 1913). Parkin (1966) has recently carefully investigated the phenomena indicated by Freud in this passage. Another form of this view was also expressed by Freud in *An Outline of Psycho-Analysis* (1940b) where he stated:

> The problem of psychoses would be simple and perspicuous if the ego's detachment from reality could be carried through completely. But that seems to happen only rarely or perhaps never. Even in a state so far removed from the reality of the external world as one of hallucinatory confusion, one learns from patients after their recovery that at the time in some corner of their mind (as they put it) there was a normal person hidden, who, like a detached spectator, watched the hubbub of illness go past him. I do not know if we may assume that this is so in general, but I can report the same of other psychoses with a less tempestuous course. I call to mind a case of chronic paranoia in which after each attack of jealousy a dream conveyed to the analyst a correct picture of the precipitating cause, free from any delusion. . . . We may probably take it as being generally true that what occurs in all these cases is a psychical *split* [italics the author's].

Freud continued at this point to describe his concept of splitting of the ego, which proved to have great theoretical power to account for borderline phenomena:

Two psychical attitudes have been formed instead of a single one—one, the normal one, which takes account of reality, and another which under the influence of the instincts detaches the ego from reality. The two exist alongside of each other. The issue depends on their relative strength. If the second is or becomes the stronger, the necessary precondition for a psychosis is present. If the relation is reversed, then there is an apparent cure of the delusional disorder. Actually it has only retreated into the unconscious—just as numerous observations lead us to believe that the delusion existed ready-made for a long time before its manifest irruption.

Melanie Klein's view of this concept has been mentioned above. Bion has the most explicit formulation; he maintains that the mental mechanisms of the paranoid-schizoid position persist in various degrees of activation and overt manifestation in every individual as a mode of mental functioning, which he calls the *psychotic personality,* side by side with the *nonpsychotic personality.* In their *Introduction to the Work of Bion,* Grinberg, Sor, and Bianchedi (1977) state Bion's basic postulate as follows:

The individual, whatever his stage of development, faces emotional phenomena of different kinds and resolves them in a particular way. For this task he uses his consciousness, which analogus to the sense organs, is considered by Freud "a sense organ for the perception of psychical qualities." Bion postulates its existence in a rudimentary form from the beginning of life. Its development requires stimuli that at first consist of feelings and later on of the whole range of mental phenomena. Contact with internal and external reality is very closely linked to this "organ" and the way of approaching such reality depends on its way of functioning. The multiple experiences of the individual in his contact with himself and with others imply an unavoidable confrontation between his tendency to "have consciousness" and not to have it, between his tendency to tolerate it and to avoid it. This confrontation and its consequences give rise to different configurations in different individual mentalities, one of which is the *psychotic personality,* or psychotic part of the personality [p. 26].

Melanie Klein's notions regarding psychotic anxieties in early childhood are unfolded and developed by Bion, whose work we may now examine in more detail.

W.R. Bion

The impression seems to be growing among clinicians that reality testing and thinking as instruments for the relationship with reality may not be as intact in borderline patients as has been reported. The work of Deutsch, Frosch, and some of the findings of Gunderson suggest that the current impression may be due to the lack of conceptual precision which does not permit finer specification of processes. The work of Bion, as far as it relates to the apparatus of thinking as a set of processes mediating the relationship to reality, has been useful as a theoretical explanation of some thought disorders, as well as other phenomena of interaction in the analytic situation (Bion 1962, Langs 1978), and may hold the promise of further applications in the understanding of borderline phenomena.

Bion's system of concepts, models, and theories flows from the theoretical headwaters of Freud's and Melanie Klein's thought. It grew out of his clinical experience with patients, in analysis as the need arose to understand their inability to make sense of their experiences and relationships with others, and this seemed to be determined by defects in their capacity for thinking. Langs has shown that its field of application reaches further than the severe thought disorders of psychotic patients and many of the processes postulated by Bion occur every day in the analytic situation.

The roots of Bion's work in Freud relate to his formulations of the pleasure and reality principles and the propositions on thinking. Grinberg, Sor, and Bianchedi (1977) in their *Introduction to the Work of Bion* emphasize that as early as 1911 Freud had established that "the beginning of the *dominance by the reality principle is synchronous with the development of the ability to think and thus bridge the frustrating gap between the moment a need is felt and the point at which appropriate action satisfies it*" (italics mine, p. 46).

Bion also credited Freud for the formulation of consciousness as "a sense organ for the perception of psychical qualities" from sense impressions as well as of emotional experiences. In characterizing the function of thinking, Freud had conceived of it as originally having the character of an evacuative mechanism to rid the psyche of excess stimulation before it acquired the capacity to contain it. An intermediate step in that evolution was provided by motor discharge which was employed in the proper alteration of reality. Then the capacity to restraint action in accordance to the requirements of reality became possible through the process of thinking.

Melanie Klein provided Bion (1962) with the conceptions of "splitting and projective identification; the transition from the paranoid-schizoid to the depressive position and vice versa; symbol formation . . . . " (p. 37).

Bion's model of thinking borrows a metaphor from the processes of food intake and assimilation which helps clarify some of the concepts he uses. Bion uses "thinking" in two senses: one refers to "thoughts" as events that are "epistemologically prior to thinking"; the second concerns the origin and operation of the apparatus for thinking which the mind develops out of the necessity to think those thoughts. If this were to sound strange it might be helpful to remember that in biological evolution, necessity creates function and the physical structures for that function. The apparatus for thinking develops through the operation of two dominant processes: one involves the relationship of container to contained; the second involves the interactions between the paranoid-schizoid position and the depressive position.

Whether the apparatus for thinking attains to normal or pathological development hinges on the capacity of the newborn to tolerate anxiety, and on the presence of a mothering object with the capacity for reverie ("good enough" mothering), who in that capacity also is, to use another of Bion's concepts, a good "container." A good container has the capacity to contain, to hold, and accept what is entrusted for a special purpose.

A state of low enough level of frustration, as it exists when a baby is beginning to get hungry, has the perceptual quality of a discomfort, a presence that cannot be made to go away. In theoretical language Bion describes this situation as the baby having a "bad breast inside" because it is caused by the absence of the breast that could make the pain disappear. With a mother (object-container) in reverie, that is, one who understands her baby's emotions, and is lovingly able to make him feel comfortable and satisfied, the baby has the possibility of evacuating the "bad breast" which he contains. This he will accomplish through one mode of projective identification (under the governance of the reality principle) into the mother who, as a good container, takes it into her and holds. The mother's calm and knowing attention to her baby's need, by giving nourishment and comfort that remove the discomforts of frustrations, is described in theoretical language as "detoxifying" the "bad breast" and returning in its place a "good breast," that is, the sense of gratification and security. The baby now, as he goes through these experiences, is said to reintroject a "detoxified" or "good breast" which alleviates his discomfort and anxieties.

To return now to the part of Bion's theory that refers to "thoughts," these events just indicated would be described, in the conceptual language of this part, as follows: The hungry state, or "bad breast" corresponds to a "pre-conception," that is, the expectation of something, not knowing what it could be but "something" that could be recognized as "fitting" when it appears. When the baby is fed and gratified, the situation would be described in theoretical language as "the pre-conception of a 'bad breast' has mated with a realization of a 'good breast' which produces a 'conception'." This newly formed "conception" now begins to take on the role of a new "pre-conception" which by mating with another conception repeatedly will come to develop into a "concept."

The relationship of contained-container, which provides the grounds for a pre-conception to mate with a realization and the production of conceptions and concepts, receives a specific theoretical label and is called a "commensal abstraction." It is called an abstraction because both baby and mother, contained and container, will abstract from this experience something that becomes internalized, which Bion calls "commensal." He states: "By commensal I mean that (contained and container) are dependent on each other for mutual benefit and without harm to either. In terms of a model the mother derives benefit and achieves mental growth from the experience: the infant likewise abstracts benefit and achieves growth" (1962, pp. 90–91). What is here internalized by the baby is an "infinitesimal increment" (to use a mathematical term actually not used by Bion) of mental structures which will go to form the apparatus for thinking thoughts. Bion states in this regard: "The activity that I have here described as shared by two individuals become introjected by the infant so that the (contained-container) apparatus becomes installed in the infant as part of the apparatus of alpha-function" (1962, p. 91). And again later he says that the growth of the relationship between container and contained, the commensal abstraction "provides the basis of an apparatus for learning by experience." Again, that relationship between contained and container "represents an emotional realization associated with learning that becomes progressively more complex as it constantly recurrs through mental development" (1962, p. 92).

There is another set of processes that is also taking place while these other events are running their course. The detoxification of the "bad breast" which takes place during its sojourn in a good container (in state of reverie) occurs through the operation of the mother's alpha-function. This is a hypothetical construct without referent in the mental apparatus, doing a service in theory similar to that performed by variables in mathematics which may take up any number of values until the fitting constants are obtained. Bion ascribes to alpha-function no other task than to transform raw sense impressions and emotional experience (i.e., metabolize) into alpha-elements. The theoretical need for these concepts arises from the existence of sense impressions that cannot be attached to any particular name of an experience, such as borderline patients have who describe anxiety by naming bodily sensations, or feel "upset," "bad," "uneasy," etc. These patients are lacking in alpha-function with which to metabolize their sense impressions into alpha-elements which are units suitable to enter as elements into other more complex mental formations such as visual, auditory, and smell images, dream thoughts, thoughts, ideas, memories, which in turn can go on to form other more complex transformations.

In the commensal abstraction, the mother has, in a manner of speaking, lent her alpha-function to her baby to provide him with the alpha-elements of a "good breast." One might compare this to the action of mothers in preliterate societies who masticate food and then place it into the baby's mouth.

As alpha-elements proliferate through the operation of alpha-function they begin to cohere and hold together, forming a structure called the "contact-barrier" with very specific functions. Its operation maintains a properly functioning boundary between consciousness and unconsciousness, filtering out from the flow of derivatives into consciousness the irrational and inappropriate fantasies and emotions. The contact-barrier, for example, permits the unfolding of a relationship and of the "preservation of belief in it as an event in actuality, subject to the laws of nature. . . . Reciprocally it preserves emotions with endopsychic origin from being overwhelmed by the realistic view. The contact barrier is therefore responsible for the preservation of the distinction between conscious and unconscious and for its inception. The unconscious is thus preserved. It is being recruited by alpha-function with alpha-elements that need to be stored, but inhibited from intrusion into consciousness on occasions when their impingement of the man's grasp of the situation of external reality would be felt as an irrelevance or a dislocation of ordered thought" (Bion 1962, pp. 26–27).

The apparatus for thinking acquires stability through the dynamic interaction between the paranoid-schizoid and the depressive postions. The paranoid-schizoid position is dominated by disruptive anxieties which are disintegrative in their effects and are responded to by fragmenting defenses, denial, splitting, and projective identification. The mode of the depressive position is one of integration, synthesis, and coherence, where the occurence of ambivalence and awareness of dependence leads to toning down destructive drives and replacing them with concern and care, which are integrative emotions. The oscilation back and forth of disintegrative and integrative processes moves toward a state of synthesis, a matrix within which a "selected fact" may appear. The meaningfulness which it imparts to a collection of facts brings them together into some kind of relationship not recognized before. The "selected fact" is an emotional experience, "the emotional experience of a sense of discovery of coherence" (1962, p. 73).

Pathology of Thoughts

The developmental course that leads to pathological thinking and the psychotic part of the personality starts from conditions of intolerance of frustration. In the paranoid-schizoid position, levels of frustration so high that they disorganize the operation of incipient reality testing set up the following conditions which constitute fertile grounds for the growth of the psychotic personality. (1) The predominance of destructive impulses becomes so pervasive that they contaminate the loving impulses, turning love into sadism. (2) The pain of frustration becomes so great that there develops a hatred of all reality, internal and external, which extends to the perceptual apparatus, and to "consciousness" as "the sense organ of psychic qualities." Consciousness is then avoided rather than accepted and experienced. Another important feature of the paranoid-schizoid position associated with the prevalence of destructive and sadistic impulses, and one that remains prominent in the psychotic personality, is (3) a dread of imminent annihilation. This dread affects the quality of object relations which then become (4) precipitate, premature, hasty, fragile, and precarious, but held onto tenaciously. These features of object relations are particularly evident in the transference with these patients.

An infant who is exposed to too great levels of frustration has a "bad breast inside" and a defective reality contact. As the baby begins to expell the "bad breast" under these conditions, a pathological form of projective identification called "excessive" by Melanie Klein comes into operation and is under the rule of omnipotent fantasy. There are two forms of this omnipotent fantasy of projective identification; one leads to flights from reality, in particular from feelings one does not want to have; the other form leads to an irrational manipulation of the environment by forcing someone to experience feelings that the baby (or the patient) does not want to have.

Without a mother in reverie, without a good container to receive and metabolize the "bad breast," the baby is denied the benefits of alpha-function and is left to endure the raw sense impressions. These unmetabolized feelings have been named beta-particles and have certain definite properties. They have a quality of things-in-themselves, a concreteness to which it is not possible to attach a name, are nameless. Bion says of beta-particles that "they are objects that can be evacuated or used for a kind of thinking that depends on manipulation of what are felt to be things in themselves as if to substitute such manipulation for words or ideas." And he adds, "They are influencial in producing acting out" (1962, p. 6). Beta-particles are not suitable for entering into other formations and are unavailable as elements for thinking. All the operations that are possible with beta-particles are limited to evacuation expulsion through projective identification.

Bion points out that beta-particles operate in the interactions of patient and analyst evoking emotional experiences in the analyst that ought not to be confused with countertransferrence reactions, which are evocations arising from the analyst's own dynamics. Bion notes these patients use association in treatment less to convey information and evoke interpretations from the analyst than to induce an emotional involvement. Langs (1978a) also has identified these dynamics or projective identification in the interactions of patient and analyst and he assigns them to a category of communicative styles that he calls the Type B communicative field, and considers them characterological features that are difficult to modify.

The operation of Bion's model of thinking has been clarified by Grinberg, Sor, and Bianchedi (1977) in these terms:

From the beginning of life, the individual's psyche has to chose between two possible alternatives. These alternatives will depend on the quality or nature of the experience of primitive thoughts and the degree of evolution reached by the apparatus for thinking. If proto-thoughts are considered "undesirable excrescences" and the "apparatus for thinking" is not sufficiently developed, the primitive thoughts will be evacuated as beta-elements through a hypertrophic projective identification. If these proto-thoughts can be accepted as "problems for solving," there will be an awareness of the state of deprivation they imply (as these are unsolved problems).

Keeping in mind that the incipient "apparatus for thinking" receives reinforcement and begins operating as the result of the successful functioning of the two formative mechanisms, the contained-container relationship and the oscillating relationship between the paranoid-schizoid and the depressive positions, we see then that the capacity for tolerating the pain of frustration allows that "aparatus for thinking" to trigger off an action in the internal and the external world that will tend to modify the state of deprivation (as a problem to be solved).

In Bion's formulation, the function of reality contact in the psychotic personality is disturbed by the operation of pathological projective identification which is activated when deprivation, anxiety, and frustration exceed the limits of tolerance of frustration. Then the external reality and the objects associated with it are experienced as persecutors and become hated. At this point pathological projective identification, in futile efforts to escape the painful reality, acts to destroy the means of registering and perceiving that reality, including the object. All other aspects that in any way serve to relate the ego to reality, what Bion calls "links," also become targets to be destroyed.

The activity of pathological projective identification actually occurs in tandem with pathological splitting which not only separates partial aspects of psychic structures but splinters them into tiny bits which are then scattered violently into external objects in the environment through projective identification. This effect turns out to be very similar to what Fiumara (1977) describes as the role of "pseudo-symbolic" processes, which she defines through the etymological sense of the word "diabolic," from the Greek verb *diaballo*. (This is a compound of the work *dia* ["across"] and the verb *ballo* ["I throw"].) Fiumara goes on to say; "Hence 'diabol' [a demon, an evil spirit] is something that flings things across and as a consequence, jumbles them up" (p. 172). This also is the result of pathological projective identification. The expelled fragments of the internal object, the ego, and the superego contain violently hostile and dangerous traces of them which become lodged in external objects, turning them into persecutory "bizarre objects." These, Bion explains, contain both hateful parts of the ego, superego, and object and also the qualities of the external objects to which they have become attached. The "bizarre objects" determine all sorts of delusions, distorted perceptions, and persecutory misperceptions of reality.

Otto Kernberg

Otto Kernberg (1966, 1967, 1972) has proposed the most comprehensive systematization of clinical observations about borderline phenomena and created an equally comprehensive theoretical structure which derives the psychopathology from a set of hypotheses about the genesis, and disturbances, of early internalized object relationships. Kernberg derived his formulations from observations of the typically tumultuous transferences these patients develop in analytic treatment. His work has been largely influential in developing a consensus that regards borderline disorders to be a specific and stable form of pathology, and not a "transitory state fluctuating between neurosis and psychosis" (1975, p. 4). To emphasize these features Kernberg coined the term *borderline personality organization* (1966, p. 250), and applied it to a group of psychopathological constellations having in common a rather "specific and remarkably stable form of pathological ego structure" (1966, p. 250). The manifestations of ego pathology characterizing the borderline personality organization have been discussed by Kernberg under four headings: (1) typical constellations of symptoms; (2) typical ego defenses; (3) typical pathology of internalized object relations; and (4) characteristic genetic-dynamic features.

Classification of Character Disorders

In a related study, Kernberg developed a classification of the varieties of character disorders, a task which had been attempted before by Freud, Abraham, Wilhelm Reich, and Fenichel.

One of the many possible applications of this classification is to serve as a reference to place borderline personality organization within a continuum of pathology generated by the composite of three areas of pathological development. These are: *(a)* pathology in the development of libidinal and aggressive drive derivatives; *(b)* pathology of ego and superego structures; *(c)* pathology of internalized object relations.

Table 3 is an arrangement of data derived from Kernberg's classification of character pathology which shows the variables used to generate the scheme and the placement of borderline personality organization at the lower level.

Borderline and Psychotics

Kernberg clarifies that the differentiation between patients with borderline personality organization and patients with psychosis who would represent a still lower level of pathology usually centers on the *(a)* persistence of reality testing found in the former group. The capacity for reality testing rests on the prior attainment of the *(b)* differentiation between self- and object representations which form the foundation for the development of adequate ego boundaries. All of these structural achievements are present in the borderline patients and not in psychotics.

The Diagnostic Process

The diagnosis of borderline personality organization cannot be made by an examination of the presenting symptoms but requires the evaluation of the characteristic ego pathology which is most manifest in the transference. Patients coming for treatment present a picture of polysymptomatic neurosis against a background of character disturbance. A combination of two or more of these symptoms provides only a presumptive diagnostic impression of borderline personality organization. Kernberg has ordered and described in great detail the plethora of symptoms that one can expect to find upon examination: (1) Anxiety which is chronic, diffuse, and free-floating; (2) polysymptomatic neurosis, such as *(a)* multiple phobias, *(b)* obsessive-compulsive symptoms, *(c)* multiple conversion symptoms, *(d)* dissociative reactions, *(e)* hypochondriasis, *(f)* paranoid trends with somatic preoccupation and associated with any other neurotic symptoms; (3) polymorphous perverse sexual trends (undifferentiated sexual preferences with sadistic and masochistic components); (4) the "classical" prepsychotic personality structures, such as (i) the paranoid personality, (ii) the schizoid personality, (iii) the hypomanic and the "cyclothymic" personality; (5) impulse neurosis and addictions; and (6) the "lower level" character disorders.

When a presumptive diagnostic impression of borderline personality organization has been made, the structural analysis will provide more definitive evidence for arriving at a specific diagnosis. The structural analysis focuses on the current level of functioning of several variables whose origin and development

TABLE 3

KERNBERG'S CLASSIFICATION OF CHARACTER PATHOLOGY

PATHOLOGY IN	HIGH LEVEL	INTERM. LEVEL	LOW LEVEL	PSYCHOSIS
Instinctual development	Achieved genital primacy	Pregenital predominance of oral fixations and regressions	Pathological condensation of genital and pregenital with predominance of pregenital aggression	
Superego	Relatively well integrated through excessive severity of superego	Varying degrees of integration, with sadistic superego	Lack of superego, predominance of forerunners	
Ego defenses	Repression predominates	Mixture of both	Primitive dissociation or splitting predominates. Denial. Projective identification. Omnipotence. Overidealization. Impaired synthetic function.	

Internalized object relations	No particular pathology of internal object relations	Generally no serious disturbance. There are some conflicts with object relations	Severe pathology of internal object relations. Relationship to part object
Maturational attainments	Ego identity. Stable self-concept and representation of world		Not achieved object constancy. Fixated at identity diffusion
Types of characters	Hysterical, obsessive-compulsive, depressive-masochistic characters	Oral character, passive-aggressive, sadomasochistic, infantile, many narcissistic. Stable sexually deviant characters	Also some infantile and narcissistic antisocial, chaotic-impulse-ridden "as if," inadequate personality. Self-mutilators. Psychotic characters. Borderline personality organization

were determined by the quality of early internalized object relationships. As a background for the structural analysis, it will be
helpful to summarize Kernberg's hypotheses about the development of internalized object relations.

Early Ego Integration and Object Relations

There are postulated four stages: (1) The earliest stage is
characterized only as the one preceding the establishment of the
primary, undifferentiated self-object constellation. Presumably
the first stage is that of the undifferentiated id-ego matrix. (2) The
second stage begins between the fourth to the twelfth week and
during this time the undifferentiated *self-object* image or representation is established. It is assumed that two sets of
opposite primitive constellations of self-object affect dispositions
are built up and fixated by memory traces as polar opposite
intrapsychic structures (1972, p. 235). One of these is the "all
good," representing positive, gratifying, comforting, love-toned
affect, and the opposite is the "all bad" with a tone of pain,
discomfort, fear, emptiness, etc. (3) The third stage is one of
differentiation and is reached when the self-image has differentiated from the object image within the core of the "all good" *self-
object* representation. The equivalent differentiation of the opposite or "all bad" occurs, optimally, later and introduces complications which may lead to pathology. These separate "good"
and "bad" object images correspond to the "part-object relationships" of British psychoanalysts (1972, p. 235). This is the stage
when ego boundaries become more firm and effective in providing the capacity to differentiate the self from the outer world. (4)
This stage is the stage of integration and begins at about twelve
months and continues through childhood and beyond. The
"good" and "bad" self-images coalesce, forming a unity which is
the incipient form of the self-concept that eventually will evolve
into a sense of identity. In a parallel development the "good" and

"bad" object images become integrated to form a representation of a "whole" object which forms the groundplan for the growth of object constancy.

Borderline Personality Organization

The achievements of the third stage include the differentiation of partial self-images from partial object images, which is equivalent to the ability to differentiate oneself from others and the nonhuman environment, which also implies the attainment of well functioning ego boundaries. These, however, are not stable, and in the borderline will not be stable, thus giving rise occasionally to a loss of reality.

The borderline personality organization is determined by disturbances in the third stage. These are initiated by the prevalence of excessive frustration, and excess of oral aggression (which may be constitutional, but also experiential) which energize the "all bad" mother image which now threatens to contaminate, damage, or destroy the "all good" mother image. In the infant's psyche this is a critical development. The threat of danger to the "all good" image raises the level of anxiety against which the defense of ego splitting is mobilized. Splitting of the ego operates by keeping apart the two mother images, the "all bad" and the "all good," so as to forestall the destructive influences. These events do not take place when frustration is mild, that is, when the "all bad" image is weaker than the "all good," but under the conditions hypothesized here, another defense is also mobilized to protect the "all good" image, namely, overidealization of the "all good" mother image as an ally. The implication of this statement is that the "ideal-object" image is irrational and omnipotent (and will eventually reappear in the transference).

The Weak Ego

When splitting is required frequently or persists into the next stage, when the partial images "all good" and "all bad" begin to coalesce into "whole" images of the self and of the object, the processes of synthesis will be disturbed and a weakened ego results.

A weak and fragmented ego consists of isolated partial images with opposite affective tones, which when activated give rise to alternating, contradictory ego states. It will remain vulnerable to diffuse anxiety because splitting does not deactivate the "all bad" threatening partial images. Nor will a weak ego be capable of synthesizing further these representations, thus slowing down the process of deneutralization of aggression which depends on synthesis.

Structural Analysis

The structural analysis appears to be a scientific procedure for organizing observations and developing a model of borderline personality organization. It consists in determining *(a)* the level of maturity and effectiveness of several ego functions which together define the variable of ego weakness, and *(b)* the specific structural derivatives of internalized object relationships. Kernberg differentiates between the "nonspecific" and "specific" aspects of ego weakness.

Nonspecific aspects of ego weakness include lack of anxiety tolerance, lack of impulse control, and lack of developed sublimatory channels.

The "specific" aspects of ego weakness consist, first, of a set of primitive defense mechanisms, vestigial but very active remnants of an inchoate stage of psychic formation; and second, of a mode of functioning, the primary process, also a regressive element, which Kernberg considers "the most important single structural indicator of borderline personality organization" (1967, p. 25).

The primitive defenses whose anachronistic operation in the adult borderline patient produce the manifestations of the pathology are *(a)* splitting, *(b)* primitive idealization, *(c)* projective identification, *(d)* denial, *(e)* omnipotence and devaluation.

Splitting was first introduced by Freud in 1923 with the meaning of a mental mechanism whose operation keeps apart two opposite mental attitudes, one rational and realistic, the opposite irrational and unrealistic. He returned to it a number of times, the last time in *An Outline of Psycho-Analysis* in 1940, as he was trying to work out its mode of functioning as an ego mechanism. It is an important concept that introduces the idea of alterations, modifications, or defects the ego may undergo as a means to preserve a certain measure of contact with reality. Melanie Klein applied the term splitting in a more general sense to keep apart the good and the bad aspects of the self and also to keep apart the good and the bad parts of the object. Splitting as a Kleinian mechanism is also involved in the process of deflecting the death instinct in the earliest period of life. It "involves the splitting of the part felt to contain the destructive impulses from the part felt to contain the libido" (Segal 1964, p. 128). Kernberg uses a more restricted definition of splitting to indicate only "the active process of keeping apart introjections and identifications of opposite quality" (1967, p. 29).

Splitting, as stated earlier in this paper, is an early defense mechanism that serves to protect and preserve the "all good" mother image, which guarantees survival against being destroyed by the overflowing destructive affects associated with the "all bad" mother image who deprives, frustrates, and is the cause of suffering. It was also mentioned that the continuation of the operation of splitting through the period of integration (see Fairbairn 1940) interferes with the integration and synthesis that would eventually lead to forming a unified self-concept, and in turn, a personal sense of identity, on the one hand, and also to a unified "whole" concept of the object, a requisite for "object constancy." Both of these unified concepts form the basis for adult object relationships.

Kernberg has established that the persistence of the splitting mechanism into adult mental functioning and its sequelae in terms of lack of integration and the retention of "partial" self-object images are the genetic factors giving rise to the borderline personality organization.

Primitive idealization was also mentioned as a mechanism to safeguard the "all good" mother image. It operates in conjunction with omnipotent fantasy to create a fantastically omnipotent object for all occasions. Its operation in the transference had already been observed and reported by Stern (1938).

Projective identification is a concept created by Melanie Klein and is rapidly being recognized as an ever-present mechanism of interaction (Langs 1978b) whereby an individual, feeling helpless to metabolize disturbing sense impressions, affects, and other mental contents, would evacuate them, metaphorically speaking, into an object, that is, he would relate to the object in an interactional mode that would literally evoke the same experience in the object. At its inception it is a mechanism that allows the baby to communicate his discomforts to the mother and evoke in her the necessary actions to alleviate his condition. In the analytic situation, the operation of this process in what Langs calls the Type B patient tends to induce feelings in the analyst that, if not under self-scrutiny, may provoke countertransference acting in. Kernberg is the first American analyst to have described the operation of this mechanism in patients with borderline personality organization.

Denial, like splitting, performs the functions of defense which at more mature stages of development will be carried out by repression. Freud at first identified denial or disavowal as the defense mechanism typical of psychosis, but in 1924 and in 1940 he extended the operation of denial to neuroses and to normal functioning. However, the predominance of denial over repression is characteristic of more serious pathology because its operation disturbs the function of consciousness as a perceptual mechanism.

Omnipotence and devaluation are also related to splitting and to the reliance on the defensive use of primitive introjection and identification. These represent aspects of identification with an "all good" object, and patients who relate in this fashion tend alternately to feel like they themselves are magically omnipotent and controlling at one moment and then at another feel that it is the analyst who has become the idealized, magically omnipotent object. At one moment the sense of personal omnipotence underlies the devaluation of the object who is regarded as not needed any longer for gratification and protection, and may be dropped and dismissed. At the next moment, the opposite happens, the omnipotent object may be needed to provide security or gratification, or to use his power to manipulate the environment (Kernberg 1967, p. 33).

Adult interpersonal relationships are the expression in the external world of internalized intrapsychic structures, of the internal object relations, which were laid down from the experiences in the relationship between the infant and his mother. From their incipient stage as partial rather than whole images representing the actual object relation, they have passed through a developmental sequence of integration and come to form the unified, "whole" units of adult object relations. These units are conceived to be structures formed of a self-representation related by an affective disposition to a corresponding object representation. The activation of these units of object relationship in the presence of an object in the external world underlies their actual interaction, as if an isomorphic relationship existed between the internal and the external world.

The operations of splitting have interfered with the formation of these "whole" aspects so that the primitive, distorted, and unrealistic "partial" aspects are the ones activated vis-à-vis the object. It must be remembered that these "partial" representations contain isolated affect dispositions of either positive "all good" or negative "all bad" affects. This lack of integration interferes with the neutralization of aggression, hate, and sadism by the interpenetration of love, that is, hate rendered harmless through love does not occur. This intrapsychic state underlies the characteristically stormy eruption of primitive affects and the impulsivity of some patients with borderline organization.

The projection of these "split-up all good" and "split-up all bad" partial images with their primitive affect dispositions upon the external world will make that world appear peopled by fantastically powerful and unpredictable objects who might at one moment be benefactors and then unexpectedly turn into persecutors.

Kernberg also accounts for the characteristic protective shallowness and lack of genuine emotional involvement in the borderline's interpersonal relationships through the persistence and activation of these unintegrated partial units of primitive object relations. The lack of neutralization of aggression which comes about by the fusion of aggression with libido, that takes place when the "all good" and "all bad" images synthesize, is also responsible for the defensive shallowness and superficiality of their emotional involvements. But there is another source also resulting from the incapacity to experience concern, remorse, and guilt which are possible after reaching the stage of ambivalence. The failure of the capacity for mourning interferes with the deepening of concern, understanding, and empathy.

The arrested integration of partial images fixates the capacity for object relations at the level of the need-gratifying object so that people are regarded as needed to attend and serve one's needs and expectations. Fixation at this level limits human relationships to manipulation, exploitation, and excessive demandingness.

The dynamics of unintegrated partial representations of the self likewise underlie the phenomenon of identity diffusion, which manifests itself most dramatically in the "as if" personality.

Kernberg's genetic-dynamic analysis refers to the persistence of pregenital, mostly early oral aggression, caused by the prolonged exposure to frustration and deprivation in the earliest period of mother-infant interactions (i.e., the lack of "good enough mothering," [Winnicott], the failure of the mother's function as "protective shield," and the occurrence of "cumulative trauma," [Khan]). Kernberg discusses two effects of these events: first, the contamination of all other developmental phases with persistent oral aggression so that anal, phallic, and genital attitudes will be tinged with aggression and sadism; and second, the consequence of excessive pregenital aggression is to provoke a premature, precipitate development of oedipal striving. These intrapsychic determinants will become expressed in the polymorphous perverse "pansexuality" with sadomasochistic involvements and in the milder heterosexual difficulties of borderline patients.

This review of Kernberg's work has been restricted to a presentation of some of his theoretical formulations of psychopathology and the operation of borderline dynamics and their overt manifestations. Kernberg's work is well known and it might seem unnecessary to state that it extends beyond psychopathology and is particularly detailed in the elaboration of the phenomena of transference and countertransference, the presentation of principles of treatment with attention to the specific requirements made necessary by the borderline's vulnerability to psychotic episodes, and their object relations difficulties, and, finally, an evaluative organization of the psychodynamic features to estimate the prognosis.

Gunderson and Singer

Gunderson and Singer (1975) conducted a review of the descriptive literature on the borderline syndrome which they conclude with a list of six features that most of the authors believe seem to be characteristic of most borderline patients and which they offer with the purpose of developing a rational basis for diagnosing these patients.

In addition, they identified four methodological issues that significantly influence those descriptive accounts. These reports were found to vary with (1) the observer who describes the patient, (2) the setting, or conditions of observation, (3) the method used to select the sample of patients for study, and (4) the type of data selected for reporting.

(1) (2) The degree of structure of the interview situation was found to have a significant effect upon the type of clinical manifestations obtained. Thus, psychoanalysts with patients in analytic treatment, and psychologists with the Rorschach test, that is, both working with unstructured situations, reported major ego defects and primitive defense mechanisms. On the other hand, reports about patients in mental institutions and from psychiatrists using structured interview techniques emphasized the stability of their personalities and interpersonal traits.

(3) The influence introduced in descriptions of clinical material by the particular criteria for selecting a sample of patients for study was explored by comparing a study of Hoch and Cattell with the one conducted by Grinker and his associates. Both groups of investigators regard schizophrenia on the basis of absence of hallucinations and delusions, life history, and mental status evaluation.

Hoch and Cattell subscribe to the view that the borderline symptomatology is a form of cover schizophrenia and prefer the diagnostic term "pseudoneurotic schizophrenia." Hoch and Cattell included in their sample severe psychoneurotic patients, but who, on closer examination in psychoanalytic therapy and eventually in hospitals, revealed primary signs of schizophrenia in their thinking, feelings, and physiological functioning. Grinker et al. selected patients on the basis of good functioning between hospitalizations and the presence of an ego-alien quality to any psychotic manifestation they presented. Grinker and his associates then hospitalized the patients in their sample in order to be able to observe them in a standard situation and under controlled conditions. The follow-up results showed that in the Hoch and Cattell sample 25 percent of the patients developed manifest symptoms of schizophrenia. By contrast, Grinker and his associates had only rare psychotic episodes among patients and virtually no cases of schizophrenia. Gunderson and Singer conclude, "It is somewhat like packing a suitcase and then being surprised later to find what is in it when it is open."

The content of the clinical descriptions revealed that most frequently and consistently reported pathological manifestations were impulsive and self-destructive behavior. Their data support the view that borderline patients (who actually tend to regress on the couch but have been described as well mannered and showing good appearance) only appear to be well adjusted in their everyday living. It seems more likely that their interpersonal relationships are superficial and lack genuine emotional involvement. Likewise the reports of work records as stable and consistent turn out to indicate on closer examination that this holds true as long as the working conditions remain structured and routine.

On the important feature of the capacity for reality testing there are various opinions, but the consensus is that psychotic episodes do occur, they are limited and fully reversible, and under ordinary conditions they are not apparent. They also stated that a scientific evaluation of the capacity for reality testing is not possible with the means available at the present time, but progress is being made.

There was considerable agreement over the phenomena of transference. In the sustained closeness of the therapeutic situation borderline patients tend to form clinging, precipitous, intense, and engulfing relationships which are not stable. They are consistently reported to be manipulative and to devaluate the therapist.

Gunderson and Singer arrived at the following six features of borderline pathology which they offer as a step in the direction of a more rational approach to diagnosis of borderline patients:

(1) *The presence of intense affect.* It is usually of a strongly hostile or depressed nature. The absence of flatness and pleasure and the presence of depersonalization may be useful in differential diagnosis.

(2) *A history of impulsive behavior.* This may take many forms, including both episodic acts (e.g., self-mutilation, overdose of drugs) and more chronic behavior patterns (e.g., drug dependency, promiscuity). Often the result of these behaviors is self-destructive although their purpose is not.

(3) *Social adaptiveness.* This may be manifested as good achievement in school or work, appropriate appearance and manners, and strong social awareness. However, this apparent strength may reflect a disturbed identity masked by mimicry, a form of rapid and superficial identification with others.

(4) *Brief psychotic experiences.* These are likely to have a paranoid quality. It is felt that this potential is present even in the absence of such experiences. The psychoses may become evident during drug use or in unstructured situations and relationships.

(5) *Psychological testing performance.* Borderline persons give bizarre, dereistic, illogical, or primitive responses on unstructured tests such as the Rorschach, but not on more structured tests such as the WAIS.

(6) *Interpersonal relationships.* Characteristically, these vacillate between transient, superficial relationships and intense, dependent relationships that are marred by devaluation, manipulation, and demandingness.

Summary

It seems unlikely, as some authors have stated in the past, that borderline pathology is a new cultural development, the product of moral, social, and cultural changes of modern societies. However, it is true that the diagnostic recognition of borderline patients is a contemporary development in psychiatry, and thus the result of more advanced clinical and theoretical sophistication ushered in by the advent of psychoanalysis. The awareness and increasing number of references of this type of disorder preceded and also grew independently and simultaneously with psychoanalysis, but the attainment of the beginning of understanding and the capacity for systematic explanations is inextricably intertwined with developments in psychoanalytic theory and practice. The unique conditions of psychoanalytic treatment that permit the manifestation and study of transference and countertransference phenomena is a new setting for observation of pathological psychic functioning that has been a factor of the greatest importance in the acquisition of understanding.

Early nineteenth century texts contain clinical descriptions of a form of insanity that differed from the other types that filled the wards of early asylums. The pattern of symptoms reported left the intellectual faculties intact and seemed limited to disturbances of feelings and behavior. The first groups of patients labeled borderline were antisocial individuals, sexual perverts, psychopathic, alcoholic, and addictive types. These patients presented a mixed symptomatology with many neurotic manifestations, but severe enough and so maladjusted to society as to be considered sicker than neurotic. However, even though the same individual would become psychotic under certain conditions, the patient would soon recover fully from the temporary psychosis, so that many questioned the appropriateness of labeling them psychotic. An early and recurrent characterization of these patients' personality included such terms as "eccentric," "idiosyncratic," "the follies of mankind," "which often could not be distinguished from the normal."

The cumulative repertoire of psychoanalytic concepts, models, and theories, particularly the developments of ego psychology and the contributions of Melanie Klein and her students, especially Herbert Rosenfeld and Wilfred Bion, finally provided the means for organizing the clinical observations into meaningful patterns that could then be explained by the operation of the psychic mechanisms postulated by psychoanalysis.

The emerging conceptualization of borderline psychopathology that is gaining ground, particularly since the work of Kernberg, regards the clinical manifestations as derivatives of primitive anxieties, the operation of defense mechanisms, and of modes of primitive internalized object relationships that persist into adult mental functioning from earlier periods of infant development. The specific character of borderline pathology is determined by the juxtaposition of these primitive modes of functioning with more mature and advanced functional capacities quite appropriate to the chronological age and life position of the patient. The combinations and permutations of the psychic mechanisms and functions in the patterning of this juxtaposition give rise to several clusters which are beginning to be recognized as subgroups of borderline psychopathology.

In terms of classical theory, the time when normal development appears to have been disturbed by excessive frustrations and cumulative psychic trauma is that following the establishment of ego boundaries and preceding the consolidation and integration of identifications into a coherent sense of identity and the attainment of object constancy. Thus fixation points have occured at, and later regressions return to, the level of the prevalence of narcissism, of diffuse anxiety of annihilation, and of the need-gratification mode of object relations.

In terms of Kleinian theory the mental development of borderline patients seems to have been disturbed as it progressed through the oscillation in the relationship between the paranoid-schizoid and the depressive positions that precedes the final consolidation and synthesis of mental structures and functioning at the zenith of the depressive position. This arrest insures the vulnerability to outcroppings of psychotic anxieties and mechanisms such as the sense of psychic death, pathological forms of splitting, projective identification, omnipotence, and overidealization.

What may seem discrepancies, but are actually variations in the clinical descriptions of borderline patients by different authors, may be accounted for by two sets of factors. First, as the work of Rosenfeld (see chapter 4 in this volume) and also Grinberg (1977) indicates, there seem to be subgroups of borderline syndromes. The second set of factors refers to the conditions of observations which evidently influences the content of clinical pictures observed. Four extraneous variables have been identified which need to be controlled to avoid spurious effects on the clustering of symptoms observed which would lead to inaccurate typologies. These variables are (1) the observer, whether psychoanalyst, psychiatrist, psychologist, or other; (2) the setting where the observations are made, hospital or outpatient facility; (3) the method used to select a sample of patients for research; (4) the type of data reported, such as results of psychological tests, material from analytic treatment, responses to structured interviews, etc.

The most consistently reported symptoms were in terms of affect: anger, anxiety, depression with a quality of loneliness and impotent rage in which the sense of guilt, self-accusation, and remorse are absent. In terms of behavior the most frequently reported forms included impulsiveness and self-destructive acts. In terms of social relations, these are precipitous, predominantly of the need-gratifying type of object choice, clinging, demanding, and at the same time superficial and fragile. The phenomena of transference and countertransference were found to be particularly useful to observe the manifestations of borderline pathology.

References

Beck, A.T. (1967). *Depression: Clinical, Experimental, and Theoretical Aspects.* New York: Harper & Row.

Bion, W.R. (1956). Development of schizophrenic thought. In *Second Thoughts: Selected Papers on Psychoanalysis.* New York: Jason Aronson 1967.

—— (1957). Differentiation of the psychotic from the non-psychotic personalities. In *Second Thoughts: Selected Papers on Psychoanalysis.* New York: Jason Aronson, 1967.

—— (1962). *Learning From Experience.* In *Seven Servants: Four Works by Wilfred R. Bion.* New York: Jason Aronson, 1977.

Bychowski, G. (1953). The problem of latent psychosis. *Journal of the American Psychoanalytic Association* 1:484–503.

Clark, L.P. (1919). Some practical remarks upon the use of modified psychoanalysis in the treatment of borderland neuroses and psychoses. *Psychoanalytic Review* 6:306–308.

Deutsch, H. (1942). Some forms of emotional disturbance and their relation to schizophrenia. *Psychoanalytic Quarterly* 11:301–321.

Fairbairn, W.R.D. (1940). Schizoid factors in the personality. In *An Object-Relations Theory of the Personality.* New York: Basic Books, 1954.

Fenichel, O. (1945). *The Psychoanalytic Theory of Neurosis.* New York: W. W. Norton.

Fiumara, G.C. (1977). The symbolic function, transference and psychic reality. *International Review of Psycho-Analysis* 4: 171–180.

Freud, S. (1913). On beginning the treatment (further recommendations on the technique of psycho-analysis). *Standard Edition* 12:123–144.

—— (1916) Some character-types met with in psycho-analytic work. *Standard Edition* 14:309–333.

—— (1923). The ego and the id. *Standard Edition* 19:3–66.

———— (1924a). Neurosis and psychosis. *Standard Edition* 19:149-153.

———— (1924b). The loss of reality in neurosis and psychosis. *Standard Edition* 19:183-187.

———— (1940a). Splitting of the ego in the process of defense. *Standard Edition* 23:271-278.

———— (1940b). An outline of psychoanalysis. *Standard Edition* 23:141-207.

Frosch, J. (1959). The psychotic character: psychoanalytic considerations. Abst. in *Journal of the American Psychoanalytic Association* 8:544-548.

———— (1964). The psychotic character: clinical psychiatric considerations. *Psychiatric Quarterly* 38:81-96.

———— (1970). Psychoanalytic considerations of the psychotic character. *Journal of the American Psychoanalytic Association* 18:24-50.

Gaw, E.A., Reichard, S., and Tillman, C. (1953). How common is schizophrenia? *Bulletin of the Menninger Clinic* 17:20-28.

Giovacchini, P.L. (1967). The frozen introject. *International Journal of Psycho-Analysis* 48:61-67.

Grinberg, L. (1977). An approach to the understanding of borderline disorders. In a *Borderline Personality Disorders: the Concept, the Syndrome, the Patient,* ed. P. Hartocollis. New York: International Universities Press.

Grinberg, L, Sor, D., and Bianchedi, E.T. (1977). *Introduction to the Work of Bion.* New York: Jason Aronson.

Gunderson, J.G. and Singer, M.T. (1975). Defining borderline patients: an overview. *American Journal of Psychiatry* 132:1-10.

Kernberg, O. (1966). Structural derivatives of object relationships. *International Journal of Psycho-Analysis* 47:236-253.

———— (1967). Borderline personality organization. *Journal of the American Psychoanalytic Association* 15:641-685.

———— (1970). A psychoanalytic classification of character pathology. *Journal of the American Psychoanalytic Association* 18:800–822.

Klein, M. (1932). *The Psycho-Analysis of Children.* New York: Delacorte Press, 1975.

——— (1952). Notes on some schizoid mechanisms. In *Developments in Psycho-Analysis,* ed. J. Riviere. London: Hogarth Press.

——— (1958). On the development of mental functioning. *International Journal of Psycho-Analysis* 39:84–90.

Langs, R. (1978a). *The Listening Process.* New York: Jason Aronson.

——— (1978b). *Technique in Transition.* New York: Jason Aronson.

Lapanche, J. and Pontalis, J.-B. (1967). *The Language of Psychoanalysis.* New York: W.W. Norton, 1973.

Mack, J.E. (1975). *Borderline States in Psychiatry.* New York: Grune and Stratton.

Mahler, M.S., Pine, F., and Bergman, A. (1975). *The Psychological Birth of the Human Infant.* New York: Basic Books.

Meares, A. (1959). The diagnosis of prepsychotic schizophrenia. *Lancet* 1:55–58.

Moore, T.V. (1921). The parapraxes: a study and analysis of certain borderline mental states. *Psychoanalytic Review* 34:252–283.

Parkin, A. (1966a). Neurosis and schizophrenia: I. Historical review. *Psychiatric Quarterly* 40:203–216.

——— (1966b). Neurosis and schizophrenia: II. Modern perspectives. *Psychiatric Quarterly* 40:217–235.

——— (1966c). Neurosis and schizophrenia: III. Clinical considerations. *Psychiatric Quarterly* 40:405–428.

Polatin, P. (1948). Schizophrenia. In *Medical Clinics of North America.* Philadelphia: Saunders.

Pulver, S.E. (1970). Narcissism: the term and the concept. *Journal of the American Psychoanalytic Association* 18:319–341.

Reich, W. (1925). *The Impulsive Character*. In *The Impulsive Character and Other Writings*. New York: New American Library, 1974.

Roazen, P. (1975). *Freud and His Followers*. New York: Alfred A. Knopf.

Segal, H. (1964). *Introduction to the Work of Melanie Klein*. New York: Basic Books.

Stern, A. (1938). Psychoanalytic investigation of and therapy in the borderline group of neuroses. *Psychoanalytic Quarterly* 7:467–489.

Weiss, J. (1966). Clinical and theoretical aspects of "as if " characters. *Journal of the American Psychoanalytic Association* 14:569–590.

Zilboorg, G. (1941). Ambulatory schizophrenias. *Psychiatry* 4:149–155.

Chapter 3

The Psychoanalytic Concept of the Borderline Organization*

James S. Grotstein, M.D.

The borderline syndrome is the clinical manifestation of what recently has come to be known as the borderline personality organization. In recent years it has come into prominence as a separate entity, in part because of renewed interest by psychoanalytic investigators who have been encouraged by their success in applying psychoanalytic principles and therapy to some psychotic disorders, and also by general psychiatrists who have realized that psychotherapy is of some benefit to a certain class of psychotics who do not seem to regress or deteriorate.

The review of the literature which Mack (1975) recently conducted on this disorder is perhaps the most nearly complete one to reveal the panorama of substrates of this disorder. He traces the connection of the borderline personality organization and borderline syndrome to early notions of the schizoid personality, the "as if" personality, psychotic character, pan neuroses, etc. In so doing, he seems to be linking the work of the British object

---

*This contribution is presented under the auspices of the Interdisciplinary Group for Advanced Studies in Psychotic, Borderline, and Narcissistic Disorders.

relations school, including Klein, Bion, Rosenfeld, Winnicott, Balint, Fairbairn, and others with their American counterparts, principally Kohut and Kernberg, who have explored and defined this area of psychopathology.

In approaching a psychoanalytic conception of the borderline personality organization I should like to offer the following understanding: What seems to give the borderline personality organization (and borderline state) its uniqueness in differentiating itself from psychoses on one hand and neuroses on the other is not so much its midplace on the spectrum but is instead a qualitative difference. This qualitative difference is characterized, in my opinion, by the presence of a psychotic personality organization *and* a normal or neurotic personality organization which have undergone a unique interpenetration with each other so that a new amalgam emerges which can well be stated as "psychotically neurotic" or "neurotically psychotic." It is as if a collusive symbiosis exists between these two twin personalities which allows for an unusual tenacity, stability, and cohesion compared to psychotic states generally. This amalgamated personality seems to be successful in preventing psychotic breaks, although momentary psychotic episodes do occur, but, expectedly, it catapults the patient into a world which he has to reorganize and rearrange in accordance with the requirements of his systematized delusional needs which are highly rationalized but maladaptive. Failing this, this patient seems to decompensate in many aspects of his adjustment and withdraws into a more constricted perimeter of living.

Other authors, particularly Kohut (1971, 1977) and Kernberg (1975), have differentiated the borderline personality organization from the narcissistic personality organization. Both contributors believe that there is even more stability in the narcissistic personality disorder and that the episodic, self-limited psychotic breaks are more characteristic of the borderline personality organization. Yet in defining separate agendas for the self and for its relationship with the object representation, Kohut has helped us to formulate some new ideas about the relationship between the narcissistic personality disorders and the borderline personality disorders.

The Narcissistic-Borderline Continuum

In other words, I believe we can now postulate that both disorders, compared with normal and neurotic states, suffer from a difficulty in cohesion of the self, to use Kohut's (1971) term, and also from a difficulty in object relations. One of the factors which seems to distinguish narcissistic from borderline personality disorders is the greater ability of the narcissist in utlizing his object relations to maintain a sense of pseudocohesion. My own personal clinical experience, and that of the Interdisciplinary Group for Advanced Studies in Psychotic, Borderline, and Narcissistic Disorders, seems to indicate that the borderline personality organization is itself a particular subtype of narcissistic disorder and is on a continuum with it (Grotstein et al. 1975–1978). We believe what have generally been called narcissistic personality disorders correspond to manic and schizoid personality subtypes, where the former is characterized by a seemingly presumptuous and invasive, emboldened attitude towards reality, exhibiting a grandiose self and/or a relationship to highly idealized objects in which there is the combined affect of triumph, contempt, and control. The schizoid personality subtype, on the other hand, is characterized by a withdrawal into the inner world, in which there is an unusually high value given to objects of the internal world, including thoughts, obsessions, and preoccupations. There is a sense of inner grandiosity in a state of secretiveness relative to the external world, and a sense of detachment from the objects of the external world. Thus the narcissistic personality disorders would seem to be characterized by a characterological manic defense, against awareness of dependency on external objects, awareness of one's inner needs, and/or a schizoid withdrawal from such awareness so as to maintain a sense of inner pseudoautonomy at the expense of one's relationship to the world.

The relative stability, upon which personality subtypes of this continuum seem to depend, is their relative adaptive capacity to utilize objects in the external world to maintain the illusion of self-intactness. They seem, in other words, to succeed in maintaining the reifications of their misconceptions about their needs and the objects of their needs because of pseudopsychopathic success in using objects to this end. In short, they are successful in getting people to believe, if they are manic narcissists, that they are indeed grandiose and/or that they are good acolytes for the object's grandiosity or, if they are schizoid narcissists, that they indeed have some rich inner thought process which is oracular or prophetic.

At the other end of the continuum of the manic and schizoid personality disorders are the borderline personality disorders. As I have earlier stated, what distinguishes them is their vulnerability to disorganizational episodes and, I should like to add, a relationship to reality and to the objects of reality which is somewhat more questionable, thin, and tenuous than is characteristic of their more successful narcissistic brethren.

Genetic Factors—the Infantile Psychosis

To me, the greatest light shed upon the nature of the borderline personality organization has been through the contributions of Klein (1948, 1952a, 1952b, 1955), Fairbairn (1954), Bion (1962, 1963, 1965, 1967, 1970), Rosenfeld (1965), Bick (1968), and Meltzer (1974). All these authors approached this area with the understanding of the vicissitudes of what I would today call the *infantile psychosis* with its *schizoid* propensities toward *splitting* of egos and objects and the creation of *bizarre objects* through *projective identification.* The latter is the prime architect of the imagination of borderline and psychotic patients (Grotstein 1978a). In emphasizing the conception of an infantile psychosis, the Kleinian object relations school offered a paradigm for understanding later psychotic and neurotic disorders on the basis of *psychic conflict* occurring from the very beginning. *Ego defect* could result secondary to psychotic conflict. This theory is at variance with classical formulations.

Heretofore the borderline personality as an entity had to be compared to the neurotic disorders on one hand and the psychotic on the other. The history of psychoanalysis began with the study of neurosis and then slowly rediscovered its relationship to psychosis. Until recently there had to be two separate theories in psychoanalysis to account for these disorders, one for psychosis and the other for neurosis. My recent monograph (Grotstein 1977a, 1977b) attempted to rectify this schism. In that contribution I sought to do away with the psychoanalytic meta-psychological infrastructure based upon instinctual drives and on later fixation points, in favor of a psychoanalytic theory based upon Isaacs' (1952) conception of genetic continuity and Klein's and Fairbairn's conception of the importance of the infantile psychotic organization. I sought to supplant the concept of the infantile neurosis with the notion of an *infantile psychosis* which is later to be superorganized by an *infantile neurosis* and then by a *childhood neurosis.* The latter corresponds to the classical notion of infantile neurosis.

I postulate, in other words, that there is an ever-evolving personality organization from the very beginning of extrauterine life corresponding to a dual-track conception; that is, that the infant is born with a sense of total separateness (track one) from the very beginning of extrauterine life—if not before—and, at the same time, thanks to Cartesian artifice, also experiences himself or herself to be a continuation of primary identification or primary oneness (track two) with what I have termed the *background object* of *primary identification*.[1] Klein and her followers have dealt almost exclusively with the former, and classical theorists up to and including Mahler seem to have dealt with the latter. It is my contention that both infantile experiences exist as different parts of one infantile composite experience and both are clinically observable.

Tustin (1978) has posited that infantile autism and childhood psychotic disorders may possibly result from a premature abruption of the sense of primary oneness by a traumatic experience in the infant's life or by a breakdown in the interrelationship between the infant and its caretaking mother. This premature abruption of the experience of postnatal oneness precipitates, according to Tustin, a premature twoness which causes, amongst other things, a precocious mobilization of ego apparatuses and future adaptive endowments which were normally meant for later recruitment. In other words, a precocious sensitivity begins to develop (Bergman and Escalona 1949).

Klein and Fairbairn were the first psychoanalytic theorists to posit an organization and a mental life for the so-called undifferentiated period of infancy. Klein suggested that at three weeks of age there exists a cluster of anxiety in the infant's mental life which can be called paranoid-schizoid because of the persecutory anxiety emanating from the awareness of disturbing feelings from within and frustrations related to them from without (in terms of objects mitigating the appearance of these needs). At four months of age, or thereabouts, it is succeeded, if all goes well,

---

[1] In other publications I have developed this conception, which corresponds to the most archaic organizing internal object which offers background support for the infant's development. My conception of it is one which is awesome, majestic, unseen, and behind one. It "rears" us and sends us off into the world. In moments of quiet repose we sit on its lap metaphorically. In psychotic illness and in borderline states it is severly damaged or compromised (Grotstein 1977b, 1978a).

by another cluster of anxiety known as the depressive anxiety of the depressive position, by which time the maternal object is more clearly recognized, realized, and missed in her absence. Simultaneously, the omnipotent schizoid defenses of the paranoid-schizoid period of infancy seem to subside in favor of a more realistic relationship to the objects, and defenses are based more on introjection than on projection and splitting. Manic defenses, which are a particular restatement of the schizoid defenses of the earlier period, seem to arise at the threshold of the depressive position to bar the infant access to it.

Thus, the paranoid-schizoid position is a primitive staging areas for infantile development and constitutes the infantile psychosis. The depressive position constitutes the infantile neurosis.

I should like to differentiate the *infantile psychosis* as a metapsychological concept from the *infantile psychotic state,* which according to Bion (1956) is the experience of *infantile catastrophe,* that is, of excessive dissolution of the ego and excessive splitting and projective identification where omnipotence fails to give the infant protection against his feelings. He therefore projects not just his thoughts, but also his mind which thinks the thoughts and is thereby all the more denuded of mental capacity. What remains is holocaustal.

The infantile psychosis, on the other hand, is, as I have stated, a metapsychological concept as well as a normal developmental series of experiences in which the infant who is born from primal oneness is called upon at birth to deal with the phenomenon of having been projected by his primal object, as it were, into external reality. He copes with this confrontation with external reality by a splitting of himself and his objects based upon his affective experiences, according to Klein (1952b). Pleasurable experiences, in other words, are organized into the conception of a good breast; and painful or unpleasurable experiences are organized into the conception of a bad breast. These two objects and the egos associated with them are split apart so that the goodness of the good object can be protected, since his growth and maturation depends upon his relationship to this good object. Projective identification, idealization, and magic omnipotent denial facilitate the protectiveness of splitting. Insofar as these are psychoticlike defense mechanisms (since they seek to evade and/or deny reality, and are omnipotent), they can be called psychotic defenses. The infantile psychosis of the paranoid-schizoid position therefore represents the crisis of the capacity to develop proper splitting of self and objects, and proper projective identification to assist the development of this splitting. Proper splitting is not only the requisite ingredient of all defense mechanisms but is also the necessary precursor of all cognitive and perceptual differentiations. Failure to negotiate this crisis properly may result in pathological splitting, that is, splitting that does not seem to obey reasonable laws but, rather, is excessive, e.g. splintering, fragmenting, etc. Pathological splitting predisposes to pathological projective identification and, therefore, the internal objects which the infant now fantasies become more terrifying and ultimately bizarre. The result is the beginning formation of an altered, psychotic personality.

An important contribution to the development of defective splitting seems to be the development of a defective sense of adhesive identification (Bick 1968, Meltzer 1975) in which the infant does not acquire a good sense of skin definition between inside and outside. Instead, these infants seem to adhere tenaciously to mother's body in order to utilize her skin surface as a defining stimulus. It is perhaps this defective sense of skin-boundary formation which inaugurates the later phenomenon of poverty of ego boundaries which characterizes psychotic and borderline personalities and separates them from other narcissistic and neurotic personalities.

Sufficient growth from a facilitating and nurturing relationship with the goodness of the good object or good breast facilitates the development of the depressive position where the infant, who is now a toddler, feels ready to abandon his omnipotent defenses in order to become more realistic. As he is able to experience the reality of the separateness of the object, he is able also to experience his own separateness. In this regard, the theories of Klein (1948, 1952a, 1952b, 1955) and of Mahler (1975) are congruent. The depressive position is characterized by the infant's pining over the loss of his object which at the same time is pining over the loss of omnipotence. This latter is the beginning of a sense of reality. As a result, the depressive position constitutes, in my opinion, the onset of the infantile neurosis because psychotic mechanisms are foresworn in favor of a more neurotic relationship to the object.

The crisis of the infantile neurosis of the depressive position is, therefore, one of *integration,* that is, of *reconciliation* of the proper splitting achieved in the infantile psychosis of the paranoid-schizoid position. The splitting and projective defenses give way to introjective and assimilative modes of relating to objects. Manic and schizoid defenses may then obstruct this reconciliatory integration and then, alternatively, form the bases of a manic-narcissistic or schizoid-narcissistic personality organization. Persistence of the altered or psychotic personality emerging from the unresolved crisis of the infantile psychosis may merge with the more neurotic aspects of the manic and/or schizoid personality organization which emerge from the depressive position so that a narcissistic personality disorder (in the way that category is generally thought of) emerges as a borderline personality disorder. The key features seem to be: *(a)* the strength of the psychotic organization from the infantile psychosis; *(b)* the strength of the normal personality from the infantile neurosis; *(c)* the strength of the personalities emerging from the manic and schizoid defenses against the reconciliatory integration of the infantile neurosis (depressive position); and *(d)* the nature of the relationship between *(b), (c),* and *(a).* In other words, a healthy personality may successfully repress its psychotic twin, but a manic or schizoid personality organization may so collude with it as to achieve a "diabolical" amalgam. If the psychotic organization from the infantile psychosis be the strongest, then it may be the organizing principle of the resultant personality, possibly predisposed to schizophrenic and/or manic or depressive illnesses. In this latter case the personality amalgamation is more like a military takeover rather than a collusive symbiosis, the latter of which is, in my thinking, pathognomonic for the borderline personality organization and the borderline state which results.

While the genetic roots of psychosis in the infantile psychosis of the paranoid-schizoid position seem clear enough, the origin and nature of neurosis may well be in need of reevaluation. The classical theory still holds that neuroses are the outcome of vicissitudes of the infantile neurosis which connotes the phallic-oedipal complex of later childhood. My own conception is as follows: the *infantile psychosis* organizes the paranoid-schizoid position (Mahler's autistic and symbiotic phases). The *infantile neurosis* (if it is to be "infantile" at all) organizes the depressive position (Mahler's three subphases of separation-individuation). I further posit that a *childhood neurosis* supervenes at the time of the phallic-oedipal stage to organize the previous phases (see Grotstein 1978b).

I further postulate (after Klein and Fairbairn) that neuroses are more sophisticated techniques of dealing with psychotic anxieties than are schizoid or manic defenses but that they are on a continuum with psychoses. In other words, it seems quite unreasonable today to suppose that all goes well with an infant until he develops oedipal-sexual feelings in childhood. Neuroses, like psychoses, develop from the beginning of life—in the infantile psychosis—and are formed by the achievement of advanced, sophisticated defenses from the more positive achievements of the resolution of the infantile neurosis of the depressive position. Thus, Fairbairn's conception of neurosis as being the phobic, paranoid, obsessive-compulsive, and hysterical *techniques* for maintaining the splits of the earlier psychotic positions is probably more nearly true than has been hitherto realized.

The normal progression through the paranoid-schizoid position into the depressive position can be fixationally obstructed by any phenomenon which interferes with the harmonious relationship between the separate self of track one and the continuing sense of primal oneness of track two. There are at least three possible etiologies in this regard: *(a)* hereditary-constitutional; *(b)* congenital (the uterine environment); and *(c)* a defect in the interaction between the infant and the caretaking mother. Owing to the fact that all infants come to the neonatal world as separately endowed individuals, the hereditarily begotten personality may very well express itself through excessive greed and/or envy and thereby, because of the misconceptions of external objects which projective identification consequently establishes, the infant may then introject internal objects of great demanding and hateful vengence, thus jeopardizing the internal world from the outset.

At the same time, a perturbing uterine world and a perturbing external world, in which the mother is, relatively speaking, unable to cope with the demands and projective cues of her infant, may so precociously confirm destructive preconceptions at the expense of the confirmation of benevolent preconceptions that the infant is overmobilized for danger, is hyperalert to predator anxiety, and has forsaken of necessity his primal blanket of postnatal oneness.

Differentiation Between the
Psychotic and Nonpsychotic Personalities

In addressing himself to the issue of psychosis, Bion has written two papers which I believe are of immediate relevance to this topic of the borderline. One is "The Imaginary Twin" (1950) and the other is "The Differentiation Between the Psychotic and Non-Psychotic Parts of the Personality" (1957a), some of the implications of which I employed earlier in this contribution. To these I would add his conception of the attacks on linking, his formulation of schizophrenic thought processes, his conception of the arrogance of stupidity in the psychotic personality, and his conception of the container and the contained. My own conception of the dual-track theory is, I believe, an outgrowth of Bion's conception of the container and the contained. Although Bion did not use the term "borderline," the patients he seems to have been dealing with in formulating his theories could today be called borderline rather than truly psychotic. Long before Kohut's (1971) notion of the separate agendas of the narcissistic and object relations aspects of the personality, Bion posited a separate agenda for a psychotic personality which had experienced infantile catastrophe and was split off for its own separate existence by a much more nearly normal or neurotic personality which had managed to survive. This normal personality is successful to one degree or another in keeping the psychotic personality in repression. The infantile psychotic state, whether it be schizophreniclike or a maniclike, seems to subside symptomatically and devolve into a smoldering, nongrowing, active and passive, stunted homunculus which periodically erupts through vents in the repressive surface of the normal personality in order to epiphanize as clinical psychosis.

I have dealt with the characteristics of the psychotic portion of this personality in another contribution (Grotstein 1977a, 1977b).

The characteristics of the schizophrenic portion of the personality are: (1) alienation; (2) premature closure of a portion of the personality, thereby causing an abnormal personality development; (3) anhedonia, as a result of the attacks on perception; (4) bizarreness, because of the formation of bizarre internal objects which in turn reflect the schizophrenic's bizarre developmental agenda; (5) conative suppression, insofar as he lacks the will to explore or to be alive, since that portion of his personality was believed to be dangerous and was therefore expelled via projective identification; (6) transitivism, a feeling of being totally dependent—biologically, emotionally, and "politically"—upon others insofar as the capacity to maturate their dependency needs is believed to be lost or absent, since that, too, has undergone projective expulsion, leaving them automatons who cannot grow from experience; adhesive (autistic) identification is its characteristic; (7) defensive or deviant perceptual transformations, with a failure of the senses to harmonize and work properly; (8) a boundary which is felt to be porously permeable to their own contents and to the intrusions of external objects; and (9) neophobia, the fear of any change in the perceptual set.

The characteristics of schizophrenic thinking are primarily bizarreness and secondarily concreteness as a result of their compromised perceptual and cognitive capacities. Their psychic space is simply insufficient to allow for the necessary maneuvers of thinking that normal personalities have.

What particularly distinguishes the borderline personality organization is, at best, the capacity of the normal aspects of the personality to contain the psychotic twin and, at worst, the tendency of the manic and/or schizoid narcissistic personality organizations to be traduced into pathological symbiosis with a psychotic personality organization so as to create an amalgamated personality which behaves "rationally irrational," is relatively stable (really, relatively immutable), and survives by a high degree of artifice, imagination, manipulation, and ingratiation. Those patients who are psychotic and beyond borderline in their organization are characterized not only by the undeniable presence of the psychotic twin but also by a pseudonormal personality which has been so compromised and interpenetrated by the psychotic self that its capacity as a container is not intact. One might say that in psychotic patients the normal personality is subordinated by the psychotic one and is felt to be a hostage within some kind of an eerie hallucinatory and delusional prison, knowing all the while what is happening but unable to give voice to its presence.

The Nature of Splitting in the Borderline

Thus, what characterizes the borderline personality organization and syndrome is the nature of the splitting between the psychotic and nonpsychotic personalities. When Kernberg (1975) states that the borderline personality organization is characterized by splitting, he is talking about the genesis of splitting in the differentiation between the pleasurable and unpleasurable, good and bad self-object representations. Actually, this kind of differentiation occurs in all personalities. According to Klein's schema it is normal. The splits which characterize the borderline personality organization are in my opinion basically between the psychotic portion(s) and the normal portion, but, because of the partial compromise of the normal portion of the personality (effected by inroads of the psychotic portion) in eschewing it from achieving cohesion, the veneer of cohesiveness of the container (normal personality) reveals the chaotic disorganization of the psychotic personality as a series of disconnected, desultory selves and objects in a chaotic nether world.

In other words, the psychotic unconscious is distinctly abnormal and quite different from the unconscious of the normal, neurotic, or narcissistic personality. Thus I would *not* see the distinction between the former and the latter as between primary process and secondary process, as has usually been stated, but would rather say that the normal personality has a reasonably harmonious relationship between primary and secondary process, and so has a normal unconscious. The psychotic personality, on the other hand, constitutes an abnormal, bizarre, and perversely reconstituted aspect of another type of unconscious which is not to be confused with the normal. To the degree that the normal personality frontier is felt to be compromised, then the bizarre splittings which comprise the abnormal unconscious make their appearance.

This compromised veneer or frontier of the normal personality vis-a-vis the abnormal personality has been dealt with by Bick (1968), Meltzer (1974, 1975), Green (1977), and by myself (Grotstein 1977a, 1977b). Bick and Meltzer have postulated that there is a stage of adhesive identification during the earliest stages of the paranoid-schizoid position in which the infant's task is to develop a sense of a skin boundary by apposing his own skin to that of the maternal object in order to get a stimulating interface. Failure to develop this—perhaps due to a failure of maternal stimulation—may result in adhesive identificatory disorders in which the infant is always apposing himself against an object in order to get a sense of skin. Failing this, he goes into a state of hypermotility in order to use activity and muscularity as a secondary skin. Thus, Bick and Meltzer posit that in psychotic illnesses a defective sense of a skin boundary and a defective sense of boundary between inside and outside may result which subsequently compromise the capacity for reality testing based upon the function of differentiation. Green (1977) has also called attention to this phenomenon in terms of the compromise of the borders in borderline disorders and relates it to a defective function of negation.

I have elsewhere dealt with the phenomenon of the compromised border in borderline and psychotic disorders (Grotstein 1977a, 1977b). In those contributions I dealt with the phenomenon of the internal objects of the normal and the psychotic internal worlds and formulated the concept of the boundary or border object. Let me derive this anew for this presentation. After Bion (1957b) I posit that there are normally four objects of the internal world. They are the *background object of primary identification,* and its three postnatal derivatives which correspond to the three instinctual organizational functions: the libidinal, the destructive, and the epistemophilic (Bion's *L*ove, *H*ate, and *K*nowledge linkages). The libidinal instinct corresponds normally to a *nurturing object,* the destructive instinct to a *boundary* or *frontier object* (for defense), and the epistemophilic object to a *stimulating object.*

Abnormal projective identification by the infant into his maternal object can be experienced by him, Bion believes, particularly if the mother's actions seem to confirm it as the presence of a *destroyed maternal object* and of an *obstructive object.* The obstructive object is one who refuses to contain his projections and interferes with his capacity to communicate with the maternal object normally in the next and subsequent sequences. It is, in short, a malevolent object. Its passive counterpart is a destroyed, handicapped, and impedimentary object which can also be seen as an object that is multiply perforated with holes so that it no longer functions as a containing object or good boundary object but rather allows intruders inside and does not help to keep internal contents inside.

One of the characteristic clinical features of the borderline personality disorder is the abnormal fear of blushing and the belief that people are staring at them. These hapless patients believe they have no sufficient ego boundary to keep the stares of external objects from the outside or to keep their shameful internal contents on the inside. Blushing is an apocalyptic revelation to them. In other words, their self-consciousness is paramount.

One of the other internal objects which emanates as a distortion from the psychotic world is the *magus object*. When the epistemophilic instinct is linked up with excesses of the libidinal instinct, the result is one of a greedy acquisition by knowledge in which the curious infant wishes to devour mother's insides by his curiosity. When the epistemophilic instinct is linked with excesses of the destructive instinct, the result is a desire to find out about objects in the world in order to detect their weaknesses so that one can dominate them, control them, or destroy them. When the libidinal, destructive, and epistemophilic instinctual organizations collude, one finds the phenomenon of the magus object.

Let me demonstrate this object with excerpts from the second analytic hour of a borderline patient. She reported to me on the second hour that, upon leaving my office after the first hour, she felt that she had had a very searching contact with me but felt intimidated and persecuted by me. She reported that when she was driving home she experienced me almost in an hallucinatory way, showing motion pictures of her thoughts on a screen which I compelled her to watch. I was felt by her to be uncanny, omniscient, omnipresent, and omnipotent. Forcing her to look at these projections of her thoughts was felt to be vengefully destructive in the sense of a diabolical accusation of her malevolence and ineptness (her sense of badness), and I was furthermore suggesting that I knew everything about her but required her to know as much as I did about her before she could be cured. I was the agent of both God and the devil, thus the magus, who was a Zoroastrian sorcerer (and the singular of "magi").

It is my impression that borderline personality disorders are characterized by a sense of a defective background object, a consequent defective cohesion of the postnatal personality, and the lack of sufficient containment. The development of a psychotic personality separated from a normal personality is thereby permitted, and there then develop abnormal objects such as the obstructive object, the defective boundary object, the magus object, and the defective background object of primary identification. As a consequence of the defective background object of primary identification and its consequences—especially defective adhesive identification—the borderline suffers utmostly from anxiety of *dissolution,* which he defends against by extreme projective identification into his image of an object for exaggerated containment. The results of this are the secondary fears of *(a)* engulfment, *(b)* petrifaction, and *(c)* impingement. *Engulfment* is the result of the projective identification of the patient's extreme neediness, which converts the object he depends on into a claustrophobically devouring, spoiling, and/or engulfing object. *Petrifaction* is the result of the patient's deadly immobilization of his object by virtue of the omnipotent power of his controlling hatred. The result is an internal object which does the same to him. *Impingement* is due to the phenomenon of impulsive helplessness which seeks at any cost to invade an object, only to create an internal object which does the same to him.

I should like to say another word about splitting in the borderline personality disorder and syndrome. I believe that patients with this disorder can be observed to have different degrees of dissociation of personalities which seem to have separate agendas of their own. One of my patients who free associates frequently in a hypnogogic state brings in dream material in statu nascendi which seems to come from varying personalities. In one hour he dreamily found himself wandering from the movie screen of one play onto the movie screen of another. Another borderline personality felt herself to be in intimate, intuitive contact with key objects in her life and felt an absolute certainty that they were trying to contact her at moments which she could predict. She also believed herself to be a reincarnation of a French poet of another age who was continuing to live within her. More commonly, borderline patients and even narcissistic personality disorder patients generally will make, in my opinion, a differentiation between the illusion of their unborn selves and of their factotum born selves which have to deal with reality to one degree or another. Their major identification is, however, with their unborn selves.

One patient obsessively-compulsively directed her well-to-do life in a manner so as to achieve a fairybook, romantic notion of family life. She prevailed upon her husband to buy her a large estate with a tennis court and other entertainment facilities so that her children could entertain other children in the extended neighborhood in such a manner as to render their home almost like a miniature Disneyland. Children would come to play in a marvelous and benevolent atmosphere so as to re-create the image of a splendid childhood which she believed she never experienced. The fanatic obsessiveness and compulsiveness which she used to achieve this end crippled her relationship to her husband, children, and friends, whom she rarely saw. It also interferred with the very function she was trying to achieve. For instance, she had such an idealized notion of the family meal that she would spend hours in its preparation. Although extraordinarily wealthy, she would not allow her numerous maids to participate in the dinner activities; she alone had to prepare the meals. As the result, the family did not eat until about eight or nine o'clock at night. Moreover, she was so busy preparing and serving the meal that they had to eat without her. She was an observer of the family meal at which she, the wife and mother, was absent.

This patient is an example of that observer function detached from the usual mainstream of reality participation which so characterizes the schizoid borderline and narcissistic disorders.

She also demonstrates the operation of the "corrupt amalgam" core of the borderline. Her manic defenses were demonstrable in her contempt for her husband on whom she was dependent for love *and* for the money required to achieve the realization of her romanticized illusions. Her schizoid defenses are shown by her withdrawal into herself and away from people, characterized by an overestimation of her inner thought content at the expense of values in the external world. Furthermore, to her, giving was the same as losing content of self, so she exhibited her good qualities, like her beautiful home, yet paradoxically did not invite anyone to enjoy her hospitality. She did not eat with the family, as I have mentioned, for fear of losing content or even of being eaten up (unconsciously). She would eat alone, but her menu was only vegetable salads and occasional chicken breasts. She ordered only salads at restaurants and often brought her own lettuce and asked the waiter merely for a plate to put it on. Her psychotic core survives under the highly rationalized and compromised guise of "eccentricity."

Another patient who typifies the schizoid aspects of the borderline personality organization was, at age thirty-three, beautiful, well-to-do, a licensed graduate from a professional school, and nowhere. She was unable to marry or work because she found herself unable to adjust to real people and occupations, which she believed to be a degradation of and compromise with her own necessarily ideal world. She frequently had dreams of returning home to her apartment and finding another woman, who reminded her of herself but was different, who rented the apartment from which she was evicted. In another dream she was chased by a maniacal driver on the freeway. She suddenly stopped and told her twin to escape while she dealt with the intruder, and then awoke in a nightmare. This patient seemed to be alienated from her feeling, needy, authentic self which was projected into others for "safe-keeping," so to speak, while she existed in this alienated state of anomie.

What seems utmostly to characterize the *Weltanschauungen* of the above-mentioned patients and other borderline patients is their dwelling in the universe of the second dimension. They are Cyclopean insofar as they see things from their point of view alone. The fantasies they foist on their real worlds seem like a blanket of naive, innocent, childlike notions where there are such things as heros and heroines, right people and wrong people, and absolute solutions to problems. More tactfully, it can be said that they frequently think, behave, and relate as if they are highly impractical. For a further discussion in depth of the *Weltanschauung* of the second dimension see Grotstein (1978a).

"Possession" in the Borderline

I have recently been able to locate a distinct kind of splitting of personalities which seems to characterize psychotic and borderline patients. This splitting is the result of the inner experience of demoniacal possession. These patients all seem to believe they have "made a pact with the devil" at one time or another in their lives, in order to achieve an invisibility, so as not to be held accountable. Their "lives" were lies, in other words; they did not occupy their bodily selves. While they disowned and disavowed their own "body souls," these same souls were believed unconsciously to have been forfeited and taken over by others (at the deepest level, the devil). In later life they then believe they have permanently forfeited hope and the opportunity to be well. In analysis one can generally find the typical manifestations of this debacle when one aspect of the patient tries to cooperate with the analyst while at the same time being reminded by another aspect that it is foolish to do so or it is too late; the future has already been forfeited. The goodness and helpfulness of the analyst cannot therefore be utilized because of belief in this forfeiture. Thus, the good and helpful analyst is transformed into a persecutory object who tantalizes and torments the patient with the goodness he cannot have. This is the diabolical envy which characterizes the *negative therapeutic reaction* so pathognomonic for the borderline patient.

It must again be pointed out that the borderline patient exhibits an unusual amalgam of neurotic and psychotic thinking and behavior by which the therapist is hard put to decide whether the patient is really neurotic or psychotic. One often suspects that the neurotic aspects of the patient are pretending, even insisting, on being psychotic, whereas the psychotic aspects seek to deny their existence and masquerade as neurotic or normal. I believe the truth lies closer to the view that there appears to be a collusion between the normal (or neurotic) and psychotic personalities in these patients which devolves into a pathological symbiosis between them, in which each can be used to further the misbegotten purposes of the other.

"Acting Out" in the Borderline

There is a particular feature of the borderline personality which comes to the forefront during psychoanalytic treatment and during hospitalization. Moreso than with frankly psychotic patients, there seems to be an instantaneous, massive regression at the beginning of treatment in which archaic aspects of the personality seem to emerge and dominate. Psychotic acting out ensues. The observers of this scenario are generally perturbed and are mobilized into stopgap measures which seek to curb the patient's behavior. The patient may be sent into seclusion, restraints, be given massive doses of drugs, and, if they are in outpatient psychoanalysis, are usually discontinued from the analytic procedure and are asked to sit up and then treated supportively rather than analytically. It is as if any kind of recognition of their mental state in which the treatment addresses itself to their inner feelings mobilizes a greedy, starved, unconscious self which suddenly rushes to the surface in order to be heard. This portion of the personality then seems to topple the stability of the normal personality and then dominates the scene. It is almost as if it is a caricature of psychosis rather than of psychosis itself. Thus, many observers have thought it to be hysterical psychosis or a manifestation of hysteria generally.

The ultimate purpose of this outflow of primitive behavior seems to be a need to engage the caretaking object in a relationship with the primitive self at the expense of the progressing, growing self. In short, the borderline personality seems to misuse and misconstrue a therapeutic relationship in order to obtain recompense for its suffering and attention to its narcissistically mistreated self rather than to use the treatment in order to emerge from oneself. (Wishnie [1975] has provided an excellent account of this phenomenon.) This apparent misuse of the treatment smacks often of *secondary gain* and has caused many observers to label borderline states as hysterical psychoses. It is this very secondary gain phenomenon which so beautifully depicts that "corrupt amalgam" conception I have been discussing.

The propensity for borderline patients to "act out" is too often met with "counter acting out" by therapists. The psychoanalytic treatment of these patients frequently stimulates feelings of despair and great psychic pain. It is often the tendency of these patients to "elope" from analysis and consult other therapists who too often may sympathetically agree that analysis is too harsh and that they should have "supportive treatment" instead. These moments in analysis generally correspond to the patient's becoming aware of the devastation to himself and his objects that exercising his propensity for negation has wrought. It also may be due to the collapse of the idealized transference and the emergence of a delusional transference which has not yet been reconverted into a transference psychosis.[2] In most cases it would seem advisable, not to say ethical, to recommend to these patients that they return to their analysts.

The Treatment of the Borderline Personality Organization

Rosenfeld (1965), Bion (1962a, 1962b, 1963, 1965, 1967, 1970) and Segal (1950), all analysands of Melanie Klein, have been pioneers in conducting the psychoanalytic treatment of psychotic and borderline disorders following the even earlier pioneering efforts of Abraham (1908, 1911, 1924), Federn (1943), and Nunberg (1920, 1921). Abraham did not particularly describe his technique but only referred to his direct id interpretations to psychotic patients. Apparently he achieved success in schizophrenic and in manic depressive psychoses. Federn, on the other hand, first discussed the use of parameters in the conducting of the treatment. For instance, he suggested female as well as male therapists, advocated avoiding interpretation of negative transference, etc. He was really more the pioneer in the psychotherapeutic treatment of psychotic disorders which has brought forth the interpersonal school, the British object relations school, etc.

Kernberg (1975), following the Kleinian experience, conducted a research program at the Menninger Foundation which was to study the psychotherapeutic treatment of borderline personalities. He and his group found, surprisingly, that borderlines did lend themselves to psychotherapeutic and psychoanalytic intervention but with certain modifications. He put restrictions on acting out, had a social worker to handle reality aspects of the patient's life in terms of advice, etc., restricted his interpretations to the here and now, and avoided reconstructions.

---

[2]The difference between a *delusional transference* and a *transference psychosis* is the presence of a therapeutic alliance in the latter.

The Interdisciplinary Group for Advanced Studies in Psychotic, Borderline, and Narcissistic Disorders has been studying treatment of such cases in hospital and office practice (Grotstein et al. 1975, 1976, 1977, 1978) and has come to the following conclusions. The formal psychoanalytic technique is the treatment of choice for borderline and for narcissistic personality disorders. Melanie Klein's contribution of the theory of projective identification and of splitting, and of the schizoid and manic defenses in general, her positing the paranoid-schizoid and the depressive positions, and her own conception of the internal world have made the interpretation of psychotic disorders more accessible to psychoanaltic technique than that of the classical technique which was based upon the structural theory in the oedipus complex belonging to later fixation points in childhood development.

We believe further that the borderline patient forms transference relationships which can and must be gathered by the analytic technique into a *transference psychosis* (Rosenfeld, personal communication), which is the analytic recapitulation of the infantile psychosis *and* of the infantile psychotic state resulting from its unsuccessful resolution. The concept of the transference psychosis connotes the expression of psychotic mechanisms and states within the perimeter of the therapeutic alliance. In other words, the conception is understood by the patient and the analyst that the psychosis within the analytic framework is all fantasy. A delusional transference, on the other hand, is one in which the patient has an overriding delusional relationship to the analyst which is believed by him not to be a fantasy but the truth! There is not therapeutic alliance. An example of the latter is that of the borderline young woman who nearly quit the analysis because of her delusional conviction that I was in telepathic communication with her at various times throughout the day, and also with her teachers. She eventually came to understand that she had an internal world as well as a picture of the external world, and that she confused them because she was also confused with me in order to avoid the consequences of separation. Eventually she came to realize that maybe the telepathy was only her idea and not an external phenomenon. She had moved from a delusional transference to a transference psychosis.

Kohut's (1971, 1977) and Mahler's (1975) recent studies of narcissistic disorders and of infantile development have greatly added to our understanding of the descriptive aspects of that phase but have not been sufficiently conjoined with Klein's phenomenology of infantile development to have become a standard feature of technique employable for the psychoanalysis of psychoses per se, in our opinion.

The Interdisciplinary Group for Advanced Studies also believes that the use of the therapist and manager in the treatment of borderline personalities is oftentimes essential, particularly in the hospital.[3]

We have found after several years experience that this is the situation which works best for hospital patients, both psychotic and borderline. We have also found, as I have alluded to above, that borderline patients in office practice generally have such a compromised relationship to reality at times that they frequently need a manager to be engaged in the relationship to the family, for advice and for other factotal needs.

A particular problem that has come to our attention in the psychoanalytic treatment of borderline patients is a paradoxical one. We have found that when interpretations are made about dynamic content, the normal portion of the personality seems to understand and make such use of them that instant progress can

[3]Currently, we are operating the Department of Psychoanalytic Studies at Del Amo Hospital, Torrance, California, in which all patients are seen on a research basis by both a psychoanalyst who is the therapist and by a manager who is also a psychoanalyst but who deals with the family, with the hospital staff, and the routine management of the patient's case.

often be seen. We have also found that negative therapeutic reactions instantly set in, however, by virtue of this very progress, because of a growing discrepancy between the normal and the abnormal personalities. It must be recalled from my discussion above that there are two levels of splitting in the borderline personality. The first is the major differentiation between the normal and the abnormal personalities, and the second is the chaotic splittings of internal objects and selves in the abnormal internal world which the relatively normal personality tries to repress and superordinate in the course of the patient's life.

The more the normal personality grabs hold of interpretations, the more it resembles the successful and greedy twin grabbing the meal from mother's breast and leaving the hapless twin behind. In other words, one of the characteristic features of the psychoanalytic treatment of borderline disorders is a growing split between the two personalities. No matter how deep the interpretations, it is as if the normal or neurotic portion of the personality understands the interpretations and seemingly runs with them. The psychotic personality's envy of its more successful twin is pathognomonic for the borderline and psychotic disorders and probably the major cause of the negative therapeutic reaction. This personality, out of a sense of danger of abandonment, seems to viciously attack, and to precipitate acting out and sabotage so as to discredit the normal personality, and undermine its progress.

This paradoxical feature brings up a very interesting, important, and hitherto unanswered question. When the psychotic makes progress in analysis, how does progress occur in the psychotic portion—or does it occur? It is our belief that this is perhaps the most important question in the treatment of psychosis. We also believe that in normal nonepisodic periods in the life of the borderline or the psychotic patient—that is, in the time between episodes of efflorescent psychosis—the psychosis is dormant in terms of the character structure of the abnormal personality. From many case reports, the abnormal personality does not seem to understand interpretations and cannot get well from analysis, as revealed by dreams and in free associations. As Bion (1967) has informed us, the psychotic portion of the personality has been able to exist only by an apparently total projective identification of its sense of mind and capacity of perception, so that it exists as a residue after evacuation of all mental, perceptual, and affective processes. It is varyingly described by many patients as a black, seething hole of expanding emptiness, a dark incineration after a holocaust, a sense of eternal raging madness and destructiveness, etc. It is either not to be reasoned with and/ or cannot be reasoned with because reason does not exist to take hold of reasonable interpretations.

It is at this point that the seeming "nonanalytic" caretaking aspects of Winnicott (1956), Balint (1953, 1968), and Kohut (1971, 1977) seem to be relevant. These investigators all seem to advocate fostering enactment of containment in lieu of interpretive analysis whereby the psychotic self can achieve a tranquil nurture within the framework of the therapeutic alliance with the analyst. It is a real relationship, not just a symbolic one. In short, these authors believe that the early object relations of these patients were really quite defective, and that there can be no progress until there is restoration (in the present) of an object relationship which can help to facilitate growth and maturation of the yet unmaturated self.

Those who still hold a psychoanalytic point of view, such as Kleinian workers on one hand and Kernberg, less rigorously, on the other, handle the situation in different ways. I am not sure how Kernberg addresses himself to the issue of the treatment of the psychotic self as differentiated from the neurotic self, but Kleinian workers seem to attempt to achieve the same thing that Winnicott, Balint, and Kohut are trying to achieve externally via an internal symbolic technique. In other words, they try through interpretations to interest the normal personality in recognizing its psychotic twin in lieu of splitting it off. It is as if the patient is reminded that he is indeed his brother's keeper. This sense of therapeutic tolerance in the depressive position in which the healthier self becomes more interested in his psychotic personality seems to foster, first, deep acceptance and later absorption of the psychotic aspects of the abnormal personality into the more normal self. As the sense of infantile catastrophe (which is repeated in the transference) is better understood, the psychotic self seems at times to be more enabled to reclaim its disavowed mind and sense organs; intelligence becomes less hypersensitive to progression and knowledge and is therefore enabled more and more to join its more successful brother as its envy is mitigated in favor of collaboration.

Other Aspects of Therapy of the Borderline Organization

It is my opinion and the opinion of the Interdisciplinary Group for Advanced Studies that one of the essential issues in the etiology and perseveration of the borderline syndrome and of the psychotic state is sensory deprivation. In the earlier monograph I have referred to (Grotstein 1977a, 1977b) I suggested that the etiology of the psychotic personality in infancy had to do with the infantile experience of a defective threshold against internal and external stimuli (defective passive stimulus barrier and/or active stimulus barrier). As a consequence, the infant found a way of attacking his capacity to integrate his somatosensory stimuli so as to achieve a higher threshold at the expense of his capacity to feel and therefore to think. With the compromise of his capacity to integrate his somatosensory perceptions, he found himself in a sensory deprivation state. This sensory deprivation released the toning effect of an active somatosensory system on the adjacent systems such as the reticular arousal and reticular suppressive, and the limbic. The release of the toning effect by the somatosensory constitutes a phenomenon not unlike a pyramidal lesion in reverse so that the limbic system and the reticular suppressive system thereafter function chaotically. The new organization which seeks to restore order is a psychotic organization which is characterized by dopaminic nerve cell hypertrophy and by other biochemical and neurophysiological phenomena which are pathognomonic of the psychotic state generally.

Of importance for this presentation is our belief in the fundamental importance of sensory deprivation for the development of psychosis. When the psychotic acts out in a mental hospital he is often put in restraints and/or seclusion, not to mention given higher dosages of psychotropic drugs. We believe that somatosensory stimulation such as used to be given in the form of wet packs, etc., can oftentimes be of much more benefit than seclusion; and that psychotropic drugs, while treating the immediacy of the abnormal biochemical state of psychosis, compromise the patient's mental state by continuing the state of sensory deprivation chemically. We believe, instead, that the psychotic needs enormous stimulation in order to establish contact. This should be done in terms of object relations as is currently the rule in most well-appointed private psychiatric hospital facilities. Those hospitals which function as intensive care units oftentimes supply a great deal of contact, which is beneficial to the patient.

Psychoanalysis, which is itself an intensely stimulating, therapeutic intervention generally, is also indicated in order to maintain a high level of stimulation. Parenthetically, I believe that electroconvulsive therapy and insulin therapy were effective because of the somatosensory stimulation which they offered. Yet an argument can also be offered that the Dauerschlaff technique also worked—as do its descendants, the psychotropic drugs—by virtue of withdrawing contact. I can only approach a possible answer to this dilemma by suggesting that maybe both techniques are necessary, stimulation on one hand in order to overcome sensory deprivation, and also a prolonged rest for the already besieged psychotic personality so as to reestablish confidence in his capacity to obtain asylum or sanctuary from overwhelming stimulation.

Summary

This contribution offers the suggestion that the borderline syndrome and personality organization are on a continuum with the narcissistic personality organization and are characterized in particular by the perseveration of a split between seemingly normal and psychotic personalities in which the normal personality is relatively effective most of the time in superordinating and repressing the abnormal personality. A further split can be seen in terms of the propensity for unresolved splitting in the unconscious of the abnormal personality as differentiated from the unconscious of the normal personality.

Psychoanalytic treatment is recommended particularly if the analyst is familiar with Klein's conception of the paranoid-schizoid and depressive positions, the schizoid and manic defenses, and particularly with the tactical deployment of projective identification and splitting. Moreover, special attention must be paid to the propensity for acting out and for the negative therapeutic reaction because of the paradoxical phenomenon in which there is a growing disparity between the normal and abnormal personality in psychoanalytic treatment.

References
Abraham, K. (1908). The psycho-sexual differences between hysteria and dementia praecox. In *Selected Papers On Psycho-Analysis*. London: Hogarth Press, 1949.

—————— (1911). Notes on the psycho-analytical investigations and treatment of manic-depressive insanity and allied conditions. In *Selected Papers On Psychoanalysis,* op. cit.

—————— (1924). A short study of the development of the libido, viewed in the light of mental disorders, Part I. Manic-depressive states and the pre-genital levels of the libido. In *Selected Papers on Psycho-Analysis,* op. cit.

Balint, M. (1953). *Primary Love and Psycho-Analytic Technique.* New York: Liveright.

—————— (1968). *The Basic Fault.* London: Tavistock.

Bergman, P. and Escalona, S.K. (1949). Unusual sensitivities in very young children. *Psychoanalytic Study of the Child* 3-4.

Bick, E. (1968). The experience of the skin in early object relations. *International Journal of Psycho-Analysis* 49:484-486.

Bion, W. (1950). The imaginary twin. In *Second Thoughts.* New York: Jason Aronson, 1967.

—————— (1956). Development of schizophrenic thought. *International Journal of Psycho-Analysis* 37:344. In *Second Thoughts,* op. cit.

—————— (1957a). Differentiation of the Psychotic from the non-psychotic personalities. *International Journal of Psycho-Analysis* 38:266. In *Second Thoughts,* op. cit.

—————— (1957b). On arrogance. *International Journal of Psycho-Analysis* 39:144. In *Second Thoughts,* op. cit.

—————— (1962). *Learning from Experience.* In *Seven Servants: Four Works by Wilfred Bion.* New York, Jason Aronson, 1977.

—————— (1963). *Elements of Psychoanalysis.* In *Seven Servants,* op. cit.

—————— (1965). *Transformations.* In *Seven Servants,* op. cit.

—————— (1967). *Second Thoughts.* New York: Jason Aronson.

—————— (1970). *Attention and Interpretation.* London: Tavistock.

Fairbairn, W.D.R. (1954). *An Object-Relations Theory of the Personality.* New York: Basic Books.

Federn, P. (1943). Psychoanalysis of psychoses. In *Ego Psychology and the Psychoses.* London: Imago, 1953.

Green. A. (1977). The borderline concept. In *Borderline Personality Disorders,* ed. Peter Hartocollis. New York: International Universities Press.

——— (1978). Negation and contradiction. In *Do I Dare Disturb the Universe? A Festschrift For Wilfred Bion* [In press].

Grotstein, J.S. (1977a). The psychoanalytic concept of schizophrenia: I. The dilemma. *International Journal of Psycho-Analysis* 58:403–425.

——— (1977b). The psychoanalytic concept of schizophrenia: II. Reconciliation. *International Journal of Psycho-Analysis* 58:427–452.

——— (1978a). *Splitting and Projective Identification.* New York: Jason Aronson [In press].

——— (1978b). Infantile psychosis and the dual-track theorem [Unpublished manuscript].

Grotstein et al. (1975, 1976, 1977, 1978). The Proceedings of the Interdisciplinary Group for Advanced Studies in Psychotic, Borderline, and Narcissistic Disorders [Unpublished manuscript].

Isaacs, S. (1952). The nature and function of phantasy. In *Developments in Psycho-Analysis,* ed. Klein et al. London: Hogarth.

Kernberg, O. (1975). *Borderline Conditions and Pathological Narcissism.* New York: Jason Aronson.

Klein, M. (1948). *Contributions to Psycho-Analysis, 1921-1945.* London: Hogarth Press, 1950.

——— (1952a). *Developments in Psycho-Analysis,* eds. M. Klein, P. Heimann, S. Isaacs, and J. Riviere. London: Hogarth.

——— (1952b). Notes on some schizoid mechanisms. In *Developments in Psychoanalysis,* op. cit.

————— (1955). On identification. In *New Directions in Psycho-Analysis,* eds. M. Klein, P. Heimann, and R. Money-Kyrle. London: Tavistock.

Kohut, H. (1971). *The Analysis of the Self.* New York: International Universities Press.

————— (1977). *The Restoration of the Self.* New York: International Universities Press.

Mack, J.E. (1975). Borderline states: an historical perspective. In *Borderline States in Psychiatry,* ed. J.E. Mack. New York: Grune and Stratton.

Mahler, M., Pine, F., and Bergman, A. (1975). *The Psychological Birth of the Human Infant.* New York: Basic Books.

Meltzer, D. (1974). Mutism in infantile autism, schizophrenia, and manic-depressive states: the correlation of clinical psychopathology and linguistics. *Internation Journal of Psycho-Analysis* 55:397–404.

Meltzer, D. (1975). *Explorations in Autism,* eds. D. Meltzer, J. Bremner, S. Hoxter, D. Weddell, and I. Wittenberg. Perthshire: Clunie Press.

Nunberg, H. (1920). On the catatonic attack. In *Practice and Theory of Psychoanalysis.* New York: Nervous and Mental Diseases Monographs.

————— (1921). On the course of the libidinal conflict in a case of schizophrenia. In *Practice and Theory of Psychoanalysis,* op. cit.

Rosenfeld, H. (1965). *Psychotic States: A Psychoanalytic Approach.* New York: International Universities Press.

Segal, H. (1950). Some aspects of the analysis of a schizophrenic. *International Journal of Psycho-Analysis* 31:1–11

Tustin, F. (1978). Psychological birth and psychological catastrophe. In *Do I Dare Disturb the Universe? A Festschrift for Wilfred Bion.* New York: Jason Aronson, Inc.

Winnicott, D. (1956). Primary maternal preoccupation. In *Collected Papers.* New York: Basic Books.

Wishnie, H.A. (1975). In-patient therapy with borderline patients. In *Borderline States in Psychiatry,* ed. J.E. Mack. New York: Grune and Stratton.

Part II

Technique of
Treatment of the
Borderline Patient

Chapter 4

Difficulties in the Psychoanalytic Treatment of Borderline Patients

Herbert Rosenfeld, M.D.

In this paper I shall discuss some of my diagnostic observations, experiences, and difficulties in the psychoanalytic treatment of borderline states. I shall also touch on the psychoanalytic view of narcissistic states with particular emphasis on differential diagnosis.

The literature on this subject has grown to gigantic proportions, ever since Hughes in 1884 spoke of the borderland of insanity. The first analytic attempt to define more clearly the group of patients who did not fit either into psychoneurotic or psychotic groups was made by Stern in 1938 in his paper "Psychoanalytic Investigation of and Therapy in the Borderline Group of Neuroses." He discussed a group of patients who were resistant to psychoanalytic treatment. He described them as highly narcissistic, greatly oversensitive, and suffering from "psychic bleeding." They were paralyzed by psychic trauma, rigid in mind and body, deeply insecure, masochistic, and suffered from deep-rooted feelings of inferiority.

Stern was particularly impressed by the strength of the negative therapeutic reactions which occurred in these patients. It predominated over their capacity to make adequate use of the treatment situation. He also observed the tendency of such patients to use projective mechanisms, and he stressed their difficulties in reality testing, particularly in personal relationships. He obviously regarded the problem of narcissism as a major factor, but one is impressed by the similarity of his patients with Freud's rigid and inert group of patients who also showed marked negative therapeutic reactions. Freud's findings were described in the paper, "Analysis Terminable and Interminable" (1937). He did not connect this deep resistance to narcissism, but rather to "the power in mental life" which he called "the instinct of aggression or of destruction."

In my papers, "On the Psychopathology of Narcissism" (1964), "Notes on the Negative Therapeutic Reaction" (1968) and "A Clinical Approach to the Psychoanalytic Theory of the Life and Death Instinct" (1971), I investigated in some detail severe chronic obstacles to treatment, including the negative therapeutic reaction created by narcissistic structures. I found that a detailed psychoanalytic investigation of a number of patients who presented chronic resistances to analysis by acting out, and by narcissistic withdrawal states, helped me to discover narcissistic structures which I linked with Freud's observations about the clinical importance of the instinct of destruction, and his contention that most phenomena of life could be explained by the concurrent and/or mutual opposing action of two primary instincts.

It would be an exaggeration to claim that all severe narcissistic patients respond to analytic treatment. Kernberg describes narcissistic patients functioning at an overt borderline level who show chronic narcissistic rage, often expressed quite openly, and in whom antisocial and sadistic sexual behavior combined with violence may be prominent. He feels that these cases usually present a contraindication for analysis, and often even for the modified psychoanalytic procedure which he recommends for most borderline patients. I agree with Kernberg that violently aggressive patients, particularly those who act out with physical violence with the analyst, are generally unsuitable for analysis, particularly if they deliberately try to wreck the treatment situation. However, some violent patients occasionally respond to analysis if there is introduced the parameter that treatment will be discontinued unless the physically destructive behavior is controlled.

There are also certain severely sadistic and masochistic patients who do not respond to analysis. I have had the opportunity to observe the treatment of at least one severely destructive narcissistic patient who preferred to continue to adhere to the idealization of his omnipotent destructive and self-destructive powers, and who after some improvement refused all analytic and psychotherapeutic help, gave up his achievements in life, including his close relationships, and drifted into a rigid, aggressive inertia which was accompanied by a constant preoccupation with and idealization of death which, after some delay, actually came about. This patient could be called a case of extreme destructive narcissism and such an outcome of analytic, psychotherapeutic, and psychiatric treatment of narcissistic patients is rare. Even an obstinately destructive attitude often softens, and life is allowed to return. Generally I have found that narcissistic patients improve considerably during analytic treatment.

During the last ten to fifteen years there have been many reports of successful analytic treatment of narcissistic patients, particularly by Kernberg and Kohut, who have differentiated the narcissistic character disorders from the borderline group of patients. These analysts feel that analytic treatment is now the treatment of choice for narcissistic patients. Kernberg's theory of narcissism is mainly based on Klein's work on internal object relations and my own work, "On the Psychopathology of Narcissism" (1964), where I stress among other factors the importance of envy in the object relations of the narcissistic patient. Both Kernberg and I have tried to clarify pathological narcissism, but there is still a great deal of work to be done. I extended the concept of narcissism when I described destructive narcissism in 1971.

I have studied Kohut's work in some detail, and believe that many of the narcissistic self-structures, such as the grandiose self, which he regards as normal archaic parts of the self, are in fact pathological narcissistic structures. I agree with Kohut that it is extremely important to diagnose narcissistic rage, and differentiate it from other sources of hate or anger. What I have found missing in his work is the description of the working-through in analysis of narcissistic rage and the negative transference which is related to this problem. Kohut (1972) discusses destructive, omnipotent, narcissistic structures and personalities in relationship to dictators and organizations such as Hitler and Nazi Germany, but he has not applied his views to clinical pathology. The understanding of destructive narcissistic structures plays a central part in the treatment of psychosis and many borderline states.

I think it is important for us to realize that there are many different types or groups of borderline states and many analysts use the term *borderline* for patients who show a number of psychotic features without being overtly schizophrenic or psychotic. I sympathize and agree with Robert Knight, who said in 1953, "The term borderline case is not recommended as a diagnostic term and a much more precise diagnosis should be made which identifies the type and degree of psychotic pathology." His paper illustrates the difficulties of a highly experienced psychiatrist and therapist in arriving at the differential diagnosis of latent psychosis, particularly schizophrenia, early schizophrenia, mixed neurotic and psychotic states, and borderline conditions.

In the diagnosis of borderline states he stresses the importance of a number of impaired ego functions, such as lack of achievement over long periods of time, combined with vagueness and unreality of plans for the future, and insufficient contrast between dream content and waking activities. He also describes the presence of multiple symptoms and disabilities, especially if these are too easily accepted as ego-syntonic by the patient, or, on the contrary, viewed as being due to "malevolent external influences."

In contrast to many other psychiatrists and analysts, Frosch (1964) and Kernberg (1975) described specific character structures to clarify the diagnosis of the borderline patient. Frosch suggested that the term psychotic character be substituted for borderline state as well as ambulatory schizophrenia, pseudoneurotic schizophrenia, schizophrenia without psychosis, latent psychosis, larval psychosis, "as if" characters, and neurotic ego distortions. He thought the symptoms or cluster of symptoms were not suitable for classification. He felt that there was a definite entity or syndrome characterized by ego functions in their relationship to reality, other objects, and other psychic structures. Under certain conditions patients may develop transient psychosis, but he found it equally possible for such an individual to go all his life without developing a psychosis. Frosch does not recommend psychoanalysis but psychoanalytic therapy for the psychotic character syndrome.

Kernberg similarly described patients who have a rather specific stable pathological personality organization which he calls "borderline personality organization." Kernberg's patients present neurotic symptoms including anxiety, polymorphous perverse sexuality, schizoid or hypomanic prepsychotic personalities, impulse neurosis and addiction, infantile and antisocial character disorders and many polysymptomatic problems such as phobias, obsessions, dissociations, and paranoid trends. All these symptoms were occasionally present in varying combinations but did not help to differentiate the syndrome. He found the borderline cases are easily differentiated from psychosis but not as easily from neurosis. He gave a very detailed picture of the ego and general character structure of the borderline patient. He stressed, for example, nonspecific manifestations of ego weakness represented particularly by lack of anxiety tolerance and lack of impulse control. He described the predominance of early ego defenses such as splitting of objects into good and bad, primitive idealization, early forms of projection, in particular projective identification, denial, and omnipotence—mechanisms which Melanie Klein described as typical defense mechanisms of the earliest phase of infantile development, which she called the paranoid-schizoid position (1946).

Kernberg found that these patients, when analysis was attempted, often developed a transference psychosis characterized by a particular loss of reality testing and even by delusions restricted to the transference situation. He also emphasized that the borderline patient often develops a particular acting out of his instinctual conflicts in the analytic transference, which gratifies his pathological need and blocks further analytic progress. Kernberg found psychoanalytic treatment often contraindicated and recommended carefully directed psychoanalytically orientated psychotherapy. He suggested a detailed elaboration of the latent and manifest negative transference followed by the deflection of the manifest negative transference away from the therapeutic interaction by systematically examining it in the patient's relationship with others.

I agree with Kernberg that many borderline patients present difficulty in relation to acting out and the development of a transference psychosis. But deflecting the negative transference away from the therapeutic interaction is often felt by the patient as rejection and confirms his deepest anxiety that there is nobody who can cope with him and bear his projections. More detailed understanding of the earliest infant-mother relationship with emphasis on the importance of the need of the infant to experience that his nonverbal communications transmitted by projection are received and contained by the perceptive and intuitive mother (Bion 1962a, 1962b) may lead gradually to a better understanding of the transference psychosis. As the transference psychosis highlights a failure of the analyst-patient relationship, it can also provide an important clue and guide to reach the patient's basic problems (Rosenfeld 1978).

I am impressed by both Frosch's and Kernberg's careful work. I do agree that, in general, symptoms are not the best guide for diagnosing the borderline patient. I have, however, seen so many different types of borderline patients that I feel some classification is necessary and helpful to me and perhaps to others. I suggest five groups of such patients.

Contrary to Kernberg's experience, in my first group I would place those patients whom I find very difficult to differentiate from latent psychotics.

In the second group I would place most of the patients whom Kernberg and Stern describe. These patients usually have an infantile character and show generalized lability and oversensitivity. They show an infantile demandingness and overinvolvement, and often an exhibitionistic dependency and clinging to objects. Sometimes a mixed depressive, paranoid, masochistic character structure predominates. Frequently they suffer from what Stern calls "psychic bleeding." They feel wounded and hurt, and their mental skin does not protect them against any slight injuries from the external world, but equally they cannot keep what they have been given. It constantly seems to leak out and so increases their demandingness.

In the third group (Grinker, Werble, and Drye 1968) I place the "as if " patient who is difficult to diagnose in a psychiatric interview, so that he is frequently only discovered in analysis.(Grinker also places the "as if" personality in a separate group of borderline disorders.)

In the fourth group of borderline patients I would place those who suffered severe mental trauma for long periods in early infancy, sometimes for years. These patients have not only experienced insufficient mothering in early infancy, but had to cope with long, drawn-out separations in later childhood. They seem to have retained many of their early infantile psychotic mechanisms, such as omniscient and omnipotent projective identification, used particularly to evacuate overwhelming anxieties into external objects and situations. These long separations from their mothers have prevented such patients from modifying their primitive modes of functioning with the help of external objects.

In addition, it seems that the later separations often increased the early psychotic anxieties and the primitive defense systems related to them. I also found that the normal oedipal problems were greatly reinforced, as absence of the parents makes it almost impossible to modify oedipal conflicts without the understanding help of the primary objects. In spite of the strength of their psychotic anxieties, such patients feel that they have an inherent strength and reality sense because they have survived. They often have an intense narcissistic pride in having almost single-handedly kept themselves alive. This type of patient often develops some psychotic transference manifestation during analytic treatment, as the slightest positive change but also the slightest misunderstanding on the part of the analyst leads to violent primitive eruptions of the early psychotic anxieties, related to the traumatic situation.

In the fifth group I would place patients who show a mixture of narcissistic modes of functioning, combined with the problems described by Kernberg, such as marked ego weakness, inability to sustain interest, and feelings of inner emptiness, which lead to excessive dependency on external object relationships, which they find extremely difficult to maintain. It is the mixture of an intense need for objects, and an overpowering narcissistic withdrawal reaction which dominates the life and treatment situations of these patients. This mixture of inertia and violent emotional reactions often has psychotic intensity and sometimes leads to diagnosing the patient as psychotic or schizophrenic, and, in turn, to long hospitalization. In my experience these patients are definitely borderline. They do not develop a severe transference psychosis, but engage in prolonged acting out within the transference. It is their acting out which may be analytically difficult to control and sometimes requires temporary hospitalization.

The five groups of borderline patients which I propose frequently overlap, and may, therefore, cause some diagnostic confusion. They all have one important factor in common: they are difficult to treat. But it is interesting and gratifying that the detailed psychoanalytic treatment of these patients is not as impossible and hopeless therapeutically as Stern (1938) and Knight (1953a, 1953b) seemed to believe. Henry Rey (chapter 12) described schizoid borderline patients who had many similarities with the patients described in this group.

I shall now turn to some clinical observations of the five different groups of patients that I have described.

Group one. In my analytic and supervisory work I have been most familiar with borderline patients who have a psychotic character structure (Group one). They use psychotic mechanisms freely and often have beliefs which do not differ much from psychotic delusions but, generally, these delusional beliefs are projected into real life situations where they can be hidden. This gives the patient a certain stability and pseudosanity. Sometimes the delusion relates to a magical union frequently erotized with an omnipotent idealized object. In my experience, once the split between a massively idealized object and the real object has been worked through in the transference, we are faced with an upsurge of severe persecutory anxieties.

There is, of course, always the danger that the real object represented by the analyst in the transference may now become the persecutor, particularly when the delusional union with the idealized object is revealed in the treatment. If this appears at a time when some trust in the helpful aspects of the analyst has developed, it is not likely that a paranoid transference psychosis will occur, but one has to be on the lookout for paranoid anxieties which will appear simultaneously with the revelation of the magically idealized delusional object, as they are often split off and acted out. If the highly erotic delusional object relation attaches itself to the analyst, there is a danger of a highly erotized transference psychosis, but this is not generally the outcome in the borderline psychotic states unless there has previously been a marked collusive relationship with the analyst.

In the successful treatment of the psychotic borderline state, the revelation of the delusional object relation often increases confidence in the analyst as a real object and a more realistic therapeutic alliance can develop. Technically, I think it essential in borderline states of this kind to be firm, open, and perceptive to the intense fear and pain that patients have to go through when they become aware of the content of their delusional dream state. This makes them feel temporarily quite mad. It is also important to realize that these patients, even if they want to be helped by the analyst to return to life, temporarily experience a breakthrough to better understanding as a persecution, and this often leads to confusion and negative therapeutic reaction (Bion 1953). The negative therapeutic reaction is generally related to the power of the delusional, omnipotent dream state which is opposed to external reality, and to any dependent relationship to the analyst generally standing for the feeding mother.

Group two. In relation to the second group of borderline

patients which bear a similarity to Kernberg's observations, I would like to stress that their main difficulties appear to relate to containing their anxieties, dealing with separations, and their oversensitivity which turns any minor difficulty in their lives into a major catastrophe. Many patients in this group are so oversensitive that one feels they have hardly any mental skin, a problem which Stern (1938) has called "mental bleeding." This problem seems related to the patient's constant entanglement with situations or objects which show in reality a striking similarity to aspects of the patient's own personality, which the patient wants to hide and disown. As a result of this projective process, the patient seems stuck and unable to feel any distance from these objects. He feels irritable and constantly obsessionally preoccupied with these persons or situations. While he cannot detach himself from the person concerned, specific aspects of the patient's character which relate to the situation become accentuated rather than diminished by this process. Analysis of this problem is very difficult since the patient feels easily criticized and rejected; he regards this problem as an inherent part of his personality which he believes to be unchangeable.

These patients often give the impression that being in analysis means being there to stay, and for a long time they react to any interpretation that the analysis will have to end one day with intense feelings of being rejected. They tend to idealize the analyst as someone into whom they can project all their problems and difficulties, and when they use the analyst as an idealized receptacle, they subtly undervalue him as someone from whom they can accept nourishment which allows them to become stronger. Insofar as they use the analysis endlessly to repeat their problems rather than learn from their experience, they act out in the way Kernberg describes.

Another important problem of this type of patient is his intense desire to be part of the analyst's life situation. The patient often admits this, and helps in the analysis of this problem, but secretly he maintains the belief that he or she is the analyst's favorite, so that he will never have to part from him. This secret conviction is often missed because it appears as projection into another patient who arouses intense jealousy. Another problem, which becomes apparent only after a long analysis, is the patient's deep conviction that he is incurable, crazy or mad, and that he has deceived the analyst about his pseudosanity. When this problem gradually is brought to light, the patient is often convinced that the analyst had colluded with him to keep this problem out of the analysis, probably because of the analyst's fear of being psychotic himself.

In the treatment of the borderline patient, the extent to which the analyst unconsciously colludes in making the treatment more difficult probably varies a great deal. I think it is important to recognize that the borderline patient chooses a particular form of projection which often has a double meaning, and has the effect of making the analyst miss the main points, which in turn increases the patient's omnipotent delusion that he can control the analyst's mind. In the analytic treatment it is essential to expose all evidence of entaglements and collusion which have attached themselves to the transference. This seems the only way to break the vicious circle. Avoiding analysis of these problems in the transference, as Kernberg seems to suggest, cannot really help the patient. Unconsciously this contrived avoidance or deflection must increase the patient's conviction of his own omnipotence, because it is a proof of his capacity to make the analyst helpless. For the patient this unconsciously means that the analyst is the carrier of the patient's own madness.

Group three. This group represents the "as if " personality. Many borderline patients have some "as if " features in their behavior. But if the "as if " features dominate the personality of the patient, the analysis becomes very difficult. One of my patients made great sacrifices for his analysis, but for a long time found it extremely difficult to cooperate. He complained that he frequently felt that he was drowning, disappearing into nothing. Whenever I wanted to confront him with any problem that appeared in the analysis, he did in fact emotionally disappear. One of this patient's difficulties was related to his doubt that any strong emotions he experienced were real. "Do I really feel anything or do I just want you to believe that I experience love, depression, or any other feelings?" I believe that the "as if" patient is intensely narcissistic but deceives himself about this. It is apparently the domination by an omnipotent self which controls the perceptive apparatus and recreates the deception in the self-presentation and also the deception in the object relationship.

These patients are difficult to treat because they are constantly misleading to themselves and the analyst. After he had improved, a patient suffering from an "as if" state dreamt that he stood near a swimming pool and noticed that a ten-year-old boy had jumped into the pool but failed to come to the surface. He decided to jump into the pool and thought he had found the boy and tried to swim with him to safety. But when he turned his head he noticed to his surprise that the drowning boy had been saved by someone else and was sitting with him on the lawn beside the swimming pool. The patient then noticed that he was holding a key and a cockroach in his hands and he felt dismayed. Analysis of the dream revealed that the patient was identified with the drowning boy because he felt so improved. But the patient omnipotently believed that he had cured himself. Through the dream he realized how reluctant he was to perceive that I had helped him.

Group four. The traumatized patient of Group four has many features in common with the psychotic borderline group. He is more in contact with the infantile nature of his feelings. All his emotions, his anxieties, pain, hate, and guilt have an overwhelming quality. He deals with emotions, in particular with overwhelming anxieties, by violent omnipotent and omniscient projection into other objects or situations, in order to deny their existence and make their content unknown. Only then does he hope to feel better. This violent expulsive process of mental content creates emptiness and incapacity to think, which he tries to overcome by omnipotently taking over (stealing) and copying the mind of an idealized object in a secret manner. This process creates intense guilt since the normal infantile self, and the relationship he tries to form to a caring object, is thus eliminated or destroyed.

Analysis with these patients creates difficulties because interpretation of the denied and unknown mental content is contrary to the patient's insistence on denial and anonymity. This insistence causes intense anxiety and resentment because the patient feels the analyst should play the role which he, the patient, assigns to him, namely, to allow the mental content to remain unknown. Consequently the analyst's interpretive function can cause a great deal of confusion and misunderstanding. As the patient mainly functions through omnipotent processes, he believes that the analyst functions similarly. This belief is reinforced through the patient's projective processes, so that the analyst's image becomes confused or fused with the omnipotent self of the patient. When this happens a transference psychosis becomes manifest which has a paranoid character, and the analyst is constantly experienced as asserting that he is right in everything he says and that the patient is wrong. The analyst's behavior, his speech, and his thoughts are constantly tested by the patient for proof that he has omnipotent characteristics himself, so that any interpretation of projection is suspected and counteracted, and then thrown back at the analyst, who is accused of denying his own problems of omnipotence.

The danger of a lasting deadlock in the analysis can be avoided by giving the patient time to get over the confusion, by allowing him to express his anger, observations, and criticisms without attempting more than tentative, infrequent interpretative work. This means that it is analytically essential to assist the patient to bring his often completely distorted image of the analyst right into the open, which helps the patient to experience the analyst as a receptive and accepting person who can contain the patient's projection. Too immediate an interpretation of projection often has the opposite effect, namely, the creation of a rejecting image of the analyst.

One has also to remember that links between different parts of the self are being violently attacked during the delusional episode. This is one of the reasons for the patient's inability to use normal self-observation. He often has the conviction that good aspects of his self have been lost forever, but he may not observe that he himself has been responsible for this attack. So he feels persecuted by the analyst's overinterpretation of aggressive parts of his personality and believes him to be responsible for the attack on his good self. If it is possible to show the patient, often through a dream, that he believes that positive, particularly loving infantile aspects of his self have been lost and killed by him forever, he may be able to acknowledge the correctness of the analyst's observations. Even if he continues in his conviction, the interpretation may shake the patient's delusional conviction that the analyst wants to destroy him with his interpretations.

My experience with some borderline patients, especially in Groups one and four, contradicts Kernberg's observation that in the borderline states there exists mainly confusion of early pathological part-object relations with the analyst as a result of splitting and projecting, particularly of bad objects. He states that such a situation in the transference may temporarily cause transference psychosis where the analyst "becomes" the bad object of the past, for example, mother. My own observations have shown that some splitting and projection of bad parts of the self occur frequently in borderline states, but it is mainly the confusion or merging of self and object which causes a transference psychosis, which may often only last a limited period, when the cause of the confusion is carefully investigated by the analyst. Interpretation of the projective process, as I previously explained, is strictly contraindicated during the transference psychosis.

Group five. These patients often present a mixture of narcissistic problems, endless repetition of negative therapeutic reactions, combined with disguised psychotic anxieties or delusions. One patient of mine whom I think belongs to this group has been in psychotherapy and psychoanalytic treatment on and off for more than fifteen years. Whenever she improved and had a chance to relate more to life she became acutely anxious, and withdrew into a sleepy state in which she felt forced to retire to bed and feed herself tranquilizers, drink, and food, and she turned on all the heating equipment she could lay her hands on. In this state her anxiety subsided and she was comfortable, but found it difficult to make any effort to return to life again. She consciously regarded her withdrawal to bed as an attempt to regain a comfortable womb or eggshell while she supplied all the warmth and food herself.

Gradually we became aware in the analysis of an entirely opposite experience from what we had previously observed in the withdrawn phase. She then felt imprisoned and dominated by an extremely powerful and destructive narcissistic organization which threatened her with death if she tried to return to life from her imprisonment. Even when she was better she was not able to experience herself as really belonging to herself. She gradually became aware that she had a disguised paranoid attitude to the world, and everybody was experienced by her as making strong demands to which she had to submit in a placatory way. This seemed to be identical to her behavior towards the ideal and persecutory withdrawal state in which helpless surrender or appeasement was the predominant feature. It then became clear that it was the domination of disguised internal and external persecutory anxieties which had prevented her from forming good object relations which could be internalized and help her grow stronger and independent.

Conclusions

It is characteristic of all borderline conditions, that the psychotic anxieties are carefully hidden in external reality situations. In addition, there is a strong desire in all borderline patients to pull the analyst into some collusive relationship where he may act out with the patient without being aware of it. I therefore suggest that it is not only the projective elements but the collusive elements, probably expressed through mutual projective identification, which makes the analysis of the borderline patients difficult.

Another essential aspect characteristic for all borderline conditions is the failure to internalize good objects which are necessary to strengthen the ego. This is not only due to the reaction of the narcissistic organizations which attack any meaningful dependent relationships to objects and the analyst, but to the excessive projection of hidden psychotic, particularly paranoid aspects of the self into external objects in a hidden way, which makes *any object dubious and uncertain.* This shows itself particularly during separations where the apparent good internalization of the analyst quickly disappears and gives rise to intense but often unknown anxiety which, if more carefully examined, reveals the hidden paranoid feelings of the patient which are carefully disguised. So I suggest that clinically it is important to pay attention to the entanglements of the projection of the patient with certain real events or characteristics of the analyst or other objects which represent the analyst in the outside world. This has to be carefully observed and fully understood to help the patient to overcome his illness and cope with life.

The traumatized borderline patient, apart from long-lasting separation from his mother or long illness, frequently experienced feeding difficulties in infancy and disturbances in the earliest infant-mother relationship wherein the infant communicates nonverbally with his mother by projective identification. The mother, who through anxieties or other impairments in her mothering capacity is incapable of receiving and perceiving the infant's need to project his anxieties and impulses into her, is experienced as intensely guilt-producing by the infant (Rosenfeld 1978).

Aspects of this problem frequently contribute to the tendency of the borderline patient to develop a transference psychosis or may lead to long-lasting, repetitive acting out. This is often a desperate attempt by the patient to repair the disturbed link of mother and infant. However, the strong reparative drives are often covered by chronic rage or despair. So the traumatic situation is repeated in the analysis. Borderline patients have many difficulties in common. There are, however, also important differences.

My description of the five groups of borderline patients may not only assist in diagnosing the patient's problems, but may be important for the clinical approach in understanding the patient's behavior which frequently hides his deepest anxieties.

References

Bion, W. (1953). Notes on the theory of schizophrenia. In *Second Thoughts: Selected Papers on Psychoanalysis*. New York: Jason Aronson, 1967.

———(1959). Attacks on linking. In *Second Thoughts: Selected Papers on Psychoanalysis,* op. cit.

———(1962a). A theory of thinking. In *Second Thoughts: Selected Papers on Psychoanalysis,* op. cit.

———(1962b). *Learning from Experience.* In *Seven Servants:*

Four Works by Wilfred Bion. New York: Jason Aronson, 1977.

Freud, S. (1937). Analysis terminable and interminable. *Standard Edition* 23:216–253.

Frosch, J. (1964). The psychotic character: clinical psychiatric considerations. *Psychiatric Quarterly* 38:81–96.

———(1970). Psychoanalytic considerations of the psychotic character. *Journal of the American Psychoanalytic Association* 18:24–50.

Grinker, R. Sr., Werble, B. and Drye, R. (1968). *The Borderline Syndrome.* New York: Basic Books.

Hughes, Z. (1884). Borderline psychiatric records—symptoms of impairments. *Alienist and Neurologist* 5:85–90.

Kernberg, O. (1975). *Borderline Conditions and Pathological Narcissism.* New York: Jason Aronson.

Klein, M. (1934). A contribution to the psychogenesis of manic-depressive states. In *Contributions to Psycho-Analysis 1921-1945,* pp. 282–310. London: Hogarth Press, 1948.

———(1946). Notes on some schizoid mechanisms. *International Journal of Psycho-Analysis.* 27:99–110.

Knight, R.P. (1953). Borderline states. In *Psychoanalytic Psychiatry and Psychology,* eds. R.P. Knight and C.R. Friedman, pp. 97–109. New York: International Universities Press, 1954.

———(1953). Management and psychotherapy of the borderline schizophrenic patient. In *Psychoanalytic Psychiatry and Psychology,* op. cit., pp. 110–122.

Kohut, H. (1968). The psychoanalytic treatment of narcissistic personality disorders. *Psychoanalytic Study of the Child* 23:86–113.

———(1971). *The Analysis of the Self.* New York: International Universities Press.

———(1972). Thoughts on narcissism and narcissistic rage. *Psychoanalytic Study of the Child* 27:360–400.

Rey, J.H. (1977). The schizoid mode of being and the space-time continuum. *Bulletin of the British Psycho-analytical Society,* January 1977. [Chapter 12, this volume.]

Rosenfeld, H.A. (1964). On the psychopathology of narcissism: a clinical approach. *International Journal of Psycho-Analysis* 45:332–337.

————(1968). Notes on the negative therapeutic reaction. (Paper read to British Psycho-Analytical Society and Menninger Clinic, Topeka.) In *Tactics and Techniques in Psychoanalytic Psychotherapy,* vol. 2, ed. P. Giovacchini. New York: Jason Aronson.

————(1971). A clinical approach to the psychoanalytic theory of the life and death instincts: an investigation into the aggressive aspects of narcissism. *International Journal of Psycho-Analysis* 52:169–178.

————(1978). Notes on the psychopathology and psychoanalytic treatment of some borderline patients. *International Journal of Psycho-Analysis* 59:215–221.

Stern, A. (1938). Psychoanalytic investigation of and therapy in the borderline group of neuroses. *Psychoanalytic Quarterly* 7:467–489.

————(1945). Psychoanalytic therapy in the borderline neuroses. *Psychoanalytic Quarterly* 14:190–198.

Chapter 5

Psychoanalytic Technique with the Borderline Patient

Hyman Spotnitz, M.D., Med. Sc. D.

Since midcentury, changing patterns of mental illness have stimulated significant advances in theory and technique. The code words commonly employed to differentiate the analyzable from the unanalyzable patient have proved to be inadequate or misleading guides. The traditional dichotomy—whether formulated as transference neurosis/narcissistic neurosis or neurosis/psychosis—appears to be evolving into neurosis/borderline/psychosis. This trichotomy reflects the widening spectrum of psychoanalytic work.

I attach the intermediate label to patients who, by and large, have maintained a strong neurotic facade but appear to be in danger of taking the road to psychosis. At times they impress me as clearly neurotic, at other times as possibly psychotic. Because of these conflicting impressions, it usually takes some time to resolve the uncertainty, particularly in the differential diagnosis of borderline schizophrenia and schizophrenia (Spotnitz 1957). The personal history and family history help one determine the potential for psychosis. In treatment borderline patients may demonstrate psychotic tendencies. Failure to deal adequately with their resistance to experiencing and verbalizing negative feelings increases the possibility of negative therapeutic reaction.

The majority of analytic therapists treating borderline patients modify the classical procedure to some extent to reduce the risk of chaotic regression, while adhering to the basic theory of technique. In my view, this model has to be amplified for preoedipal patients to take account of their oscillating transference states and their unresponsiveness, in the early stages of the case, to interpretive procedures.

Both factors are provided for in modern psychoanalysis. (The term is not used here in a temporal sense, but to distinguish a specific approach from classical psychoanalysis.) Successive stages in the elaboration of this theory and related clinical concepts and techniques have been described elsewhere (Spotnitz 1976). The application of modern psychoanalysis in the treatment of schizophrenic patients has been reported (Spotnitz 1969). My purpose here is to discuss and illustrate its application in borderline cases. The therapeutic principles will be briefly reviewed to facilitate understanding of the case presented.

Modern Psychoanalysis

Adhering to Freud's basic framework of systematically resolving transference resistance, modern psychoanalysis is a general operational theory for the treatment of severe preoedipal disorders. It extends the basic theory of psychoanalytic technique to delineate the technical implications of narcissistic transference and its gradual transformation into object (oedipal type) transference.

The major working concepts of resistance and transference are utilized in a more discriminating way. A broad range of interventions, including emotional communication, is sanctioned for dealing with preoedipal resistance patterns.

In primitive narcissistic states, the patient is responded to in ways that permit him to reexperience symbolically the negative and positive aspects of the ego in the process of formation. He thus reveals basic maturational needs for object relations that were not met during the first two years of life. The modern psychoanalyst therefore attaches much significance to narcissistic transference.

Countertransference is recognized not only as a source of counter-resistance but also as a source of therapeutic leverage. (The terms "countertransference" and "counter-resistance" are therefore used as reciprocals of "transference" and "transference resistance.") The analyst's feeling-responses to the patient's transference attitudes and behavior (objective countertransference) are sustained and are selectively communicated to resolve resistance. It is presumed that these induced feelings encompass the patient's own pre-ego feelings and also those that he experienced from significant objects during the preoedipal period.

Modern psychoanalysis integrates post-Freudian findings on the role of aggressive impulses in the early evolution of the mind. Aggression internalized in an ego damaging way to protect the object is identified as the primary problem to be dealt with in cases of schizophrenia and borderline schizophrenia. In other severe preoedipal disorders, the problem may be emotional deprivation, but this also mobilizes aggressive impulses. Obstacles to their discharge in language are focused on from the beginning of the case.

In positive transference states, the borderline patient tends to bottle up his hostile feelings. Therefore, the analyst maintains a reserved attitude and limits his interventions. With the development of negative transference, he conveys the message: Verbally communicated feelings are not too hurtful; I can tolerate them. In positive transference states, the patient is educated to communicate so as to obtain narcissistic supplies on demand. These are two ways the analyst works to resolve narcissistic-transference resistance.

The maximal development of narcissistic transference in borderline cases usually takes at least six months but may require two years. Its dissolution begins in what is commonly regarded as the middle phase of analysis. The patient then relates more consistently to the analyst as a separate object. Manifestations of object (oedipal) transference become increasingly prominent, but the patient tends to oscillate between the two states. Narcissistic-transference resistance is worked through first. Since object transference is the source of the analyst's decisive influence, it is retained as long as it is needed.

Modern psychoanalysis is a unitary approach, applicable to all psychologically reversible conditions, but it is not employed routinely. While understanding without technique does not help the patient, technique without understanding is guesswork. The treatment is based on accurate understanding of the patient and his therapeutic needs. The goal in mind is to help him discover the forces underlying his disorder and master them so that he can evolve into emotional health.

Case Report

In the presentation that follows, successive developments in the case of a borderline patient are discussed in terms of ten discrete steps. These, it should be borne in mind, are actually stages of treatment that overlap to some extent; they are listed in the order in which they begin. This schema, reflecting the major psychodynamic events in a treatment relationship oriented to meet the therapeutic needs of patients with preoedipal problems, enables the analyst to take soundings of progress as the case evolves.

The report focuses on the major themes of the patient's communications, the strategies engaged in to deal with her resistance, and the feelings she induced in the course of the relationship.

Mrs. C. was in her late thirties when she entered treatment with me. Her somber dress and diffident manner somewhat obscured her attractiveness. The wife of an attorney and mother of two teenage daughters, she worked in the editorial department of a well-known publishing house specializing in childrens's literature.

There was a strong element of depression in her personality. She was given to periods of weeping and said she had contemplated suicide on several occasions. She had paranoid ideas. In the initial interview, she voiced fears of falling apart.

Continuous combat with her mother was characterized as the primary event of her childhood. She was an only child. She had little to say about her father, a retiring and submissive individual who died when she was sixteen. She still felt uncomfortable in her mother's presence and avoided contact with her as much as possible.

A bright girl, she had done well academically at high school and college, but her relations with her schoolmates were shallow. Her college years were marked by periods of withdrawal alternating with periods in which she felt intact and capable.

She described her husband as an overbearing bully who compelled her to comply with his sexual demands. They quarreled continually about the upbringing of their daughters and financial matters.

Several years of treatment with her two previous analysts had afforded some relief but had not helped her resolve her conflicting feelings about divorcing her husband. She contemplated analysis again because her present situation was intolerable; she feared that she would become psychotic or kill herself if it continued much longer. She had a desperate need to understand her current difficulties; she wanted to make up her own mind what to do about them so that she could accomplish something for herself. At this point she was not considering her husband and children. "My main concern now," she said, "is my own survival."

The treatment of Mrs. C. extended over a period of five years. I saw her once a week for the first three years, during which the acute stress that aroused her fears of loss of identity and thoughts of suicide were substantially relieved. Thereafter I saw her once every two weeks. In the last two years, she moved forward into constructive adjustment in her personal and professional life.

Step one: Narcissistic transference develops and is analyzed (silently)

During the first two years of our relationship, Mrs. C. related to me primarily as the "influencing" part of her mind. Three years later, in looking back at this period, she explained simply, "My ego boundaries wavered continually. Sometimes you were part of my ego, sometimes outside it." Time and time again, she said she knew exactly what was on my mind. Early in the relationship she was usually wrong about this. Later on, there were times when she accurately described my immediate thoughts and feelings.

She talked freely about her marital difficulties. Her husband was an impossible man to live with. He forced her to have sexual relations with him regardless of her wishes. He accused her of being a harsh and demanding mother. She complained that he was niggardly. To avoid arguments about her inability to manage the household on the meager allowance he provided, she supplemented it from her more modest earnings, approaching him only when her own funds were exhausted. They did not talk for days on end.

Seeking solace, she had indulged in brief erotic episodes with several professional acquaintances. These had proved disappointing, and a long-term relationship with another man had ended in fiasco. Her husband also engaged in extramarital relationships, but steadfastly denied doing so when she confronted him with evidence. In an emotionally explosive situation, she admitted to her affairs but he continued to deny his own. States of withdrawal and depression followed such confrontations.

She had married him, she said, to escape from her mother's clutches. Her mother treated her as a puppet, telling her what to think and feel and how to behave. Her early life had been tolerable as long as she submitted to this dictation; but attempts to assert herself had provoked violent quarrels, after which she would isolate herself in her room.

She felt that her marriage was destroying her and that she had to get out of it. She insinuated over and over again that I was trying to force her to stay with her husband.

She reported a dream in which someone was overpowering her and she was suffocating. In another version, the attacker was choking her. For many years she had dreamed of being in this terrifying situation. I attached great importance to this dream because of its frequent occurrence. She responded to my questions and interest in it by reporting many dreams.

The analogy between the recurrent dream and these insinuations was striking. Consciously and unconsciously, she was telling me that she was in danger of being overpowered, with life-threatening consequences.

Changes in her conscious attitudes paralleled changes in the character of her dreams. The waning of her fears of being controlled in the relationship dovetailed with dreams of being able to defend herself. Eventually, when she experienced me as a cooperative object, nonthreatening encounters with people she knew figured in her dreams. Because they tied up so closely with Mrs. C.'s clinical symptoms in the case, her dreams served as a barometer of her progress in treatment and in life.

During the first few months of the relationship, Mrs. C. did not interrupt her ruminations to ask questions or elicit comments. I asked her four or five inconsequential questions in each session— brief verbal feedings to alleviate her suffering and eliminate the danger of destructive acting out.

*Step two: The patient's attempts to get in contact with the analyst
are studied to determine their origin and history, and responded
to as necessary to control the intensity of resistance*

In those relatively brief interludes when Mrs. C. related to me
as the controlling mother, my occasional interruptions of her
repetitive complaints were viewed as attempts to influence her.
She also seemed to object to those brief verbal feedings when she
perceived me as part of her mind. She was educated to the idea
that I would remain the narcissistic object in her mind until she
initiated verbal contact with me.

Her failure to engage in contact functioning (ask questions or
say something that would indicate awareness of my presence)
suggested that she had not been trained to assert herself and make
her wants known. They had been anticipated by her mother, who
had ministered to them as she thought best. When the child did
not submit to the mother's will, she was squelched. Deprived of
opportunities to express her own wishes, she formed a pattern of
withdrawing and nursing her resentments in silence. She still
seemed to be trapped in this pattern. There was evidence for this
in her dealings with her husband.

She continued to report dreams of situations in which she was
being overpowered and could not utter a word. These dreams
seemed to be related to a traumatic experience in the preverbal
period.

*Step three: Narcissistic countertransference resistance is recog-
nized and analyzed*

During the sessions with Mrs. C., I often became aware of
feelings that seemed to have nothing to do with her. Other feelings
I experienced could definitely be attributed to her presence.

She behaved like a "very good girl," trying her best to please me
and scrupulously observing the routines of treatment. Punctual
in attendance, she lost no time in getting on the couch, and she left

promptly at the end of each session. She was equally prompt in paying for the treatment.

It gradually dawned on me that she was a very attractive woman. Her generally demure manner and air of innocence tended to belie her age and her sexual experience.

As she talked about her helpless compliance with her husband's sexual demands, she induced desires to rape her. At a moment when she impressed me as discreetly flirtatious, I asked if she was trying to get me to seduce her. Her unconscious wishes to be dominated, so strongly suggested by her dreams, made me aware of urges to exercise authority.

When she accused me of siding with her husband in a family dispute, I became aware of feelings of annoyance. These feelings were not verbalized. At times she thought she sensed them from the tone of my voice or reserved attitude. Her suspicions were not confirmed or denied.

I experienced other emotions that were not as easy to account for. At times, when she remained out of contact, she aroused feelings that seemed to have nothing to do with her.

Because of the elusive quality of the narcissistic countertransference, it required considerable effort to figure out the source of these feelings and deal with them appropriately.

Step four: Narcissistic transference resistance is effectively influenced by joining the patient's resistive attempts to establish contact

You are like my mother; you either starve me or stuff me with food I don't want. This unconscious attitude, the dominant theme of the narcissistic transference, was communicated interminably, with numerous variations: I was trying to manipulate and control her; I was not telling her what she wanted to hear; I was not talking because I did not like her; there must be something wrong with our relationship if I did not talk to her; I made her do what I wanted her to do; she was a prisoner in my power; I had hostile wishes for her.

My occasional verbal feedings had prevented this resistance to progressive communication from becoming too intense (Step two). But the full evolution of the narcissistic transference dictated a new stategy: to help Mrs. C. recognize and relate to me more consistently as a separate person. The process of retraining her to establish contact with me was one of the major battles of the analysis.

The ground rules were communicated at times when she said that, rather than helping her understand her problems and make her own decisions, I was trying to influence her to do what I thought would be best for her.

"I'm not playing that game," I said. "I won't impose my will on you in any way. I will talk to you only when you want me to, and tell you only what you want to know" (breast feeding on demand). Mrs. C. agreed to these terms.

Her complaints gradually gave way to questions. When she asked whether she should submit to her husband's sexual demands, the question was reflected: "If you want to, why not have sex? If you don't want to, why not refuse it?" Questions about other immediate problems in her life were reflected in the same neutral manner.

Thereafter, when she complained that I did not talk to her, she was reminded that I was respecting her wishes. During a session when she talked for forty minutes without contacting me, she said my silence proved that I disliked her. I told her I had been waiting for her to ask me to talk. After a brief silence, she said, "That's true. I didn't ask you anything."

When she accused me of keeping silent to increase her misery, I reminded her that she was making herself miserable by operating so that I would not talk to her.

Frequently I repeated her questions and asked, "Is that the

information you want me to give you?" Eventually, I was able to answer the questions precisely as she wanted them answered.

Step five: Narcissistic transference resistance is worked through

Mrs. C. was now convinced that she was in the presence of someone who really wanted to help her find her own solutions to her problems. She functioned more comfortably in the relationship. As my questions and interest stimulated her to communicate, she explored the relation between her early life experience and current situtation. She wondered whether her attitudes of helpless submission and passive acceptance might have incited others to manipulate and control her. She thought that might be so.

As she began to assert herself to obtain what she wanted in the treatment relationship, she became interested in operating in the same way in her dealings with her husband, daughters, and the professional associates whose intrusive attitudes distressed her. Her original description of her husband as an unmitigated scoundrel was somewhat modified. She began to consider that her submissive attitudes might have influenced him to treat her as a child.

She would have no more of that. She wondered whether she could influence him to treat her as an equal, and whether it would be worth the effort. She thought that it might be possible to preserve the marriage and to transform it into a true partnership. She began to move in that direction.

She reported new versions of the recurrent dream of being overpowered and speechless. In one she struggled with a man trying to rape her, and she managed to scream at him. Her husband awakened her and asked her what she was yelling about. Later she dreamed that she was able to defend herself. In subsequent versions, she ran away from the attacker or someone came to her rescue. Gradually, the dream lost its terrifying quality.

I asked many questions at this stage of the relationship. Mrs. C. evinced less interest in obtaining information about herself than in attacking me or finding out what was on my mind at the moment. What she wanted primarily was reassurance that I would not try to control her. Although I gave few interpretations of the narcissistic transference resistance, I asked questions based on my impressions.

Step six: Object transference resistance develops and is studied
Oscillating transference states characterized this transitional period. Mrs. C. rarely regarded me now as the influencing part of her mind. I became the good parent she had always needed. Her reports of what was going on in her life suggested that she was making progress in applying the understanding she had achieved. Improvements in her relations with her husband and children were mentioned.

Nevertheless, she felt lost. She had entered a strange new world and had yet to find her bearings. She was confronted with the necessity of taking charge of herself and leading her own life.

The major problem that emerged was her own inadequacy. Over and over again, she expressed doubts about her ability to accomplish anything worthwhile.

But there were times when, instead of bemoaning her inadequacy, she regarded herself as a superior human being: The kind of person I preferred to anyone else and would overcome all obstacles to marry.

She was reluctant to cope with the subject. She spoke in glowing terms about the help I had given her, but hemmed and hawed rather than verbalizing her feelings for me as a real person. She also resisted giving open expression to her feelings toward her husband and children.

She reported several dreams about her father.

Step seven: Countertransference resistance is recognized and analyzed

I was very challenged by Mrs. C.'s vague allusions to intensely positive feelings for me that were too painful to talk about. I became aware of strong desires to put her under pressure to verbalize them—in other words, to resort to Freud's technique of overcoming resistance. (Occasionally I intervene in that manner at a late stage of treatment when there is every indication that the patient has a need or urge to be forced to make a disclosure. At such times, the intervention may have a therapeutic effect; but in general, it does not facilitate the analysis and is not good for the patient.) Instead of yielding to that temptation, I worked on the resistance indirectly, asking Mrs. C. why she objected to giving the information, what reaction she wanted to avoid, and similar questions.

By and large, I was in a pleasant frame of mind during the sessions with her. It was no longer necessary to consider the possibility that one or another circumstance extraneous to the relationship might be responsible for it. At this stage, my good mood was clearly identified with her presence.

I became aware of a tendency to talk to Mrs. C. more than necessary. I took pleasure in her company and our sessions seemed to go by more quickly. I felt regret when she had to leave.

I found myself looking forward to the next session with her. On two occasions I made a mistake of expecting her when we did not have an appointment. When I phoned to inquire about the first "absence," she reminded me of a change in time that had been agreed to. She remarked, "My, you must really like me." The second time, I did not phone but checked my appointment book.

In analyzing the positive impulses she aroused, I recognized that Mrs. C. was not consciously seductive. Indeed, her behavior was demure and her manner shy. This train of thought led me back to the myth of Narcissus. Mrs. C. reminded me of the nymph

Liriope in her chance encounter with the river god Cephisus while innocently enjoying a swim in his preserve. Liriope did not conceive Narcissus because she tried to seduce Cephisus. What caused him to rape her was her naturally exciting presence.

Continuing analysis of the induced feelings diminished any urge to act on them.

Step eight: Object transference resistance is interpreted

At this stage the whole relationship was clarified. Both the preoedipal and oedipal configurations of the case were explained.

As the narcissistic transference evolved, Mrs. C. had the idea that she would be controlled and coerced in the analysis. She suspected, in particular, that she would be forced to do my "bidding," that is, to remain with her husband.

When she became aware of me as a separate object, she was fearful that she would have to repeat with me the painful experiences of her childhood. After I agreed to follow her directions (contact functioning), treatment became a painless experience except as she induced pain in herself. As her awareness of my separate identity continued to develop, the fear of being hurt was reversed: She did not want to hurt me. She had a need to protect the good object who rescued her when she was suffocating or unable to talk (recurrent dream)—as her mother or father had rescued her in childhood.

The feelings she attached to me were discussed. Some were feelings for her mother at one time and for her father at another time. Her resistance to verbalizing them was explained. It was pointed out, in essence, that she thought I was so enamored of her that I might be motivated to break up her marriage and separate her from her children if she revealed her affection for me. She was trying to protect me from recognizing that situation; calling it to my attention, she thought, would expose me to narcissistic injury. She was educated to the idea that I did not object to her hurting me; wasn't being hurt a fact of life?

Mrs. C.'s initial fears that I would compel her to do what *I* wanted had thus given way to the attitude that I would be compelled to do what *she* wanted, even more than she wanted.

Other interpretations centered on the vicissitudes of the relationship. The preoedipal and oedipal configurations that were reenacted in the transference drama were explored in the context of the immediate situation.

As an infant, she had been very submissive to a domineering mother, trying to please her whatever the cost. At that time, she related to her mother as the better part of herself (preoedipal configuration). This pattern, so dominant when the treatment began, still reappeared, usually when Mrs. C. was in a regressed state.

Later she identified at times with her father as her significant object (inverse oedipal), and at other times with the controlling mother (positive oedipal).

The narcissistic transference resistance took two forms. I was first cast in the role of the controlling mother (and presently controlling husband). But when I refrained from talking until Mrs. C. gave me permission to open my mouth, the situation was reversed. She then took over the mother role, relating to me as someone like herself (the baby and father). But when I responded to her signal to talk, she complained that I was trying to influence her; when she did not signal me, she complained that my silence made her miserable.

When I demonstrated that she could get me to talk when and how she wanted me to, Mrs. C. moved out of both patterns (transitional period). She began to relate to me as a separate person—someone she could control, as she and her father had been controlled, and as she now wanted to control her husband. Later the idea of controlling me became as distasteful to her as that of being controlled. She began to crave a mutually cooperative relationship. She would not try to control me and I would not try to control her. In this partnership, she wanted me to be spontaneously cooperative—talk when *I* wanted to talk.

Step nine: Object transference resistance is worked through

The resistance patterns just outlined were dealt with repeatedly and in different ways. Interpretatons were supplemented by other interventions (Spotnitz 1969, chapter 10). Emotional communication was engaged in to highlight the patterns; they were reflected; questions were formulated to help Mrs. C. verbalize her own insights. When her self-interpretations coincided with my understanding, I registered approval; when our views differed, they were discussed at length. At times we agreed to disagree.

At a time when she was totally preoccupied with an immediate difficulty and seemed unaware of my presence, I asked if she wanted me to talk. That intervention enabled her to work herself out of the state by talking.

Her difficulties in asserting herself were repeatedly investigated. It was suggested that her views might command more respect if she expressed them more forcefully. To my surprise, when I demonstrated how she should talk to her husband (paradigmatic strategy), she said, "I always talk that way when I blow up at him." Although she usually fumed in silence, it was true that, when sufficiently goaded, she demonstrated some capacity to release negative emotions—involuntarily. Her problem was inability to regulate the release, and this was what we worked on. She came to recognize the distinction between exploding in rage—a self-defeating pattern—and expressing her resentments in a controlled way to make clear how she felt or what she wanted. She learned to raise her voice and tell off her husband when she was angry.

Her impressions of the people she worked with were vague; she was inclined to lump them together and respond to them in the same way. She developed more appreciation of their personal qualities. As she became aware of them as different individuals, she found it easier to get along with them.

She verbalized her feelings with increasing ease. She recalled her fears that she might estrange me from my wife. At that time, Mrs. C. seemed to be reliving her awareness of how painful it would be for her mother to know that her husband cared more for his daughter than for her.

Other memories of her father emerged at that time. She recalled her mother's tendency to belittle him. Her disparaging attitude had ill-prepared Mrs. C. for her mother's overwhelming reaction to his death. In retrospect, her father became a significant figure in her life.

She no longer needed to avoid contact with her mother. She viewed her more objectively now and could assert herself comfortably in her mother's presence.

Step ten: Resistance to termination is resolved

Mrs. C. often talked about the novel she was writing. It had been "in her head" for many years, and now she had the energy to put it on paper. Two short stories she had written at college had been published in a literary journal. Her husband was encouraging her to get on with the novel.

Her home life was not as tranquil as she wanted it to be. She reported spats with her husband and daughters in which it was hard for her to hold her ground. But she was adjusting to her new posture; and they seemed more considerate. She felt more comfortable in her job. Most of her dreams were about love relationships.

But after we agreed that the time to terminate the relationship was drawing near, she demonstrated a need to prolong it. The early complaints were reiterated and she brought up new problems which she felt incapable of solving without my help. Her husband still rode roughshod over her; and one of the women she worked with was scheming to unseat her. The reappearance of her early symptoms enraged her.

Actually, no new problems were presented during this final phase. What she brought up were new variations on the old themes. These were worked through repeatedly, each time in the context in which it had cropped up. As each situation was explained to her, she said she knew exactly how to handle it.

The immediate dilemma was often solved in the course of a single session. Distressed or dejected on arrival, she would walk out feeling fine.

Interpretations, interspersed with the types of emotional communications, questions, and joining techniques that had resolved her resistance patterns earlier in the case, brought her out of this relapsed state relatively quickly. Toxoid responses were administered; that is, the feelings she induced in me were fed back to her, in graduated doses, to immunize her against the return of her narcissistic attitudes in stressful situations.

Her idea that I would do anything she wanted was occasionally discussed. She was helped to recognize that I enjoyed working with her, but that she was not all-important to me. She came to accept the realities of our relationship: I was just her analyst, and she had outgrown her need for me.

Concluding Remarks

I agree with Boyer that failures in the treatment of patients with severe preoedipal disorders "are often iatrogenic, resulting from problems in the countertransference or the therapist's failure to use his emotional responses adequately in his interpretations" (Boyer 1977, p. 388). His description of his emotional responses to a borderline patient is an excellent illustration of what I refer to as narcissistic countertransference.

When I began to treat schizophrenic patients, I was in personal analysis. This was a fortunate coincidence because I was totally unprepared for the weird feelings they induced. When I described them to my analyst, she asked, "Why are you so afraid to feel psychotic for a few minutes?" She helped me understand these feeling-responses and how to deal with them so that I would not be swayed into interventions that might be destructive to the patient. At that time I usually repressed my feelings, but on some occasions when they were involuntarily communicated they had a therapeutic effect. Years later I got to recognize that the release of feelings in a controlled way, to accomplish a specific objective, often resolves a therapeutic impasse. Planned spontaneity is desirable when one is working with a preoedipal patient.

It is my impression that some analysts take the opposite route—from intellectual to emotional understanding. They are demonstrating more awareness of the feelings induced by borderline patients and more interest in determining their signficance. The main deterrent is the fear of the consequences of impulsive behavior and of the loss of identity.

There is less risk of this when they understand the narcissistic countertransference state; intellectual defenses reduce the threat of disintegrated ego functioning. Since these defenses are becoming more adequate to dilute the threat of the feelings induced by borderline patients, a growing number of therapists are accepting these cases and reporting good results with them. The prognosis for these patients is brightening.

By and large, however, analysts prefer to avoid the more turbulent emotions experienced in a case of psychosis. Particularly objectionable are feelings of therapeutic impotence and destructiveness. It is often difficult to recognize that these are induced by the schizophrenic patient's feelings that he is incurable and that the therapist is wasting time on him.

I disagree with current views that patients in the borderline category are radically different from clearly schizophrenic individuals. It is my impression that the differences between the two groups are purely quantitative. In a case of schizophrenia, the narcissistic countertransference is more intense, the danger of chaotic regression is greater, and treatment is much more time-consuming. Nevertheless, the schizophrenic patient responds to the same types of interventions as the borderline patient, but these need to be employed more persistently. An analyst who works comfortably and effectively with borderline cases can eventually provide schizophrenic patients with the kind of object relationship they need.

In the evolutionary process of achieving more consistently favorable results in the treatment of schizophrenia, the steadily improving prognosis of the borderline patient is a significant milestone.

References

Boyer, L. Bryce (1977). Working with a borderline patient. *Psychoanalytic Quarterly* 46:386–424.

Spotnitz, H. (1957). The borderline schizophrenic in group psychotherapy. *International Journal of Group Psychotherapy* 7:155–174. Reprinted in *Psychotherapy of Preoedipal Conditions.* New York: Jason Aronson.

———(1969). *Modern Psychoanalysis of the Schizophrenic Patient.* New York: Grune & Stratton.

———(1976). *Psychotherapy of Preoedipal Conditions.* New York: Jason Aronson.

Chapter 6

The Many Sides of Helplessness:
The Borderline Patient

Peter L. Giovacchini, M.D.

There is an urgent need to understand as much as we can about patients suffering from characterological problems, patients who have been loosely thrown together under the rubric of the borderline syndrome. This term is imprecise, but our increasing recognition that patients with structural problems are by far the most common group that turns to psychotherapists and psychoanalysts for help requires that we find some anchor around which to organize our thinking so that we do not feel even more helpless than the patient.

Clinical understanding usually begins with classification that enables us to recognize what types of phenomena we are encountering. I believe that much confusion still exists at this early diagnostic phase of our thinking, although most of us seem to agree that the patients we are considering are distinct and different from the psychoneuroses and the psychoses.

The fact that these patients seem to be suffering from severe emotional problems which may be so crippling that they cannot survive in the ordinary world causes us to view them as similar to psychotic patients who may require hospitalization. Yet, they are not really psychotic; they do not have the same distortions of affect and thought disorders that are characteristic of schizophrenics. In many instances, the degree of the patient's incapacity seems to place him on the brink of a psychosis, as if he were hovering on the edge of one. So we go along with Knight (1953) and refer to the patient as borderline.

Unfortunately, the term *borderline* has been applied to all types of characterological disorders. I believe there is some rationale in using it, but, rather than a diagnostic category, as a quality that is found in patients suffering from structural problems. By this, I mean that these patients can decompensate into a psychosis and in this sense they are borderline, but the diagnosis, borderline, can be especially apt for a specific group.

I wish to outline the main adaptive defenses or lack of such defenses, and developmental arrests which distinguish the group of patients I choose to call borderline from other patients suffering from character problems. This can best be done in a clinical context which also highlights some of the technical and countertransference problems encountered in the psychoanalytic treatment of patients who have usually been considered unanalyzable.

Developmental Aspects

The main elements of the clinical picture of borderline patients are reactions to early failures, to the lack of gratifying experiences, to privation. I am distinguishing privation from deprivation in the same way Winnicott (1963) did. With privation, there never have been experiences of satisfaction to any significant degree and thus the patient's responses will be different from patients whose infantile months were characterized by a series of frustrating experiences. To be frustrated means that there has been some gratification. A person feels frustrated because he misses gratification. He feels thwarted because he is not receiving what he *knows* he needs or, later in life, wants. Needs become wishes and he is then vulnerable to frustration.

By contrast, the patient who suffers from privation has not been able to develop *the capacity to feel frustrated.* He does not have sufficiently established memory traces of gratifying experiences that will cause him to react to the lack of such experiences. His adaptive techniques and defenses will correspondingly suffer.

I am, of course, exaggerating when I say that these patients lack the memory of gratifying experiences. They had to have some gratification for, otherwise, they would have perished as did the children Spitz (1965) studied. But, relatively speaking, these patients have little assurance that they can be gratified since they had so little gratification. Inasmuch as there is a structural defect, specifically the lack of memory traces of interactions which lead to satisfaction of inner needs, both needs and techniques of satisfaction are poorly developed and psychopathologically distorted.

Elsewhere, I have described in detail the nature of various structural lacunae (Giovacchini 1963, 1967). I traced how an interaction with the external world becomes part of the ego as an introject (Giovacchini 1972) which later is amalgamated, that is, loses its boundaries and becomes part of the executive system. Thus, a satisfying experience becomes an adaptive technique. The borderline patient's ego has not registered such experiences and, as a consequence, has not developed adaptive techniques that would enable it to profit from potentially helpful experiences in the external world.

The adjustment to the outer world is borderline: He has an awareness of what surrounds him, but it is dim because he cannot find anything in it that would enhance his security. He feels vulnerable but literally does not know what actions and relationships might cause him to feel comfortable. In fact, in extreme instances, he cannot really grasp what either comfort or discomfort means. He cannot even perceive his needs in a structured fashion nor have the vaguest idea as to how he can pursue satisfaction. He does not believe he is capable of being gratified and this adds to his sense of helplessness.

The clinician is struck by the patient's lack of adaptive techniques which is manifested in treatment as an urgent and clinging demand that the therapist do something. What that something is cannot be articulated or understood by either patient or analyst. This can create a tense, disruptive atmosphere which, in many instances, causes insurmountable thereapeutic impasses if they are not properly understood.

More specifically, from a developmental viewpoint, the patient has not yet passed through the phase of symbiotic fusion. He is fixated at a presymbiotic level. Those elements of his psyche that have passed through the maternal fusion, for fixation is never absolute, have only an imperfect and rudimentary awareness of the external world. Since the patient's psyche has incorporated so little, it is diffusely organized, it is somewhat amorphous and lacks the ability to deal with the complexities of the surrounding reality. I recall one patient who expressed this situation graphically when he stated that he had an arithmetic mentality as he was living in a world of calculus complexity.

Kernberg (1967) and Masterson (1972) have a different character constellation in mind when they describe borderline patients. They consider the borderline patient to have a somewhat stable ego organization, perhaps with narcissistic elements and a tendency to act out. Kernberg describes the extensive use of splitting mechanisms similar to the adaptations employed by psychotic patients, and in spite of superficial stability these patients can have brief psychotic episodes. I prefer to reserve the term borderline for a different type of character structure. The patients I have described are borderline in two senses: they can, as other patients suffering from ego defects, decompensate into a transient psychosis, and they are also borderline in that they minimally adapt to the external world, that is, they relate to their environment in a borderline fashion.

I do not believe these nosological distinctions are particularly important. They help us order our thinking and when clinicians communicate with each other, it helps to know what group of patients we are studying. I am referring to a different group than the one Kernberg and Masterson have concentrated upon, but whatever subcategory of character disorders on which we choose to focus, they all have sufficient similarities that confront us with specific technical problems during the course of psychoanalytic treatment. Furthermore, there is also considerable overlapping between one group and another and diagnostic distinctions become blurred.

The best method I know to illustrate the borderline phenomenon is by presenting clinical material derived from the psychoanalytic treatment of a helpless patient. I have discussed this patient elsewhere (Giovacchini 1978) but here I will be viewing her from another perspective.

Clinical Material

I will never forget the first session I had with a young housewife in her late twenties, the stormy volatile atmosphere she created and her attempts to disrupt the well-ordered calm and equanimity that often characterize analysis. Analytic sessions can often be turbulent, but not usually at the very beginning.

In the first place, she arrived over an hour and a half early for her first appointment. When I saw her in the waiting room, she looked tranquil enough and composed, but when she recognized me as the person she was to see, she underwent a sudden transformation. She immediately became tense and anxious and I found myself feeling obliged to console her. However, I restrained myself. Instead, I directed my efforts to helping her understand the correct time for her appointment and, for a moment, it seemed that this would be just too difficult a task. I was beginning to feel some dismay because I knew my scheduled patient was due to arrive at any moment. When the patient did arrive and all three of us were standing in the waiting room, she experienced another amazing transformation. She was able to ascertain that she had mistaken the time and reconciled herself to wait. She now regained her former composure. I was not particularly pleased to have her wait in the waiting room for two patients' sessions, but I tried not to think about it.

When she finally came into the office, she once again reverted to her distressed state. She entered the consulting room in a melodramatic fashion. Though her behavior was obviously histrionic, her anguish seemed genuine and she was suffering intensely. I did not feel the annoyance that I might have expected at having my balanced routine upset, or having to deal with a disturbed woman about whom I knew nothing. I felt compassionate and would have liked to have been able to offer help immediately, but I had absolutely no idea where to begin.

At first, she barraged me with a series of physical complaints. She stressed that she was feeling an odd mixture of somatic pain and the physiological accompaniments of anxiety. Her face was flushed and her eyes had a peculiar exophthalmic quality to them, (she was not actually exophthalmic). She continued staring hard at me and held me fixedly with her eyes as she enumerated her various pains. She first complained about her gastrointestinal system—very severe stomach cramps, as well as milder "butterfly" sensations. All this time she was clutching her abdomen and she frequently moaned, sometimes so much that it was difficult to understand what she was saying. I began to wonder whether she had come to see the right person, whether she should be seeing an internist or a surgeon rather than a psychoanalyst. I found myself thinking in a medical frame of reference, trying to understand her symptoms as manifestations of some gastrointestinal disorder.

No sooner was I able to assure myself that her symptoms did not suggest such familiar entities as gastritis or peptic ulcer, than she jumped to another organ system. She went into great detail about her headaches. She spoke of "splitting headaches," which, as far as I could determine, included both migraine and tension headaches. She then went on and explained visual and equilibratory disturbances.

I find it easier to maintain analytic calm if the patient is lying on the couch, so, during the latter half of the first session, I motioned her toward it. As has been true for other agitated patients, she protested that this would only aggravate her various aches and pains, but her protest was only verbal. She thrashed around considerably but she stayed in the supine position.

As I reflect back on this initial contact, I believe I had some rather definite reactions. I must have had the impression that I was dealing with a demented woman. As she increasingly felt that her brain was not working, she kept manufacturing symptoms. Of course, she was not demented. She was really quite bright, but this is the way she appeared to me.

I was confronted with a puzzle. I really did not understand this patient. The usual formulations about somatization, the conversion process, or hypochondriasis just did not seem apt, though I could not even say why.

Actually, I did not conclude anything. That seemed to be my most prevailing feeling. I was unable to reach any kind of understanding that would cause me to feel secure in my professional orientation toward her. On the other hand, I did not feel insecure either; I simply did not have reactions of any particular intensity and knew that I did not understand what this patient wanted. I did not know what she expected from treatment or, for that matter, why she came to treatment at this time. I knew something about the husband's supposed improvement during his therapy, but the changes did not seem so impressive that they would have upset the marital equilibrium. In general, things seemed to be pretty much as always.

Because of the patient's quick mood changes, I apparently did not take her distressed moments seriously enough. I was confident of her capacity to reintegrate, so I did not appreciate the extent of her suffering when she was in what might be called a decompensated state. At least, that is how she saw it, and I suspect that she was right. Here was an instance where a low-key, casual approach can be overdone.

I also probably expected too much from her. I attributed a degree of competence to her that was beyond her capacities. Inasmuch as there was such a wide discrepancy, such an intense contrast, between her insane and sane ego states, it was easy to view the latter as being more structured, integrated, and capable than actually was the case. She complained that my expectations of her were unrealistic and that I was ignoring her fundamental helplessness and vulnerability.

Recently, she had done a good deal of traveling in foreign countries, sometimes on vacations with her husband and children, and sometimes on business trips with her husband alone. She really hated traveling, but went along because her husband insisted. When they went alone, he did not pay much attention to her; he just wanted to have her there with him, but did not care to relate to her. I call attention to this material because she saw it as the recapitulation of a recurrent and distressing childhood fantasy.

In her fantasy, she was standing in a strange street in a foreign country, a country that was totally unknown to her. She knew nothing about the people, their language, mores or customs. She had the task of surviving in this alien environment but did not know how to approach anyone for assistance. There were no Traveler's Aid Societies or United States embassies in this country. If she approached someone, as she sometimes did in the fantasy, he would not understand her, since he did not know English. After perfunctorily listening to her, the stranger would walk away, showing no interest whatsoever. Clearly, he did not know how to help her and he would just go about his daily business, ignoring her and her needs. Sometimes, she would find herself in a restaurant, but, of course, the menu was in an incomprehensible foreign language. Furthermore, no one understood that she wanted something to eat, so no one would try to help her.

She apparently was stressing her inability to communicate, but more than that, the fantasy was a rather direct replication of how she always felt, yet she had no problem with language. Although as a vehicle of communication she handled language well, she basically did not know what to communicate. In the fantasy, too, she did not know what she wanted to ask the stranger in the street, and though it seemed that in the restaurant her needs were clear enough, she stated that she was not really certain whether she was hungry.

After about six months of analysis, the patient became less agitated, and relatively calm. Up to this time she cried helplessly in practically every session and often experienced considerable anxiety. She gradually stopped this and was able to behave pretty much like any other patient. Now, as she lay motionless on the couch she remained silent for long periods of time.

The intrapsychic focus helped me weather these early trying months. I had indicated to her time and again that all of her reactions, especially the most distressing ones, were designed to prove to me how miserably helpless she felt. In view of my apparent calm, she had to become increasingly agitated in order to capture my attention, which she felt was either limited or easily distracted. I was emphasizing the adaptive and reactive features of her behavior and the patient was able to understand and agree with me. She remarked that she had to go to great lengths to be noticed and was well aware of her propensity for manipulation.

I felt less need toward the end of this period of analysis to emphasize how well integrated she could be. Instead, I turned to her fantasy and interpreted how she must feel that I would not be able to understand her needs *in the same way* she could not understand them. The patient would then demonstrate how introspective she could be. She accepted my interpretation as a new insight and was able to apply it to many situations and relationships. She would immediately relate it to her husband; although as she pondered about him, she did not feel he was that important. Later, she related this incapacity to deal with needs to her childhood relationships with her family.

In spite of her insight, she continued feeling some anger toward me. Though she no longer felt I underestimated the importance of her symptoms, she resented what she observed to be my calm and, to her, complaisant self. She related this to control. She felt she was not able to control her impulses because she did not understand them, and this made her feel miserably helpless. She surmised, on the other hand, that I did understand and this put me in control, a position she envied. She was afraid of my having such power over her.

She viewed my control also as a control of my impulses, that I was not vulnerable to them. During one session, she made associations about a mother with engorged breasts feeding herself and this made her angry. She was also afraid that her demands on me might render me helpless, perhaps destroy me, and that would be catastrophic. She saw a baby nursing at a mother's breast and depleting her, drying her up, and then the mother died. These were all painful, frightening and anger provoking associations which were followed by long periods of silence, in which it was important for her not to communicate.

This phase of her analysis, which lasted for more than two years, can be considered her silent period in contrast to her previous noisiness. She seemed to alternate between timidity with a certain tremulous quality about it, and rather unpleasant bitterness, a surly anger that was usually not openly expressed. She was, on occasion, sarcastic and devious in her depreciation.

Throughout the beginning phase of analysis, I was able to reconstruct the following history. I include it now because I believe it is crucial to our understanding of what had been happening up to this point in the treatment and will help us understand how the transference was developing.

Her early childhood was highly traumatic from both an emotional and physical viewpoint. In a way, it was a chamber of horrors in which she was constantly on the threshhold of death, especially the first three months of her life. She was marasmic, because she could not retain food. She vomited after every feeding and apparently experienced intense pain after trying to eat since she screamed and kicked, obviously suffering from colic.

She was the first child and the mother insisted on breastfeeding her. While in the hospital, she had been advised to consider formulas and bottle feeding because her breasts were not producing sufficient milk. However, she paid no attention to this advice and continued doggedly trying to breastfeed her infant.

Part of the mother's behavior was based upon determination, but another part based upon confusion. It seemed as if she had not heard the pediatrician when he first suggested and then prescribed the bottle. It was later discovered that the mother felt that she would not have been capable of preparing a formula, that such a task was beyond her limited capacities. Putting an empty breast into her daughter's mouth was much simpler.

The events I have described took place in Europe. The patient did not come to the United States until late adolescence. In this European setting, the patient's mother was constantly surrounded by relatives. This was an extended family, a closely knit one, and this was fortunate for the patient, for otherwise she undoubtedly would have died.

One of the mother's sisters became exasperated and concerned with the situation and took charge of making the formula. The patient has to this day kept in touch with this aunt, who also emigrated to the United States, and it was from this aunt that she learned how inept her mother was, especially in matters involving maternal care.

The aunt recalled how difficult it was for her sister, the patient's mother, to prepare the formula. It was a momentous ordeal. First, it was almost impossible for her to follow instructions about mixing the ingredients. She just did not understand them and then seemed to be bewildered by the enormity of the task. The aunt told how it could take hours to prepare a single feeding and then, because of the inordinate length of time involved in preparation, the mother would have to start working on it all over again immediately after the feeding. This became an interminable and tiring process, which brought her to a state of utter depletion and pathetic exhaustion.

My patient did not thrive. She became thinner and thinner and was obviously dying of starvation. At the age of three months, the mother suddenly decided that something was wrong, although the relatives and the aunt, in particular, had been hammering at her to take notice. She still was not able to do anything about it, which would have meant seeking medical help. The mother suddenly began feeling extremely guilty, but instead of motivating her to find out what was wrong, the guilt further immobilized her. She simply could not bring herself to do anything. Her husband also did nothing. From what I could gather, he was an isolated man, a depressed nonparticipant.

The aunt felt that she was watching murder being committed. She finally could not stand it any longer and one afternoon she practically kidnapped the patient and took her to a pediatrician. The pediatrician was instantly alarmed and personally took her to a surgeon, who operated upon her the next day and repaired a pyloric stenosis.

When she returned home, the vomiting abated, but it did not disappear completely. The colic also continued, but apparently it was not as intense as before. She was able to retain some food and slowly started gaining weight. However, she gained weight very slowly and the surgeon was not at all satisfied with her progress.

He gave the mother elaborate instructions, but, according to the aunt, she did not seem to understand a word. The only difference in the mother's attitude, if it can be considered a difference, was that she was more anxious and guilty than ever.

The patient somehow managed to survive, but she attributed this to the aunt's intervention. She was always slender, and when she consulted me she was very thin, just on the edge of being emaciated. She stated that, since her psyche could not really understand what surrounded her and, therefore, could not take it in, her stomach could not "receive" food either. Her stomach symptoms never really went away. She often felt nauseous, occasionally vomited, and she frequently had abdominal cramps which seemed to be extensions of her early colic.

As stated, she managed to survive but she had always felt "empty," weak, and vulnerable. Furthermore, she thought of herself and of her mother as hollow shells with thin, egglike coverings that could crack at any time.

Apparently the mother had sufficient guilt that she tried in her way to take care of her daughter. The child, for many reasons, especially her pyloric stenosis, was extremely difficult to care for, and this only added to the mother's sense of inadequacy and guilt. These disruptive feelings caused her to be even more inadequate in her mothering, creating a vicious circle.

When the patient reached puberty, she discovered that her mother was an alcoholic. The mother felt that she was so inadequate that she could get through a day, that she could not function, without a fifth of liquor.

In the meantime, the father underwent a remarkable metamorphosis. He had been a passive, depressed man who had also been incapable of functioning. He had isolated himself from everybody. He did not want to bother to relate to anyone or to become engaged in his profession. He had accepted living off his wife's money. All of a sudden, he changed. He went back to work and in a few years became immensely successful. Apparently his depression lifted and he went out into the world and dealt with it well at all levels, socially and economically.

He amassed a fortune and then abruptly left his family. He set aside a large sum of money to take care of his wife, because he believed she would need nurses and housekeepers to take care of her and the children. He had also predicted that she would, at some time, need hospitalization or a nursing home and, though his wife had considerable money of her own, she did not have enough for such contingencies. Other than these materialistic connections, he had practically nothing to do with the mother or the patient.

The mother's course was downhill. She seemed to be drinking more every day and was perpetually drunk. The care of the house was finally completely taken over by maids and practical nurses around the clock. When the patient was twenty years old, the mother died of a stroke. The last time she saw her father was at the funeral.

Returning to the analysis: as I stated, the patient stopped making pleas for help, stopped being overtly demanding, and gradually became aware of some resentment toward me. Initially, this was a reaction to what she considered to be my "good organization" and "absolute and rational control." I saw this in two lights. First, I surmised that she was angry at me for withholding from her. In essence, I felt this was the usual situation of frustration of dependency needs. She wanted me to take care of her and provide nurture, but I had chosen not to do so and consequently she hated me. The second reason could concern the management of her anger. She might feel loss of control, weakness, and vulnerability in face of emerging destructive impulses. She could resent my control but also welcome it, because I would have the strength to protect her against her inner destructive impulses. To some extent, these formulations had some elements of truth about them, but at this point in the analysis, they were both wrong.

I am glad that I did not make any interpretations at this time, because I am certain they would have been misleading. Most likely, I would have reinforced the feeling that I did not understand her, which in fact I strongly believed. Probably this feeling made me reluctant to speak out. So I decided to do the only thing I knew how to do, that is, to wait and see.

Before proceeding with what will be a summary of the remainder of the analysis, I want to comment further about my feelings. As might be evident, from feeling relatively calm at the beginning of the analysis, I was becoming gradually uneasy. I liked the patient and I was glad to see her and, since she had become calmer, she was much more pleasant to be with. She was intelligent and capable of making fairly rational judgments about matters which seemed in no way related to her. This was a respite from her previous crying and clinging demandingness. Nevertheless, the feeling that I did not know what she wanted continued to grow on me. It was not that I felt acute confusion or anxiety. I was not uncomfortable in an active sense nor did I feel desperate as I have with other very needful patients. Perhaps the best way to describe my reaction is to compare it with trying to solve a very difficult puzzle or riddle, working on it for a while and then reaching an impasse and being completely stymied. For a while, there is a feeling of utter loss, not knowing which way to turn. That is the way I reacted to my patient. I wanted to do something to help her, but I knew that anything I would try to do would be irrelevant, not harmful or even wrong, just beside the point. There was something about her that seemed very synthetic and I was eager to relate to her as if she had the same basic affects of any ordinary human being. That was a mistake.

Regarding her feelings, she reminded me of some adolescent patients I have treated. They are not sure of their feelings. I can recall several young men who wanted to be told how to feel on specific occasions (Giovacchini 1967). This patient convinced me that she had a very poor definition of her affects. She revealed that she frequently did not know how she felt or how she was supposed to feel when confronting particular circumstances. Although she often experienced irritation and confusion, she had never felt object-directed anger. She knew what rage was but could never fit it in a specific context. She would tell me about events where one would have expected an angry reaction, where most of us would have felt some degree of frustration, but her reactions were, at best, diffuse. I realize that this does not describe much, but, then, it is hard to describe.

During the second year of treatment, the patient had become aware of the fact that she did not have the same "emotions" that others have and this is where her resentment entered the picture. Though there might have been some elements of truth in my two conjectures, basically she resented me because she saw that I was able to feel like other people while she could not. She had not known this consciously but it became gradually clear as her dreams and associations focused upon this deficit.

She frequently spoke of being dead or frozen inside, a theme which I have often encountered in patients suffering from characterological problems, but not always necessarily borderline patients (Giovacchini 1967). She emphasized her inability to distinguish between various bodily sensations. For example, she was not able to identify the type of sensory perception that would be associated with hunger. She might have a colicky-like pain and believe this to mean that her "body wanted to eat," but she really did not know if this were the case. This uncertainty caused her to feel anxious because she had no security that she could control her inner feelings. If she could not identify them she was at a complete loss. On the other hand, as she saw it, I had certitude as to what was going on within myself and was in absolute control. In view of my strength and her weakness, she resented me. She was afraid of me as well because I might use this power of control to exploit her. Again, she did not know what she meant by being exploited. She was not a good paranoid. She just had some paranoid tendencies which were involved in her resentment toward me, but basically she was placing my control and power alongside her weakness and vulnerability. This stimulated some feeling within her which is reminiscent of anger, but, as with the rest of her feelings, it was not clearly defined. For lack of a better term, I call it resentment.

I had commented many times throughout the beginning course of the analysis that I did not understand what she was asking for, but recently I had been stressing more and more that my lack of understanding was a fundamental characteristic of the transference. In a sense, I was making her responsible for the situation and emphasizing that there was something about her psychic makeup that led to my dilemma. My comfort increased considerably as I became more firmly convinced that my feelings were reactions to her psychopathology and not due to inhibitions stemming from untoward countertransference feelings.

With the approach of the Christmas holidays during the third year of analysis, her condition rapidly degenerated. She admitted that analysis worked within a particular framework and intrinsic in it were certain limitations. She also believed that she had received, without being able to explain what was meant by "receive," everything analysis could offer with its limited boundaries. However, she needed more; it was just a "trickle of sustenance given to a starving body." Of course, I was fascinated by this sequence, and began to recognize that it involved a replication in the transference of the infantile situation of an inadequate mother trying to minister to an infant with pyloric stenosis, an infant who literally could not be fed. The patient's course continued rapidly downhill. She considered herself to be paralyzed and became totally unable to function.

I did not sufficiently connect her present attitude toward me with the events preceding her hospitalization for gastrointestinal surgery. This was partly due to the fact that I had not, as yet, seen these similarities. It seems clear enough now, but amidst her consternation and speedy disintegration, I was not entirely aware of all of the transference implications of her regression. I was aware of some of them, but I doubt if I had interpreted what I had been able to put together that she would have been capable of understanding and integrating it in view of her distraught and functionless state. The family and husband could no longer tolerate her. They cancelled her appointments and had her hospitalized.

This was not the first hospitalization. She had entered this same hospital four times in the last six years and each time for ostensibly the same reason. She would be emotionally paralyzed, on the brink of starvation, and diagnosed as an acute schizophrenic reaction with anorexia nervosa.

This patient's decompensation was undoubtedly part of a repetitive pattern which was aimed at reliving past traumatic events; perhaps with some attempt at mastering them. I needed this positive viewpoint of the adaptive significance of her decompensation in order to make the best I could of it and this also helped me put it into a transference context. The personality disintegration that occurred before my eyes had occurred many times before, but now it was possible to see how it was the outcome of our relationship. She was able to organize it around me and, in spite of the severity of her physical condition and the chaos of her feelings, I preferred to accept what was happening as an inevitable part of the treatment and, to make progress, we had to live through such a regression.

Unfortunately, I could not see her while she was in the hospital since I was not on the staff and the administration would not bend their rules. However, I did discuss the patient with the attending psychiatrist and expressed my extreme antipathy about shock therapy. He agreed that it was contraindicated and also believed that it would be contrary to her general welfare and to her analysis. Even though I could not continue regular sessions while she was hospitalized, he gave her telephone privileges, allowing her to call me daily for the same amount of time of an ordinary session. During the second week of hospitalization, he had somehow managed to have an attendant bring her to my office to continue her sessions with the same frequency (five times a week) as before. I found the differences in her rational manner of relating to me on the telephone, and in her behavior in my office, amazing.

In the hospital, she seemed to have relaxed considerably and had even begun to eat a little. She had told me this during our last telephone conversation. The next day she saw me at the office and the atmosphere she created was entirely different. She sat on my big armchair and curled into the fetal position, and for fifteen or twenty minutes, she babbled incoherently. Saliva was running out of the corners of her mouth and when I asked a question—I suppose because I did not know what else to do—she looked at me with the same fixed exophthalmic stare that I had noted at the beginning of analysis. The feeling I got when she looked at me in this fashion was that I was facing a confused, terrified person unable to comprehend or control incomprehensible, dangerous, and overwhelming outside forces that threatened to devour her. Devouring her was my idea, but, her terror and confusion were unmistakable. Now, I felt more acutely the impulse to do something to pull her out of utter helplessness, isolation, and panic. Still, as usual, I did not know what to do, which was hard for me to accept in view of her agitation. I told her that she was trying to create a world, with me as a central figure, that I could not understand or respond to her needs, because she could not understand them herself. I added that by creating crises where she plunged herself into the depths of misery and uncertainty as to whether the world could support her survival, she was somehow testing that world. As I had become representative of all forces that were attempting to care for her, she was testing me, to see if I could overcome my lack of understanding and inability to get through to her so that she could feel her needs directly and gain some confidence that they would be met. As I could have predicted, she ostensibly ignored everything I said.

Back in the hospital following this interview, she deteriorated further, according to the staff. She became phenomenologically catatonic, in a classical sense. She was mute and immobile, lying in bed, staring in front of her, again with the same exophthalmic intensity, but never moving. The staff could move her limbs at will, but they would fall down to her side when released. I wondered what I should do now and what would happen at our next appointment, which was the following day.

I was not completely surprised when she appeared as scheduled for the appointment. She said absolutely nothing and lay down on the couch. I said nothing either and noticed that she was asleep, at least she seemed to be asleep, as evidenced by her heavy and regular breathing. She continued this pattern of curling up on the couch and sleeping throughout the entire interview for several sessions.

The last time she slept, she awoke during the middle of the session, sat up and looked at me with a dreamy expression. I could almost see her stretching and yawning, although in reality she did neither. I asked her if it were a restful sleep and whether she had been dreaming. She nodded and stated it was the most refreshing sleep she ever had, but she either could not or would not tell me her dreams. I sensed that it was vitally important that I not press her for anything. She then indicated that sleeping in my office was much more restorative than sleeping for longer periods under the influence of sedatives.

For the next several sessions, she talked quite easily about various events in her daily life and her relationships with members of her family and some friends. She also spent a good deal of time emphasizing how painful eating was and though she knew it was important for her to eat, she found it such a chore. I tried to relate her current difficulty in eating to being unable to take in a complex external world which had become equated with eating, because she did not believe she had the capacity for such an integration or the memory of a previous experience when she had been able to do so. Again a hopeful note, and bringing in the transference, I stressed that she was experimenting with me, trying to find out how much of me she could take in. Now, she seemed to be listening, though she never made any comment in response to what I had interpreted.

I do not know how to fit what happened next into a technical context. The same thing happened once again with the same results. At the beginning of a session, I had a cup of coffee on the table next to my chair and I would take a sip now and then. I had coffee many times before while she was there, and never offered her any. I never do with any of my patients, and am only infrequently accused of being rude or ungenerous. The patient usually brings such feelings in an analytic context and discusses them. This time she asked if she could have a sip of my coffee. I did not think she would like it since it was just plain black coffee without any cream or sugar, but without any deliberation, I simply handed her the cup. She was startled by my unexpected response, but she took the cup and sipped it once. She then returned it to me and I noticed that she had drunk very little, only a few drops.

Those drops must have been a magic potion, a powerful elixir, because, as I subsequently learned, from that moment she was able to eat with both comfort and pleasure. On the ward, she became outgoing and involved with the staff and other patients. The staff found her helpful in the total treatment program rather than needy. She started gaining weight and both the ward psychiatrist and the internist agreed that she was sufficiently improved that she be granted her request for discharge.

I do not mean to imply that anything miraculously dramatic occurred or that she was suddenly cured. In comparison to her previous confusion, terror, starvation, and catatonia, these changes were indeed impressive, but from an overall viewpoint, I was still dealing with a woman whose ability to adapt to the external world in terms of her needs was tenuous. Furthermore, I am not advocating that analysts drink plain black coffee when treating borderline patients, although in this instance it seemed to be crucial. Of course, it was not the coffee drinking itself that was important; it was the significance of the interchange that was meaningful and the patient's continuous experience within the analytic setting paved the way for her to take something concrete from me. Analysis represented a confirmation that she had achieved a degree of security and a sense of safety that gave her the temerity and allowed her to extend herself to ask for something directly.

As so often happens with patients suffering from characterological problems, she had vivid fantasies of our relationship between sessions. She had long conversations with me, but was unable or unwilling to tell me about what was discussed. In general, the patient felt much calmer and somewhat secure about herself. That is, she considered herself better able to deal with the world. She need not be frightened about coping with it and she would not be rejected.

This security was especially interesting because it appeared that, in fact, she was being rejected by her husband. After the coffee sipping episode, their relationship markedly deteriorated. He went out of his way to ignore his wife and to treat her as if she were a nonentity. The relationship continued worsening and the patient was glad when their divorce was finalized.

Whereas during the early phases of analysis, the patient was always preoccupied with the gastrointestinal system and had immense difficulties with digestion, now there was a shift in focus. She was still concerned about things being inside her, but, rather than food, she was now thinking in terms of sex. Things inside meant penises or babies, and, for the most part, they were perceived as dangerous. She had anxiety dreams whose content involved assault and rape. She had fantasies of her abdomen being torn apart as she was violently penetrated, or that a deformed baby inside of her would rip her uterus to shreds.

In terms of the transference, she experienced considerable anxiety as she ambivalently pursued her efforts to internalize me. At this point in treatment, this involved more than an inability to form endopsychic representations of external object relations. There were still problems caused by her limited capacities, but these were not as limited as they had been. She had developed considerable ability during the course of treatment to hold my imago without needing to keep me in her sensory field. She had finally become able to be relatively comfortable during our recent separations, whether they were initiated by me or by her. The difference was that she was experiencing an active conflict as I entered her psyche and this was manifestly expressed in erotic terms.

I believe that her material consisted of a mixture of pregenital and sexual elements. She was still dealing with her inability to make outside experiences helpful, but due to some developmental progress, she viewed them less as useless and more as dangerous. It may seem odd that this reaction of incorporating danger in her feelings and perceptions should be considered progressive.

I wish to compare the apprehension of danger with the development of affects. This patient's developmental fixation, mainly a prementational one, resulted in an ego that had only a minimal capacity to structure affects. It will be recalled that all of her sensations, that is, inner feelings, were only dimly and vaguely perceived. They were amorphous in quality and she was barely able to discriminate between different types of bodily tensions and needs. As for feelings which are manifestations of psychological processes and mentational responses, she was just as constricted. Joy, sorrow, anger, despair—such affects were foreign to my patient. She had some feelings which seem to be akin to these affects, but they lacked depth and one might say they were monochromatic. She was a most colorless person and she complained about her inability to feel with the richness and intensity she attributed to others.

Such affective constriction also gave her a constricted view of her surrounding world. She saw it in the same narrow way she experienced the inner world. Her reality was gray and her corresponding mood was also gray. There was no verve or vibrancy to the way she related or reacted. Extremes were not part of her life.

A dull, colorless world is not a dangerous world. It is not a safe world either. It is barren, "like the moon," she used to say, and "one could starve there." She could not, however, be attacked nor did she have to fear hidden destructive forces.

From a conceptual viewpoint, the ability to perceive a situation as dangerous requires an ego that knows something about anger, organized anger that can be experienced as a definitive affect rather than a general feeling of being overwhelmed or out of control. The destructive aspects of anger also have to be perceived and evaluated in a circumscribed fashion in contrast to diffuse, global waves of destructive feelings. The ego must have reached a sufficient degree of structuralization that inner danger can be relatively well discriminated, a necessary condition to be able to judge whether external situations are dangerous.

It follows, then, that to percieve outer danger means that there is considerable capacity to see the outer world as separate and distinct from the psyche. This structural integration would be characteristic of an ego that could support so refined an affect as anxiety as a signal. It also means that the ego has a well-developed capacity for projection. It is able to project inner danger into the outside world, while inner and outer danger are well delineated.

In this discussion I am making only one simple point, and that is that the pressure of affects such as anger and the ability to view an external situation as dangerous, whether this is a realistic appraisal or the outcome of projection, indicate that the ego has attained sufficient structure so that it can retain mental representations of external objects, interactions, and functional modalities without requiring continuous reinforcement from the surrounding world. In addition, these findings signify that the ego has developed or is developing the capacity to experience intrapsychic conflict rather than just adaptational failures which are the outcome of difficulties between the ego and reality (Freud, 1924a, 1924b). Intrapsychic conflict lends itself well to expression in sexual terms, and the content of danger can also be conceptualized in terms of a hierarchal continuum.

The patient continued bringing in sexual material associated with moderate anxiety. I could observe a shift from fear of annihilation and obliteration of her identity to more circumscribed concerns about her integrity as a woman. She revealed how insecure her basis for womanhood was in view of the identification that she had made with her mother. To be sexually involved meant to be destroyed because of her frailness, as she incorporated her mother's weaknesses and inadequacy. She saw me as threatening her shaky sexual identity as her erotic feelings toward me intensified. She showed many similarities in behavior and attitude to those seen in some hysterical patients.

She acted as though she were trying to repress, something that had never occurred previously in the analysis. For example, she would be visibly anxious at the beginning of a session, sometimes bordering on panic. She would have to force herself to be on the couch and then she might say nothing for the entire session. She was not devoid of associations. On the contrary, many thoughts and feelings were racing through her mind, but she could not bring herself to verbalize them. She was very critical of herself for not saying what was uppermost in her mind and, on occasion, she would severely revile herself.

Her silence had a different meaning from that which she presented early in the analysis. Then, not communicating was the expression of her early infantile orientation and dilemma where she was not able to make her needs known to her mother or herself. From an unconscious viewpoint, her primary purpose was to be silent.

Now, she visibly struggled against silence. She still had a need to be silent, but this time it was the outcome of conflict rather than the direct replication of a childhood pattern. She was so disturbed on one particular occasion that she walked out of a session before it was half over. She apologized profusely for leaving, but she found it impossible to continue lying on my couch and suppressing her associations. She was also well aware that I had probably heard similar material many times and that I would not be shocked, horrified, or critical, but this did not help her much.

I tried to emphasize the transference aspects of what she was suppressing. I stressed that it was not the feelings and thoughts in themselves that were all that difficult to deal with, but the fact that they were directed toward me frightened her to the extent that she had to keep them hidden. The patient would usually sob loudly when I gave her such explanations and from time to time would bring forth little bits of sexual fantasies. They were mainly involved with performing fellatio on me and occasionally they were connected with an experience usually occurring the previous night where she had picked up a man at a bar and had, in fact, performed fellatio. She had less frequent fantasies of having intercourse with me and she also engaged in the sexual act with the men she picked up, but not as often or as consistently as she had oral sex.

As stated, this material came out in bits and pieces, and again I seemed to be dealing with a mixture of pregenital and sexual elements. The patient was beginning to equate tender feelings and sexual feelings in the transference.

She had been able to hold a mental representation of me within her psyche as one who had some ability to care for her needs, and this had a positive feedback effect in that she began structuring her needs so that she could perceive them. As she gained some security about the world being able to recognize her basic survival requirements, she began to direct sexual feelings toward my imago and this characterized the transference, which in many ways seemed to develop into what Freud would have called a tranference neurosis (Freud 1914).

She even began struggling with a three person relationship. Her father's later success and colorful career was, in her fantasies, moved back in time and she was able to merge him with me as an oedipal object. In the meantime, the mother's imago was also distorted in that she became strong, but prohibitive and villainous. As I write this, it seems reasonably clear and simple, but the patient had practically to drag it out of herself to present to me. I was puzzled as to why she was suffering so much with it.

She told me of how terribly confused and sad she felt. She spoke of being alone one weekend and crying incessantly. She claimed that she did not know why she was crying. She considered herself crazy and was ashamed to tell me how one afternoon she went into her garden and hugged a tree.

She then met a man, a person she had known slightly when she was a young girl in Europe, who showered her with a fantastic amount of attention. He declared his love for her and wanted to marry her immediately. She responded by feeling exuberant and reacted as an ecstatic adolescent, but she hesitated about marriage. She put him off, preferring to have an affair rather than to make a permanent commitment. She was uneasy about the relationship in spite of feeling some happiness about being with her lover.

I surmised that she was afraid of intimacy, that she expected that if she allowed herself to get what she considered to be too involved, she, myself, or her lover would be destroyed. Whereas previously she could not relate to anyone because she did not have the "equipment" to relate, that is, the adaptive and executive ego capacities, she now was afraid to get close to another person because she feared the consequences.

She had now been in analysis five years and decided she did not want to go on any further. I did not want her to discontinue and told her that I would like to see her make further progress, which I believed was a distinct possibility. She understood that these were my feelings and opinions and that she was in no way obligated to abide by them. I was simply exercising my freedom to express my attitudes about the analysis, but ultimately her decision had to be respected. Perhaps out of deference or because she wanted to, she stayed in treatment another six months and then terminated. She married before our final appointment, in a sense indicating that she did not need me anymore and that she had overcome her problems about intimacy.

This was not the end. In fact, there is no end. Three years later, she called for an appointment. She looked well, remarkably so. She was smartly dressed, had a sophisticated air about her and, in general, was relaxed and poised. This was a marked contrast to the day eight years ago when I first saw her. There was nothing of the helpless, confused, frenetic attitude and behavior that had been so conspicuous. Instead, she told me about herself almost casually.

Ostensibly, she wanted to see me because her husband was relatively impotent. She sought me out, because he adamantly refused to see an analyst. She did not exactly explain why this would necessitate treatment for her, but I did not question it. It was obvious that was what she wanted. We resumed the analysis as if our last session had been the previous day. This was initially very difficult for me because of my schedule, but I sensed that it was important that I work it out.

She had functioned rather well the past three years. I even gathered the impression that she had been functioning exceedingly well. She had developed many skills covering a broad range of activities. She had become an excellent housekeeper and cook, an amateur violinist and an expert photographer, to mention just a few of her accomplishments. Her only problem now was her husband's lack of sexual responsiveness. As she explained further, he had largely withdrawn from her, remaining immersed in his business, spending much time on the telephone with his male friends, and participating vigorously in sports such as handball, golf and tennis.

She continued talking in a composed way, her material well-organized and mostly confined to a recitation of everyday events. She complained a good deal about her husband and asked many questions as to what she should do about him. During her previous treatment with me she had also asked many questions, but they were impossible to answer, and in spite of the anguished and pressing quality of her demands, I did not feel any particular need to answer them. Now her questions were quite concrete and in tune with reality and their content and her way of asking them made it much more difficult for me not to answer them. I resisted this inclination. They were questions that I might have been able to answer, but this would have changed me from an analyst to a dispenser of advice.

What gradually dawned on me was that I was working with a patient who seemed to have no idea whatsoever as to what constitutes an analytic relation. This amazed me in view of the fact that I had seen her practically daily for five years and had witnessed deep regressions and many variations of transference. I also recalled how quickly she responded to some interpretations and how she had violently rejected others, and then slowly incorporated them. Although she usually operated at fairly primitive levels and was generally unable to function, there was a certain fluidity to her mind that had made her analytically accessible. The present picture seemed to be lacking some vital ingredient.

It took me some time, several months, before I realized that something was wrong. Our relationship was pleasant enough, but I was somehow dissatisfied with it. I must confess that she was annoying me with what I considered to be meaningless chatter and questions which I experienced as intrusive. The intrusive impact of her material caused me to look at our relationship from a fresh perspective. I realized that I was confusing this woman with another, whom I had known some years back and who bore some superficial resemblances to my current patient. Although the same, they appeared to be two different people.

Whereas my former patient had been infantile and helpless, my present patient was seemingly mature and capable. No longer did she seem to be on the borderline of a psychosis. However, this made the situation, analytically speaking, difficult if not impossible. I had been more comfortable with her in the past when we were in contact with the primitive within her, parts of her personality which now seemed quite remote and unavailable. In spite of her competence in dealing with the external world, she still seemed to be quite needy and, as before, not really any more capable of expressing her needs verbally.

This patient is still in treatment with me and I believe she is getting along quite well. She is maintaining something that resembles analysis with me, although I would be the first to admit that it lacks many qualities that are intrinsic to analysis. She is only coming once a week now, sometimes more often as she feels the need, but it is not the frequency of sessions that I am referring to. Rather, it is her concrete style, a particular type of rigidity that does not permit a true analytic reaction.

This woman initially sought treatment because she could not cope with the external world, with reality. Now she seems very much involved, perhaps too much so, with her environment. Rather than withdrawing or feeling helpless, she keeps herself immersed in all kinds of activities. She is functioning at a very high level of efficiency and competence. As I have been hinting, her involvement with so many external activities and relationships seems to be imitative, a caricature of a well functioning person. In contrast, to her prevous self, she is hyperfunctioning. She is overly realistic in that she focuses all of her attention on external reality and has become cut off from her inner world.

She has achieved considerable psychic structure in that she has been able to incorporate some gratifying experiences and acquired various adaptive techniques that have become part of the ego's executive system. These would be definitive structural accretions, but I do not believe they are well integrated. As with any newly acquired skill, one that has not yet become completely part of oneself, it is clumsily exercised or defensively handled.

My patient has not smoothly amalgamated all these techniques of dealing with various segments of reality and she relates in an exaggerated fashion, what I have called a caricature, in order to adapt herself to reality. Her behavior can be compared to the situation of someone who has learned English in another country, a foreigner who has just arrived in this country and is suddenly forced to communicate in a strange tongue. This person may have studied English for many years and comes here well-trained. However, he has not yet made the new language part of himself; it is not smoothly integrated into his repertoire of communication skills. It has not become ego-syntonic, and he has to make an effort to speak and understand the new language. A native is much more relaxed and need not make any such efforts, because comprehension and use of the language is so well ingrained in his general personality and is so much a part of his general functioning that he speaks without conscious thought or effort. He handles his language as an automatized habit. The foreigner may speak flawless English. His diction and grammar could be perfect. He allows himself no careless errors or indulges in sloppy speaking patterns. He does not have the freedom to do so, but there is a rigid, stereotyped quality to his speech that easily identifies him as someone who is not using his mother tongue.

So it is with my patient. She is rigid and there is something awkward about the way she conducts herself both in the outer world and in my consultation room. She continues in this fashion and I am seeing her regularly although infrequently. I am not too concerned as to whether what I am doing is analysis. To some extent, she is getting some satisfaction out of life, but she feels she needs some contact with me to be able to carry on.

Apparently, she needed a constant contact with the treatment setting to maintain this equilibrium. If I made even the weakest suggestion or subtly hinted that we should consider termination, as I had done sometime after her return, she would become extremely upset and violently oppose it. Fortunately, I was impressed by a colleague's experience with a similar situation. When he protested about the interminability of treatment, his patient retorted that she had no problems about remaining in treatment indefinitely. If he had such problems, he had better go back to his analysis and work them out there rather than acting them out in her therapy. He did just that. I learned from his experience and stopped suggesting to my patient that she should try getting along without her sessions.

Ego Defect and Helplessness

My patient, an example of borderline psychopathology, could rather easily regress to psychotic states characterized by helpless vulnerability and almost total inability to function. She had never really been very far from a functionless state and her hold on reality was tenuous. Though tenuous, it was just as quickly reinstituted as it was relinquished. These qualities practically define the borderline syndrome.

The structure of the ego can be examined in greater detail. Regarding the perceptual system, she demonstrated a reduced capacity for distinguishing inner stimuli. She often felt tension, but she frequently did not know what sort of inner needs were responsible for her discomfort. This led to an inability to express herself, to let others know what she required, and this increased her privation.

During neonatal periods, every infant has limited modes of expression at his command. The mother, because of her more coherent and integrated organization, and in touch with her own needs, is able empathically to sense what her child has to have. The mother's caretaking and nurturing response enables the infant to structure his needs so that they can be more easily understood by both the mother and child. The neonate develops a sense of security that he will be taken care of.

Inability to make one's needs known and lack of gratification cause the child to feel helpless, vulnerable, and unloved. This was particularly true for my patient who in addition to being cursed with an inadequate mother also had a physical defect which literally blocked her access to external supplies. When one's needs are imperfectly understood and the external world does not or cannot respond, the patient at some level begins to believe that something is missing inside of him which makes him incapable of being gratified.

The mother of my patient could not, because of her psychopathology and her child's physical defect, respond appropriately or respond at all to her infant's primitive needs. Because of this neonatal impasse, the patient never received satisfaction adequate to give her assurance and security that gratification would be forthcoming. The chief ego defect that she had before treatment was that *she did not form memory traces of satisfying experiences, and, therefore, she could not structure a current experience so that it would represent potential gratification.*

In adult life, the patient displayed her helplessness and needfulness openly and directly, and she brought these feelings and orientations into the therapeutic relationship. Such an orientation, however, was pervasive, and as far as could be ascertained, was typical of all of her relationships. She not only displayed her helplessness, but insisted that I do something about it. Her frantic demands of me were particularly interesting because, inasmuch as she lacked, in a relative sense, endopsychic registrations of gratifying experiences, they were inevitably doomed to fail.

Here, as often happens with patients suffering from structural defects, we have a negative feedback sequence. They seek reassurance that they are capable of being gratified. As was the situation with my patient, she wanted some protection from the profound feeling of helplessness that engulfed her. She did this in the only way that she knew, that is, by asking for help. But this could not help since basically she did not know what help meant. Consequently, she felt more helpless than ever when I was unable to respond to her pleas.

As discussed in the clinical section, there were several reasons why the patient should feel helpless. Here, I wish to emphasize how helplessness is the outcome of the lack of structure of ego subsystems, brought about by defective mothering. Defective mothering, in this instance, means that the patient's nurturing source was unable to provide what was required for emotional growth. It does not necessarily refer to a hostile, attacking mother or a mother who uses her child to enhance her narcissism. These situations would be errors of commission whereas with borderline patients we are faced with *errors of omission*. Borderline patients do not feel assaulted, intruded upon, or manipulated and used at the expense of their autonomy, as is common with so many patients suffering from other character disorders. Their chief dilemma is a hopeless feeling of inadequacy in feeling their needs or having any security that they can take in and avail themselves of experiences with the outer world that others would find helpful.

I am aware that some borderline patients have felt assaulted and intruded upon and that their early lives were also punctuated with errors of commission as well as omission, but this is not typical of the borderline patient. I repeat that patients suffering from characterological problems seldom present themselves as clear cut diagnostic entities. There is usually considerable overlapping as is true for most patients with emotional problems. Here I am emphasizing the features that I believe are the essence of the borderline personality.

The borderline patient feels as if he were a stranger. He finds reality, to a large measure, incomprehensible. He is, unlike some primitively fixated personalities, aware of his surrounding world but he cannot become involved with it. He cannot integrate it. This causes him to feel further helplessness.

Technical Factors

As is the situation with all patients suffering from ego defects rather than predominantly from intrapsychic conflicts, the question, analytically speaking, is whether a patient during psychoanalytic treatment can acquire psychic structure. If basic structures are missing, can the analytic relationship somehow supply them or help the patient achieve them?

It is well known that if proper learning experiences are not supplied at specific periods of childhood, the child will have difficulty in acquiring certain functions. Langer (1942) writes about a chattering period around the first year of life when it is extremely important, much more important than previously thought, that the parents actively converse with the child so that he will learn how to speak. Once a basic language is established, the child can learn other languages relatively easily and without accents up until adolescence. After the age of sixteen, however, the adolescent or adult may learn other languages, but not as facilely, and he will cling to the patterns and accent of his mother tongue.

To return to the clinical situation of the borderline patient, if he has not had the proper nurturing experiences at the appropriate time, then how can an analytic relationship enable him to incorporate what we might call the nurturing modality? The analyst may attempt to provide helpful experiences, but, as my patient illustrated, the ego of the borderline patient is not prepared to accept them. The fundamental state of helplessness persists.

Analysis, however, creates a unique situation in which earlier ego states are reexperienced through the transference regression. When she slept on my couch, my patient dramatically illustrated the reproduction, in essence, of her infantile psychic orientation at the time of her surgery. As the surgeon repaired her pyloric stenosis, she gained the capacity to be nurtured in a physical sense. In my office, she acquired some ability to incorporate certain aspects of our relationship as she relived this crucial period of her past. Thus, in analysis, the ego can once again relate to the external world in the same fashion as it once did when it was particularly receptive and able to integrate experiences which could lead to the acquisition of important functions and psychic structure. The world failed the patient then.

The analyst need not fail the patient but he often feels that he has. As is so common with patients who lack certain elements of psychic structure, the analyst feels frustrated because he seems to be unable to make contact with the patient. I believe the borderline patient is also unique in that he stimulates particular countertransference reactions which may have somewhat similar results as those stimulated by other patients but which have different mechanisms.

Usually, the therapist reacts to the patient's projections or his attempts to fuse with him. This also occurs with the borderline patient, but to a much lesser extent. As stated, the borderline patient has a deficiency, an inability to introject, and, correspondingly, his abilities to project are limited. The analyst, however, does not lack these psychic mechanisms and, in turn, he introjects the patient's helpless ego with its lack of memory traces of gratifying and helpful experiences. The analyst then finds himself in the same situation as the patient; he faces an identical dilemma.

The professional elements of the analyst's self-representation seem to have disappeared. During such phases of treatment, the therapist feels that he knows nothing or that he has forgotten everything he has ever learned. At least that is how he feels about himself when dealing with the borderline patient. He has now become a borderline analyst, and does not have, so he believes, the analytic adaptive techniques that would enable him both to understand and interpret to the patient. If this countertransference reaction is not understood in terms of how the patient's fundamental helplessness has become part of therapist's ego structure, then all kinds of disruptive situations can occur which will lead to collapse of the analytic relationship.

From this discussion, it would seem that if the analyst did not let the patient's helplessness invade his psyche, he would be able to create an optimal situation in which analysis can proceed. This is often the case, but he runs the risk of leaning too heavily in the opposite direction. Fearing the consequences of introjecting the patient's helplessness, he may reactively pull away from the patient. In order to maintain separateness and distinct ego boundaries, the analyst may withdraw from the patient. The patient then finds him remote and unable to fathom, a feeling which is typical of the patient's orientation to external objects, one which is accentuated by the analyst's defensiveness. The world becomes even more complicated and incomprehensible to the patient as the analyst moves away from the patient, emotionally speaking. In turn, the analyst knows less and less about the patient and though he insulates himself to protect himself from feeling helpless, he is still virtually helpless as far as being able to conduct analysis with his borderline patient.

What I am emphasizing is that with the borderline patient, disruptive countertransference reactions are more apt to occur when the analyst makes the patient's ego defects his own. The analyst views his professional self in the same fashion the patient generally views himself. This may become unmanageable for both patient and therapist and then the borderline patient is considered unanalyzable. What creates even greater frustration for the analyst is that any other approach, such as one based upon deliberate attempts to be supportive, is doomed to failure.

Countertransference problems can occur with all patients and the more primitively fixated the ego, the more likely that they will lead to technical complications. I cannot generalize, however, nor make more than a loose correlation between early fixation points and disruptive countertransference. It is true inasmuch as the earliest fixations are accompanied with more intense feelings of vulnerability and helplessness and the pervasiveness of such feelings in the analytic setting obscures the therapist's vision. He literally becomes unable to learn from the patient and in this sense the patient fails him by being unable to teach him what is going on within himself. The patient fails the therapist in the same way the world failed the patient (see Searles 1975). This is fundamental and characteristic of the transference of borderline patients, but, unfortunately, the analyst has lost sight of the transference.

These countertransference factors, in my opinion, are responsible for most of the difficulties encountered in the therapy of borderline patients and explain why we consider them to be difficult patients. They are also difficult because of their psychopathology, and their lack of structure underscored by the relative absence of introjects and adaptive techniques. Still, many borderline patients are treatable, especially in an analytic context, because the analytic attitude can be applied to both patient and analyst and disruptive countertransference reactions can be used for therapeutic advantage.

Summary and Conclusions

I single out a particular group of patients and designate them as borderline states. I choose this group because they are borderline in two respects: (1) as with other patients with character problems, they can decompensate fairly easily into a psychotic state but they can just as quickly reintegrate and regain their former equilibrium; and (2) they make a borderline adjustment to the external world inasmuch as they lack the adaptive techniques to deal with an inordinately complex reality.

I present in some detail the analysis of a patient who I believe to be typically borderline in the two respects that I have described.

She was especially noteworthy because during infancy she suffered from an organic condition which literally made it impossible for her to be gratified, to be nourished.

Finally, I discuss some of the complications we might expect when treating borderline patients analytically or, for that matter, in any therapeutic context. Understanding how the patient causes us to feel helpless can restore our analytic orientation and create a setting in which the patient can feel secure enough to regress to a position when he felt most abandoned but also most needful. The analysis can capitalize from the patient's needfulness by creating a new dimension for him, that is, by helping the patient achieve the capacity to be receptive, one that is more easily evoked in a fluid regressed ego. The patient slowly realizes he can be understood; he learns that there is something inside of him which deserves understanding and learns to perceive himself as a deserving person who can integrate helpful experiences.

References

Freud, S. (1914). Remembering, repeating and working through. *Standard Edition* 12:145–157.

———— (1924a). Neurosis and psychosis. *Standard Edition* 19:149–155.

———— (1924b). The loss of reality in neurosis and psychosis. *Standard Edition* 19:183–191.

———— (1926). Inhibitions, symptoms and anxiety. *Standard Edition* 20:75–177.

Giovacchini, P. (1963). Integrative aspects of object relationships. *Psychoanalytic Quarterly* 32:393–407.

———— (1967). The frozen introject. *International Journal of Psycho-Analysis* 48:61–67.

———— (1972). The symbiotic phase. In *The Psychoanalysis of Character Disorders,* 148–177. New York: Jason Aronson, 1975.

———— (1979). *The Treatment of Primitive Mental States.* New York: Jason Aronson.

Kernberg, O. (1967). Borderline personality organization. *Journal of the American Psychoanalytic Association* 15:641–685.

Knight, R. (1953). Borderline patients. *Bulletin of the Menninger Clinic* 19:1–12.

Langer, S. (1942). *Philosophy in a New Key.* New York: New American Library.

Masterson, J. (1972). *Treatment of the Borderline Adolescent.* New York: John Wiley and Sons.

Searles, H. (1975). The patient as therapist to his analyst. In *Tactics and Techniques in Psychoanalytic Treatment,* vol. 2, ed. P. Giovacchini, pp. 95–152. New York: Jason Aronson.

Spitz, R. (1965). *The First Year of Life.* New York: International Universities Press.

Winnicott, D. (1963). The mentally ill in your caseload. In *The Maturational Process and The Facilitating Environment,* pp. 217–230. New York: International Universities Press, 1965.

Chapter 7

Technical Considerations in the Treatment of Borderline Personality Organization[*]

Otto F. Kernberg, M.D.

General Principles of Treatment

Opinion regarding the treatment of borderline pathology remains divided. At one extreme are those who would follow Zetzel's (1971) approach, which implies that borderline pathology is related, at least in an important part, to defective development of ego functions and therefore requires a supportive psychotherapeutic approach. At the other extreme are those who would consider a nonmodified psychoanalysis the optimal treatment for all cases (Segal 1967). A majority of clinicians who have worked intensively with borderline patients have been shifting in recent years, it seems to me, from a supportive approach inspired by Knight's earlier work (1953a, 1953b) to modified psychoanalytic techniques or psychoanalytic psychotherapy for most patients,

*Presented at the New York Psychoanalytic Institute and Society, November 1975, and at the Fall Meeting of the American Psychoanalytic Association, December 1975. The author thanks Drs. Jacob Arlow, Leon Shapiro, Martin Stein, and Arthur Valenstein for their criticisms and suggestions. Previously published in 1976 in the *Journal of the American Psychoanalytic Association* 24:795–829.

while still considering the possibility that some patients may be treated by nonmodified psychoanalysis from the beginning of treatment, and others with a modified psychoanalytic procedure which might gradually evolve into a standard psychoanalytic situation at advanced stages of the treatment (Stone 1954, Greenson 1970, Jacobson 1971, Frosch 1971, Giovacchini 1975).

One problem complicating a review of where various writers stand regarding the issues mentioned is that some of them, in my opinion, do not sufficiently differentiate psychoanalysis proper from psychoanalytic psychotherapy; and many of them, when discussing psychotherapy, imply such a broad spectrum of psychotherapeutic tools and techniques that it is hard to know whether they are employing an expressive or supportive strategy. In attempting to clarify some of these issues, I shall utilize the following overall frame of reference, which should permit the reader to place my approach within the various alternatives just summarized.

First, I think that, while some borderline patients may respond to a nonmodified psychoanalytic approach, the vast majority respond best to a modified psychoanalytic procedure or psychoanalytic psychotherapy, which I have described in detail elsewhere (Kernberg 1968, 1975a). I believe that for some borderline patients a psychoanalytic approach—standard or modified—is contraindicated, and these patients do require a supportive psychotherapy, this is, an approach based upon a psychoanalytic model of psychotherapy relying mostly on the supportive techniques outlined by Bibring (1954), Gill (1954), and Zetzel (1971).

Second, I think that psychoanalysis and psychotherapy should be most carefully differentiated, and I follow Gill (1954) in this regard. I also believe that the psychoanalytic psychotherapy I have proposed for borderline patients can indeed be differentiated from broader psychotherapeutic approaches which include both expressive or interpretive and supportive measures, and I will dedicate a good part of this paper to spelling out the specific characteristics of my approach.

Third, I think that much of what appears as "ego weakness," in the sense of a defect in these patients, turns out, under a psychoanalytically based exploration, to reflect conflictually determined issues. For example, what first appears as an inability to establish object relations or the unavailability of drive derivatives, or lack of affective response, or simply lack of impulse control eventually reflects active defenses against very intense and primitive object relations in the transference. Obviously, this conviction underlies my stress on the value of an interpretive, in contrast to a supportive, approach with borderline patients. A major additional source for this conviction stems from the Psychotherapy Research Project of the Menninger Foundation (Kernberg et al. 1972), which revealed, contrary to our initial expectations, that borderline patients did much better with an interpretive or expressive approach, and much more poorly with a purely supportive one.

Fourth, while I believe that, in addition to the effects of interpretation, there are also therapeutic effects of the patient-therapist relationship per se which are crucial in the treatment of borderline conditions—and which include ego-supportive effects if not techniques—these nonspecific effects can be best activated in a psychoanalytic atmosphere that combines the therapist's technical neutrality with an interpretive approach. Again, this point will be elaborated upon in what follows.

The focus of this paper is mostly on patients who would not be able to undergo and/or benefit from a standard psychoanalysis, at least not initially or for extended periods of their treatment. I am strongly convinced, however, that only psychoanalytic theory and technique and a solid grasp of normal and pathological psychic development permit the carrying out such modified

treatment procedures as are indicated for these patients. Psychoanalytic psychotherapy, therefore, is a legitimate and even essential technique for the psychoanalyst; it broadens the spectrum of
psychoanalytic work and should not be regarded as a diluted or
even distorted analytic approach. I think we need a strict delim-
itation between psychoanalysis as such and other modalities, a
precise definition of psychotherapeutic procedures, and an integrative theoretical and clinical frame for all psychoanalytically
derived psychotherapeutic approaches. Wallerstein (1969) has
raised some fundamental questions regarding these issues and
comprehensively summarized the literature.

As one effort in this direction I will now attempt to define
"psychoanalytic psychotherapy," referring here to that limited
approach which is based mostly on clarification and interpretation and which corresponds to what Bibring (1954) and Gill (1954)
referred to as exploratory psychotherapy. The implication is that
this interpretive approach should be differentiated sharply from
other psychoanalytically derived procedures. I would tentatively
define psychoanalytic psychotherapy (thus restricted) as the carrying out of interpretive work, including transference interpretation, in the context of a treatment setting of technical neutrality
limited only by the need (stemming from the patient's reality) to
safeguard the patient's immediate life situation and to block
damaging effects of transference acting out: the setting up of
parameters of techniques (Eissler 1953) is determined by these
requirements. I agree with Brenner (1969) in the restricted definition of acting out as transference acting out, and I use the term
"transference acting out" to lay emphasis on the restrictive meaning of the term. "Blocking" of acting out does not refer to
moralistic or omnipotent efforts to control the patient's life, but
to technically required disruption of self-perpetuating behavior
patterns that would otherwise threaten the patient's life, the
treatment itself, or produce chronic therapeutic stalemates. With-

out such "blocking," treatment would not be possible. (The dynamic tension between such measures and the still crucial requirements for moving into a direction of technical neutrality will be dealt with later on.)

Interpretation in psychoanalytic psychotherapy, rather than being determined by the natural sequence of evolving transference paradigms (so that a full-fledged transference neurosis might be systematically worked through), is determined by (1) the requirements of the dynamic combination of the predominant transference paradigm, (2) the urgency of immediate life problems, and (3) the specific overall goals of the treatment.

Considerations of time and space do not permit detailing the reasons that underlie my stress on the importance of these three elements. In brief, I consider the severity of transference acting out of these patients to imply an additional dimension of danger to the continuity of the treatment situation, a danger either nonexistent or much less acute in the ordinary analytic situation. Acting out in borderline patients often includes a dimension of magical playing out of the transference situation in external reality, as part of an effort to deny or destroy all reality that goes counter to the transference wishes; and this needs to be interpreted. With regard to treatment goals, stubborn, long-term treatment stalemates can often be uncovered only in the context of the patient's denial of the passage of time, his treatment of the psychotherapeutic relationship as an "eternal" one, so that a long-range transference acting out may become diagnosable only in terms of comparison of the treatment goals with where the treatment situation has become immobilized over a long period of time.

Insofar as the psychotherapeutic technique proposed still requires a technical position of (or persistent movement toward) neutrality of the analyst and a consistent interpretation of the transference and other resistances, the *tactics* of therapeutic interventions are quite similar to psychoanalysis proper, although the treatment goals and *strategy* are different.

Because this paper focuses on tactical rather than strategical issues, particularly on the interpretation of the transference, the technical considerations included may apply, at least in part, to both a standard psychoanalysis and psychoanalytic psychotherapy of borderline patients. I am emphasizing that some borderline patients may indeed be treated by a nonmodified psychoanalytic procedure. I have outlined my proposals for the treatment of borderline personality organization elsewhere (1968, 1975a, 1975c), and shall only stress here that *the essential task is the diagnosis and resolution of primitive transference paradigms.*

Particularly in the early stages of treatment, the transference is either characterized predominantly by overwhelming chaos, meaninglessness, or emptiness, or it is consciously suppressed or distorted. This usually results from the predominance of "primitive transferences," that is, the activation in the transference of "part-object" relations—or units of early self- and object images and the primitive affects linking them—not characteristic of internal object relations of neurotic patients and normal people. The transference reflects a multitude of internal object relations of dissociated (or split-off) aspects of the self, and highly distorted and fantastic dissociated (or split-off) object representations.

The strategical aim in working through the transference is to resolve these primitive dissociations of self- and internalized objects and thus to transform primitive transferences into higher level or integrated transference reactions, more realistic and more related to real childhood experiences (1975c). Obviously, this requires intensive, long-term treatment along the lines I have suggested, usually not less than three sessions a week over years of treatment. First, the dissociated or generally fragmented aspects of the patient's intrapsychic conflicts are gradually integrated into significant units of primitive internalized object relations.

Second, each unit (constituted of a certain self-image, a certain object image, and a major affect disposition linking these) then needs to be clarified as it becomes activated in the transference, including the alternation of reciprocal self- and object reenactments. Third, when these units can be interpreted and integrated with other related or contradictory units—particularly when libidinally invested and aggressively invested units can be integrated—the process of working through of the transference and of the resolution of primitive constellations of defensive operations characteristic of borderline conditions has begun.

When such a resolution of primitive transferences has occurred, the integrative affect dispositions that now emerge reflect more coherent and differentiated drive derivatives. The integrative object images now reflect more realistic parental images as perceived in early childhood.

Two Clinical Illustrations

Case 1

A thirty-year-old architect had begun psychoanalysis four months earlier with the following major symptoms: chronic feelings of depression, emotional inhibition in group situations, fearfulness of being criticized, and a general feeling of lack of authenticity. The diagnosis was depressive personality with strong paranoid features, and possibly borderline personality organization. In spite of severe pathology of object relations and a strong predominance of primitive—particularly paranoid—defenses, there was sufficient evidence of nonspecific ego strength to warrant a standard psychoanalysis.

From the beginning of his analysis, the patient rapidly shifted from one subject to another during the sessions. What he talked about seemed important, but the manner of presentation seemed to me inauthentic. Either the patient stayed with one subject but talked in an intellectualized way about it, or the subject matter sounded authentic enough, but would only appear for fleeting moments in the middle of other material. The patient seemed distant, almost strangely aloof, and yet had moments of great emotional intensity—gone too fast to be fully understood. He was constantly preoccupied with any possible criticism from me and with the possibility that I might not understand him or might show him a "phony" friendliness.

In one session, the patient began by remembering the impossible situation he felt himself in when he was about ten years old. At this time his mother, a chronically depressed alcoholic, failed to display any warmth or even the merest interest in him. Her interest occurred only when she was under the effect of alcohol, and he experienced it as false and embarrassing; when she was sober, she was cold and distant. Another subject then appeared in his associations, namely, his feelings of dread and guilt over the incapacitating illness of his cousin, who was reduced to almost complete immobility without any hope of improvement. This cousin had been competing with the patient throughout their adolescence, and the patient was quite conscious of his sense of triumph—and yet deep guilt—about this illness. In the past, the patient had experienced fear of my criticizing him because of his sense of triumph over his cousin, and he had once felt irritated at my acknowledgment of his feelings of guilt toward his cousin: the patient felt that my understanding was an expression of phony concern on my part.

In the hour under discussion, the following developments took place in rapid succession: as I was thinking that the patient was irritated at what he saw as my concern over his conflicts with his cousin because he experienced me as being as phony as his mother was when she was seemingly interested in him under the influence of alcohol, the patient said that he was sure I was speculating about this (indeed, guessing my thoughts) and that it reflected my complete lack of understanding of what was going on in the analytic situation. He reminded me that the day before he had accused me of being very critical although attempting to hide that criticism. (I had said something, not critical, which he construed as criticism in response to telling me that he had been smoking pot.) He then said that he really wouldn't mind if I did not understand or were indifferent to him, but he resented what he saw as the rigid, petty, provincial quality of my criticism, a reflection of my rigidity and puritanism related to being part of the psychoanalytic establishment.

He then thought of his wife, a businesswoman whose functions took her out of town for several days at a time, and speculated whether she would ever have an affair while being away. In contrast to the earlier associations about his mother and his cousin, these latter ones seemed to contain more direct, strong, although fleeting, emotions. A silence ensued, and the patient said that he could imagine my clicking away various interpretations and trying to hide from him my insecurity.

My conviction gradually strengthened that the most important thing going on was the patient's almost desperate need to fill the hour with material that would seem important to me—while he would remain "one step ahead" and attempt to keep control over my thinking and feeling. Something very actively going on in the transference was being submerged by the patient's attempt at "thought control." I finally told him I thought he was trying to bring up a number of matters that were meaningful, indeed, but that now served the purpose of preventing the emergence of a more dreaded emotional experience regarding me.

He then became anxious, started to breathe rapidly, and said that something was terrorizing him but he couldn't explain it. He had had moments when he experienced terror when his mother—who had died during the patient's preadolescent years—looked at him shortly before the time of her death. He then remembered the administrator of the building he lived in, whom he thought was dishonest and tried to control people in surreptitious ways (and, if that were not possible, by force); the patient said that he felt like terminating his analysis right then and there. It turned out that, at one level, the patient was identifying me with the sick cousin and his dying mother, while he identified himself with the controlling, sadistic, dishonest administrator. This relationship, in turn, was a defense against the opposite one: on a deeper level, he was the potential victim and I, the persecutor.

It eventually became clearer to him that he was attempting to escape from an experience of undefinable dread in the hour, related to the image of me as somebody who would hatefully attack him after pretending either indifference or phony interest. What I wish to stress is the uncanny nature of this emotional experience, the overwhelming fear and dread of my aggression, the fantastic nature of the image of me, and the difference between this essential primitive aspect of the transference, on the one hand, and the various more sophisticated transference dispositions related to his guilt and aggression toward his mother, his competition with the cousin, and the jealousy of his wife, on the other.

The rapid shift of his associations, the "invasive" quality of his focus on my thinking, his disqualification of my comments, and the rapid shift of his feelings and attitudes, all brought about a chaotic combination of material in the middle of which it was hard to say what object relation activated in the transference was predominant. The reconstruction of that dominant object relation on the basis of the examination of the total situation in the hour—including my emotional reactions to the material—permitted clarification of the nature of the primitive transference activated in the psychoanalytic situation. This case, it needs to be stressed, was still a rather "standard" analytic case; the next one is a more typically regressed borderline patient.

Case 2

A graduate student in her late twenties had begun psychoanalytic psychotherapy (three sessions a week) a few weeks earlier because of a severe depressive reaction—with weight loss and suicidal ideation, alcoholism, and a general breakdown in her functioning at school, in her social life, and in her love relation with her boyfriend. The diagnosis was infantile personality with borderline features, severe depressive reaction, and symptomatic alcoholism. This treatment was carried out in "face-to-face" sessions. (For reasons I have mentioned in an earlier work [Kernberg 1975a], I only utilize the couch in cases of standard psychoanalysis, and never in cases of psychoanalytic psychotherapy as defined, or with any modality of psychotherapeutic treatment.) In the beginning of the treatment, I had established a number of conditions under which I would be willing to see her on an outpatient basis. If she could not fulfill these conditions, I would see her in psychotherapy and she would remain in the hospital until she became ready to fulfill these conditions. Hospitalization had been suggested by other psychiatrists who had seen the patient, and I, too, had contemplated it as an alternative, in case she proved unable to take responsibility for her immediate functioning in reality.

Insofar as I made these preconditions, one might say that a selective process took place and that only a limited range of borderline patients would accept and be able to undergo the kind of treatment approach proposed. However, it must be pointed out that this patient had available as an alternative the possibility of short-term (or long-term) hospitalization, and that, if needed, I would expect hospitalization at a minimum to develop the patient's capacity to take responsibility for such functions as are indispensable in any case for outpatient treatment. The implication is that the opposite approach, namely, to accept outpatient treatment on a less than realistic basis, would bring about a more complicated and potentially disastrous course of treatment. In other words, a therapist cannot do justice to his patient's needs if the therapist does not have the minimum requirements and freedom for full deployment of his special technical knowledge and capabilities.

This patient had committed herself to stop drinking, not to act on suicidal impulses while discussing them openly with me (if and when they occurred), and to maintain a minimum weight by eating sufficiently, regardless of her mood and appetite. A psychiatric social worker was beginning an evaluation of the patient's total social situation, including her relations with her parents (who lived in a different town) and was available to the patient for any suggestion and advice, if needed, regarding any problem in her daily life. Our understanding was that the social worker would convey full information about the patient to me, and that I would communicate to the social worker only such information I considered crucial and that the patient had explicitly authorized me to transmit. My psychotherapeutic approach was essentially psychoanalytic, and I attempted to maintain a consistent position of technical neutrality (further discussion of which will follow).

In the session to be described, the patient looked haggard and distraught; it had been raining, and she had not taken precautions to dress correspondingly, so that she came without raincoat or umbrella, drenching wet, the thinness of her body showing under the wet clothes. Her blouse and pants were dirty, and she looked somewhat disheveled. She began talking immediately about a difficult test she would have to take at school that she was afraid she would not pass. She then talked about a serious fight with her boyfriend; she felt jealous because of his interest in another woman, a former girlfriend of his whom, the patient had discovered, he had met with secretly. She also expressed concern over her parents' sending her the monthly check (which produced in me the fantasy that she wanted to reassure me: she would be paying for her treatment, and therefore, even if I were fed up with her otherwise, it would still be in my interest to continue seeing her in spite of her "unlikable" nature).

The patient's flow of verbal communication seemed to be disrupted by a variety of nonverbal behaviors. Sporadically, she fell silent and looked at me with a searching, distrustful, and somewhat withdrawn expression; there were moments of inappropriate, artificial gaiety, and a forced laughter, which conveyed to me her conscious efforts to control our interaction. She became "confused" in telling me where she had met her boyfriend and the other woman—which made me wonder whether she had been drinking without daring to let me know about it. Information from the psychiatric social worker came to my mind: the patient had casually observed to her that she had had stomach aches and had been vomiting in recent days, and the social worker wondered whether the patient would need another medical check-up.

I now oscillated between moments of concern and strong urges to express this concern to the patient in terms of the deterioration of her physical appearance, her health, and the question whether she would really be able to maintain the outpatient treatment setting we had agreed upon. I was also tempted to confront her with those aspects in her behavior which made me wonder whether she was telling me the truth. I felt an underlying fearfulness in her, and an experience of me as a potentially critical and inflexible parental figure who would scold her for not being truthful or for behaving poorly. (All this was superimposed on my feeling that she desperately wanted me to take over and run her life.) I now became aware of a growing sense of impatience in myself, a combination of worry for the patient and yet irritation that the treatment program as set up was falling apart, and that inordinate demands were being made on the psychiatric social

worker and on me to change the treatment arrangements, mobi-
lize her parents, and protect her against the impending threat of
dismissal from school (another reality aspect which had brought
her into treatment).

I finally felt that the predominant human relationship enacted
at that moment was of a frightened little girl who wanted a
powerful parental figure (the particular sexual identity of whom
was irrelevant) to take over and protect her from pain and fear,
from suffering in general. At the same time, I thought she hated
that parental figure because such a taking over could only be
forced by extreme circumstances of the patient's suffering and not
by natural concern, love, and dedication to her. And she was
afraid of a retaliatory attack from that needed and yet resented
parental figure because she projected her own angry demands
onto it. Therefore, I felt, she had to escape from that dreaded
relationship, perhaps drink herself into oblivion, and create a
situation of chaos in which she would be rescued without having
to acknowledge or emotionally relate to the rescuer as an enemy
to fight off.

I now said to the patient that, on the basis of what she seemed
to be communicating, I had the feeling that she was expressing
contradictory wishes: she wanted to reassure me that she was still
in control over her life, while at the same time she was conveying
almost dramatically that things were falling apart, that she was
unable to handle her life, and that she was running the risk of
illness, expulsion from school, and loss of her boyfriend. I added
that, if I were correct, whatever I might do under these circumstances would be disastrous to her: on the one hand, if I explored
further whether she was really able to handle her immediate life
situation, she would experience this as an attack. For example, if
I raised the question whether, under these circumstances, she felt
able to continue not to drink, it would be a "cross examination"
revealing my basic harshness and suspiciousness of her. If, on the

other hand, I sympathetically listened without raising any of these questions, it would be like an indifferent, callous expression of a psychiatrist mostly worried about whether he would be paid by the patient's parents. In either case, she could expect only suffering and disappointment from my potential reactions to her.

The patient replied that she had been worried because she had been drinking and was afraid I would hospitalize her if I knew. She had also thought that, because of her parents' lateness in sending her the money, I might be worried about receiving my fee, and she had been angry at her parents and embarrassed about this lateness. She said she felt completely hopeless about herself, and didn't know how this psychotherapy could help her. I said I thought she was not so much worried about whether the psychotherapy would help her, but whether I was genuinely interested in her, or just concerned about getting paid for the sessions. I also said that I wondered whether she felt that the only way of obtaining anything from me was by forcing it from me, extracting it, so to speak, by presenting herself as if she were a completely helpless human wreck. I added that, under the circumstances, any help from me would be like the irritated, angry reaction of a parent who would prefer not to be bothered, but had no alternative but to take care of an unwanted child.

The patient burst into tears, said how desolate she felt because her boyfriend was leaving her, adding with real feeling that she felt she had no right to be helped by me, there were many people like her, and only because of the fortunate circumstance that her parents had money was she able to afford treatment that would otherwise be unavailable. Why should she be treated, when there was so much suffering in the world? It was better to give up.

At this moment, I felt that a change had occurred in the hour: now her verbal communications and her behavior coincided. She had become open in telling me about what had actually happened during the last two days, and there was an awareness of and worry over her sense of failure, mixed with a strange sense of relief at failing because she felt she did not deserve better. I felt that the patient was becoming concerned for herself in the process of this interchange, that the pressure on me for taking over was decreasing, and that she was beginning to feel guilty for having failed to keep her part of our agreement, while beginning to understand that this failure was an expression of her sense that she did not deserve to be helped.

What I wish to stress is that the situation now became a more coherent transference situation in which a masochistic character pattern was expressed in a mostly pregenital, conflictually dependent relation to a frustrating parental image. The intersystemic conflict between superego features (unconscious guilt) and the dependency conflictually expressed by her ego now reflected a rather typical neurotic object relation in the transference. This development, then, needs to be contrasted with the earlier, chaotic, contradictory manifestations of implicit suspicion, projected anger, aggressive demandingness, concealment, and withdrawal. I would also stress that the reduction of the chaotic transference manifestations into the predominant object relation expressed in the transference permitted the full exploration of the transference and life situations and the activation of ego resources that made it unnecessary for the analyst to intervene on the patient's behalf. In other words, the approach from a position of technical neutrality permitted a strengthening, if only temporarily, of the patient's ego and a fostering of her capacity to combine understanding in the hour with an increasing sense of responsibility for her life outside the treatment hours.

Further Considerations Regarding the Characteristics of Primitive Transference and Their Interpretation

What follows are some technical considerations that seem to me of particular relevance for the psychoanalyst treating bor-

derline patients with psychoanalysis or psychoanalytic psychotherapy, and an attempt to elucidate further some of the implications of the general principles of treatment mentioned earlier in
this paper.

Borderline patients characteristically present primitive transferences. In practice, this means that the activation of an ordinary
transference is replaced by an impulse derivative of a more
primitive nature, often by peculiar condensations of aggressive
and libidinal drive derivatives reflected in diffuse, overwhelming
affect states. Instead of a definite projection of a certain infantile
object image onto the analyst while the patient reactivates aspects
of the infantile self in that relation, borderline patients reactivate
dissociated self- and object images, with rapid oscillation of the
projection of either self- or object component of that relation
onto the analyst. The projected object image is often highly
unrealistic or strange, and does not reflect the repetition of a real
infantile or childhood experience; the patient's self-experience in
regard to this object image projected onto the analyst also reflects
a bizarre, strange experience of the self that is not linked to or
integrated with a more global infantile self activated in the
transference.

In other words, the ordinary object relation in the neurotic
transference is replaced by a fantastic relationship in primitive
transferences, within which subject and object are easily inter-
changeable and remarkably unrelated to the usual or predominant characteristics of the particular infantile self or parental
figure involved. The diffuse, overwhelming, nonmodulated characteristics of the affects involved are particularly striking in
regard to the intensity of anxiety, which frequently borders on
panic; the affects reflecting dependency, love, and aggression are
dissociated from other, contradictory feelings toward the same
object that may be present in the transference only minutes or
hours before or after that particular affect is present. In short,

affects, self-images, and object images shift rapidly and chaotically, and the reconstruction of more complex and integrated past object relations requires that the analyst try to integrate the mutually dissociated transference aspects into what eventually reflects more realistic childhood experiences.

What complicates the picture further is that, not only is there a rapid escalation or change of transference dispositions (which gives an overall chaotic picture to the transference developments), but the very nature of primitive defensive operations—particularly severe forms of splitting (leading to fragmentation of all emotional experience), omnipotent control, and devaluation, etc.—all bring about a general deterioration or destruction of human experience in the hours, so that even the dissociated primitive internalized object relations are at first unavailable and may need to be reactivated or reconstructed by means of the interpretation of these primitive defenses. In other words, often the analyst's task is first to work through meaninglessness, generalized dispersal of emotions, and paralyzing emptiness or distortions in the hours, in order to permit the full development, later, of the primitive transference manifestations mentioned. Only later still, and very gradually, may these chaotic transference dispositions be integrated into broader transference paradigms of the usual neurotic kind.

The implications for the technique of diagnosing and interpreting the transference are that the analyst has to focus sharply on manifestations of emptiness, meaninglessness, distortion, and control, which stand in the way of the full deployment of primitive transference dispositions. Once a human relationship has been activated in the transference so that the experience of the analyst is of being part of a primitive, overwhelming, emotionally charged relationship, the analyst has to diagnose and verbalize the nature of this relation and to define the self- and object component in it. The questions one may ask regarding any transference manifestation, namely, "Who is saying or doing what to whom now and why?" (Heimann 1956) will have to be answered, under typical circumstances with borderline patients, in terms of a highly unrealistic, primitive interaction between an aspect of the self and fantastically distorted object representations. It is only after such primitive relations have been diagnosed, clarified, and spelled out repeatedly—while their self- and object aspects are exchanged, as it were, between patient and analyst—that the defensive quality of the mutual dissociation of these primitive transferences can be diagnosed and interpreted and an integration of self- and object components can occur.

The characteristics of the transferences of borderline patients make genetic reconstructions very difficult or impossible. Insofar as the primitive transference dispositions reflect fantastic, unreal, internal relations of dissociated aspects of the self with "part objects," what is reconstructed is really an internal world of object relations expressed largely in primary-process thinking, with qualities of timelessness and condensation of various stages of psychosexual development, all of which make genetic reconstructions highly speculative, to put it mildly. It is only at later stages of treatment, when more realistic childhood experiences are reactivated in more advanced levels of transference manifestations, that efforts to reconstruct genetically significant childhood conflicts become possible and effective. It is a typical characteristic of the clinical study of borderline patients that the initial history reveals little of what later on turn out to be the main transference paradigms in the treatment, and the differences between initial information and genetic reconstructions are much sharper than is the case with the average neurotic patient.

Therefore, the analyst has to tolerate a state of ignorance and uncertainty about the genetic continuity of the material activated in the transference that exceeds by far that of the ordinary psychoanalytic treatment. What makes the situation even more difficult is the very intensity of primitive transferences and the weakening of reality testing in the area of projection onto the therapist of primitive impulses and self- and/or object images. Primitive types of projection, particularly projective identification, bring about a confusion, on the part of the patient, of present interaction with past internal object relations. The reason for this is the patient's confusion of what is "inside" and what is "outside" under these circumstances, so that ego boundaries, reality testing, and secondary-process thinking are all weakened. Any premature efforts to achieve immediate genetic reconstructions of such fantastic transferences may induce in the patient the conviction that the fantastic internal object relation was at one time—and is again now—a real one, and past and present are just the same. In other words, premature genetic reconstruction may foster transference psychosis.

The nature of primitive transferences in borderline patients presents certain technical problems and dangers. The analyst may be tempted to interpret these transferences directly, as if they reflected the actual, earliest, or most primitive human experiences; he might even go so far as to interpret them as a genetic reconstruction of the first few years or even the first few months of life, thus confusing or condensing primitive fantasy and actual earliest development, characteristic of some Kleinian work. The Kleinian approach combines, in my opinion, two errors: first, the mistaking of the primitive, bizarre intrapsychic elaboration of psychic experience with actual developmental features, and second, the telescoping of complex, slowly developing structural organization of internalized object relations with assumed (and highly questionable) developments in the first few months of life.

A second danger can result from assuming a simplistic ego-psychological approach. The intense activation of affects in a patient with little capacity for observing what he is experiencing may lead the analyst to focus on ego functioning, to the neglect of the object-relations implications of what is activated in the transference. The analyst may focus, for example, on the patient's difficulty in experiencing or expressing his feelings or overcoming silence, his tendency to impulsive actions, or his temporary loss of logical clarity, instead of on the total primitive human interaction (or the defenses against it) activated in the transference. A mistake in the opposite direction would be to interpret the object relation "in depth" without paying sufficient heed to the patient's ego functions. A further danger is of focusing exclusively on the "here and now," in the context of conceptualizing the transference as a corrective emotional "encounter" and neglecting the task of gradually integrating self- and object images into more realistic internalized object relations and advanced types of transference that will permit more realistic genetic reconstructions. Here, the analyst unwillingly or unwittingly may contribute to the stability of primitive transferences (as the treatment replaces life), thus interfering with the patient's ego growth.

To give simultaneous attention to the "here and now" and to the underlying primitive internalized object relations activated in the transference, so that what is on the surface and what is deepest are integrated into human experiences of ever-growing complexity, is implicit in the technical approach I have proposed. In this process, whatever remnant the patient has of a capacity for self-observation and autonomous work on his problems must be explored, highlighted, and reinforced, so that attention is given to the patient's ego functioning, particularly to his self-observing ego function, hand in hand with the clarification and verbalization of primitive object relations reflected in his conscious and unconscious fantasies.

Fenichel's (1941) general rule of interpretation—to proceed from surface to depth—certainly applies to borderline patients. It is helpful if we first share our observations with the patient, stimulate him to integrate them a step beyond what is immediately observable, and only interpret beyond his own awareness when it is clear that he cannot do so himself. Further, whenever we interpret beyond the patient's awareness of the transference situation, we should include in our interpretation the reasons for his unawareness. Inasmuch as primitive transference dispositions imply a rapid shift to a deep level of experience, the analyst working with borderline patients must be preapred to shift his focus from the "here and now" to the fantasied object relation activated in the transference—one that often includes bizarre and primitive characteristics which the analyst has to dare to make verbally explicit as far as his understanding permits. Moreover, one must also be alert to the danger that the patient interpret what the analyst has said as a magical statement, derived from a magical understanding, rather than a realistic putting-together of what the patient has communicated to him.

Integrative aspects of the interpretations, therefore, include consistent interpretation of surface and depth. The same procedure applies to the patient's communications, so that when apparently "deep" material comes up in the patient's communications it is important to clarify, first, to what extent the patient is expressing an emotional experience, an intellectual speculation, a fantasy, or a delusional conviction. One question the analyst often has to ask himself in the treatment of borderline patients, "Should I now clarify reality, or should I now interpret in depth?" can usually be answered by evaluating the patient's reality testing at the moment, his capacity for self-observation, and the disorganizing effects of primitive defensive operations in the transference. Ideally, clarification of reality and interpretation in depth should be integrated, but that is often not immediately possible.

Surprisingly enough, as one's experience with this kind of treatment of borderline patients grows, one finds more and more that what seemed at first a simple manifestation of ego weakness or ego defect turns out to be the effect of very specific, active, primitive defensive operations directed against full awareness (on the part of the patient) of a dissociated transference relation reflecting intrapsychic conflicts. In other words, this treatment approach permits us to diagnose areas of ego weakness, to evaluate the ego-weakening effects of primitive defensive operations and of dissociated internalized object relations, and to foster ego growth by essentially interpretive means. Clarifications of reality made by the analyst often subsequently turn out to have been an unnecessary support feeding into a certain transference situation. Whenever this is the case, it is very helpful to interpret to the patient how an apparently necessary clarification by the analyst was actually not necessary at all.

Often the question arises whether to further clarify the reality of the patient or interpret the meaning of the patient's distortion of reality. If one proceeds from the surface to depth, first testing the limits of the patient's understanding, and then interpreting the defensive aspects of the patient's lack of awareness of an appropriate perception of (or reaction to) reality, one can usually resolve this apparent alternative in a basically analytic fashion. The danger always exists that the patient will interpret our interpretation of his defensive denial of reality as a subtle attempt to influence him. Therefore, in addition to our introspective evaluation of whether the patient may be right in this regard, this distortion of our interpretation has to be interpreted as well. In essence, technical neutrality, interpretation of the transference, the analyst's introspective exploration of his countertransference, and focus on the patient's perceptions in the hour are all intimately linked technical tools.

A related problem of the analyst working with borderline conditions is to what extent he should intervene quickly in an interpretive fashion or wait until the patient is ready to do further work on his own. In general, once operational understanding has been achieved, I think few advantages are gained from simply waiting. Insofar as primitive transferences are activated rapidly in the hours and tend to perpetuate themselves in a repetition compulsion which often defies long-term interpretative work, there is an advantage to interpreting the material fully as soon as it is clear enough and whenever a certain transference disposition becomes a predominant transference resistance. There are borderline patients who activate one kind of transference pattern in an endless repetition over many months and years, and an early interpretive stance may not only save much time, but protect the patient from destructive acting out. At the same time, an interpretive approach that deals rapidly with the developing transference resistances does not imply bypassing the patient's own capacity for self-observation: I wish to stress again that interpretation in depth should include an ongoing evaluation of the patient's capacity for self-observation and never justify the patient's hopes (or fears) of a magical relation with an omnipotent therapist. Very often, simply waiting for the patient to improve in his self-observing capacities is of little usefulness and creates the danger of bringing about chronic countertransference distortions which gradually undermine the analyst's position of technical neutrality.

I have mentioned elsewhere (1975c) the need to rapidly deepen the level of interpretation when the patient begins to act out. Although there is a risk of interpreting beyond the level of emotional understanding reached by the patient at that point—and a risk, therefore, that the interpretation be either rejected or incorporated in intellectualized or magical ways—the focus on the patient's relation to the interpretation will make it possible to correct such potential misfirings of quick interpretations of the transference at such time.

Another important aspect of the analysis of the transference of borderline conditions is the tenuous nature of the therapeutic alliance as compared with that of ordinary neurotic cases in a standard psychoanalysis. The therapeutic alliance (Greenson 1965, Zetzel 1956) links the analyst as such—a professional in a special work relation with the patient—and the observing part of the patient's ego, however small or limited, in the treatment situation. Insofar as there is a sufficient observing part of the patient's ego in the ordinary neurotic case, the therapeutic alliance or, one might say, the task-oriented alliance between the patient's observing ego and the analyst, is a given, ordinarily not requiring too much attention. However, even under ideal circumstances in the typical psychoanalytic case, there are times when the intensity of the transference relation threatens to overwhelm temporarily the patient's observing ego, and it may be necessary to focus the patient's attention on that complication. In contrast, the observing ego in the typical borderline case is so limited and frail that the question has been raised to what extent there is a need to focus attention strongly, consistently on the therapeutic alliance. Are there times when the analyst needs to take active measures to strengthen the therapeutic alliance by reality-oriented, supportive comments or by providing the patient with information regarding the analyst's reality aspects?

In my opinion, to focus on the defensive use or nature of the distortions of the patient's perceptions, and, particularly, on his distortions of the analyst's interpretations, is the best means of strengthening the patient's observing ego without shifting from an essentially analytic model. The various aspects of the real relation between analyst and patient are, it seems to me, a nonspecific, potentially therapeutic aspect of the treatment in all cases. However, this aspect of the total treatment relationship is rather limited in the ordinary psychoanalytic case, and the systematic analysis of all transference paradigms in the unfolding transference neurosis should lead to a systematic working through of the patient's efforts to use the therapeutic relationship as a parental function in the transference. In other words, the nonspecific supportive implications of the real aspects of the relationship in terms of the patient's unfolding transference will automatically become part of the analytic work and remain in the background. In borderline patients, on the other hand, the nonspecific, "real" human relationship reflected in the therapeutic alliance may constitute an important corrective emotional experience, not in the sense of the therapist's adopting an active, manipulative stance, but in the sense of the normally gratifying nature of such a positive human and working relation, which often goes far beyond anything the patient had previously experienced. Insofar as chronically traumatizing or frustrating circumstances of early development and, therefore, of the patient's former relations with the real parents, are an important aspect of the genetic and historical background of borderline patients, the real relation with the therapist may carry out parental functions the patient has never had before.

In addition, the therapist's being available to absorb, organize, and transform the patient's chaotic intrapsychic experience (which the therapist first attempts to clarify in his own mind and then reflects back to the patient as part of his interpretive comments) does provide cognitive functions which the ordinary neurotic patient undergoing a standard psychoanalysis is expected to carry out for himself. In other words, the therapist does provide auxiliary cognitive ego functions for the borderline patient in addition to the implicit reassurance given by his abilities to withstand and not be destroyed by the patient's aggression, to neither fall apart nor retaliate, to maintain a general attitude of concern and emotional availability toward the patient. Others have stressed the importance of the therapist's "mothering" functions with borderline patients (Little 1958, 1960, Winnicott 1958). These aspects of the therapeutic relationship undoubtedly play an important role in the psychoanalytic psychotherapy of borderline patients, and, as long as they occur within a setting of technical neutrality, constitute a legitimate use of the psychotherapeutic relationship. This use has to be differentiated from the patient's intense transference demands that the analyst gratify those needs that were previously frustrated, and carry out active parental functions, thus abandoning the position of technical neutrality and increasing the supportive aspects of the therapeutic relationship. I cannot emphasize strongly enough the need for the psychoanalyst working with the borderline patient to carefully analyze all these attempts on the patient's part. What really strengthens the patient's ego is not the gratification of needs in the "here and now" that were denied in the "there and then," but coming to terms with past frustrations and limitations in the context of understanding the pathological reactions, impulses, and defenses that were activated under those past traumatic circumstances and which contributed importantly to the development and fixation of ego weakness.

Technical Neutrality and Interpretation

I have stressed (1968, 1975a) how crucial it is that the psychotherapist of the borderline patient remain in a position of technical neutrality—equidistant from external reality, the patient's superego, his instinctual needs, and his acting (in contrast to observing) ego (A. Freud 1936). It is necessary to set limits for many borderline patients so that they do not act out in ways that threaten their treatment or safety. Sometimes the therapist has to spell out certain conditions the patient must meet in order for outpatient psychoanalytic psychotherapy to proceed. The setting up of such conditions for treatment represents, of course, the setting up of parameters of technique (Eissler 1953). By the same token, the setting up of such parameters implies a reduction of the position of technical neutrality, and, beyond a certain point, it is questionable whether a standard psychoanalysis can be carried out. Even when the treatment is psychoanalytic psychotherapy rather than analysis proper, if the therapist remains constantly vigilant to his deviations from technical neutrality, it will help him to evaluate the extent to which transference acting out is occurring, and the extent to which chronic countertransference distortions are complicating the treatment situation.

It may be helpful to stress that, as Freud pointed out (1963), technical neutrality does not mean "listless indifference," or lack of spontaneity and natural warmth. Neutrality implies, rather, a sufficient degree of objectivity combined with an authentic concern for the patient. It also implies a relative degree of freedom from impingement of general theoretical formulations that would interfere with his immediate attention to the patient, and from pressures of any kind to move, push, direct, or coach the patient into any particular direction. Technical neutrality, thus conceived, guarantees not only the analyst's freedom to carry out psychoanalytic work, but maximal protection of the patient's autonomy and independence and his capacity to carry out work on his own (in contrast to acting out excessive dependency in the transference).

In the treatment of borderline patients, neutrality constitutes an "ideal" but ever-transitory situation, which is threatened continuously from various sources. The danger of acting out and reality conflicts of borderline patients which threaten their well-being, the treatment itself, or even their life, may induce in the analyst an urge to act rather than interpret. The effect of primitive defensive operations, particularly of projective identification, is not only to attribute a certain mental disposition to the analyst, but to induce in him a certain emotional disposition which complements the patient's own affective state, an urge to act in a certain direction which complements the transference needs. Neutrality is thus challenged or threatened, although by the same token, every momentary threat to or deviation from technical neutrality imparts important transference information.

The primitive nature of the transference activated in borderline patients leads the analyst, as he strives to empathize with the patient, to whatever capacity he may have for awareness of primitive emotional reactions within himself. This is reinforced by the patient's nonverbal behavior, especially those aspects of it that attempt to control the analyst, to impose on him, so to speak, the role assigned to the self or to an object image within the primitive activated transference. We probably still do not know enough about how one person's behavior may induce emotional and behavioral reactions in another. The analyst's emotional empathy, his creative use of evenly hovering attention—a function akin to daydreaming—and the direct impact of behavioral perception, all combine to bring about a temporary regressive reaction that permits him to identify with the patient's primitive levels of functioning.

In order to maintain an optimal degree of inner freedom for exploring his own emotional reactions and fantasy formations in connection with the patient's material, the analyst who treats borderline patients must be particularly concerned that he intervene only when he has again reached a technically neutral position. It is especially important to maintain a consistent attitude of "abstinence"—in the sense of not giving in to the patient's demands for transference gratification, and rather to interpret fully and consistently these transference demands. The analyst's humanity, warmth, and concern will come through naturally in his ongoing attention to and work with the patient's difficulties in the transference, and in his ability to absorb and yet not react to the onslaught of the demands stemming from primitive dependent, sexual, and aggressive needs.

In short, technical neutrality, attention to abstinence in the transference, preservation of the internal freedom for analyzing the transference, and, introspectively only, the counter-transference components of the analyst's emotional reaction are intimately linked aspects of the overall technical approach to borderline patients.

Psychoanalysis or Psychoanalytic Psychotherapy?

The analyst's position of technical neutrality in the treatment of borderline patients may be helped by an early, informed, and well-considered decision as to whether the patient will be treated with standard psychoanalysis, or modified, psychoanalytic psychotherapy will be the treatment of choice. The implication of such an early decision is that a degree of ego weakness that would contraindicate a psychoanalysis proper, or a potential for severe acting out that would interfere with the maintenance of a standard psychoanalytic situation, can be evaluated as part of the diagnostic process, and one can thus prevent or foresee excessive pressures on the analyst, once the treatment has started, for moving away from a position of technical neutrality.

While most borderline patients, in my opinion, do best with modified psychoanalytic psychotherapy along the lines I have proposed for these conditions, there are borderline patients who can be analyzed without modifications of technique, and I have become more optimistic in this regard in recent years. Perhaps the most important criteria of whether a borderline patient is analyzable are, in addition to the potential for early severe acting out and the extent to which there is an observing ego, two considerations. First, the extent to which there exists a certain superego integration, so that the patient presents only very limited antisocial trends. When antisocial trends are marked, there is usually a danger that conscious distortion and lying will become an important feature of the treatment: under these circumstances, psychoanalysis proper becomes very difficult indeed, or impossible.

Second, the extent to which object relations have evolved so that at least some advanced, neurotic transferences—in contrast to more primitive ones—are available.

The implication is that, when the patient has some capacity for differentiated relationships in depth with other human beings, there is less risk of the disorganizing effects of primitive transferences on the analytic situation. In simple terms, when differentiated oedipal features are strongly present from the beginning of treatment, and realistic, integrated kinds of transferences are available in addition to the chaotic, bizarre, and fragmented ones of borderline conditions, a standard psychoanalysis may be indicated. This is particularly the case in infantile personalities with hysterical features functioning on a borderline level.

Care in diagnosis and equal care in deciding on the mode of treatment to be used will help to resolve some of the potential sources of complication in the treatment. Once the decision has been made that a psychoanalytic psychotherapy, rather than psychoanalysis proper, will be carried out, the next question is, to what extent there will be a need for structuralization of the patient's life outside the treatment hours, for setting of limits and the introduction of auxiliary therapists, hospital setting, or psychiatric social work as part of the treatment arrangement. The issue is the extent to which the analyst will be free to deal with the transference in a technically neutral way in the hours (because the dangerous, destructive or self-destructive potential of the patient will be taken care of elsewhere). Many of these arrangements represent significant parameters of technique, and the analyst's clear awareness of them and their strategic consideration as situations he should eventually try to interpret will also help to maintain neutrality in other areas.

The therapist's deviation from technical neutrality in the form of directive behavior may be of such intensity and/or duration that technical neutrality cannot be achieved or recovered, and modifications—rather than parameters—have been established. Under optimal circumstances, gradual interpretation of temporary deviations from technical neutrality are possible, leading to a reversion to a neutral stance which maximizes the possibility for transference interpretation and resolution of primitive transferences.

Paradoxically, it may be very helpful for the analyst who treats borderline patients in long-term psychoanalytic psychotherapy or in analysis to also have an active, general psychiatric experience with brief, crisis-intervention type treatments with other such patients. In other words, when the analyst feels secure doing short-term, supportive psychotherapy or crisis intervention and can remain firmly in an analytic stance, the pressure on him for "action" decreases. A broad level of experience, the capacity to carry out alternative modalities of treatment, and a careful, complete diagnostic evaluation, all contribute to permitting the analyst to maintain a serene and firm position while interpreting the patient's acting out and complex transference developments.

One rationalization for countertransference acting out is the analyst's impression that the patient is not able to handle a certain situation analytically because it corresponds to a particular "ego defect." Frequently, such ego defects turn out to be complicated transference resistances that were not fully analyzed because, in part, of countertransference developments interfering with full analytic exploration at periods of acting out. If the patient does present important ego defects, these should be evident enough to make it possible to evaluate them as part of the diagnostic process, and then to explore them in the early stages of treatment as part of the evaluation of the patient's perceptions in the hours, particularly, his perceptions of the analyst's interpretations.

At times, mistakes in indicating psychoanalysis or psychoanalytic psychotherapy for borderline patients are unavoidable, and there are cases which, after a period of time, require a revision of the treatment modality. If a psychoanalysis that seemed at first indicated later appears contraindicated, it is relatively easy or safe to shift the modality into psychotherapy. The principal reasons for this shift may be the analyst's awareness that persistent severe acting out cannot be controlled by interpretation alone and threatens the continuity of the treatment or even the patient's physical or psychological survival. At times, reality conditions (often brought about in part or totally by the patient's illness) deteriorate, and create vicious circles that interfere with analytic work. At other times, the prevalence of primitive transferences and primitive defensive operations evolve into a full-fledged transference psychosis, with a loss of reality testing in the treatment hours and the impossibility of reconstituting an observing ego on the basis of an interpretative approach. Under these circumstances, the analyst may re-evaluate the situation with the patient, clarify the nature of the problems that unexpectedly changed the total therapeutic situation, and transform the analysis into a psychotherapy. In practice, this usually also means sitting the patient up and carrying out face-to-face interviews: I see no advantage and only disadvantages in carrying out a psychoanalytic psychotherapy on the couch rather than face to face (1975b).

In the case of the opposite situation, this is, when what started as a psychoanalytic psychotherapy should in the therapist's opinion be transformed into a psychoanalysis, the situation is more difficult. Usually, under these circumstances, there has been a development of non-neutral stances on the part of the analyst, and the establishment of parameters or even modifications of technique which may distort the transference relation to such an extent that analysis becomes difficult or impossible. Therefore, the more technically neutral the position of the psychotherapist in a psychoanalytic psychotherapy with borderline patients, the easier will be such a shift into psychoanalysis if indicated. Now the analyst has to ask himself searchingly to what extent he has utilized supportive techniques (in the form of manipulative or suggestive comments) or made supportive use of the transference rather than analyzing it. If the analyst can answer these questions satisfactorily in the sense that the major transference distortions or departures from neutrality can be resolved analytically, the case may still be shifted into psychoanalysis.

At other times, particularly if a shift from psychotherapy to psychoanalysis seems indicated after months or even years of treatment, this is, when the patient has sufficiently improved in psychotherapy to make psychoanalysis possible, it may be preferable to evaluate the situation fully with the patient, set up certain goals that should be accomplished in psychotherapy itself before terminating it, and then consider the possibility of a termination of psychotherapy with indication of starting a psychoanalysis—if still needed—later on. Under these conditions, it is ideal if the patient remains without treatment for a period—at least six to twelve months—so that the total effect of the psychotherapy can be re-evaluated after the patient has functioned independently for a time and the mourning processes connected with termination of psychotherapy have a chance to resolve. Ideally, under these circumstances, the patient should start psychoanalysis with a different analyst.

The application of psychoanalytic theory and technique to the diagnostic study and treatment of borderline conditions has, it seems to me, opened new modalities of psychotherapeutic treatment for these patients, and has extended the indications of psychoanalytic treatment itself. I would hope that some of the findings derived from applying a psychoanalytic technique to borderline conditions have applications in nonborderline conditions as well. There are many situations in the psychoanalytic treatment of basically nonborderline patients where primitive transferences and defenses become apparent, and the understanding gained in psychoanalysis and psychoanalytic psycho-therapy of borderline conditions should be helpful for these other situations as well. A task still wide open is the formulation of an integrative, comprehensive theory of psychotherapeutic technique on a psychoanalytic basis.

References

Bibring, E. (1954). Psychoanalysis and the dynamic psychotherapies. *Journal of the American Psychoanalytic Association* 2:745–770.

Brenner, C. (1969). Some comments on technical precepts in psychoanalysis. *Journal of the American Psychoanalytic Association* 17:333–352.

Eissler, K. R. (1953). The effect of the structure of the ego on psychoanalytic technique. *Journal of the American Psychoanalytic Association* 1:104–143.

Fenichel, O. (1941). *Problems of Psychoanalytic Technique.* Albany: Psychoanalytic Quarterly Inc.

Freud, A. (1936). *The Ego and the Mechanisms of Defense. The Writings of Anna Freud,* vol. 2. New York: International Universities Press, 1966.

Freud, S. (1963). *Psychoanalysis and Faith,* ed. E. L. Freud and H. Meng. New York: Basic Books.

Frosch, J. (1971). Technique in regard to some specific ego defects in the treatment of borderline patients. *Psychiatric Quarterly* 45:216–220.

Gill, M.M. (1954). Psychoanalysis and exploratory psychotherapy. *Journal of the American Psychoanalytic Association* 2:771–797.

Giovacchini, P.L. (1975). *Psychoanalysis of Character Disorders.* New York: Jason Aronson.

Greenson, R.R. (1965). The working alliance and the transference neurosis. *Psychoanalytic Quarterly* 34:155–181.

————(1970). The unique patient-therapist relationship in borderline patients. Presented at the Annual Meeting of the American Psychiatric Assn. (unpublished).

Heimann, P. (1956). Dynamics of transference interpretations. *International Journal of Psycho-Analysis* 37:303–310.

Jacobson, E. (1971). *Depression.* New York: International Universities Press.

Kernberg, O.F. (1968). General principles of treatment. In *Borderline Conditions and Pathological Narcissism,* pp. 69–109. New York: Jason Aronson, 1975.

————(1975a). *Borderline Conditions and Pathological Narcissism.* New York: Jason Aronson.

————(1975b). Overall structuring and beginning phase of treatment of borderline patients. In *Borderline Conditions and Pathological Narcissism,* pp. 185–211. New York: Jason Aronson, 1975.

————(1975c). Transference and countertransference in the treatment of borderline patients. *Strecker Monograph Series No. XII* of the Institute of Pennsylvania Hospital. Reprinted in *Journal of the National Association of Private Psychiatric Hospitals* 7:14–24.

Kernberg, O., Burnstein, E., Coyne, L., Appelbaum, A., Horwitz, L., & Voth, H. (1972). Psychotherapy and psychoanalysis: Final report of the Menninger Foundation's psychotherapy research project. *Bulletin of the Menninger Clinic* 36:1–275.

Knight, R.P. (1953a). Borderline states. In *Psychoanalytic Psychiatry and Psychology,* ed. R.P. Knight and C.R. Friedman, pp. 97–109. New York: International Universities Press, 1954.

————(1953b). Management and psychotherapy of the borderline schizophrenic patient. In *Psychoanalytic Psychiatry and Psychology,* ed. R.P. Knight and C.R. Friedman, pp. 110–122. New York: International Universities Press.

Little, M. (1958). On delusional transference (transference psychosis). *International Journal of Psycho-Analysis,* 39:134–138.

———(1960). On basic unity. *International Journal of Psycho-Analysis* 41:377–384, 637.

Segal, H. (1967). Melanie Klein's technique. In *Psychoanalytic Techniques: A Handbook for the Practicing Psychoanalyst,* ed. B. Wolman, pp. 168–190. New York: Basic Books.

Stone, L. (1954). The widening scope of indications for psychoanalysis. *Journal of the American Psychoanalytic Association* 2:567–594.

Wallerstein, R. (1969). Introduction to panel: psychoanalysis and psychotherapy. *International Journal of Psycho-Analysis* 50:117–126.

Winnicott, D.W. (1958). *Collected Papers.* New York: Basic Books.

Zetzel, R.R. (1956). The concept of transference. In *The Capacity for Emotional Growth,* pp. 168–181. New York: International Universities Press, 1970.

———(1971). A developmental approach to the borderline patient. *American Journal of Psychiatry* 127:867–871.

Part III

The Psychotherapeutic

Situation and the

Borderline Patient

Chapter 8

The Countertransference with the Borderline Patient*

Harold F. Searles, M.D.

A working definition of what I mean by "countertransference" is provided by the first sentence of a lengthy definition in *A Glossary of Psychoanalytic Terms and Concepts,* edited by Moore and Fine, and published by the American Psychoanalytic Association in 1967: "Countertransference: Refers to the attitudes and feelings, only partly conscious, of the analyst towards the patient. . . ." The rest of their definition is one with which I largely concur, but is unnecessary to reproduce here.

For many years, I have found that the countertransference gives one the most reliable approach to understanding patients of whatever diagnosis. My monograph (Searles 1960) on the nonhuman environment and many of my previous papers have contained detailed data and discussions of the countertransference in my work with frankly psychotic patients; this contribution will not attempt to condense those earlier writings.

As an example of the usefulness of the countertransference,

---

*This paper is excerpted from two lectures delivered at the Advanced Institute for Analytic Psychotherapy, New York, October 1976.

consider the question of whether it is well for the borderline patient to use the couch. For nearly thirty years now it has seemed to me that the patient is unlikely to be panicked by this experience if the analyst himself, sitting behind the couch, does not give way to panic.

Comparably, in my work with an ambulatory schizophrenic woman who had moved from sitting in a chair to sitting on the couch, I found that the next analytic-developmental step, her becoming able to lie down on the couch, involved not merely *her* ability to adapt to the isolation attendant upon no longer being able to see my face. I came to realize after she had started lying down, but sitting up from time to time to get a look at my face, that my relief at these "interruptions" was fully comparable with her own. I had been myself repressing the feelings of deprivation attendant upon no longer being able to watch her fascinating, mobile facial expressions while she was lying on the couch.

Recently, when a borderline patient who had been sitting in a chair for some months began lying on the couch, I found that, during the first session sitting behind it, I was speaking to her much more than had been my custom. My first thought was that I was supplying, empathically, sufficient verbal feedback to help her become accustomed to this new and, for her, much more emotionally isolated situation. Only some time later in this session did I realize that, again, I myself evidently was repressing abandonment anxiety, and struggling to keep such anxiety repressed and projected upon her.

In work with the borderline patient, there are several readily apparent reasons why the realm of the countertransference is so important. I intend to discuss in this paper additional, more subtle reasons; but first I shall make brief mention of some of the more obvious ones.

The intensity of the borderline patient's repressed emotions is so great as to make unusual demands upon the emotionality of the analyst. The demands are greatly accentuated because of the patient's wide gamut of ego developmental levels at work in his mode of relating with the analyst, such that the latter finds himself called upon to relate with the patient upon unpredictably shifting levels which vary from relatively mature, healthy-neurotic modes to extremely primitive modes essentially akin to those found in the transference psychoses of frankly schizophrenic patients. Not uncommonly, the analyst feels related with the patient upon two or more such levels simultaneously.

So much of the borderline patient's ego functioning is at a symbiotic, preindividuation level that very frequently it is the analyst who, through relatively ready access to his own unconscious experiences, is first able to feel in awareness, and conceptualize and verbally articulate, the patient's still-unconscious conflicts. Though these conflicts inherently "belong" to the patient, they can come to be known to and integrated by him only through his identification with the analyst into whom they have been able to flow, as it were, through the liquidly symbiotic transference.

Because the *borderline* patient does indeed seem, during much if not most of our work with him, to be walking a tightrope between neurosis and psychosis, he requires us to face our fear lest he become psychotic, our envy of him for his having this avenue so widely open to him, our hateful desire for him to become psychotic, as well as our ambivalent fear and wish to become psychotic ourselves.

Because the normal phase of mother-infant symbiosis in him never has been resolved into predominantly individuated ego functioning, we find that in the transference-symbiosis which naturally ensues over the course of the analysis, we are cast not only as the symbiotic mother in the transference but, equally often and by the same token, as the symbiotic infant. We must accustom ourselves, therefore, to experiencing symbiotic-dependency feelings toward the mother-patient such as are only relatively subtly present in our work with neurotic patients.

The Impact Upon the Analyst of the Patient's Split Ego Functioning

Gunderson and Singer (1975) in an article entitled, "Defining Borderline Patients: An Overview," provide a helpful survey of the extensive literature of descriptive accounts of borderline patients. Among several features which they found that most authors believe to characterize most borderline patients, foremost is the presence of intense affect. Now in entering into more detailed discussion, I want first to highlight the impact upon the analyst of the patient's unintegrated ambivalence—or, perhaps better expressed, the impact of the unintegrated affects which the patient expresses toward him, referable to splits in the patient's ego functioning such that intensely hateful affects are not integrated with (and thus modified by) intensely loving affects, and vice versa.

I cannot fully convey here this impact, for the reason that I cannot achieve, at will, such a complete splitting of intense emotions as prevailed at the level of ego functioning in these patients on these occasions; I must elaborate upon the following comments, therefore, with some brief description. One woman patient said, "I can't tell you how much I love you or how much of a shit I think you are." In saying, "how much I love you," her affective tone was one of glowingly unambivalent love; but in saying only moments later, "how much of a shit I think you are," her affect was unambivalently one of hostile contempt. Another woman, reminiscing that her mother used to address her as "my darling rat," conveyed by her tone that the words "darling" and "rat" had been expressive of forcefully contrasting emotions without any acknowledgment, in the mother's ego functioning, of any conscious conflict between these two images of her daughter. A chronically schizophrenic woman once said to me, "You should have the Congressional Medal of Spit." The first seven words of that eight-word sentence conveyed heartfelt admiration; but the last one, said with no break at all in the rhythm of her speech, was uttered in unalloyed contempt.

The examples of patients' affective expressions which I have just cited are expressions which switch instantaneously from loving to hateful ones. Even more unsettling, oftentimes, are a patients' expression of highly incongruous emotions simultaneously. Such phenomena comprise a part of what is not only difficult but also fascinating in the work with borderline patients, for one discovers that there are combinations of intense emotions never before encountered within one's conscious memory.

For example, I have come to realize that two of the part-aspects of one of my patients comprise what I experience as an irresistibly funny homicidal maniac. I had long been aware of his quick-tempered fury at any perceived insult, and of his underlying murderousness; but as the work went on it became evident that he possessed also an enormous ability to be funny. At times I felt overwhelmed by the urge to laugh at some of his raging comments, and yet, simultaneously, felt that it was of life-and-death importance not to let him detect my amusement. On rare occasions with him and comparable patients, I have been seized with strangled, epileptic seizurelike laughter, and on some of these occasions have managed, apparently successfully, to disguise it as a cough or somatically-based fit of choking. My underlying terror of being detected in some instances is that I will be murderously attacked physically or—hardly less frightening—subjected to a demolishing verbal attack. More often, the terror is lest the outraged patient sever, instantly and irrevocably, the treatment relationship which he and I have built up so slowly and arduously.

In my work with one such patient after another, it becomes evident that the patient's largely unconscious sadism has had much to do with my finding myself in so tortured a position. Only somewhat milder forms of this same phenomenon are to be found in one's work with a supervisee who, with a simultaneous hawklike sensitivity to any increment of somnolence, is reporting the clinical material in a soothing, boring, or some similar tone which drives one almost irresistibly toward sleep.

To return to borderline patients, a woman was reporting a dream in her usual overmodulated tone which was thoroughly enigmatic as regards emotions. She said that in her dream: "We were all under some kinda interstellar influence, some kinda unseen force that was controlling things . . . kinda malevolent force hovering around. . . ." As I was writing down the dream, I noticed that each time I wrote the word "force," I had a momentary thought, either that it was written "farce" or else that I had to be careful not to write "farce." I sensed there to be an unusual theme, here, of a murderous or sinister farce. The patient gave a brief chuckle at the beginning of her description of the parts of the dream which I have quoted; but in the main she sounded to be feinding off an awed, whistling-in-the-graveyard feeling. Later in this session she commented, without identifiable emotion of any sort, that her former roommate, years ago in law school, had been electrocuted in a strange "accident." During the years of her analysis, her fear lest she possess an omnipotent destructiveness proved to be one of the major themes of our work together.

To simply mention other unusual affective combinations, I have been struck by the diabolical naïveté of one of my male patients, and by this same patient's ferocious idealizing of me— his idealizing me with ferocity. I have felt one patient to give me a slashing smile when she walked in from the waiting room, and another (far more ill than borderline) to give me a decapitatingly saccharine verbal greeting when I walked into the seclusion room for my usual session with her. Another female patient has often provided me gratification with the caustic warmth of her so ambivalent responses to me.

I have found this same phenomenon (of strange-seeming combinations of affects) at work in many teaching-interviews I have had with patients who were manifesting pathologic grief reactions. That is, I have found myself experiencing sadistic urges toward depressed patients who clearly were repressing intense grief; only gradually did my initial shock at finding these sadistic urges in myself, in that setting, give way to an understanding that I was experiencing something of the sadistic feelings at work on an unconscious level in the patients themselves, and which thus far had been preventing further accomplishment of their grieving.

Surely some of these instances of patients giving expression simultaneously to so intensely incongruous emotions are manifestations of incongruously nonfitting introjects, within the patient, derived from the two parents; the disharmoniously wedded parents have counterparts (however exaggerated or otherwise distorted) in comparably poorly married parental introjects largely unintegrated in the patient's ego functioning. But even more pathogenically, neither parent was well-integrated within himself or herself. Thus the mother alone, or the father alone (or both), presumably presented to the child, as a model for identification, the embodiment of intensely incongruent emotionality such as we find in the patient himself. Hence either parent, taken alone, can have been the source (so to speak) of an abundance of nonfitting parental introjects within the patient.

Amusement

In relation to those occasions, which I mentioned earlier, when the analyst finds himself in the grip of amusement which he experiences as crazily incongruous with the more predominant and explicit aspects of his interaction with the patient, I wish to emphasize that, during the childhood of such a patient, some of the most traumatic effects of his family-relatedness derived from having to maintain under repression essentially healthy laughter. It is this healthy laughter which, more often than not, in the patient-therapist interaction is experienced first by the analyst, and only after much resistance on the latter's part. Laughter is, after all, precisely one of the most appropriate, healthiest kinds of response to the crazy things that have gone on in the childhood families of borderline patients, and that transpire not infrequently during their analytic sessions in adult life.

In the many teaching-interviews I have done, it is usual for there to emerge some occasion, during the interview, for the patient and I to laugh at least briefly together. Not rarely, this is the first time the therapist and other hospital staff members, for example, have seen such a capacity for humor in the patient. It is rare indeed for me to encounter a patient in whom I am unable, during a single interview, to perceive a sense of humor, no matter how straight-faced or laden with lugubriousness, or however sadistic or psychotically distorted its means of expression.

Our traditional training, as well as the mores of our culture, have so schooled us with the rigorous taboo against laughing *at* the poor victim of psychosis that it is difficult for us to realize that some of his most grievous warp, in childhood, derived from the family-wide taboo against healthy laughter, lest such laughter do violence to the so vulnerable sensibilities of the other family members. If we can dare to let our "own" healthy laughter come into the patient-therapist interaction, we can help him to find access to his "own" long-repressed healthy capacities in this regard. Parenthetically, in many years of work with a chronically schizophrenic woman, there have been many sessions in which I felt that the only solidly healthy responses she manifested consisted in her occasional belly laughs, unaccompanied by any verbal communication. It is amusement which I have shared at such times, however uncomprehendingly in any secondary-process terms.

The Analyst's Experience of Transference Roles Which are Both Strange in Nature and Inimical to His Sense of Reality and to His Sense of Personal Identity

Turning from the subject of the impact upon the analyst of the patient's emotions *per se,* I want briefly to delineate the integrally related topic of the analyst's experience of the strange transference roles in which he finds himself, by reason of the patient's developing transference, at times psychotic or near-psychotic in its reality value for the patient.

The major roots of the patient's transference reactions are traceable to a stage in ego development prior to any clear differentiation between inner and outer world, and prior to the child's coming to function as a whole person involved in interpersonal relationships with other persons experienced as whole objects. Hence the analyst finds that these transference reactions and attitudes of the adult borderline patient cast him, the analyst, in roles strangely different from those he commonly encounters in working with the neurotic patient whose transference casts him, say, as a domineering father or sexually seductive, masochistic mother. Instead, the analyst finds the patient reacting to him as being nonexistent, or a corpse, or a pervasive and sinister supernatural force, or as God, or as being the patient's mind, or some anatomical part-aspect of his mother (her vagina, for example, or her fantasied penis). My monograph concerning the nonhuman environment (Searles 1960) contains many examples of schizophrenic patients' transference reactions to the therapist as being one or another of a wide variety of nonhuman entities, and one finds an equally wide range in the work with borderline patients.

Not only the bizarre content or structure of the patient's transference images of him, but also their near-psychotic reality value for the patient, at times formidably threaten the analyst's own sense of reality and his own sense of identity. For example, I found that one of the sources for my persistent hatred of one such patient was his intense transference to me as being his highly obsessive mother, which exerted upon me a powerful pull toward my earlier, much more obsessive, only partially outgrown self. A woman reported, several years into our work together, that for the first time the thought had just occurred to her that perhaps I was *not* crazy, and went on to associate the craziness, which she now realized she had been attributing to me all along, with that which she had perceived in her father since early childhood. All along I had had to cope, alone, with the patient's persistent but unconscious transference image of me as being crazy. Another woman, whose childhood was lived in remarkable isolation from both parents, and who used to talk with insects and birds, manifested transference reactions to me as being one or another of these creatures, and I never was able fully to determine whether, even in childhood, the conversations she had were with real creatures of this sort, or fantasied ones.

The omnipotent creativity, for good or evil but predominantly for evil, which frankly psychotic patients attribute to their own and the therapist's thought processes, is only to a somewhat lesser degree true of the borderline patient. Whereas the borderline patient possesses, most of the time, sufficient observing ego to not fully misidentify the therapist as being someone, or a part-aspect of someone, or something, from the patient's real past, he nonetheless comes sufficiently close to doing so that the therapist may feel submergedly threatened lest this transference role become, indeed, his—the therapist's—only subjective reality.

In a session several years into her analysis, a middle-aged woman said during a brief interchange between us as to whom

various persons in a just-reported dream personified or represented: "People are never to me who *they* think they are. They are
who *I* think they are." She said this in a tone of small-childlike
grandiosity and without appearing consciously disturbed or
threatened. She said it by way of pointing out or reminding me of
an obvious fact. The charming little child quality of this expressed
recognition on her part was in marked contrast to the genuinely
threatening effects upon me, many times in earlier years, when
her negative transference had been much more intense and her
ability to differentiate between mental images and flesh-and-
blood outer reality had been much less well established. During
those years I had felt anything but charmed by her reacting to me
with the full conviction that I was (to give but one example)
literally a stone-hearted witch.

To the extent that a patient is unable to distinguish between the
analyst as, say, a mother in the transference situation, and the
actual mother in the patient's early childhood, he is likewise
unable to differentiate between *mental images of persons* (i.e.,
images within his own head) and the corresponding *persons in
outer reality*. This is another way of understanding why the
analyst reacts to the borderline patient's transference images of
him as being such a threat to his sense of personal identity—that
is, why the patient's transference *image* of him, which the patient
experiences as being so fully and incontestably real, carries with it
the threat to the analyst that it will indeed fully create or
transform him into conformity with that image.

I shall turn again to my work with frankly and chronically
schizophrenic patients for relatively unambiguous examples of
this point. Each of the following two instances occurred relatively
early in my work with such patients, at a time when more areas of
my own identity existed at a repressed or dissociated level than I
find to be the case in my work these days. One chronically and
severely assaultive woman asked me, at a time when I was

conscious of feeling toward her only a wish to help her and a physical fear of her, "Dr. Searles, *why* do you hate me?" She asked me this in a tone that assumed it to be an incontrovertible fact that I hated her, that hatred was the predominant—if not the only—feeling I experienced toward her, and that this was something we both had known all along. In response to her question I felt thoroughly disconcerted and at a loss to know what, if anything, to say. I thought that theoretically I must hate her, but was entirely unaware of hating her and—most pertinent for the point I am making here—I felt completely alone, without any ally in her, as regards any attempt on my part to question, with her, whether her view of me was not at all exaggerated, oversimplified, or otherwise distorted.

Another chronically ill woman, who for several years in our work perceived me most of the time as being, in flesh-and-blood reality, a woman, and who was herself the mother of several children, once said to me in very much the same tone as that used by the woman I have just mentioned, *"You're* a reasonable woman; what do *you* do with a daughter who . . . " She was speaking for all the world in terms of our being two women comparing notes, companionably, about the problems of rearing daughters.

In the neurotic patient it may be that an unconscious *personality aspect* such as hostile domineeringness, based upon an unconscious identification with the domineeringness, say, of the father, is projected during the course of treatment upon the analyst, who meanwhile is perceived by the patient as essentially the same person as before but with—so the patient now perceives—a hateful and perhaps intimidating, domineering aspect. The analyst may sense himself, in response to these developments, to have an uncomfortably domineering personality aspect, but does not feel his basic sense of his own identity to be appreciably disturbed.

Although such a state of things may be true in psychoanalytic work between a neurotic patient and the analyst, in the borderline patient there is insufficient ego integration for the unconscious domineeringness to exist as merely a repressed component of the patient's ego identity. It exists, instead, in a dissociated, split-off state as a largely unintegrated introject derived from experiences with the parent in question. It exists as a separate self, as it were, a component with its own separate identity. Now, when the analyst becomes involved in psychoanalytic psychotherapy with such a patient, he finds that the latter, through projecting this introject upon the analyst, comes not merely to perceive him as being the analyst with a newly-revealed hateful domineeringness. The analyst finds, instead, that the patient becomes more or less fully convinced that the analyst has been replaced by the hateful and intimidating, domineering father.

That is, in the work with the borderline or schizophrenic patient, the unconscious affect is encapsulated in, or pervades, an introject structure which has an identity value all its own. This affect-laden structure which the patient, to the extent that he is schizophrenic, is convinced *is* the real identity of the analyst has, by being projected forcibly and persistently upon the latter for many months or even years, an effect at times formidably shaking the analyst's own sense of identity.

But on the positive side the analyst, attentive to the resultant fluctuations in his sense of his "own" personal identity in the course of sessions with these patients, finds that he possesses a priceless (and, more often than not, previously unrecognized) source of analytic data. In a paper entitled, "The Sense of Identity as a Perceptual Organ," I mentioned that,

Somewhere midway through my own analysis, after I had undergone much change, I visualized the core of myself as being, none the less, like a steel ball bearing, with varicolored sectors on its surface. At least, I told myself, this would not change. I have long since lost any such image of the core of my identity. . . . In a succession of papers I have described the process whereby my sense of identity has become sufficiently alive to change . . . so that it is now my most reliable source of data as to what is transpiring between the patient and myself, and within the patient. I have described . . . the "use" of such fluctuations in one's sense of identity as being a prime source of discovering, in work with the patient, not only counter-transference processes but also transference processes, newly-developing facets of the patient's own self-image and so on; and in supervision, of discovering processes at work not only between the supervisee and oneself, but also between the supervisee and the patient. [Searles 1965b]

For a number of years during the analysis of a young woman, I felt, more often than not, somnolent during the session and much of the time indeed sensed that her transference to me was, even more, as being comatose, moribund. Many of the sessions felt endless to me. After several years, her transference to me began to emerge into her own awareness through such dreams as this:

I was at a dinner party. This woman seated across the table from me seemed to fluctuate between being dead and being alive. I was conversing with her and it was almost as though the more involved I became with her, the more dead she would become. That kind of thing went back and forth several times. From a distance she seemed vigorously alive, but up close she seemed lifeless and dull.

Associative connections between that woman in the dream, and myself as a representative of a number of personality aspects of various persons from the patient's childhood, as well as connections to components of herself which were identified with those emotionally dead figures from her past, emerged in the subsequent analytic work.

A childless woman, after detailing how moved she had felt at the aliveness of a pair of twin babies she had seen the day before, became somberly philosophical and said, with an undertone of fear and awe in her voice, "There's always the death in the background." I heard this as a clear but unconscious reference to me, behind her, as being death; I said nothing. She went on, " . . . I do have a lot more thoughts about the finiteness of my own life."

Other patients, of various diagnostic categories, have associated me—partly by reason of not feeling free to look at me during the session—with those parts of a parent's body which they had not been permitted to look at during their childhood, most frequently the parent's genital.

Parenthetically, it seems to me not coincidental that in those very frequent instances in which such transference responses as I am citing prevail in work with borderline patients for years, the analyst seldom indeed finds it feasible to make effective transference interpretations. The patient is largely deaf, unconsciously, to verbalized intelligence from an analyst who is powerfully assumed, again at an unconscious level in the patient, to be something quite other than a whole human being.

Further, in a number of patients with varying degrees of illness, I have found that *words*—from either patient or analyst—are equivalent to *father,* intruding unwanted into a nonverbal mother-infant symbiosis. This transference "father" is most significantly traceable to components of the biological mother herself, in these instances of split mother-transference, wherein intense jealousy permeates both the transference and the countertransference. Such jealousy phenomena are detailed in chapter 8 of this volume.

The borderline patient's impaired sense of reality is another typical factor which makes the development, and work of resolution, of the transference psychosis stressful for both participants. Helene Deutsch's classic paper on "as if" personalities (Deutsch 1942) is highly relevant here. One woman emphasized to me that "I am very different in person from the way I am here." This curious phrase, "in person," seemed to indicate that the analytic sessions possessed for her the reality value merely of a television show or a movie, for example. Later in the session she commented that her relationship with her father was so stormy that she sometimes felt an urge to write a novel about it; my own private impression was that, in that relationship, she was indeed living a novel. I have found it commonplace for these patients to emphasize that "in my *life*" or "in my *real* life" they are quite different persons from the way they are in the analysis. Admittedly, an analytic relationship commonly can be seen to be in many ways different from other areas of a patient's life; but these patients refer persistently to the analytic relationship and setting as being not really part of their lives at all. Many times, while reminiscing about events earlier in their lives, they will recall that, "In my *life*. . . ," saying this as though from the vantage point either of a very old person whose life is essentially *all* past now or—very often, in my experience—of one who has already died and can therefore look back upon his own life in its totality, as something now behind and quite apart from him.

The Analyst's Reactions to the Development of the Transference-Borderline-Psychosis in the Patient

Now I shall discuss various of the emotions which the therapist comes to experience in consequence of the development of the transference-borderline-psychosis in the patient, and some of the sources of those emotions. While the literature is not in full and explicit agreement that a transference psychosis typically develops in psychoanalytic therapy with the borderline patient, it seems generally agreed that he brings into the treatment relationship a vulnerability (or, one might say, a treatment need) for this development, and that the emergence of so intense and primitive a constellation of transference reactions is at the least a standard hazard in the therapist's work with these patients. I think it fair and accurate to say that the borderline patient needs to develop and, if treatment proceeds well, will develop a transference-borderline-psychosis in the course of the work.

Certainly in my own work with borderline patients, and in my supervision of analytic candidates and psychiatric residents concerning their work with such patients, as well as in my study of the literature regarding psychoanalytic therapy with borderline patients, I find that a transference-borderline-psychosis commonly develops over the course of the work and needs, of course, to become resolved in order for the treatment to end relatively successfully.

My own clinical and supervisory experience strongly indicates to me that there are certain intense, and intensely difficult, feelings which the therapist can be expected to develop in response to the patient's development of the transference-borderline-psychosis. It may well be that, as the years go on, we shall become able to do psychoanalytic therapy with borderline and schizophrenic patients with increasing success in proportion to our ability to accept that, just as it is to be assumed an inherent part of the work that the *patient* will develop a transference-borderline-psychosis or transference-psychosis, it is also to be assumed no less integrally that the *therapist* will develop— hopefully, to a limited, self-analytically explorable degree, appreciably sharable with the patient—an area of countertransference-borderline-psychosis or even countertransference psychosis. It should be unnecessary to emphasize that going crazy, whole hog, along with the patient will do no good and great harm. But I believe that we psychoanalytic therapists collectively will become, through the years, less readily scared and better able to take up this work and pursue it as a job to be done relatively successfully, as we become proportionately able, forthrightly and unashamedly, to take the measure of feelings we can *expect* ourselves to come to experience, naturally, in the course of working with these patients.

Pao (1975) reports his project concerning a schema, devised at Chestnut Lodge by himself, Fort (1973), and presumably others on the staff there, for dividing schizophrenia into four subgroups. Pao, the Director of Psychotherapy at the Lodge, describes that in the course of this project he interviewed each new patient shortly after admission. It is of much interest to me that, evidently without having encountered my (1965b) paper concerning the sense of identity as a perceptual organ, his experience led him in what seems to me the same general direction: "My emphasis is that the diagnosis should begin with the study of the interviewer's own emotional reactions in the interaction between the patient and himself. . . . Such personal experience must be supplemented by a careful scrutiny of the patient's background, the course of illness, the patient's ability to tolerate anxiety, etc." I can believe that the time will come in our work with neurotic patients when, just as we now use as a criterion of analyzability the patient's capability for developing a transference neurosis, we may use as an additional criterion, of earlier predictive significance in our work with the patient, his capability to foster a countertransference neurosis, so to speak, in the analyst.

Having said this much by way of preface, I shall detail some of the therapist's expectable feeling-experiences in the course of his work with the borderline patient.

The therapist comes to feel guilty and personally responsible for the patient who, appearing initially relatively well, becomes over the months or years of the transference evolution appreciably psychotic or borderline psychotic in the context of the treatment sessions. It is only in relatively recent years, after many years of tormented countertransference experiences of this sort, that I have come to realize how largely referable is the therapist's guilt and remorse, in this regard, to unconscious empathy with the patient's own child-self. That is, the patient in childhood tended to feel that only he possessed the guilty awareness of how deeply disturbed the mother is and that, moreover, he personally was totally responsible for driving her to the edge of, or even into, madness. The father may have been the more central parent in this regard; but much more often it was, from what I have seen, the mother.

It is garden variety experience for children in our culture to hear reproaches from a parent, "You're driving me crazy!" and, of course, I do not mean that such words alone, even with more than a modicum of appropriately maddened demeanor, cause the child any serious and lasting trauma. But the parents of borderline patients have themselves more than a mere garden variety, neurotic degree of psychopathology. Hence it is a formidably serious degree of parental psychopathology for which the child is assigned, day after day, totally causative personal responsibility.

The therapist's guilt in this same regard stems partly from his finding, over the course of the work, that the patient's crazier aspects provide him (the therapist) covertly with much more of lively interest, and even fascination, than do the patient's relatively dull areas of neurotic ego functioning. Although the therapist's conscientious goal is to help the patient to become free from the borderline-schizophrenic modes of experience, privately and guiltily he feels fascinated by these very sickest aspects of the patient, and fears that his fascination with them has led him to foster, to deepen, these most grievously afflicted components of the patient's personality functioning.

Typically the treatment process itself, in work with these

patients, becomes highly sexualized, such that the patient reveals newly-experienced and fascinating borderline symptoms in a basically coquettish, seductive manner, while the enthralled therapist struggles to match this priceless material with brilliantly penetrating interpretations. Typically, too, the treatment process becomes laden with acted-in aggression. For instance, as I have mentioned in a recent paper (Searles 1976b) the therapist who develops formidable quantities of hatred toward the patient comes to feel for a time that the only effective "outlet" for his hatred is to be found in seeing the patient suffer from persistent symptoms.

All these details of the therapist's countertransference have had, so my clinical experience indicates, prototypes in the patient's childhood experience with the parent in question. As one simple example, the child could not help deriving gratification, no matter how guilt-laden, from feeling himself capable of bringing mother out of her depressive deadness into a highly animated and vocal state verging upon madness.

My work with a patient far more ill than borderline had shown me another point relevant for this discussion. She is a chronically schizophrenic woman with whom I have worked for many years. After the first few years of our work she refused to acknowledge her name as her own and, although she has improved in many ways over subseuent years, it has become rare for her to be conscious of bits of her own real, personal childhood history such as were relatively abundantly available to her, despite many already-present delusions, at the beginning of our work. For many years now, one of the harshest of my countertransference burdens is a guilty and remorseful feeling that I personally have long since destroyed her only real and sane identity—destroyed it out of, more than anything else, my hateful envy of her for her many and extraordinary capabilities, and for her childhood lived in a setting far different from my own small-town, middle-class one.

It is only as she has been improving, recently, to such an extent that some of her psychotic transference reactions have become clearly linked with newly remembered childhood experiences, that I have felt largely relieved of this burden of guilt and remorse. Specifically, I have come to see that my long-chafing feeling, often intensely threatening to the point of engendering in me fantasies of suicide, of having destroyed her sense of identity, has a precise counterpart in *her* having been given to feel, by her mother, that as a child she had destroyed the mother's so-called real and true identity—an identity based, in actuality, in the mother's ego-ideal as a woman of myriad magnificent accomplishments, above all in the field of dramatics. The mother had been given to maniac flights of fancy, and her fantasied accomplishments were not to her so much ambitions thwarted by the patient; rather, she reacted to the daughter as having destroyed these supposedly actual accomplishments and, in the process, destroyed the mother's supposedly real, true identity.

The Analyst as Unwanted Child

To return to the discussion of borderline patients *per se,* I have indicated that the therapist is given to feel that he has had, and is having, a diabolically, malevolently, all-powerful influence in the development and maintenance of the patient's transference-borderline-psychosis. But I have found, in my work with a reliably long succession of patients, that such an experience of myself in the work comes in course of time to reveal, at its core, the experience of myself as being an unwanted little child in relation to the patient. It gradually dawns on me that this is who I am, in the patient's transference relationship with me, as I listen month after month and year after year to the patient's reproaches that all the rest of his or her life is going relatively well these days, with my being the only fly in the ointment. If only he were rid of me, he says more and more explicitly, his life would be a breeze. In case after case, I become impressed, inevitably, with how much the patient sounds like a mother reproaching and blaming her small child, giving him to feel that, had he only not been born, her life would be a paradise of personal fulfillment.

In the instance of my work with one patient after another, the awareness of my unwanted child countertransference comes to me as an excitingly meaningful revelation and, although its appearance has been made possible only by my having come to realize, more fully than before, how deeply hurt and rejected I am feeling in response to the patient, this phase comes as a relief from my erstwhile grandiose and guilt-ridden countertransference identity as the diabolical inflictor of psychosis. In some instances, more specifically, I no longer hear the patient as reproaching me with diabolically *spoiling* his otherwise satisfactory life, but hear him saying, as the stronger, parental one of the two of us, that I, as the smaller one, the child, am not, and never was, loved or wanted.

All these processes in the patient's childhood regularly involved his becoming the object, beginning in early childhood or infancy or even before birth, of transference reactions on the mother's (and/or father's) part from her own mother and/or father (or sibling, or whomever) to the patient. Typically, the more ill the adult patient is, the more sure we can be that such transference responses on the parent's part were powerfully at work remarkably early in the patient's childhood. I have written a number of times of the schizophrenic patient's childhood in this regard, and I am aware that a number of other writers have done so. But I feel that we are only beginning to mine this rich lode of psychodynamics.

Here is, I believe, a prevailing atmosphere in the background of many borderline patients. Beginning when the patient was, say, two years of age (or even younger; I do not know just when), his mother had an unconscious transference image of him as being, all over again, her own mother and/or father, in relationship to whom she had felt herself to be an unwanted child, and whose love she had despaired of evoking. Now she blames and reproaches her little son (or daughter) for all sorts of events and situations which are far beyond his realistic powers to control, as if he were God Almighty; just as later on, in psychotherapy, the adult patient who was once this child comes to vituperate against his therapist as being a diabolical god. During the patient's childhood the mother does this basically because she unconsciously experiences herself as being an unwanted child to this transference "parent" of hers, who is actually her little child. I sense that as we come to understand more fully the poignancy of such mother-child relationships, we will discard the crude and cruel "schizophrenogenic mother" concept (to which I, among many others, devoted much attention in my early papers) once and for all.

The Analyst's Guilty Sense of Less-than-Full Commitment to His Therapeutic Role

A countertransference experience which has been long-lasting in my work with one patient after another is a guilty sense of not being fully committed, inwardly, to my functional role as the patient's therapist, despite my maintenance of all the outward trappings of therapeutic devotion. Any thoroughgoing discussion of this aspect of the countertransference would require a paper in itself, since it has, undoubtedly, so many connections to the patient's primitive defenses of fantasied omnipotence and of splitting, with powerfully idealized or diabolized transference images of the therapist. It is my impression, in essence, that it is only in proportion to a deflation of grandiosity, in the transference and the countertransference, that the therapist can come

to feel fully committed to his now human-sized functional role as
the patient's therapist. My treatment records abound with data
from earlier phases in the work with, for example, schizophrenic
patients who would talk adoringly and loyally of a delusional
construct hallucinatorily conversed with as "my doctor," while
shutting me out of any functional relatedness with them; but at
those rare moments when I would feel he or she was giving me an
opportunity, supposedly long sought by me, to step into the shoes
of "my doctor," I would quail at doing so.

In this same vein, but in work with a much less ill female
patient, she developed a headache during a course of a session,
and in association to this headache reported conjectures about
"rage at myself—*at you, maybe my mother*" [my italics]. I sensed
that she was manifesting an unconscious transference to me as
being her mother who was only *"maybe* my mother," which fit not
only with my frequent countertransference reactions to her, but
also with her childhood experience of a mother who persistently
remained tangential to the mother role, rather than more fully
committed to it. It fit also, needless to say, with her own unresolved, fantasied omnipotence, which allowed her to acknowledge only grudgingly, at best, any mother figure as being *"maybe*
my mother."

*The Analyst's "Own" Feelings as Comprising Layer Under Layer
of Countertransference Elements*

I cannot overemphasize the enormously treatment-facilitating
value, as well as the comforting and liberating value for the
therapist personally, of locating where this or that tormenting or
otherwise upsetting countertransference reaction links up with
the patient's heretofore unconscious and unclarified *transference*
reactions to him. In other words, the analyst's "own" personal
torment needs to become translated into a fuller understanding of

the patient's childhood family events and daily atmosphere. I find it particularly helpful when a "personal," "private" feeling-response within myself, a feeling which I have been experiencing as fully or at least predominantly my "own," becomes revealed as being a still deeper layer of reaction to a newly-revealed aspect of the patient's transference to me.

For a case in point, I shall turn briefly to my very long work with a previously mentioned chronically schizophrenic woman. I felt on many occasions over the years how seriously disadvantaged I was, as her therapist, in trying to function, since my role in her life precluded responding to her in the only manner appropriate to her behavior toward me, that is, by administering a brutal physical beating such as her mother frequently had given her. Only after many years did I come to realize that, in so reacting, I was being her transference-father; she had come by now to clearly portray me, in the transference, as a diabolical, omnipotent father who controlled from a distance both her and her mother, and who delegated to the mother the physical punishment of the child. His godlike, aloof role forebade, by the same token, that he dirty his hands with such matters.

A borderline man expressed, during a session after a number of years of work, the realization, at an unprecedentedly deep level, that "you are not my father." What I found fascinating about this was the attendant evidence of still-unresolved transference which revealed to me that, in saying this, although he was consciously expressing the realization that I was actually his therapist rather than his father, unconsciously he was expressing the realization that I was his uncle, who had provided most of his fathering following the death of his actual father, early in the patient's boyhood. Experiences such as this have led me, incidentally, to assume that any presumed "therapeutic alliance," supposedly involving relatively transference-free components of the patient's ego functioning in a workmanlike bond with the analyst, needs constantly to be scrutinized for subtle but pervasively powerful elements of unconscious transference.

Suspense; Choice Between Illness and Health; the Patient's Acting Out on Basis of Identifications with the Analyst

Suspense is prominent among the feelings of the analyst who is working with the borderline patient: suspense as to whether the patient will become frankly psychotic or will commit suicide, or both; whether he will leave treatment suddenly and irrevocably; or even, at times when the transference is particularly intense and disturbing to analyst as well as patient, whether the analyst himself will fall victim to one or another such outcome.

In the writings of Kernberg concerning borderline conditions I find much to admire and from which to learn. But one of the major differences between his views (in those writings of his which I have read) and mine is that he does not portray the suspenseful aspect which seems to me so highly characteristic of the analyst's feelings in working with the borderline patient. Kernberg (1975) says, for example, that patients with borderline personality organization "have in common a rather specific and remarkably stable form of pathological ego structure. . . . Their personality organization is not a transitory state fluctuating between neurosis and psychosis" (p.3) In a similar vein, he (Kernberg 1972) comments: "Under severe stress or under the effect of alcohol or drugs, transient psychotic episodes may develop in these patients; these psychotic episodes usually improve with relatively brief but well-structured treatment approaches" (p. 255).

Kernberg's writings on borderline states are in part the product of his work in the Psychotherapy Research Project of the Menninger Foundation, and I do not doubt that his experience in that project helps to account for the widely-admired soundness, both theoretically and clinically, of his writings. But in those passages which I have quoted, in their tone typical of a recurrent emphasis in his work (and, incidentally, passages the validity of which I am not contesting here, as far as they go), Kernberg fails to convey how very far removed indeed the analyst feels, in his work, from any such statistician's or theoretician's cooly Olympian view. All too often, for example, the analyst feels desperately threatened lest his patient become frankly psychotic, and the analyst finds little or no reason for confidence that, in such an event, the psychosis will prove transitory.

Any in-depth discussion of this area of the countertransference would include an exploration of the analyst's envy of the patient for the latter's psychopathology, his hateful wishes to be rid of the patient by the latter's becoming frankly psychotic and hospitalized somewhere, and his own—the analyst's—fears of, and wishes for, becoming psychotic himself. I have discussed (Searles 1965a) various among these countertransference phenomena, as regards the work with frankly psychotic patients, in a number of earlier papers.

In several years of work with a woman who showed a borderline personality organization at the outset, I found that she recurrently held over my head, mockingly, year after year, the threat that she would become frankly and chronically schizophrenic. She did not say this in so many words; but her behavior conveyed, innumerable times, that implicit, sadomasochistic threat. In many of the sessions during those years, I felt a strong impulse to tell her that I had felt for years, and still did, that she could become chronically schizophrenic if she would just try a little harder. Essentially, I wanted at such times to somehow convey to her that this was a *choice* she had. I suppressed this urge each time; but had I given way to it, this would have been an attempt to deal with her infuriating, year-after-year expressions of defiance and mockery and of, above all, the highly sadistic, implicit threat of her becoming chronically psychotic.

The following comments of mine in a recent paper concerning psychoanalytic therapy with schizophrenic patients are also in my opinion fully applicable, in principle, to such work with borderline patients. I wrote there of

> the crucial issue of *choice*—of the patient's coming to feel *in a position to choose* between continued insanity on the one hand, or healthy interpersonal and intrapersonal relatedness on the other hand. In order for the analyst to help the patient to become able to choose, the former must be able not only to experience, indeed, a passionately tenacious devotion to helping the latter to become free from psychosis, but also become able to tolerate, to clearly envision, the alternative "choice"— namely, that of psychosis for the remainder of the patient's life. I do not see how the patient's individuation can ever occur if the analyst dare not envision this latter possibility. The patient's previous life-experience presumably has proceeded in such a manner and his therapy at the hands of a too-compulsively "dedicated" analyst may proceed in such a manner likewise, that chronic psychosis may be the only subjectively *autonomous* mode of existence available to the patient.
>
> An analyst who, for whatever unconscious reasons, cannot become able to live comfortably with the possibility that his patient may never become free from psychosis cannot, by the same token, foster the necessary emotional atmosphere in the sessions for the development of the contented, unthreatened emotional oneness to which I refer by the term therapeutic symbiosis (Searles 1961), a form of relatedness which is of the same quality as that which imbues the mother-infant relatedness in normal infancy and very early childhood. Any so-called individuation which occurs in the patient which is not founded upon a relatively clear phase of therapeutic symbiosis in the treatment is a pseudo-individuation, and only a seeming choice

of sanity, with the urge toward psychosis, the yearning for psychosis, subjected to repression rather than faced at all fully in the light of conscious choice. Essentially, at the unconscious level, the patient chooses to remain psychotic [Searles 1976a, pp. 400-401].

Although these passages may be reminiscent of what I have termed the Olympian quality of the passages from Kernberg, most of my writings have emphasized—as I emphasized in the bulk of this recent paper—the struggles which even the experienced analyst must go through, as an inherent part of his countertransference work with one patient after another, to come to any such harmony with his own feelings, formerly so ambivalent, which have been at the basis of his experiencing so much of a threatened suspensefulness.

Along the way, it is especially threatening to the analyst to feel kept in suspense as to whether the patient is headed toward destruction precisely by reason of functioning loyally as being a chip off the old block—namely, the analyst as perceived by the patient in the transference. That is, the analyst finds much reason to fear that it is exactly the patient's identification with one of the analyst's qualities, no matter how exaggeratedly perceived because of the patient's mother- or father-transference to him, which is carrying the patient toward destruction. Thus the analyst feels responsible, in an essentially omnipotent fashion, for the patient's self-destructive acting out behavior outside the office. The analyst feels that the patient's behavior vicariously manifests his—the analyst's—own acting-out proclivities.

For example, although I seldom feel inordinately threatened lest any one of my psychiatrist analysands act out sexual fantasies toward one or another of his or her own patients. I had a more threatened time of it in my work with one analysand. This man was convinced, for years, that I had sexual intercourse with an occasional patient, casually and without subsequent remorse or other disturbed feelings. When he became strongly tempted to give way to his sexual impulses toward one or another of his own current patients, he reported these impulses during his analytic sessions with me as being in the spirit of his overall wishes to emulate me as an admired, virile father in the transference. Not to leave the reader in any unnecessary suspense, here I can report that this aspect of his transference became analyzed successfully.

Another example of this same principle is to be found in another recent paper of mine, "Violence in Schizophrenia" (Searles. 1975), in which I describe my single teaching-interviews with a number of schizophrenic patients whose histories included seriously violent behavior. In the instance of one particularly frightening man, with whose therapist I worked subsequently in supervision, the role of a threatened suspensefulness, in both the therapist and me, was especially prominent. My paper describes the end of the therapy with this man, who had run away from the sanitarium previously:

> He again ran away, was found and taken by his parents to another sanitarium, and ran away from there and joined the Marines without divulging his psychiatric background. Our last bit of information about him was a telephone call to the therapist from an official at an Army prison, stating that this man had stabbed a fellow Marine three times, that his victim was barely surviving, and that an investigation was under way to determine whether Delaney was mentally competent to stand trial. The therapist and I agreed that he had finally committed the violent act which we both had known he eventually would. . . . I want to emphasize the aspect of relief, of certainty, which this clearly afforded me and, I felt, the therapist also. It was as though the distinction between the patient's actualized murderousness and our own murderous fantasies and feelings was now clear beyond anyone's questioning it . . . .

Both the therapist and I, in relating to him, evidently had mobilized in ourselves such intensely conflicting feelings of love and murderous hatred that a regressive de-differentiation occurred in our respective ego-functioning, such that we attributed to the patient our own murderous hatred, and unconsciously hoped that he would give vicarious expression to our own violence, so as to restore the wall between him and us. More broadly put, such a patient evokes in one such intensely conflicting feelings that, at an unconscious level, one's ego-functioning undergoes a pervasive de-differentiation: one loses the ability deeply to distinguish between one's self and the patient, and between the whole realms of fantasy and reality. Thus the patient's committing of a violent act serves not only to distinguish between one's own "fantasied" violence and his "real" violence but, more generally, serves to restore, in one, the distinction between the whole realms of fantasy and outer reality [pp. 14–16].

Still concerning the matter of the analyst's experiencing suspense, to consider it less globally (e.g., whether the patient will become psychotic or commit suicide), and more particularly as regards any symptom or personality trait or current transference reaction, I find pertinent the following note I made half a dozen years ago concerning my work with a man who manifested a predominantly narcissistic form of ego functioning.

Regarding the therapist's experiencing *suspense*. Thinking back on the hour yesterday with Cooper, it occurs to me that, in reacting to his projection upon me of his own sadistic unfeelingness, I tend to function as distinctly *more* so than I actually feel—partly for the reason, as I see it now, of trying to make this issue become clear enough so that he can see it and we can thrash it out, analyze it, resolve it.

In other words, one of the major reasons why it is so difficult to maintain a genuinely neutral position, not reacting in tune with the patient's transference, is because it is so very difficult to endure the tantalizing ambiguity, the suspense, of the unworked-through transference reactions which one can see in the patient, and to which one *does* react genuinely. That is, I do experience myself as uncomfortably sadistic, unfeeling, unlikable and unadmirable to my self in reaction to Cooper's transference.

In a paper subsequently, "The Function of the Patient's Realistic Perceptions of the Analyst in Delusional Transference" (Searles 1972), I describe some aspects of my work with a far more ill patient, in terms both of her delusional transference perceptions of me, and of my own subjective experience of what I was "really" feeling, and communicating to her, in the therapeutic sessions. That paper mainly emphasizes my discovery, over the course of years, that again and again seemingly purely delusional perceptions of me on her part proved to be well rooted in accurate and realistic perceptions of aspects of myself which heretofore had been out of my own awareness.

What was mentioned above, concerning my work with the narcissistic man, suggests something of why the analyst may introject (unconsciously, of course, for the most part) some of the patient's psychopathology, in an attempt to hasten its resolution and thereby end the feelings of suspense which permeate the treatment-atmosphere in one's work with so tantalizingly ambiguous a patient.

It has seemed to me that some of these same psychodynamics have applied in a considerable number of instances of my work with patients who have been involved in chronically troubled marital situations where there is a chronic, suspense-laden threat of divorce hanging over the marriage. In the course of my work with each of these patients, it has appeared to me no coincidence that, concurrent with especially stressful phases of the analytic work, my own marriage has felt uncharacteristically in jeopardy. My strong impression is that the analyst under these circumstances tends to regress to a level of primitively magical thinking, whereby if his own marriage were to dissolve, this would end the years-long suspenseful question as to whether the patient's verge-of-divorce marriage will or will not endure. Whether the analyst were thereby to bring about, vicariously, the disruption of the patient's marriage or, on the other hand to preserve the patient's marriage by sacrificing his own, the tormenting element of suspense in the analytic situation—so goes in my speculation, the analyst's primitively magical reasoning—would be brought to a merciful end.

Differing Kinds (Repressive Versus Nonrepressive) of the Analyst's Sense of Identity as an Analyst

Lastly, I want explicitly to discuss a point which has been implied throughout this paper—namely, that the analyst's sense of identity as an analyst must be founded in a *kind* of analyst-identity which in major ways is different from the analyst-identity traditionally striven for and consonant with classical analysis. For the sake of this discussion, at least, it is not an oversimplification to say that classical analysis enjoins the analyst to develop, and strive to maintain, a sense of identity as an analyst which constrains him to evenly hovering attentiveness to the analysand's productions, and to participating actively in the analytic session only to the extent of offering verbal interpretations of the material which the analysand has been conveying to him. Such a traditional analyst-identity is neither tenable for the analyst who is analyzing a borderline patient, nor adequate to meet the analytic needs of the patient.

Knight (1953) described that in a relatively highly structured interview, the borderline patient's basic difficulties in ego functioning tend not to become available for either the patient or the psychiatrist to see and work upon:

> During the psychiatric interview the neurotic defenses and the relatively intact ego functions may enable the borderline patient to present a deceptive, superficially conventional, although neurotic, front, depending on how thoroughgoing and comprehensive the psychiatric investigation is with respect to the patient's *total* ego functioning. The face-to-face psychiatric interview provides a relatively structured situation in which the conventional protective devices of avoidance, evasion, denial, minimization, changing the subject, and other cover-up methods can be used—even by patients who are genuinely seeking help but who dare not yet communicate their awareness of lost affect, reality misinterpretations, autistic preoccupations, and the like. [pp. 102–103]

To be sure, Knight's comments suggest that a relatively free form of analytic-interview participation on the part of the patient most facilitates the emergence of the latter's borderline difficulties, and with this I am in full agreement. But his comments suggest, too, that such a patient is unlikely to be helped much by an analyst who himself is clinging, in a threatened fashion, to some rigidly-constructed analyst-identity. I hope that this present paper, when considered with my previous writings concerning countertransference matters, will serve forcefully to convey my conviction that the analyst must far outgrow the traditional, classical analyst-identity in order to be able to work with a reasonable degree of success with the borderline patient—to be able, for example, to utilize his sense of identity as a perceptual organ in the manner I have described here; to enter to the requisite degree into (while maintaining under analytic scrutiny) the so necessary therapeutic symbiosis; and to be able to preserve his analyst-identity in face of the extremely intense, persistent, and oftentimes strange transference images which, coming from (largely unconscious) processes at work in the patient, tend so powerfully to dominate the analyst's sense of his actual identity.

I have seen that various psychiatric residents and analytic candidates who, partly because of a relative lack of accumulated experience, have not yet established a strong sense of identity-as-therapist, are particularly threatened by the intense and tenacious negative transference images wherein the patient is endeavoring, as it were, to impose upon the therapist a highly unpalatable sense of identity. By the same token, it should be seen that an analyst who is struggling to maintain, in his work with such a patient, a professional identity untainted by such emotions as jealousy, infantile-dependent feelings, sexual lust, and so on, is undoubtedly imposing, by projection, such largely unconscious personality components upon the already overburdened patient. In essence, I am suggesting here that, in the analyst's work with the borderline patient, he needs to have or, insofar as possible, to develop a kind of professional identity which will not work on the side of the forces of repression but will, rather, facilitate the emergence from repression of those feelings, fantasies, and so on which the borderline patient needs for his analyst to be able to experience, on the way to his own becoming able, partly through identification with his analyst, to integrate comparable experiences within his—the patient's—own ego functioning.

Summary

The countertransference provides the analyst with his most reliable approach to understanding borderline (as well as other) patients. The impact upon him of the patient's split ego functioning is discussed. His experience of transference roles which are both strange in nature, and inimical to his sense of reality and to his sense of personal identity, is explored; in the latter regard, the value of his sense of identity as a perceptual organ is highlighted.

There are detailed some of the analyst's reactions—his guilt, envy, and so on—to the development of the transference-borderline-psychosis in the patient. The analyst finds that, underneath the patient's transference to him as being an omnipotent, diabolical inflictor of psychosis, is the patient's transference to him as being an unwanted child.

The analyst's guilty sense of less than full commitment to his therapeutic role is described briefly, as is the general principle of his finding, time and again, that what have felt to be his "own" feelings toward the patient include layer under layer of responses which are natural and inherent counterparts to the patient's transference responses and attitudes toward him.

The prominent role of suspense is discussed at some length, as is the related issue of choice between illness and health. The phenomenon of the patient's acting out on the (partial) basis of unconscious identifications with the analyst, and the impact of this phenomenon upon the countertransference, is mentioned.

Lastly, the significant role, in the countertransference, of the analyst's sense of identity as an analyst is discussed, and it is suggested that the borderline patient needs for the analyst to have, or, insofar as possible, to develop, a sense of identity as analyst which will predominantly enhance derepression rather than repression of countertransference attitudes and feelings.

References

Deutsch, H. (1942). Some forms of emotional disturbance and their realtionship to schizophrenia. *Psychoanalytic Quarterly* 11:301–321.

Fort, J. (1973). The importance of being diagnostic. Read at the annual Chestnut Lodge Symposium, October 5, 1973.

Gunderson, J.G., and Singer, M.T. (1975). Defining borderline patients: an overview. *American Journal of Psychiatry* 132:1–10.

Kernberg, O. (1972). Treatment of borderline patients. In *Tactics and Techniques in Psychoanalytic Therapy,* ed. P. Giovacchini, pp. 254–290. New York: Jason Aronson.

——— (1975). *Borderline Conditions and Pathological Narcissism.* New York: Jason Aronson.

Knight, R.P. (1953). Borderline states. In *Psychoanalytic Psychiatry and Psychology,* eds. R.P. Knight and C.R. Friedman. New York: International Universities Press, 1954.

Moore, B.E. & Fine, B.D., eds. (1967). *A Glossary of Psychoanalytic Terms and Concepts.* New York: American Psychoanalytic Association.

Pao, P-N. (1975). On the diagnostic term, "schizophrenia". *Annual of Psychoanalysis* 3:221–238.

Searles, H.F. (1960). *The Nonhuman Environment in Normal Development and in Schizophrenia.* New York: International Universities Press.

——— (1961). Phases of patient-therapist interaction in the psychotherapy of chronic schizophrenia. In *Collected Papers on Schizophrenia and Related Subjects,* pp. 521–559. New York: International Universities Press, 1965.

——— (1965a). *Collected Papers on Schizophrenia and Related Subjects.* New York: International Universities Press.

——— (1965b). The sense of identity as a perceptual organ. Presented at Sheppard and Enoch Pratt Hospital Scientific Day Program, Towson, Maryland, May 29, 1965. Reprinted in "Concerning the Development of an Identity" *Psychoanalytic Review* 53:507–530, Winter 1966–67.

——— (1972). The function of the patient's realistic perceptions of the analyst in delusional transference. *British Journal of Medical Psychology* 45:1–18.

—— (1976a). Psychoanalytic therapy with schizophrenic patients in a private-practice context. *Contemporary Psychoanalysis* 12:387–406.

—— (1976b). Transitional phenomena and therapeutic symbiosis. International Journal of Psychoanalytic Psychotherapy 5:145–204.

—— (1977). Dual- and multiple-identity processes in borderline ego functioning. In *Borderline Personality Disorders,* ed. P. Hartocollis. New York: International Universities Press.

Searles, H.F., Bisco, J.M., Coutu, G., and Scibetta, R.C. (1975). Violence in schizophrenia. *Psychoanalytic Forum* 5:1–89.

Chapter 9

Jealousy Involving an Internal Object*

Harold F. Searles, M.D.

In one of the popular songs of my high school years, a lover is giving expression to his possessive jealousy of all that impinges upon his beloved. He sings, for example, of his jealousy of the moon that shines above, and ends with the rueful realization that "I'm even getting jealous of myself."

This romantic ballad in no way prepared me for the discovery, conveyed to me by various of my patients decades later, that one's jealousy of one's "self" and analogous experiences of jealousy, which are related to such an internal object within either oneself or the other person in an ostensibly two-person situation, are at the heart of a great deal of severe and pervasive psychopathology and account, in psychoanalytic treatment, for much of the unconscious resistance, on the part of both patient and analyst, to the analytic process.

*Earlier versions of this paper were presented at the Department of Psychiatry of the University of Wisconsin, Madison, October 4, 1974, and at the New York Conference on Borderline Disorders, under the auspices of Advanced Institute for Analytic Psychotherapy, New York, November 20, 1976.

This "internal object jealousy" is a significant element in the psychodynamics of patients of any diagnosis, and therefore cannot be considered specifically characteristic of borderline patients. But psychoanalytic therapy with these latter individuals provides the arena *par excellence* for the study of this jealousy. In a paper (Searles 1977) entitled "Dual- and Multiple-Identity Processes in Borderline Ego Functioning," I described those processes as being among the fundamental features of borderline ego functioning. The type of jealousy I am describing here is a major factor in maintaining the disharmony of the borderline patient's internal object world and in preventing him, therefore, from experiencing a single, whole, and continuous identity.

My first clinical experience of this strange jealousy phenomenon occurred in the course of my work, about thirty years ago, with a young man whom at the time I regarded as suffering from nothing more severe than an obsessive-compulsive neurosis, but whom I now know to have been manifesting a borderline schizophrenic degree of impaired ego functioning. During one session he began venting intense jealousy in the process of describing, with much hatred and bitterness, that his mother used not infrequently to converse aloud, in a spirit of warmly adoring intimacy, with an hallucinated image of Jesus Christ. The patient's jealousy of her hallucination was unmistakable.

After the session I was left with a sense of how strange was the nature of his jealousy: when one considered that her hallucination was a projected component of her own unconscious contents,[1] one saw that he was essentially jealous of her relationship with a part of herself.

---

[1]In more recent years I have come to believe that an hallucination is referable, in significant degree, not only to the patient's projection of his "own" unconscious personality components, but also to his unconscious perceptions of actual outer reality, perceptions which take the form of the hallucination. But for the purposes of this paper, that does not diminish the relevancy of the early clinical vignette mentioned above.

Some years later, in the course of my work at Chestnut Lodge with a hebephrenic young woman, I felt even more strongly the memorable impact of her saying, on one occasion, "I guess I'm jealous of myself." She confided this to me partly in the spirit of a painful confession; but it went far deeper than that. It clearly had a connotation of a split in her functional ego, with her ego being in two parts, her "I" and her "myself," equal in valence and in a state at hopelessly jealous odds with one another.

My first remembered experience of feeling within myself jealousy of essentially this same nature—jealousy involving an internal object, in this instance an internal object in the other person, precisely as had been felt by the borderline schizophrenic young man I first mentioned—occurred some years later, in my work with a hebephrenic middle-age man. This man had been hospitalized constantly for about fifteen years when my work with him began, and for many months his demeanor was marked mainly by silent dilapidation and apathy, punctuated only by sudden and brief streams of vitriolic cursing, seemingly at the world of people around him—for example, when he was impelled to leave the couch at the end of the corridor, where he customarily reclined during the day, to walk rapidly to the nurses' station for a cigarette.

But after several months of four hours per week of psychotherapy (which for the first one and a half years of my experience with him was conducted in a four-person situation involving two therapists and another chronically psychotic patient), the daily nurses' reports indicated that Eddie (as he was commonly known) was sleeping poorly, waking up repeatedly during the night and cursing furiously for prolonged periods at, evidently, hallucinatory figures. During the therapy sessions, however, his continued apathetic silences, while the other patients conversed volubly, were among the factors which led to the abandonment of the four-person treatment endeavor, and I went on working with Eddie on an individual basis for an overall period of nine years.

As those years went on, he became more and more alive in the sessions with, however, from my point of view an oftentimes frightening unpredictability, for his aliveness consisted in suddenly becoming involved, time and again, in trading curses, insults, and belligerent threats with, evidently, one or more hallucinatory figures. For many months after this development had come to dominate the sessions, he seemed still so oblivious of me that I was given to feel like part of the woodwork or, one might say, a passerby who sees and hears a man in a nearby phone booth wholly immersed in a loud and vitriolic telephone conversation, utterly unaware of the passerby. On one occasion during this era, when I pressed more strongly than usual to make my presence felt with some loud comment to him, he retorted in absolute fury, "Shut up! I got company!" and immediately reimmersed himself in his only momentarily interrupted, and very lively, dialogue with the hallucinatory figure(s).

But as the months and years wore on I came gradually to know, from innumerable, largely indirect and nonverbal, cues, that I was of real interpersonal significance to him. It was in this new era—lasting at least several months—that I found myself prey to the strange jealousy which is the focus of this paper. He had become by now relatively verbal in speaking directly to me, and on those many occasions when he would turn away suddenly and start conversing with one or another hallucinatory figure which had more powerfully wrested his attention, I was left feeling helplessly jealous of his hallucination(s). In the closing two years or so of my work with him, I had become so sure of my personal significance to him that it was easy to perceive data indicating that his hallucinatory experiences, during the sessions, were secondary to the vicissitudes of the relationship between him and me, such that I no longer felt susceptible to jealousy, and was able to work with him concerning his hallucinations as (of course, I knew intellectually they had been all along) transference-based psychotic symptoms, rather than quasi-real rivals of mine. Perhaps I should make plain that at no time did I hallucinate during our sessions; but during the era when I was feeling jealous I had the strange and unsettling *sense* that there were several—not merely two—persons in the room. In the instance of a chronically schizophrenic, severely ego-fragmented woman with whom I have worked for many years, the feeling-atmosphere of the sessions has been, on more than a few occasions, that of a group-relatedness, precisely as was the case for a time in my work with Eddie.

The experiences with these few patients, each of them more than merely neurotically ill, have served for me as a springboard into innumerable subsequent experiences with more subtly evidenced, but nonetheless centrally pathogenic, manifestations of this same kind of jealousy in schizoid and neurotic patients. With this mushrooming accumulation of clinical experiences in more recent years, I have come to see that the jealousy phenomena with which the analyst is accustomed to working, namely, those occurring in a context of three whole persons, are merely—to resort to Breuer's metaphor (Breuer and Freud 1893-1895) for the predominance of unconscious over conscious living—the tip of the iceberg, of which the far greater portion, invisible to surface view, is comprised of those vastly more frequent and varied jealousy phenomena which involve but two actual persons and an internal object in one or another of them, an internal object which is invested with the feeling-significance (often if not always on a transference basis) of an actual whole and separate person.

To complete my introductory remarks I shall give an example from my work with a schizoid patient—that is, a patient whose degree of illness is common in an office practice. I quote from an earlier paper (Searles 1973):

For several years I found this man infuriatingly smug. But the time came when, to my astonishment, I realized that what I was feeling now was jealousy; *he* so clearly favored his *self* over *me* that I felt deeply jealous, bitterly left out of this mutually cherishing and cozy relationship between the two "persons" who comprised him. I emphasize that this did not happen until after several years of my work with him. In retrospect, I saw that I previously had not developed sufficient personal significance to him . . . to sense these two now relatively well-differentiated "persons" in him and to feel myself capable of and desirous of participating in the "three"-way, intensely jealousy-laden competition. It is my impression that such schizoid patients usually prove so discouragingly inaccessible to psychoanalysis that the analyst and the patient give up the attempt at psychoanalysis before they have reached this lively but disturbing (to analyst as well as patient) stratum, this stratum in which the patient's ego-fragmentation becomes revealed and the nature of the transference becomes one of a murderously jealous "three"-way competitiveness [pp. 256-257].

These jealousy phenomena are so varied, and their childhood etiology so diverse, that I can present only a few typical examples. As regards the diagnoses of those patients whose analyses have yielded the clinical vignettes which follow in this paper, it is not to be assumed that their illnesses were of a *preponderantly* borderline-schizophrenic order of severity. Several of these patients were functioning in a largely normal-neurotic manner. In my experience, significant *areas* of splitting of ego functioning come to light in the analyses of patients of whatever diagnosis, just as does the "internal object" jealousy which is based upon such splitting. I share Fairbairn's (1952) opinion that everyone has schizoid factors in his personality. As he puts it,

The fundamental schizoid phenomenon is the presence of splits in the ego; and it would take a bold man to claim that his ego was so perfectly integrated as to be incapable of revealing any evidence of splitting at the deepest levels, or that such evidence of splitting of the ego could in no circumstances declare itself at more superficial levels, even under conditions of extreme suffering or hardship or deprivation . . . [p. 8].

Jealousy Involving a Body Part or Whole Body Upon Which an Internal Object is Being Projected

One category includes instances wherein a part of one's own body is, at an unconscious level, not a part of one's body image but is reacted to, instead, as being a separate person to whom one reacts with intense jealousy. By now I have become convinced that a male patient's jealousy of his own penis is a frequent, if not regular, factor in the dynamics of men who suffer from sexual impotence and castration anxiety. In the histories of such patients, one learns after some years of their analyses that, in each instance, in childhood his penis had been involved in, as it were, an adoringly intimate relationship with the mother, a relationship from which he had felt jealously excluded, much as though his own penis were a favored younger sibling who had displaced him. Further, in such a patient, his penis, when erect, proves in the analysis to have a transference significance to him as being the personification of the rigidly autocratic qualities of one or both his parents. The analysis comes to reveal these heretofore unconscious determinants of the symptoms only when the analyst has become approximately as important to the patient as is the latter's penis, and the analyst finds to his astonishment that he is feeling jealous as regards the patient's intimate and fascinated relationship with the latter's own penis. The analyst, that is, first comes to feel as his own the jealousy which the patient himself has dissociated for so many years—jealousy referable to his mother's relationship with his penis.

Frequently indeed, a woman patient will prove after long analysis to have been repressing jealousy of her own breasts, breasts which at her puberty—or in some instances, at the level of the parent's mental imagery, even at her birth—had been the object of such exclusively focused interest on a parent's part that the girl herself had felt jealously excluded from that intimate "interpersonal" relationship between the parent and the girl's biologically-own body parts. Similarly, a woman's unconscious jealousy of her well-turned legs which are the focus of men's fascinated interest to the large-scale exclusion of the rest of her body (not to mention her nonsomatic aspects), may interfere with her integrating these legs into a whole body image. Again, it is inherent in the successful analyzing of this "intrapsychic" jealousy that the analyst become able to experience it vis-à-vis the relationship between the patient and the body part(s) in question, before the patient can be expected to become aware of, and integrate, this strangely jealousy-ridden relationship between herself and one or another introject represented by the body part(s) in question.

One borderline woman, whose body image was comprised of a number of different parts in at times murderously jealous war with one another, said of a personnel manager whom she had seen in a job interview, "He kept looking at my *legs,*" in a tone implying that all the rest of her had felt largely ignored. The course of her analysis brought to light a kind of dismembering, largely internalized, jealousy in her which was at times of frighteningly self-destructive proportions.

Just as the analyst's becoming aware of feeling jealousy toward a patient's penis, for example, can provide an indispensable clue to a major determinant of the patient's sexual impotence, so can the analyst's recognition of his own jealousy of the patient's *whole body* help in understanding the patient's symptom of depersonalization—his sense of not really inhabiting his own body but of experiencing it, rather, as an alien external object. The unconscious jealousy in the patient which is keeping that body alien from him is first experienced by the analyst.

I first became aware of the role in depersonalization of internal-object jealousy during my supervision of a female therapist's treatment of a chronically schizophrenic woman. It became evident, through the therapist's demonstration to me of the patient's posture and gestures in their largely silent treatment sessions, that the patient was tantalizingly offering her body to the therapist, not predominantly in an adult lesbian sense, but rather in a far more primitive sense, as a physical housing for the therapist's self to occupy. Various of the patient's symptoms of chronic schizophrenia became relatively understandable in terms of the hypothesis that her mother thus had dangled her own body tantalizingly before the patient for her to psychologically inhabit, as the indispensable context for the girl's (as infant and young child) establishment of her first human identification, while at the same time (because of the mother's own emotional difficulties, probably including depersonalization) being unable really to share her body, psychologically, with the daughter for the kind of infant-mother symbiosis which occurs in healthy infancy.

Another way in which a body part proves to have had a fundamental role in the childhood etiology of a wide variety of clinical symptoms is through the child's being given reason to feel jealously excluded from the relationship between a parent and one of the latter's own body parts (entirely as the analyst may come to feel jealous, as described above, of a patient's relationship with the latter's own penis). The hypochondriacal parent who nurses for years a chronically ailing stomach or limb, for instance—a body-part having the unconscious significance, for the parent, of a possessively loved transference parent in turn—is typical of the parents in the histories of such patients, as becomes revealed in the evolution of the transference and corresponding countertransference.

Jealousy Involving a Mental Image as the Third "Person"

In a second broad category of these jealousy phenomena, it is not a body part but a mental image which is the third "person" involved in the jealousy-laden transference-countertransference relationship in which patient and analyst come to participate—a mental image within either patient or analyst. In the examples previously given, mental images have been involved, of course— unconscious mental images of internal objects, mental images which are being projected upon, for instance, a body-part. But this category is comprised of instances wherein the mental image in question is relatively readily recognizable as such, in consciousness, by the person in whom it exists.

The etiologic sources from which such images derive are of limitless variety. For example, it developed that the father of one male patient had given the boy to feel jealous of the middle-age father's own idealized, youthful "self," still so tangibly alive in the father's nostalgic preoccupation. This same patient subjected my analyst-"self" to such incessant derision, while expressing admiration of my author-"self," that I experienced uncomfortable stirrings of jealousy of the relatively admired author Searles whose works this scornful man was sure I could not possibly have written or, had I done so, then the brain cells which had made this possible had long since died inside my skull. Another patient was placed in jealous competition, as his boyhood and young manhood proceeded, with his parents' and older siblings' remembered images of his own baby-self, a self with whom he felt now, as a result, more at jealous odds than in any really well-integrated oneness. His mother never tired of saying fondly, "You were the cutest baby I've ever seen," and this made him feel less cherished and appreciated, in the present, than rejected and jealous of this "cutest baby" she had in her mind's eye.

Not infrequently, so patients' histories and tranference evolutions indicate, a frank psychosis has been precipitated in a setting where the patient comes to realize that he is not, after all, at the center of the life of a mother or father who has appeared, heretofore, selflessly devoted to him. He now realizes that the parent's interest in him has been, all along, essentially narcissistic and that, to the extent that he has been a truly separate person at all to the parent, he has been not cherished but, rather, the object of covert, intense jealousy. He himself must now cope with his own jealous realization that the parent has a self, after all, a self "who" in fact is far more beloved to the parent than is he. When I wrote of this development in an earlier paper (Searles 1962) I had not yet come to see the element of internal-object jealousy:

> The schizophrenic illness first becomes manifest, typically, in a setting of the individual's coming face to face with overwhelming disillusionment. Specifically, he is no longer able to maintain a symbiotic relatedness with a parent, a relatedness perpetuated into chronological adulthood, long past the time when the mother-infant symbiosis is normally resolved, perpetuated partly in the service of maintaining intense scorn, and other negative emotions, under repression. He now becomes confronted with a weight of evidence which can no longer be denied, evidence showing that the parent's ostensibly altruistic interest in him has been basically narcissistic in origin—that this interest has been invested not in him as a real and separate person, but in him only as an extension of the parent's self . . . [p. 619].

Early in my work with a middle-age borderline-schizophrenic

man, I became aware of jealousy of his intimate, buddy-buddy, comfortable-old-shoe relationship with his "self "; this "self " of his proved to be an introject with multiple childhood-derived transference significances referable to his relationship with his mother and older brother, among others. Not only did he give me to feel, during the sessions, that in his daily life between them he was on far more companionable terms with his "self" than I felt to be with him—for I felt walled out, and incapable of making any personal impact upon him a high percentage of the time—but also he seemed to treat himself, all things considered, with a kinder intimacy, for all his roughly blunt ways of talking to himself in his daily life internal dialogues, than the far harsher condemnation and vilification I commonly vented privately upon myself over those years of his analysis.

As the analysis wore on, he came to dialogue, internally but consciously, in daily life between sessions, oftentimes and in loving leisure, with an idealized image of me, such that during the sessions I came to feel, on more than one occasion, jealous of my "self"—of, that is, the Dr. Searles with whom, in fantasy, he often talked between sessions, talked in entirely the same intimately companionable spirit in which he had long been accustomed to dialoguing with his "self," while continuing during the analytic sessions to maintain the same wall of resistance to my own efforts. This latter phenomenon I have encountered sufficiently often, in work with borderline patients, to convince me that it is typical indeed for the analyst of the borderline patient to come to find himself pitted in jealous competition with such a transference-derived introject, or image, in the patient, of the analyst "himself."

In the instance of a narcissistic woman whom I had known socially, but relatively distantly, for some years before she entered analysis with me, I quickly found that an intense and seemingly ever-present jealousy was at work within her character structure, and I came to have the odd experience of finding that my analyst-self was vulnerable to feeling jealous of my social-acquaintance-self vis-à-vis the patient. In one session, for instance, in which I found myself experiencing a kind of tension that had become very familiar to me over the course of my work with her, she was making clear that she had made her boyfriend jealous by holding in his presence a prolonged telephone conversation with a male co-worker of hers, and had made another male co-worker jealous by some other means. Before the end of the hour I had become convinced that she tended to cause me, as *analyst,* to feel jealous of my*self* ("my*self*" consisting in the nonanalyst, social acquaintance aspects of myself). This came about, I saw now, partially through her so-characteristic large-scale ignoring slips of the tongue (giving me to feel *neglected* as her analyst), and in her usual chatty social way of reporting during the session, talking to me much as she would with *any* social acquaintance or friend.

Since my discovery of this kind of countertransference jealousy phenomenon in my work with this woman, I have recognized the same phenomenon in my work with a number of other borderline patients—patients who foster this split in the analyst's subjective ego functioning, such that he feels that the patient either warmly accepts him, or is quite ready warmly to accept him, as social acquaintance or social friend (or as fantasied lover), but makes him feel jealously excluded and depreciated in the identity area which he occupies, subjectively, by far the majority of the time—as analyst.

I have seen evidence that, in a marriage in which one or both persons is in analysis or psychotherapy, either partner's developing the paranoid suspicion that there is "someone else" is his or her way of experiencing the impending realization that the spouse is developing, for the first time, a separate *self*—becoming an individual person for the first time—and is therefore no longer selflessly devoted to the partner. He or she perceives this self of the spouse as displaced onto some delusionally or quasi-delusionally suspected rival. This phenomenon is essentially the same as that which I described years ago concerning the young person's realization, at times so shattering as to precipitate psychosis, that the "selflessly devoted" parent has, after all, a self, and a highly narcissistic one at that.

In a paper in 1964, I reported upon another dimension of this same symbiotic-marriage phenomenon:

> In a number of married patients who were bent on divorce, I have seen that the patient's determination to "get a separation from" the marital partner consisted basically in a striving, long unrecognized as such by the patient, to achieve a separation at an *intra*psychic level, to achieve a genuine individuation *vis-à-vis* a wife or husband with whom a symbiotic mode of relatedness had been existing. In such instances, the marital partner had been responded to not predominantly as a real other person, but rather as the personification of the unacceptable, projected part-aspects of the patient's self, or, one might say, as the personification of his own repressed self-images. Thus the patient does have a need, however unrecognized as such, to achieve a separation between those repressed and projected aspects of himself, on the one hand, and the marital partner as a real and separate person on the other [p. 721-722].

I have learned that patients can be expected to come to manifest jealousy, in the context of the analytic session, of *whomever* they themselves have come, seemingly at their own initiative, to spend much of the session discussing. One sees this particularly readily in work with borderline patients, and most often as regards the patient's talking incessantly of his or her spouse. That is, during those phases of the analysis in which the patient spends much of the analytic time in reporting to the analyst details about the patient's marriage (and I refer here not merely to details about the couple's sexual adjustment, but to details about any marital interactions), the patient in this analytic situation is unconsciously a jealous child, reacting to his actual spouse as one parent (his mother, say), and to the analyst as the other (his father, say). The patient is jealous, at this unconscious level, of how much of the analyst-father's interest is being devoted to this image of the spouse-mother.

Such patients function in such a manner, during the sessions, as to powerfully give the analyst to experience the jealousy toward the spouse which the patient is striving unconsciously to keep under repression. One such man, for instance, had said something to which he was apparently hoping for a response from me, and I had maintained my usual silence. He then went on, after a brief pause, "One thing, in my *relationship* with *Margaret* . . . . " His intonation was such as to smugly and jealousy-engenderingly imply that, whereas I have no relationship with him, his wife Margaret and he *do* have a relationship. He was still successfully defended, unconsciously, against the awareness of his jealous feeling that Margaret (to whom so much of his analytic time was being devoted) and I had a relationship with one another, whereas he had none with me.

In reality, I never met this man's wife. Since the patient's spouse on the one hand, and analyst on the other hand, rarely if ever have set eyes upon one another, and remain year after year miles apart, it is at first startling to discover how powerful is the transference reaction to these two as his parents. But in one instance after another it becomes clear, as the childhood origins of this transference distortion are brought to light, that his parents had been perceived by him as being, in psychological terms, fully as remote from, as unrelated to, one another as are his spouse and his analyst, geographically and in other regards, in his adult life.

The wishful aspects of such a perception of his parents, on the

child's part—beyond a generous basis in reality for this perception, particularly on the part of the more ill patients whose
parents were, indeed, highly schizoid—are largely a product of
the child's unresolved positive and negative oedipal ambitions.
His largely unconscious, rageful jealousy gives rise to an unconscious denial, on his part, of the relationship, sexual and otherwise, which the parents actually have with one another.

There is an additional form which the patient's unconscious,
oedipal jealousy takes, in the analytic situation, which I find to be
frequent indeed and a powerful source of resistance to the
analytic process: he unconsciously fosters, and obstinately maintains between himself and the analyst, the gulf of unrelatedness
which, so his oedipal ambitions—both positive and negative—
dictate, held sway between his two parents.

Such a form of transference-resistance to treatment is one of
the phenomena which render work with borderline patients
extremely difficult, and work with chronically psychotic patients
next to impossible. A chronically psychotic woman with whom I
have worked for many years (Searles 1972) has conveyed an
image of her father as being a Pharaoh of Egypt, existing in a
time-dimension thousands of years earlier than that of her mother, the latter being a queen of various different European countries. Thus a seemingly unbridgeable gulf, as regards time as well
as distance, is maintained. In the transference situation, the most
difficult among many difficult aspects of the treatment is the high
degree of unrelatedness which prevails, most of the time, between
us (she being largely fused with the mother, and I with the father)
and which, as has become increasingly clear, serves for her as an
unconscious defense against remarkably intense oedipal ambitions (both negative and positive) and terrors, from various
sources, which attend those ambitions.

Another woman with whom I have worked for many years was, during the first several of them, chronically schizophrenic, but in more recent years has been manifesting a borderline degree of impairment of ego functioning. She has long been subject to experiencing auditory hallucinations, both during and between her treatment sessions, and I have been given to feel on occasion jealous of her hallucinations, as in the instance of the hebephrenic man whom I mentioned near the beginning of this paper. In my work with this woman I have discovered a different form of these jealousy phenomena than I had seen before.

I had long known that her parental family had had idealized images, ostensibly of her but in actuality of themselves, which, evidently largely unconsciously, they had imposed harshly upon her and to which they had tried coercively to make her conform. I had long known, too, from my own work with her what a sadistically disappointing person she is. She is a person of little accomplishment by any conventional standards. Time after time I would sense, or clearly visualize, a larger, healthier, more capable, intelligent, mature, talented, more loving and lovable person, nascent or latent in her, than the relatively ineffectual and colorless one she was presently. But time after time, my hopeful efforts to help her to realize these capabilities which I perceived in her met with bitter disappointment as she failed to take this or that forward step into greater maturity of functioning, either within the sessions or in her daily life between them.

The unconscious-jealousy component of these failures did not come to my attention until the following seemingly trivial incident occurred in one of the sessions. I was shortly to go on a modest summer vacation. While sitting on the couch as she often did, she said, looking at me, "You'll get tanned, won't you, Dr. Searles? . . . attractive . . . bronzed . . . " I felt, as she talked, that she was clearly visualizing my looking so, in her mind's eye, and this definitely tended to make me feel jealous of the attractively bronzed image of me which she was visualizing, quite tangibly, as she gazed at my face. That experience with her left me well able to believe that similar jealousy was mobilized within her on occasions when she sensed that I was visualizing her as being a person capable, for instance, of driving a car, becoming married, and so on.

As regards the hebephrenic man I mentioned early in this paper, during the course of the work with whom I became aware of jealousy of his hallucinations, he broke one of his usual silences, after several years of our work together, by saying reproachfully, "You're jealous of my shadow." At the time, long accustomed by now to my feelings of jealousy in our work, I nonetheless heard "my shadow" only in its literal meaning, and was unaware of any jealousy of his shadow itself. I was not aware of any jealousy feelings during this particular session, nor had I been conscious of any for several months; things had been progressing slowly but well in the work with him during those months, and I was feeling relatively content. But in retrospect I surmise that "my shadow" was his only way of conceptualizing the tenuous individual self which was developing in him as a result of his labors, mine, and those of the innumerable other persons who had endeavored to help him during his years in the sanitarium. I think he was quite correct that, much as I was consciously endeavoring to help such an individual self to emerge in him, I did indeed react with jealousy to his relationship to this new and still-shadowy presence. On another occasion, when I broke the silence by asking what he was thinking or feeling, he explained, touchingly, "I'm playin' possum, tryin' to catch myself."

In my work with one narcissistic woman, who was enrolled in a doctoral program in psychology, it became evident that her

functioning during the analytic sessions for years was the equivalent, at an unconscious level, of the two parents in copulation
with one another, while I was cast as the personification of herself
as a child, torn by jealousy on both negative oedipal and positive
oedipal bases. She had had several years of largely unsuccessful
analysis prior to coming to me, and I quickly and enduringly
found her to be extremely resistive to the analytic process. Her
character disorder contained readily discernible narcissistic and
sadomasochistic features as defenses against—among other conflicts, of course—her repressed homosexual strivings. It was
evident, from the nature of the daily life material which she
reported, that she functioned in that setting, as she surely did in
the analytic one, in an intensely jealousy-engendering fashion—a
defense, of course, against her own largely-repressed feelings of
jealousy. She proved highly resistive, year after year, to experiencing awareness of this jealousy, or of being able to discern her
characteristic jealousy-engendering ways of relating, either outside or within the analytic setting. My own expressing to her
repeatedly the jealousy engendered in me by our work together
helped to bring all this relatively much into her awareness before
the termination of her analysis. But for years the sessions had a
highly sadomasochistic quality, and only after several years did it
become evident to me that her usual tortured demeanor on the
couch was in part a reaction-formation against the unconscious
copulatory pleasure being enjoyed by the two "persons"—parental introjects—within her.

In a session late in the analysis she reported a dream in which
she unwittingly intruded into a situation wherein her parents were
having intercourse, with the mother on top of the father, and the
patient feared her mother's wrath at this intrusion. The analytic
work had progressed sufficiently far, despite many difficulties,
that I was able to interpret—although with only limited effectiveness—her wish to be overpowered and raped by her phallic

mother, who was equivalent, I interpreted, to the university, toward which the patient was more than a little paranoid and by which she felt chronically wronged, after her several years of still-unsuccessful attempts to gain a Ph.D. there.

As this session went on she spoke, in reference to the dream, of her fear that she would be beaten up by her powerful mother "if I intruded upon her pleasure." Upon hearing this I immediately thought that it nicely described the way I recurrently still felt intimidated, more often than not, from "intruding upon" the analysis, lest she become exceedingly wroth (over some inter—pretation which would prove premature) and beat me up— *literally;* I still found reason for such physical fear of this woman who, like her mother, was powerfully built. I did not tell her of this thought, which in my mind was associated with early child-hood fear of my perceivedly phallic mother. Nor did I call her attention to her implied assumption, in the dream, that if she were further intrusive, her mother would in a sense *prefer* to beat her up, rather than continue copulating with the father; in this sense, the daughter apparently assumed that her mother would find her more arousing (even though to a form of sexual involvement disguised as aggression) than the father. No doubt my own chronically intimidated manner of functioning in the analytic work sprang from similarly unconscious, masochistic homosex-ual longings toward her (with her equivalent, as my associations suggested to me, to the phallic mother of my early childhood, whose beatings of me with a yardstick were commonplace; my father's much less frequent, and relatively unfeared, spankings were done with a simple foot-long desk ruler).

As I have been exploring these jealousy phenomena with one patient after another more and more deeply, year after year, I find it more understandable why a male patient is so vulnerable to feeling jealous of "Edith" (the name of his wife, whom I have never met). It becomes more and more clear, in this and comparable cases, that "Edith," of whom he talks endlessly in the sessions (usually in an intensely condemnatory, rejecting, hateful spirit), is essentially, in the context of the analytic interaction, not predominantly a reference to his wife in outer reality, but rather is a projected image of his own subjectively feminine self. I have found, long since, much reason for compassion toward and appreciation of "Edith" and I have many times felt, privately, that, for all his vituperation against "her," "Edith" is a basically more lovable "person," in my view, than is the patient "himself" ("himself" being those conscious identity components which are subjectively masculine and need not be projected into "Edith"). He is in a sense realistic in feeling jealous of the esteem which "Edith" enjoys in my eyes, for I do find, increasingly, his subjectively feminine self ("Edith") to be a gentler, more loving and lovable "person" than his hypermasculine, ruthless, rejecting "self" is during our sessions. It is unnecessary to detail, here, that this image to which he refers as "Edith" is comprised to a generous degree, as well, of components of his repressed transference images of the analyst.

The Role of These Jealousy Processes in Negative Therapeutic Reaction

I have been discussing here jealousy phenomena which, when maintained under repression or dissociation on the part of either patient or analyst, undoubtedly contribute importantly to many otherwise inexplicable instances of negative therapeutic reaction. I surmise that in many an instance wherein the analytic work founders, both patient and analyst have proved unable to integrate their unconscious jealousy of the patient's (and analyst's, as well) potentially healthier "selves."

An attorney in his late twenties, who in the course of his analysis gave me cause many times to feel anxiety lest he suicide, was reminiscing about his first attempt to obtain counseling. As a senior in high school he had "decided to see someone about myself " and had gone for an interview with the minister of the church his family attended. "He was used to seeing people who were in really grievous situations, and I guess I was one of the few he'd seen who had been so successful in school and all. I sat there in his study, and all sorts of intellectual insights came out of this murk [that is, the "murk" which prevailed in his head whenever he was severely depressed] that I hadn't known I knew. . . . He said [at the end of their interview, in a brisk and admiring tone], 'Well, you surely do have an excellent grasp of what's troubling you!'" The patient went on to say that what he had been saying to the minister had seemed entirely unreal to himself. All this seemed to me a beautifully expressed example of a person's ostensibly healthiest, most capable ego aspects functioning, in actuality, on the basis of an unintegrated introject which does not feel to be part of the patient himself, and thus does not enhance his self-esteem.

This young man's analysis revealed that he tended to feel murderously jealous of the much more successful person, so to speak, within him. It seemed to me not coincidental that, later in the above-mentioned session, he commented upon a recent item in the news, concerning an unusually gruesome suicide on the part of someone who evidently had been, as the patient put it, "bound and determined to die." His own analysis brought to light much evidence that his suicidal urge consisted, in large part, in an unconscious determination to kill the jealously hated, intellectually successful but emotionally remote mother-introject within him. This kind of clinical material, concerning repressed jealousy involving an introject, is relevant to the literature concerning imbalances in the development of various ego functions (James 1960, Ross 1967).

A man in his thirties, who had worked for several years with a previous analyst, said early in a session with me, "I had a dream last night. I *have lots* of dreams; *my* trouble is that I can't *remember* my dreams. It's an uncooperative part of me that I resent, because they [i.e., his dreams] say things more clearly and succinctly that *I* do when I digress throughout my sessions." He had expressed furious exasperation toward both himself and me, innumerable times, for making—so he felt—little constructive use of our time together; he recurrently found it maddeningly difficult to express cogently his voluminous free associations. It seemed to me strongly implied, in what I have quoted here, that he was unconsciously jealous of his dreams, as equivalent to persons more articulate than himself; his difficulty in remembering his dreams apparently was based, in part, upon this unconscious jealousy of them.

A woman who not infrequently manifested, during her sessions, the sudden onset of transitory headaches (clearly linked with the threatened derepression of explosive rage, and other unconscious affects), said on one such occasion, "I sorta envy the headaches, because they seem to belong to another existence, and not to the life I'm trying to lead. . . . "

A woman whose resistance had withstood, largely intact, several years of an eventually seven-year analysis commented at the beginning of a session that she felt that each of us had greeted the other, in the waiting room, with "disinterest. The analysis was what I was looking forward to, and what had brought me here today," adding that I had seemed to feel uninterested in her, as she had felt toward me, and that she had "assumed that your thoughts would turn toward my *associations,* rather than toward *me.* . . . " She said all this in a thoughtful, largely dispassionate tone; but I sensed an underlying feeling of hurt in her, and an underlying feeling, also, of jealousy of her own associations—her own analytic productions, so to speak. I heard this as linking up with her childhood experiences of (for example) enormous interest on the part of her mother during the piano lessons to which she daily had subjected the daughter.

This same woman said, many months later, that she had been hurt, during and following the previous day's session, by my having said so little, and in this session she had repeatedly expressed wishes to kill me. Parenthetically, for years she had expressed toward me, on inumerable occasions, murderousness of a paranoid-delusional intensity which I often had found very threatening. On this occasion she went on (without comment from me) to concede, however, that "It may be very beneficial for the analysis that . . . you don't respond to everything I talk about. . . . " This last statement I heard as conveying, significantly, a hint of her unconscious jealousy of the analysis. On another occasion, when she ruminated, "It's weird how different I feel in here, than I feel outside the analysis . . . , " I heard this comment as revealing that she evidently was equating, at an unconscious level, "in here" (my office) with her analysis—as though her analysis were confined to my office and did not participate, as it were, in her life elsewhere. Her unconscious jealousy of the analysis would help account for her isolating it thus—her refusing to let it share the rest of her daily living, but her leaving it behind, instead, every time she left my office at the end of a session.

A woman whose intense homosexual longings were largely defended against by paranoid mechanisms ended some characteristically contemptuous, bitter statement derisively with: " . . . *psychoanalysis!*" and added, in an assertive, competitive, triumphant flourish, "*—my ass!*" The tone and sequence of her words clearly indicated that she unconsciously experienced her ass to be in competition with psychoanalysis (including her own psychoanalysis) and that once again she had demonstrated the primacy, in the competition, of her ass. There had emerged, in the earlier years of our work, abundant material to support this formulation. It had become evident how strong a resistance she had against receiving *analytic* help from me, since this would constitute unmistakable evidence of my being able to resist the lure of her ass sufficiently to enable me to function as her analyst.

In more general terms, and widening the focus to include extra-analytic situations also, it had become evident that she functioned, in many interpersonal settings, in terms of her brain's having to compete (as regards the arousing of the other person's interest in her) with her body. For example, she many times reported to me, in analytic sessions, that in the most recent seminars in her master's degree program in nursing, she had scarcely begun to express the many theoretical and clinical observations which she was eager to contribute, before all the others present (most of whom were women) had "jumped on me" or "descended on me."

Not rarely, the analysis itself proves to have become for the patient, as I have already mentioned in brief, the personification of the jealously-fought internal object. One borderline woman made an apparently ordinary, but highly significant, comment about "my attempts to link up things [i.e., daily-life events] *with you, or with the analysis"* [italics mine]. As the session went on, she provided data which indicated a transference to *me* as mother (relatively interpersonally responsive, accessible, tangibly *there),* and a simultaneous and contrasting transference to the *analyis* as father (for the most part an extremely emotionally-remote person in the patient's childhood—inaccessible, impersonal, enigmatic). Even though jealousy did not emerge into awareness during the session, either in myself or, so far as I could discern, in her, I knew this to be the kind of splitting of the transference, as between the analyst on the one hand and the analysis on the other hand, which typically enables the dissociated internal-object jealousy to emerge, in course of time, from dissociation, as I had found, and continue to find, occurs quite explicitly in my work with a number of patients, work wherein the analysis emerges as a jealousy-engendering rival for either patient or analyst.

One man said ruefully at the end of a session during which, bored as usual, I had said little or nothing, "I've done it again. I've filled up the hour with grinding boredom. I've rendered the hour ineffective. I've rendered the analysis ineffective. . . . " Our work together had given me reason to hear, in these seemingly ordinary expressions of futility and discouragement, an important oedipal jealousy significance. It was becoming increasingly clear to me that the analytic hour, the analysis generally, and the most formal-analyst components of myself, represented to him, at an unconscious level, an oedipal rival parent (either father or mother, varyingly), while the less formally analytic, more simply and spontaneously personal, aspects of me were equivalent to the oedipally desired parent (again, varyingly either mother or father, so the genetic data indicated). Thus, for example, in such a session as that just ending, he apparently had been involved in an unconscious effort to unman the father components of the analyst ("the hour," or "the analysis") and possess, sexually, the mother components of the analyst. It eventually became clear that there was not only a transference but also a coun-tertransference component in this, for I discovered in myself a certain submerged appeal in his remaining rocklike, immune to my analytic efforts, with the implicit promise, as I tended to experience it, that he would eventually wear down my analyst-defense and possess me sexually in a setting of my surrendering my long-sustained attempt to analyze him successfully.

All this seems to me relevant to the literature concerning the "real" relationship between patient and analyst, and concerning, similarly, the therapeutic alliance (see Greenson 1965, Greenson and Wexler 1969, and Stone 1967). From my experience with such patients as the one just mentioned, it seems to me highly illusory to think that there is much of an extra-transference, "real" relationship between the two participants until relatively late in the analysis, after the patient's oedipal conflicts have largely emerged from repression and become integrated. Prior to that time, the so-called "real" relationship between the two is all too likely to be comprised, to an appreciable if not predominant degree, in the patient's unconscious experience of it, of a transference relationship to those pertinent aspects of the analyst's functioning as being equivalent to one parent, and the more formal analyst components of the analyst equivalent to the other parent, referable to the patient's unresolved oedipal era of development.

Still another form of transference jealousy, which I have seen most readily in schizoid and narcissistic patients, is one in which the patient reacts to the analysis as being a parent whom the patient is determined to keep all to himself; whenever the analyst does succeed in participating perceptibly in the analysis, the patient reacts with jealous rage against this perceivedly sexual rival for the beloved parent.

In ostensible contrast to the phenomenon I have just cited, but on closer scrutiny an example of that phenomenon, is the following instance of a patient for whom the analytic process proved to be the unconscious equivalent of many years of a medical nursing process in his parental home, centered upon a slightly younger sister who had been born with a serious cardiac-valvular disorder. He remembered in detail, many times during the analysis, how greatly the treatment of this sister, carried on primarily by his mother but largely dominating the life of his whole family, had cast a shadow over his own whole remembered upbringing. His jealousy of this grievously afflicted sister was, of course, difficult for him to face and integrate. But what I wish to emphasize here is some of the evidence that his erstwhile unconscious competitiveness had not only to do with the sister herself but, farther from the conventionally human realm, with the *care of* this sister.

In one session he was saying, "There was *nothing* about the care of Esther in our home that did *any*thing to rally our family together.... It was a *destructive* thing .... It was just a nightmare from beginning to end .... " Because what he said here reminded me of how he had spoken oftentimes of the analysis (which he often had come close to stopping), I interrupted him, asking, "If you were to stop the analysis at this point, and were to look back on it, I wonder to what extent this would serve to express one of your feelings about it: 'There was *nothing* about the analysis that did *any*thing to rally our family [here meaning his marital family, as I felt sure was clear to him] together—it was a *destructive* thing—it was just a nightmare from beginning to end'?"

He replied promptly, thoughtfully, and convincingly, "I wouldn't the last part; but the rest of it I would," and went on to say that the analysis—like, he implied, the care of Esther during his childhood—is "something that keeps you [referring consciously to himself; it was maddeningly difficult to bring him to see that the "you" indeed referred, unconsciously to me] in turmoil. No matter how much you try to wall it off, it's always present, it's always a source of contention. . . . "

I thought of this man's unconscious resistance to the analysis as being equivalent to "the care of Esther in our home. . . . a destructive thing . . . " when on a later occasion I was interviewing, in the presence of a group of residents, a borderline schizophrenic woman. About this woman, both at that hospital and the previous one from which she had been transferred, there had been unusually diverse opinions concerning her diagnosis, and it seemed to me that this uncertainty was related to her clearly severe identity-uncertainty. During the interview she asked me if she were "a guinea pig," which of course was not an unusual question from a patient being interviewed in such a setting; later on she said, uneasily, "I wonder if I'll walk out of here feeling like a piece of liverwurst." But what particularly reminded me of the previously-described man was this patient's next question: "Am I a teaching process?"—the term "teaching process" being so much on a par, in its bizarrely nonhuman-identity connotation, with "the care of Esther."

The patient whom I was interviewing in the hospital had (like, in certain regards, my analytic patient) childhood experiences clearly relevant to her presently poorly established identity as a human being. In her childhood she had lived under the serious threat that she would be given to the Negro ice man who, she told me, "beat his horse" and, after he died, to the garbage man. She tried repeatedly, and equally seriously, to give away her baby brother, whom the mother left much in her care. By the time of my interview with her she had had the experience of working for two years as a prostitute, during which time she had obtained an abortion of an eight and a half month fetus.

One point which I wish to emphasize here is that patients whose own sense of identity is so distorted—patients who at an unconscious level have self-images as being various nonhuman entities, such as a *process* of one sort or another—are entirely capable of developing transference reactions, in the treatment setting, to various aspects of the situation in addition to the analyst himself, transference reactions in which the particular identity component in question is being projected upon the nonhuman object or process in question.

In the instance of a middle-age woman with a narcissistic character disorder, whose upbringing had involved a father who had been only tangentially and elusively present psychologically, and a mother with multiple sclerosis which had caused her to become progressively disabled over the years of this daughter's growing up, I discovered an element in her resistance to the analytic process of which I had never been aware in my work with any patients before her: she clearly was manifesting a *transference* (tenacious and multirooted) *to transference*. That is, to the whole realm of transference phenomena, of whatever childhood origin, she reacted with certain unconscious, and therefore automatic, reactions which made her conscious recognition of these phenomena extraordinarily difficult. For her, at an unconscious level, transference phenomena were equivalent, by reason of their elusive and subtle presence on the scene, to her elusive father, for whom her contempt and antagonism were enormous. Further, any transference reaction on her part, toward the analyst, implied a three-person setting—herself, the analyst, and the childhood predecessor of the analyst—and three-person situations inherently were imbued with intense jealousy for this woman, whose narcissism was serving as a defense against (among other emotions) much paranoid jealousy.

Jealousy Toward Nonhuman Objects

In these jealousy phenomena which involve an internal object in one of the two actual persons, that internal object frequently is projected upon some nonhuman thing (as I indicated earlier) which thereby acquires the psychological impact of a third person in the jealousy-ridden triangular relationship. It is not rare, for example, to discover that the analytic patient is jealous of a plant in the analyst's office, a plant reminiscent of those to which the patient's mother had devoted loving care, plants which had represented, for the mother, unconscious transference objects, the externalized representations of internal objects with which she had been involved in intimate and loving relatedness, to the jealous exclusion of the child himself.

The involvement, here, of an ingredient of what is in actuality the nonhuman environment is traceable to an incomplete differentiation, in the ego-developmental history of one or both of the two persons involved, from the nonhuman environment. That is the subject to which my first book (Searles 1960) was devoted;

in it, I tried primarily to portray how manifold are the human strivings or emotional conflicts which are given expression through, or defended against, by identification with or non-differentiation from the nonhuman environment.

A borderline woman's statement, "I felt very envious of their house" (referring to the new home of a couple who are friends of her and her husband) is typical of the phraseology which, no matter how commonplace in its grammatical usage, betrays the speaker's unconscious lack of differentiation between animate and inanimate, and her unconscious longing to *be* the inanimate possession of the persons who are, at a conscious level, the objects of her envy for the possession of it. In other words, the phraseology reveals that although the speaker *consciously* envies the other person for possessing the object in question (the new house, in this instance), *unconsciously* she wishes to be not the human possessor of that inanimate object, but the object itself, possessed and cherished by the other person(s). Unconsciously the envy is based on a far more primitive identificational longing than appears on the surface to be the case.

Experiences with many patients have convinced me that, in this admittedly commonplace phraseology for the expression of envy ("I envy his new car"; "I envy her new dress"; and so on), we are dealing not merely with a grammatical shorthand to obviate the necessity for the more cumbersome, "I envy him his new car" or "I envy her her new dress." In many instances, such seemingly mundane comments have served to alert me to the fact that this or that patient has an important if not predominant realm of his personal identity existing, at an unconscious level, subjectively in the form of an inanimate object or other nonhuman entity, in envious competition not with other human beings—for subjectively, he had not achieved a predominantly human ego identity—but with actually nonhuman ingredients of the world about him.

In general, it seems to me, the envy-dominated patient is less far along, in achieved differentiatedness, from the nonhuman environment, than is the jealousy-dominated patient. The patient who envies a colleague's new *car,* for instance, is a patient who tends to feel so akin to his nonhuman environment, so far from feeling established as a human being among his fellows, as to feel readily thrown into competition with cars and other material possessions of those around him. On the other hand the patient who is envious *of his colleague for possessing* a beautiful car, and even more, the patient who is jealous of an acquaintance for "possessing," so to speak, a beautiful wife, is reacting in terms more of burning to be the *person* who possesses these; his human identifications, and with these his identity as a human being, are stronger than is the case with the former patient whose identifications are more with various ingredients of the nonhuman world.

Space does not allow any comprehensive discussion of the determinants of a patient's having developed a sense of identity based more upon kinship with the nonhuman environment than with the human environment; my monograph concerning this subject explores that topic at length. Here I want simply to mention that as regards external causes for this, a child's seeing his parent to be lovingly related more with plants, animal pets, the furniture of the household, and various cherished material possessions, for example, than with the other human members of the family, tends to pit the child in competition with these nonhuman ingredients of his childhood surroundings. A frequent internal cause has to do with the child's attempt to take refuge from the world of people in his environment, an interpersonal world perceived by him—undoubtedly in part realistically, not merely through projection—as being permeated with murderously jealous competition, fleeing into identifying with the less frightening, more stable, nonhuman world about him—by being or remaining, for example, part of the woodwork in the home, rather than taking any identifiable part in, for instance, violent arguments between his parents, or competition with feared, or parentally much preferred, siblings. This flight into such a refuge tends—as one can see most clearly in schizophrenic patients—eventually to boomerang, to greatly worsen the patient's situation, for the nonhuman environment itself comes to personify, for him, the menacing objects of his jealous rivalry, such that the whole nonhuman world may come to feel terrifyingly inimical to him.

The ego functioning of a woman in her late forties remained, over a very considerable number of years of analysis, essentially schizoid, with her emotionality of a contrived, "as if" quality. The only emotions she manifested which seemed to me indubitably real were a relentless, grinding rage, admixed at times with self-pity; and even these emotions she seemed not to acknowledge within herself as a part of her identity. The point relevant for this paper is the dénouement: after many years of analysis, a long-repressed jealousy of all of outer reality (as epitomized by the world outside the parental/marital home), experienced as being a sexual rival in her oedipal striving for her father, was one of the determinants of this flaw in her relatedness with reality. Her denial of outer reality was, at this level of ego functioning, tantamount to massive depreciation of this oedipal rival.

Near the beginning of her analysis, she made it clear that her father had suffered throughout her upbringing, and still suffered, from a number of phobias—of flying, of traveling at all far from his house, and so on—which rendered his life largely constricted to the house itself. It was clear to me, and I felt sure that it was to her also, that his need to repress promiscuous sexual impulses, as well as rageful impulses, was one of the major causes of his phobias. It was early clear, that is, that the world outside her father's home had represented, in his unconscious, a tempting but frightening myriad of ragefully uncontrollable sexual objects.

The patient herself loved gardening. It became clear early in her analysis that her chronic, diffuse rage was expressed, on the innumerable occasions when it became unbearably intense, in a stereotyped urge to "carve up a rosebush," an urge which she had carried into action on many occasions over the years. Many times during the analytic sessions, when this always-tense woman was feeling even more tense than usual, she would become immersed in a vivid fantasy of slashing a rosebush into bits with a sickle.

Incidental to the present point, but by no means unimportant, at a deeply pregenital level this woman also manifested powerful "prehuman" identifications with her father, experienced here as a mother, and these identifications became manifest, about two months prior to a session I shall shortly discuss, in a self-image as a beautiful rosebush covered with blooms, an image I found both esthetically beautiful and emotionally moving.

In the pertinent session two months later, about fifteen minutes into it she was surmising that "It's envy or jealousy that makes me want to carve up rosebushes." She went on to say that one time in New Hampshire, where she and her marital family had lived before moving to the Washington area, her husband (who, like her father, was subject to severe phobic anxiety) had come to feel very frightened of the overgrowth of shrubbery outside the house into which they had just moved, and had said something fragmentary, and not fully intelligible, about his mother; the husband's parental home was not far away. The patient went on to speak of the jealousy she had felt in that setting. Her jealousy clearly had a reference to her husband's relationship with his mother; but, of particular interest, she hinted strongly that her jealousy had been of the shrubbery also. She all but said that she had been jealous of the shrubbery for its evoking a more intense response (of phobic anxiety) in her husband than she herself had felt capable of evoking. Relevant here is the fact, long known to both of us, that throughout her upbringing she had felt maddenedly unable to compete successfully with her father's adored image of his long-dead mother. In adult life she felt chronically belittled and ignored by her husband, much as she had felt treated in childhood by her father.

She went on to say, during the same session, that the "ferocity" with which she carved up rosebushes, with the sickle, would frighten her husband and two young sons. Parenthetically, some of the most stressful of our sessions had a kind of impending axe-murder atmosphere, an atmosphere so undemarcated by any firm ego boundaries that on occasion the murderousness felt not localized clearly within either one of us, but permeating the room.

Still later in this same session, she went on to say, without any intervening comments from me, that sometimes it seems to her that she is in her head, having dialogues with herself, and "perceiving the world in the third person."

Obviously I cannot prove incontestably here a hypothesis, based in important part upon clinical intuition, which proved pertinent and useful in my work with her. But it does seem to me that the above mentioned fragments of data, taken together, strongly suggest that she long had been reacting, at an unconscious level, to the outer world as being a person, the object of her murderous jealousy and therefore attempted denial, because this "person" represented to her (oedipally-striven-for) father his own sexually desired but tabooed mother, with whom the patient was furiously unable to compete successfully. I am reasonably confident that my records of my work with frankly schizophrenic patients can yield much analogous data, pointing toward essentially the same kind of contribution of oedipal conflicts to the later development of psychosis in many patients.

I have encountered closely comparable data in appreciably less ill patients also—patients whose ego functioning was of a predominantly normal-neurotic variety—in the depths of their analyses.

The Loneliness of the Analyst's Work

The strange emotions against which borderline and frankly schizophrenic defenses are maintained are, by definition, too stressful for the patient's relatively weak ego to tolerate in awareness. In the analyst's work with such a patient, the analyst's own relatively strong ego must become able to admit into awareness these emotions before the patient can become able, partly through identification with the analyst, to do likewise. Intrapsychic jealousy is one of these strange emotions.

As regards the difficulty for the analyst in coping even with the more obvious forms—the three-actual-person forms—of jealousy, it should be seen that the loneliness, in reality, of the analyst's work is such as to make him highly prey to feeling reality-based jealousy in the analytic setting. This lonely nature of one's work as an analyst is an immensely powerful reality factor which tends to require one to repress the feelings of jealousy to which the work renders one so vulnerable—including feelings of jealousy of that partially split-off aspect of *oneself* which enjoys, transitorily at least, relatively close communion with the patient, as one or another of the clinical examples given here have detailed.

Far more than by the ritualized structuring of tne analytic situation, which prohibits or severely limits any usual social intimacy, the analyst is rendered lonely by his necessarily predominant attunement to aspects of the patient which are unconscious, and may not emerge into relatively full awareness for years. As regards the patient's conscious self, the analyst is, to the degree that he is attuned to these unconscious components of the former, alone in the office. Moreover, to the extent that the patient concomitantly is related, during the session, with a projected transference image which the analyst feels to have little basis in his own subjective personal identity, he feels unrelated-to by the patient. Still another factor in the analyst's loneliness may have to do with the probable fact that, oftentimes, the greater part of his analytic work is being carried on at an unconscious level in *himself*—at a level of ego functioning which is relatively split off from, and therefore inaccessible as any potential working companion to, his lonely consciously-functioning ego-aspects.

Many patients spend their analytic sessions as though the analyst were a diary in which to record the daily life events which have transpired since the previous session. It has seemed to me that one of the underlying affects which impel the patient compulsively to do this is his anxiety lest the perceived recluse-analyst feel barred out from even this vicarious living-through-the-patient, and become murderously jealous of him.

Quite beyond the matter of any predominantly *symbiotic* transference, *any* analytic situation in which the transference neurosis or psychosis has become well established, leaving the rest of the patient's daily living relatively undisturbed by his most intense emotional conflicts, now safely focused predominantly in the transference relationship, is a setting in which the patient tends to feel threatened by the analyst's presumed readiness to feel jealous of him. The patient's extra-analytic daily life is now relatively enjoyable, whereas the analytic sessions—the only aspect of the analyst's daily living which the patient has an opportunity to perceive—are relatively filled with anxiety and conflictual feelings. Thus the patient tends to fear that the analyst, who leads—as judged by this immediate sample—so difficult, unpleasant, and perhaps highly anxious life—is jealous of him for the gratifications which the patient's life outside the analytic sessions has come to provide him.

Under such circumstances as I have been describing, the following typical comment came from a married woman who had been in analysis for several years. Upon arriving ten minutes late she said, after lying down on the couch, "I hadn't tried to be late;

but I hadn't tried not to be late, either. It seems like something of a paradox: I feel like I'm doing very well in general, and at the same time it seems like it's more difficult to come here."

Four months later this same woman, predominantly schizoid in her personality functioning, mentioned, "My birthday is coming up on Wednesday; I'll be thirty. It is twenty years since my mother died. Somehow that seems very striking to me—that I've been living twice as long as the number of years I lived when my mother was living." At the juncture when she said, "Somehow that seems very striking to me," I found myself wondering whether—and very much doubting that—she had *ever* felt equally struck by *any*thing *I* had ever said to her, and I began sulking in jealousy, even though I felt sure that she was vigorously fostering this reaction in me. I said nothing as she went on speaking, and a few minutes later she was saying in a semiamused but otherwise dispassionate tone, "I feel like we're running a small hospital— Bill [their toddler-age son] with his broken leg, Marjorie [their four-year-old daughter] with her eye infection, Eddie [their eight-year-old son] with his recent tonsillectomy . . . " She was saying this from her customary posture of lying comfortably curled on her side on the couch, staring absently toward the nearby window. By the end of the session, I was left feeling that this had been one of those innumerable sessions in which she had functioned in a maddeningly, infuriatingly aloof manner, a manner which often fostered my feeling bitterly left out and deeply jealous of the contrastingly lively interaction among the personality components (introjects having the subjective identity value, and interpersonal impact, of persons) within her. The family, so to speak, of her unconscious introjects were often projected, during sessions such as this one, upon the other members of her marital family—persons who in daily life may have found reason, as I often did, to feel jealously shut out of what was going on within her.

In a paper in 1971 concerning pathologic symbiosis and autism, I reported that.

In both my own analytic (i.e., therapeutic) work and in doing supervision, I have encountered many instances of the patient's functioning as though he were the only link between the analyst and a real world where there are real people who are living, who are involved in doing things and experiencing feelings. In short, the patient functions as though he were the analyst's aliveness, as though the analyst could gain access to living only vicariously, through the patient's own living outside the office.

To some degree this is a realistic reaction on the part of the patient to the sedentary aspects, the recluse aspects, of the analyst's living as the patient can only limitedly know it. But it is more significantly a transference reaction to the analyst as personifying the more schizoid, detached, preoccupied components of one or another figure from the patient's early life, and as personifying, by the same token, the patient's own detachment from living. That is, the schizoid part of the patient himself, the part which participates little in his own daily living, he projects upon the analyst.

Thus the patient, in his recounting of various daily-life incidents, communicates these in a fashion which tends to make the analyst feel a recluse, in this garret, secretly jealous of all the living the patient is doing; or secretly guilty because he cannot be filled, as he feels he should be filled, with altruistic joy on behalf of the actually narcissistic patient immersed in this recounting; or secretly grateful to the patient for speaking in a fashion which enables him to share the "reliving" of the incident. Neither the subtly schizoid patient nor the analyst may realize that the former was not at all fully living the original incident now being "relived"—that he is only now really living it for the first time, in this setting of "reliving" it in

connection with the analyst who symbiotically personifies his
own unconscious and projected schizoid self [Searles 1971, pp.
73–74].

The symbiotic, preindividuation, ego-developmental aspect of
the analyst's jealousy, as described in the foregoing quote, is
evident enough. But it seems to me probable that, as in the clinical
example of the woman who repeatedly experienced urges to
"carve up a rosebush," there is a determinant of this jealousy
from, also, the oedipal level of ego development. That is, just as in
that woman's girlhood all of reality outside the home had been
reacted to by her, unconsciously, as being an oedipal rival favored
by the father, so the analyst as I have described him in the above
passage is being given by the patient to feel unconsciously jealous
of the patient's extra-analytic reality, as being an oedipal rival of
the analyst, a rival favored by the patient.

Commentary Concerning Psychoanalytic Technique

The clinical vignettes already presented have served, I hope, to
emphasize the importance of the analyst's becoming open to
experience, during the analytic session with the patient, moments
of intrapsychic jealousy such as I have described. As the years
have gone on in my own work with patients, I have found
increasingly frequent occasions for reporting to the patient,
moreover, my inner jealousy experience, as data of importance to
be shared with him in our mutual exploration of what is transpiring between us and thus, most importantly of course, within him
at less than conscious levels. Whereas at the beginning of my
psychoanalytic career it would have been unthinkable for me to
reveal to a patient that I was feeling jealous in any regard, this has
become a relatively commonplace occurrence in my work and,
particularly if I have already begun to form at least some tentative

impression of the nature of the transference context in which I am experiencing this, and if I reveal this affective experience of mine in a relatively unanxious, nonguilty, nonaccusatory fashion but rather in an interested-collaborator fashion, the patient will find this response to be, in a high percentage of instances, predominantly illuminating and helpful rather than disturbing.

It may well be that my psychoanalytic technique in general, in my work with nonpsychotic patients, involves a marked degree of underinterpretation of the analysand's productions; certainly more than one of my training analysands has thought so. Whereas it might be thought that one's discovery of the vastness of this realm of intrapsychic jealousy, so frequently glimpsed now in one's daily work, would provide one with a profusion of opportunities for making interpretations—not of the transference in the usual sense of postindividuation object-relatedness between patient and analyst, but rather concerning aspects of the interrelatedness between, or among, different parts of the patient's self—in actual practice I do not find this to be the case.

I still find that it requires a great many hours of predominant silence on my part before the patient can achieve a sufficient degree of object-relatedness with me to be able to experience me as being an entity at all separate from him and an entity, at the same time, of sufficient significance to warrant his *(a)* hearing what I can convey to him, in verbal interpretations which are a product of my thoughts and my feelings; *(b)* listening attentively to what I am saying; and *(c)* associating constructively to what I have said to him. Prior to such a phase in the analysis, the final paragraph of my paper quoted above (Searles 1971) still seems to me valid. I discussed not only the blatant autism so evident in patients suffering from schizophrenia of whatever degree of severity, but also the subtly present autism that emerges in the depth of any neurotic patient's analysis:

As the months and years of the analyst's work with the autistic patient wear on, the analyst is given to feel unneeded, incompetent, useless, callous, and essentially *nonhuman* in relation to his so troubled and beseeching and reproachful, but so persistently autistic, patient. It is essential that the analyst be able to endure this long period—a period in which, despite perhaps abundant data from the patient, transference interpretations are rarely feasible—in order that the patient's transference regression can reach the early level of ego development at which, in the patient's infancy or very early childhood, his potentialities for a healthy mother-infant symbiosis became distorted into a defensively autistic mode of ego-functioning. At that level of ego development, the infant or young child had not yet come to achieve a perceptual and experiential differentiation between himself and his mother, *nor between his mother and the surrounding nonhuman world.* When in the evolution of the transference that early level of ego-functioning becomes accessible, then it is possible for therapeutically symbiotic processes to occur between patient and therapist, and be interpretable as such. In due course, this phase of therapeutic symbiosis will subsequently usher in the phase of individuation [pp. 83–84].

In other words, as regards this present paper's thesis, it continues to be my experience, concerning psychoanalytic technique, that it is predominantly silence on my part—a silence which involves as high a degree of accessibility as possible to communications from my own unconscious as well as from that of the patient (for example, my relatively freely becoming aware, within me, of such intrapsychic jealousy phenomena as this paper reports)—which facilitates the patient's coming to experience his internal objects, and me in the transference-relatedness, as being of approximately equivalent psychological significance to him.

Once this degree of therapeutic symbiosis has developed in the transference relationship, the analyst has achieved a position, in the patient's eyes, from which he can make powerfully effective interpretations concerning the interrelatedness among the patient's internal objects and the analyst as a transference object. Prior to the emergence of this primitive level of ego functioning in the evolution of the patient's transference regression in the analytic situation, the analyst's utilization of verbal interpretations, no matter how accurate their content may be, still seems to me to have the effect, more often than not, of temporarily severing such symbiotic relatedness as has been developing between patient and analyst and postponing, therefore, establishment of the necessary degree of therapeutic symbiosis. All too often, that is, the analyst's delivering an apparently highly perceptive, seemingly highly intelligent verbal interpretation is in actuality a predominantly unconscious defensive response on his part, impelled by his unconscious need to demonstrate to himself that he has not lost his individuality—that he and the patient are not fully at one.

In the instance of one narcissistic or schizoid patient after another I have come to realize, as the analysis reveals splits in the ego which at the beginning of his analysis had long been sealed over, that at the outset the patient had been so powerfully defended against feeling consciously dependent upon me not simply for the reason that he would be exposing himself otherwise to the risk of feeling rejected, hurt, disappointed, angry, and so forth but, far more, for the reason that he would be exposing himself to the tangible danger that he would become psychotic. One way of construing this risk is that, having exposed himself to symbiotic relatedness with the other person and then having lost the other person, he thereby loses him*self*. One can say, as well, that he is defended against the inner danger of being torn to pieces by intrapsychic jealousies which become intensified in a setting of increasing intimacy with a real other person, the analyst.

It is the task of the analyst, as over the years the patient's regression deepens in the increasing intimacy (partly transference intimacy but partly real intimacy also) of the analytic work, to foster the emergence of these previously buried ego splits in a controllable, ego-integratable manner, partly through being able to go ahead steadily while the patient is projecting his own ego-fragmented inner state upon the analyst. The analyst's going ahead steadily, in this process, involves his being able both to experience in awareness, and maintain under analytic scrutiny, such intrapsychic jealousy as had been in part responsible for the maintenance, heretofore, of the splits in the patient's ego functioning—responsible, that is, for the fact that the patient's internal object world has been permeated by jealousy-ridden disharmony.

In the instance of one highly schizoid woman, it required nearly ten years of analysis for her to become aware of feelings of jealousy toward anyone; the realm of her own dissociated feelings of jealousy became accessible to her through becoming aware of jealousy toward her legs, for which she had developed an overt, intimately-cherishing fondness, as comprising essentially a person separate from her. Such tenacious dissociation of the realm of jealousy feelings suggests to me how essential it is for the analyst to become open to experiencing jealousy of the patient's relationships with the latter's introjects, in order that the patient, in turn, will become able to emerge from her interpersonal autism, through starting to face and experience the intense jealousy against which (among other dissociated emotions) the autism had been maintained as an unconscious defense.

The point I made three paragraphs ago, concerning the determinants of narcissistic or schizoid patients' dissociation of their dependency needs seems to me sufficiently important to warrant restating in somewhat different terms. As I have encountered more and more intrapsychic jealousy phenomena, in diverse forms, in my work with patients, I have come to have what seems to me a fuller appreciation of what before had seemed to me a relatively simple repression of dependency needs in many patients. I now understand that a schizoid man, for example, functions in an emotionally sealed-off manner not so much to keep dissociated his dependency needs (and attendant frustration-rage, and so on) toward the outer world per se as, rather, to keep dissociated his intense intrapsychic jealousy which increasing intimacy with the outer world would tend to activate, and which tends to tear him apart into the component internal objects which comprise his "self " and which (paralleling the mother's internal state in his early childhood, and paralleling the state of the unconscious interpersonal relationships in the childhood family as a whole) have been existing in a state of defensively distant nonrelatedness from one another within him. In the work with such a patient, I come to see that his childhood-family psychodynamics had involved the family's living, over the years, on a powder keg of collectively dissociated jealousy. When the analyst is working with a patient who is intimately involved in relatedness with (for example) an hallucination, and the analyst is consciously content to be treated as insignificant to that relatedness, he, the analyst—just as in the instance of the walled-off schizoid patient—is unconsciously defending himself against the fear or terror of becoming torn to pieces by jealousy from intrapsychic sources.

In addition to many clinical experiences of finding how devastating to the patient had been his realization that his mother had a separate self, I have encountered instances in which it had seemed hardly less devastating to discover that the mother and father, formerly perceived unconsciously as one fused parent-figure, were in actuality two separate persons who were involved in a relationship—a relationship very jealousy-engendering for him—with one another. Such analytic material is of essentially the same nature as my description, quoted early in this paper, of my coming to perceive the two "persons" intimately involved with one another in my jealous view, who comprised the schizoid man who previously, in his impact upon me, had been a maddeningly walled-off but single, nonjealousy-engendering, individual.

I am mindful that a patient's unconscious perception of the analyst as being comprised of the two parents not fully differentiated from—that is, safely fused with—one another, has as one of its determinants the unconscious need to defend against both positive and negative oedipal strivings toward the parents. More than eight years ago, in my supervisory work with a psychiatric resident who was treating a young borderline schizophrenic woman, it became evident that, for her, individuation carried with it the threat of fulfillment of incestuous strivings, such that she unconsciously clung to a transference-image of her therapist as being both parents, safely fused together in sexual union. I do not doubt that the analytic data presented above is expressive of this determinant also.

Melanie Klein (1932) stated that fantasies of "the combined parent figure" normally form part of the early stages of the oedipus complex. She reported later that

> I would now add that the whole development of the Oedipus complex is strongly influenced by the intensity of envy which determines the strength of the combined parental figure. . . . The influence of the combined parental figure on the infant's ability to differentiate between the parents, and to establish good relations with each of them, is affected by the strength of envy and the intensity of his Oedipus jealousy. For the suspicion that the parents are always getting sexual gratification from one another reinforces the phantasy—derived from various sources—that they are always combined [Klein 1957, pp. 197–198].

For the analyst to become aware of the whole multifarious world of internal objects within the patient and within himself—to become aware of this at a more than merely intellectual level—requires him to allow himself to experience again at least a sample of what was, for him as for all human beings, his earliest and greatest loss, the loss (through large-scale and decades-long-maintained dissociation) of the so-largely nonintegrated world of very early childhood, a world comprised of a mother experienced in some such largely nonintegrated and nondifferentiated manner as Winnicott repeatedly has conceptualized, as here (1945) for example:

In regard to environment, bits of nursing technique and faces seen and sounds heard and smells smelt are only gradually pieced together into one being to be called mother. In the transference situation in analysis of psychotics we get the clearest proof that the psychotic state of unintegration had a natural place at a primitive stage of the emotional development of the individual [p. 150].

The adult's unconscious resistance in this connection must be based in major part upon his unconscious unwillingness to open himself up, once again, to the loss he experienced in early childhood at having largely to give up (repress or dissociate) this predominantly nonintegrated and nondifferentiated world, as the price of his coming to function, in his daily waking life, as a single and whole human individual. The kind of gratification he has had in this process so largely to relinquish becomes manifest, in my experience, in the therapeutically symbiotic phase of the individual patient's psychoanalysis and, similarly, in a comparable phase in the family therapy of schizophrenic patients. In both settings, the participants come to experience, among less comfortable emotions, a kind of gratifying playfulness relatively

unfettered by adult stability of ego-boundaries, playfulness permeated by an overflowing affection and *joie de vivre* which are, at
least in my experience, at best tangential to adult daily life—
except for the adult's relatively common but largely vicarious
pleasure of this sort in watching, say, little children or puppies at
play with one another.

Review of Relevant Literature

The literature concerning jealousy is in large-scale agreement
that jealousy is found in a context of three (or more) persons, in
contrast to envy, which occurs in a two-person context; Sullivan
(1953), Farber (1961), Pao (1969), and Spielman (1971) are among
the writers who have made that point.

The present paper presents a relatively few examples of the
myriad of constellations in which jealousy is at work in a context
of two actual persons, with a third "person" in the triangle
consisting in an internal object within one of the two actual
persons.

Between 1971–1975 I wrote the rough draft of a monograph on
this paper's title subject, and only very late in the writing did I
discover that anyone else had done any appreciable work in this
field before me. I came across Melanie Klein's little book, *Envy
and Gratitude* (1957), then out of print but subsequently republished in 1975.

In that book, Klein draws the usual distinction between envy
and jealousy, in stating that "envy implies the subject's relation to
one person only," whereas jealousy "involves a relationship to at
least two people" (p. 181). But in writing of what she terms the
primary envy of the mother's breast, and the consequences of that
envy, she makes a fundamental contribution to the subject to
which my present paper is addressed.

Klein cites Joan Rivière as having introduced, in a paper

entitled, "Jealousy as a Mechanism of Defence" (1932), the concept that envy in women is traceable to the infantile desire to rob the mother of her breasts and to spoil them. According to Rivière's findings, jealousy is rooted in this primal envy. Klein reports, similarly, "My work has taught me that the first object to be envied is the feeding breast, for the infant feels that it possesses everything he desires and that it has an unlimited flow of milk and love which the breast keeps for its own gratification" (p. 183).

Klein further points out that

We find this primitive envy revived in the transference situation. For instance: the analyst has just given an interpretation which brought the patient relief and produced a change of mood from despair to hope and trust. . . . This helpful interpretation may soon become the object of destructive criticism. . . . The envious patient grudges the analyst the success of his work . . . .

Destructive criticism is particularly evident in paranoid patients who indulge in the sadistic pleasure of disparaging the analyst's work, even though it has given them some relief. . . . What happens is that the patient has split off the envious and hostile part of his self and constantly presents to the analyst other aspects that he feels to be more acceptable. Yet the split-off parts essentially influence the course of the analysis, which ultimately can only be effective if it achieves integration and deals with the whole of the personality. . . .

In these ways envy, and the defences against it, play an important part in the negative therapeutic reaction . . . . [pp. 183-185].

Of her experience with one such patient who became, as Klein puts it, "able to experience the analytic session as a happy feed," the author reports that

It was by enabling her gradually to bring the split-off parts of her self together in relation to the analyst, and by her recognizing how envious and therefore suspicious she was of me, and in the first place of her mother, that the experience of that happy feed came about. This was bound up with feelings of gratitude [p. 206].

Klein found, as have I, that "to enable the patient to face primary envy and hate only becomes possible after long and painstaking work" (p. 221).

I do not find in Klein's book an appreciation of the power and depth of splitting such as I experience in my own work with patients. She reports a patient's *dream* material as showing the analyst to be two different, split figures (p. 213); but one looks in vain, in her material, for clinical vignettes which document, in a tangible way, that the patient is reacting to the analyst as being two (or more) different persons *during the analytic session,* although she mentions this phenomenon. Part of the explanation may be that Klein did not treat patients as ill as have been some of those whom I have treated (for example, see my previously-mentioned 1972 paper). Further, Klein's writing reports relatively little of what the analyst feels in doing analytic work; I could find no instance of her becoming aware, herself, of experiencing jealousy during a session with a patient.

Herner (1965), in a paper entitled, "Significance of the Body Image in Schizophrenic Thinking," reports his having found that

The split body image observed in schizophrenic patients is the introjected, disorganized, interpersonal relationships perceived by the infant to whom the family is the world. In therapeutic work with such a patient, unsolved problems of relationship to immature parents are delineated. He struggles for liberation from these maleficent figures, who appear in his dreams and hallucinations. In the course of treatment, the incomprehensible symptoms can be explained and a unit [i.e., unity] of the split body image effected. It is possible to meet the crippled and weak ego of the schizophrenic in a new way [p. 465].

I have worked with a considerable number of patients who manifested such disturbances of body-image formation, and disturbances of childhood-family interpersonal milieu, as were entirely consonant with Herner's to me convincing hypothesis.

If the first installation of internal objects occurs, in the child's development, in a setting or atmosphere (in the relationship with the mother and in the family as a whole) of intense jealousy, then presumably this emotional connotation attaches to any subsequent elaboration of the internal world, any subsequent installation of new internalized objects. The whole process of internalization becomes laden with unworked-through jealousy, which interferes with the internal assimilation and integration of these internal objects. Here again, we get some glimpse of the extent to which the present and future welfare of the adult analytic patient's whole internalized world is dependent upon the degree to which the analysis helps him to gain access to, and thus become better able to integrate, this affective realm of intra-psychic jealousy.

In my paper, "Concerning Therapeutic Symbiosis" (1973), in a subsection entitled, "The Role of Jealousy in the Fragmented Ego," I made my first published report on an aspect of the present paper's title subject, and in 1974 made my first oral presentation concerning the present subject as a whole, under this paper's same title, "Jealousy Involving an Internal Object."

Scott (1975), in a lengthy paper, "Remembering Sleep and Dreams," entitles the eleventh subsection (pp. 333–338) of his paper, "Self-envy and Envy of Dreams and Dreaming." In the

ensuing few pages he presents a number of ideas and clinical
findings which have precisely to do with the subject of my present
paper. He presents from his analytic practice an example of self-
envy:

> His associations seemed to make it clear that the part of himself
> which had been anxious and incapable in the past was now
> envying the ego which had developed [during the course of the
> analysis thus far], just as this same part had previously envied
> his father, first the external father, later the internal one. . . . His
> old symptomatic anxious and reproachful self now envied his
> capable ego . . . .
>
> His father had also been envied. The patient's developing ego
> had now new assets which were identified with the envied
> aspects of his father.

Concerning envy of dreams and dreaming, Scott reports that

> After working with the concept of self-envy for a few years,
> eventually (during the summer of 1973) it occurred to me that
> the waking ego might envy the dreaming ego and break the
> link, spoil the connexion and have none of it—or, at the most,
> only the memory of a token dream. Obviously it was an
> exciting wait until practice was resumed and I could discover
> whether or not the concept was useful.

He then presents two brief examples from his subsequent
analytic practice in which he was able to discern, and successfully
interpret, the presence of such envy. Regarding one of the two
patients in question, he describes that "in subsequent weeks'
analyses [i.e., analytic sessions] many more dreams were remembered [by this analysand who had made relatively little use of
dreams earlier in the analysis]. Many of them were long and . . .

some were clearly indicative of situations in which envy and ambition played a role." In his concluding remarks concerning that subsection of his paper, Scott mentions that "I am asking for the reader's indulgence since the clinical data presented is not copious."

For good surveys of the standard literature concerning envy and jealousy (surveys which essentially do not deal with that aspect of jealousy about which I am writing here), I particularly recommend the papers by Pao (1969), Joffe (1969), and Spielman (1971).

It is my hope and belief that this present paper adds a fundamentally clarifying dimension to overall portrayals, such as those by Kernberg (1975) and Volkan (1976), of primitive internalized object relations.

Summary

Jealousy which is related to an internal object within either oneself or the other person in an ostensibly two-person situation is at the heart of much severe and pervasive psychopathology and accounts, in psychoanalytic treatment, for much of the unconscious resistance, on the part of both patient and analyst, to the analytic process. These jealousy phenomena, derived basically from inordinately powerful ego-splitting processes in the original infant-mother relationship wherein the infant's earliest ego-formation was taking place, comprise a much more powerful source of severe psychopathology than do those jealousy phenomena referable to the oedipal phase of development.

These primitive jealousy phenomena are among the most powerful determinants of, for example, ego-fragmentation, depersonalization, castration anxiety and, in the transference relationship, negative therapeutic reaction. These phenomena, being referable to the earliest infantile phases of ego development when no clear differentiation between human and nonhuman, or between animate and inanimate, ingredients of the experienced self-and-world had yet been achieved, often are found in the transference-relationship to involve nonhuman objects which have the jealousy-engendering connotation of actual human beings.

Such jealousy phenomena may become detectable only after prolonged analytic work has occurred, by which time the analyst and patient have come to possess a degree of emotional significance for one another approximately equal to that which the internal object—or ego fragment—in question has for its possessor.

Melanie Klein's concepts concerning the infant's primary envy of the mother's breast, his resultant feeling that a good and a bad breast exist, and the consequences of these experiences for his later ego development, are of fundamental relevance for the formulations which I have presented here.

References

Breuer, J., and Freud, S. (1893–1895). Studies on hysteria. *Standard Edition* 2:240–252.

Fairbairn, W.R.D. (1952). *An Object-Relations Theory of the Personality.* New York: Basic Books, 1954.

Farber, L.H. (1961). Faces of envy. In *The Ways of the Will.* New York: Basic Books, 1966.

Greenson, R.R. (1965). The working alliance and the transference neurosis. *Psychoanalytic Quarterly* 34:155–181.

Greenson, R.R. and Wexler, M. (1969). The non-transference relationship in the psychoanalytic situation. *International Journal of Psycho-Analysis* 50:27–39.

Herner, T. (1965). Significance of the body image in schizophrenic thinking. *American Journal of Psychotherapy* 19:455–466.

James, M. (1960). Premature ego development: some observations on disturbances in the first three months of life. *International Journal of Psycho-Analysis* 41:288-294.

Joffe, W.G. (1969). A critical review of the status of the envy concept. *International Journal of Psycho-Analysis* 50:533-545.

Klein, M. (1932). *The Psycho-Analysis of Children.* London: Hogarth.

——— (1957). *Envy and Gratitude. A Study of Unconscious Sources.* New York: Basic Books. Republished in 1975 in England by the Hogarth Press and the Institute of Psycho-Analysis, and in U.S. by Delacorte Press/Seymour Lawrence, under the title, *Envy and Gratitude and Other Works 1946-1963.*

Knight, R.P. (1953). Borderline states. In *Psychoanalytic Psychiatry and Psychology,* eds R.P. Knight and C.R. Friedman. New York: International Universities Press, 1954.

Pao, P.-N. (1969). Pathological jealousy. *Psychoanalytic Quarterly* 38:616-638.

Rivière, J. (1932). Jealousy as a mechanism of defence. *International Journal of Psycho-Analysis* 13:414-424.

Ross, N. (1967). The "as if" concept. *Journal of the American Psychoanalytic Association* 15:59-82.

Scott, W.C.M. (1975). Remembering sleep and dreams. *International Review of Psycho-Analysis* 2:253-354.

Searles, H.F. (1960). *The Nonhuman Environment in Normal Development and in Schizophrenia.* New York: International Universities Press.

——— (1961). Phases of patient-therapist interaction in the psychotherapy of chronic schizophrenia. In *Collected Papers on Schizophrenia and Related Subjects,* pp. 521-559. New York: International Universities Press, 1965.

——— (1962). Scorn, disillusionment and adoration in the psychotherapy of schizophrenia. In *Collected Papers on Schizophrenia and Related Subjects,* pp. 605-625. New York: International Universities Press, 1965.

———— (1964). The contributions of family treatment to the psychotherapy of schizophrenia. In *Collected Papers on Schizophrenia and Related Subjects,* pp. 747-757. New York: International Universities Press, 1965.

———— (1965). *Collected Papers on Schizophrenia and Related Subjects.* New York: International Universities Press.

———— (1971). Pathologic symbiosis and autism. In *In the Name of Life—Essays in Honor of Erich Fromm,* eds B. Landis and E.S. Tauber, pp. 69-83. New York: Holt, Rinehart and Winston.

———— (1972). The function of the patient's realistic perceptions of the analyst in delusional transference. *British Journal of Medical Psychology* 45:1-18.

———— (1973). Concerning therapeutic symbiosis. *Annual of Psychoanalysis* 1:247-262.

———— (1976). Psychoanalytic therapy with schizophrenic patients in a private-practice context. *Contemporary Psychoanalysis* 12:387-406.

———— (1977). Dual- and multiple-identity processes in borderline ego functioning. In *Borderline Personality Disorders,* ed. P. Hartocollis. New York: International Universities Press.

Spielman, P.M. (1971). Envy and jealousy—an attempt at classification. *Psychoanalytic Quarterly* 40:59-82.

Stone, L. (1967). The psychoanalytic situation and transference. *Journal of the American Psychoanalytic Association* 15:3-58.

Sullivan, H.S. (1953). *The Interpersonal Theory of Psychiatry.* New York: W.W. Norton.

Volkan, V.D. (1976). *Primitive Internalized Object Relations—A*

Clinical Study of Schizophrenic, Borderline, and Narcissistic Patients. New York: International Universities Press.

Winnicott, D.W. (1945). Primitive emotional development. In *Collected Papers,* pp. 145–156. New York: Basic Books, 1958.

Chapter 10

The "Glass Bubble" of the
Narcissistic Patient

Vamik Volkan, M.D.

It is not unusual for a patient with narcissistic personality organization to report having a long-standing fantasy of living, to all intents and purposes, in a "bubble" in which he is self-sufficient and impregnable in his solitary glory. Such a fantasy first came to my attention (Volkan 1973) when a narcissistic patient in analysis whose adaptation was rather effective on the surface described how it felt to be surrounded by an "iron ball" which constituted his kingdom, a kingdom in which he was solitary and omnipotent. Since then I have observed similar situations. For example, one patient had since childhood clung to the fantasy that he dwelt within a plastic bubble as "Mighty Mouse," an omnipotent representation of himself two feet tall.[1] This patient throughout his life had variations of his plastic bubble, which might become a space ship or a submarine but was

[1]The resemblance between this small manikin and the omnipotent "little man" described by Kramer (1955), Niederland (1956), and myself (1965, 1976) is striking. The "little man" has been described as an "inner fossil" separated from the rest of the ego and turning it into a mother equivalent from which separation is never required.

always for one passenger only. Another patient whose care I supervised for a long time was unable to fall asleep without entering into a specific fantasy which he named "Robinson Crusoe Without a Man Friday." This was what I have described as a "transitional fantasy" (Volkan 1973, 1976), one selected by him to be used as a teddy bear or similar transitional object. This patient was addicted to his fantasy, which he played out each night with slight variations here and there in its unfolding. In it he fantasied himself alone on an island, building his own house, catching fish for his own food, etc. Contemplating the possible advantages of a Man Friday, he would decide that his great self-sufficiency made the presence of another man on the island unnecessary.

Guntrip (1968) reported seeing something similar to what I describe in patients who perceived themselves as living behind a sheet of glass. Modell (1968, 1976) noted this phenomenon and described the narcissistic patient's intrapsychic perception of being in a state of self-sufficiency as a feeling of being encased in a "plastic bubble" or "cocoon."

What interests me here is that when such a patient comes to analysis his fantasy is "actualized" in the analyst's office; the patient brings his bubble with him, places it on the couch, as it were, and settles back inside it, denying his analyst any of the usual approaches. Since he appears to be relating emotionally not at all to his analyst, he induces in the analyst a typical countertransference response that I (Volkan 1973) as well as Modell (1976) have described as sleepiness, boredom, and indifference. This response has also been noted by Kernberg (1974) and Kohut (1971). Analysts who work with such patients thus learn the technique that Winnicott (1969) has described as having "to sit and wait for the natural evolution of the transference." It is necessary to tolerate this narcissistic transference without interfering in its development if one is to analyze such patients.

Modell (1976) divided the psychoanalytic process of patients with narcissistic character disorder into three phases, and suggests that the first is the "cocoon" phase," in which it is implicitly understood that the analyst has the power of rescuing the patient and preserving the analysis in spite of his patient's efforts to sabotage it. Modell suggests that what he sees in this first phase corresponds to some aspects of Kohut's (1971) description of the idealizing transference, in which "the analyst implicitly possesses some powerful qualities so that change may be effected merely by being in his presence." During this phase, which lasts a year or so, interpretations are regarded by the patient as intrusive; he dismisses or fails to hear them. Toward the end of the first phase or at the beginning of the second, something like Kohut's mirror transference appears in its less archaic form. It can be anticipated when rage against the external reality represented by the analyst emerges. Such rage is genuine and advances the process of individuation (Winnicott 1969). It arises, as both Modell and Kernberg (1974) suggest, when the patient's grandiosity is confronted and when the cocoon fantasy begins to give way before a systematic interpretation. The dissolution of the cocoon transference by means of interpretation is analogous to that of the transference neurosis by the same means. During the second phase, which lasts for months, a year, or even longer, the patient emerges from his cocoon feeling considerably more alive than before, and a therapeutic alliance is achieved, ushering in the third phase, which approximates that of classical analysis in which the oedipus complex is dealt with. Modell is quick to emphasize that the vicissisitudes of the oedipus complex may not emerge as completely as in a classical case, and to say that during this phase the possiblility of regressive movement is ever-present. The cocoon transference may be renewed in response to weekend separation, for example.

Here I will give an account of the analysis of a young woman from its beginning to its termination and follow-up to demonstrate my basic agreement with Modell's observations concerning the analytic process with narcissistic patients. I will, however, elaborate on certain areas that seem divergent from his report in some degree. Before going into this case it would be well to offer a brief formulation of my understanding of the meaning of the "glass bubble" fantasy and others like it. My formulation will be further illuminated in my case report.

The Protection of the Grandiose Self

Two separate but interrelated considerations appear whenever a narcissistic patient activates his fantasy of living within a glass bubble; one concerns the integument within which the patient retreats, and the other concerns what can be found within this integument. One recognizes, of course, that the "glass bubble" is a fantasy of metaphor, but it takes on "reality" insofar as the patient's behavior is directed by his supposedly unique and impregnable locus.

Throughout history man has built walls to surround a personal or collective domain in order to protect himself or his people from real dangers lurking without. The Great Wall of China, the eighth wonder of the world, reaches about 1500 miles to protect China, and more limited walls have been built for the protection of cities and castles in all lands. Our era has the Berlin Wall, which was erected to keep those in East Berlin from escaping to the West—in other words, to protect the cohesion of East Berlin itself.

The walls we encounter in psychoanalysis are the invisible ones our patients have built. The most common in daily practice are erected by the obsessional patient's "isolation" or "intellectualization" or, in the case of the hysteric, his "dissociation." In neurosis such walls are mainly to protect against what is happening within the patient's psychic structure—for example, to protect him against dangerous affects he is experiencing. Other invisible walls differ from these, reflecting fundamental disturbances of object relationship (Modell 1976), and it is this type that we see in narcissistic as well as psychotic patients. The cover of the bubble controls the psychological distance (Volkan 1976) between what the patient keeps within himself under the bubble—his self-concept and suitable internalized objects—and what he externalizes onto his analyst. My formulation here is that the continuing fantasy of living within a glass bubble reflects a continuous effort to protect the grandiose self, which is a pathological development. (I describe other ways of protecting the grandiose self elsewhere [Volkan 1979].) Thus, our twofold technical task in analyzing the narcissistic patient's fantasy that actualizes itself in his analyst's office requires analysis of what the protective cover means and analysis also of the content of the grandiose self in order to effect its resolution.

Kernberg (1970, 1974, 1975) holds that, apart from a possible inborn intensity of the aggressive drive, oral aggressive conflicts, and unbearable rage and envy are the usual determinants of the narcissistic personality. He sees the grandiose self, to use a term borrowed from Kohut (1971), as a pathological structure that compensates for the failure to integrate a normal self-concept, a failure attributable to the underlying borderline personality organization. The defensive organization of narcissistic patients is strikingly like that of borderline personalities. Kernberg points out, however, that the reliance of the former on such primitive mechanisms as primitive splitting, denial, projective identification, pathological idealization, and omnipotence differs in a particular way. The narcissistic person may, of course, function rather well socially because he differs from the borderline patient in having an integrated, albeit pathological, self-concept. The individual with a narcissistic personality typically has a cold, narcissistic mother who induced in her child a self-concept of being hungry, and an image of the world as being devoid of sustenance and love, while at the same time overprotecting him and encouraging him to believe that he is someone "special." It is around this "specialness" that the grandiose self is built.

A like suggestion concerning the interplay of the human environment on the vicissitudes of development and the sense of self is provided by Modell (1976), who states that the child is forced into premature self-sufficiency in the absence of any "holding environment" (Winnicott 1965) that can provide an illusion of safety and protection implemented by the bond of affective communication between the child and his caretaker. These two writers, then, unlike Kohut (1971), rely on object relations for a fuller understanding of narcissistic character disorder, and my clinical experience in such cases inclines me to agree (Volkan 1973, 1976, 1979).

Kernberg (1975) understands the contents of the grandiose self from a metapsychological point of view. It includes a fusion of some aspects of the real self (the specialness of the child, reenforced by early experience), the ideal self (the self-image of beauty, power, and wealth that compensates the small child for the experience of oral frustration, rage, and envy), and the ideal object (the fantasy of an ever-giving mother). Certain realistic aspects of the self-concept may be maintained, coexisting with the grandiose self—or they may be split off. Certainly, unacceptable aspects of the real self are split off and this process is accompanied by generalized devaluation of external objects and their representations. Clinging to the grandiose self gives the patient the ability to function better than a borderline individual. Insofar as the grandiose self is developed defensively, its cohesiveness must be maintained throughout life. The main function of the related fantasies is to put an integument around it. Modell, concerned with the necessity of a holding environment for the psychological life of the child, used the metaphor of "cocoon" in describing the narcissistic patient's intrapsychic self-sufficiency; in the cocoon he saw an implication of potential life. Although I think this is important, my analysis of my patients' invisible walls has led me to believe that their main function is to control the distance between the grandiose self and other representations. I am struck by a certain cold, dead quality of the barrier in the fantasy that is well compared to a surface of transparent plastic or glass.

The glassy shell in the fantasies of the patients we are considering serves two functions; it not only protects the grandiose self from what lies outside, but it invites relatedness, in spite of the patient's outward indications that he expects the analyst simply to care for him. An appreciation of this second aspect will help the analyst not to be totally overwhelmed when the fantasy is actualized in the treatment situation and the patient seems to relate to him not at all. It was the "watershed" (Modell 1970) aspects of the glassy case, corresponding to acceptance and nonacceptance of external objects, that suggested to me (Volkan 1976) that its function might be compared with that of a reactivated and ideational transitional object.

As Greenacre (1969) noted, the transitional object is an illusory bridge that "comforts and fortifies the young venturer in taking his first steps into the expanding realities of the outer world. . . . It offers a cushion against distress or frustration before reality testing is at all secure, and provides dosages of omnipotence according to infant needs."

Modell (1976) noted the transitional nature of the analytic process. He says: "Although the qualities of the holding environment are generated by the analyst's technique, they may become separated from the analyst and take on a life of their own. The analytic process is not infrequently observed in dreams as a more or less protective container, such as a house or an automobile."

What I suggest here is that the narcissistic patient comes to analysis with his own fantasied container, and when the analysis starts, the cover of the container may assume the transitional role. As my case report will clearly show, the symbolic aspects stemming from structural conflict may be condensed in the fantasied and "activated" meaning of the cover, but in the narcissistic patient its role as protector of the grandiose self needs the scrutiny of analysis.

A Flower in a Glass Vase

A beautiful woman in her mid-twenties sought analysis after being frightened by an aggressive act of her husband. The couple had been vacationing at the shore when her husband became angry at her as they swam together and held her head under water long enough to terrify her. He was known to have a "paranoid condition" and had been for years in psychoanalytic psychotherapy with one of my psychoanalyst colleagues. The couple had been married for two years. Before her marriage my patient had consulted her husband's therapist, who discussed with her the psychological condition of her husband-to-be. He implied that marriage to him would not be easy, but she reacted as though the warning had gone in one ear and out the other. Now, however, the incident that had aroused her short-lived but very real terror gave her a sense of anxiety about what she was doing with her life. She wanted analysis not only to indicate whether or not she should stay with her husband, but also to explain why she had no desire for children. In spite of the conscious seriousness of her reasons for seeking psychoanalysis, she presented her concerns in a nonchalant way as though she were talking about the problems of someone else.

She was the elder daughter of a wealthy gynecologist who practiced in a traditional southern town. The patient's mother was a very beautiful woman, and the parents' life seemed centered around the constant competitive struggle for social recognition, with all the country club and other social activities that would assure it. The physician father occasionally drank to excess and displayed his hot temper by aimlessly shooting a gun. Neither he nor his wife were close to their children in the usual parental manner, or warmly interested in them as children. The patient and the sister three years her junior were treated by their mother as though they were *special* dolls. They were unusually pretty, and their mother openly competed with them from their childhood on. The mother and her daughters talked of little else than the superiority of one over the other in dress and appearance, and their relationship held so much envy and malice that the slightest favor given to one was deeply resented as an injury by the others. The usual mothering functions such as hugging her baby, feeding her, changing her diapers, etc., had, according to my patient, never been included in her mother's self-perception. Her tolerance of her daughters was limited to those occasions when they did her credit by being beautifully dressed and groomed without, however, eclipsing the effect she herself was making on others.

A black housemaid fed the children, and my patient still recalled as an adult the savor of the food she prepared. The maid sang to the little girl on occasion, and rocked her. Later, she played hide-and-seek with her. The child's relationship to the maid was a secret solace that she denied altogether while being her mother's "doll." As a doll she was unable to play and thus had "an impoverishment of capacity to experience in the culture field" (Winnicott 1966). All of her memories of warmth given her when a child referred to the black woman, any emotional attachment to whom had to be denied because of her lowly station and the disdain principal family members felt toward her. The patient's situation was very like that of those who had multiple mothering in the "old South" as described by Smith (1949) and Cambor (1969). The child who has in effect two mothers has "a greater tendency for a delay in the establishment of stable object representations, and this delay may be re-enforced by interference with the process of fusion of good and bad maternal object representations. This interferes both with the process of separation-individuation and the progressive maturation of identification processes, and encourages the regressive wish for fusion with the idealized good mother only" (Cambor 1969).

It took a long time for my patient to reveal to me the mothering she had received from the black maid. Most of her memories of this, while not repressed, were avoided. It was while my patient was in her latency years that the black woman left the household. By that time, having left her early childhood behind, largely displaced in the black woman's attention by a sister, and now able to take care of her own personal needs, she had moved away from any intimacy with the black woman and had become her mother's "doll," and a competitor with her mother and her sister.

The gynecologist father had a clinic next to his home, separated from it by a garden. Since many deliveries took place there, my patient had been accustomed during her oedipal years to hearing women scream in labor; she had fantasied that they were being mutilated and had concluded that to become a mother was to suffer. These barely repressed fantasies and notions helped her to maintain the "doll-child" concept and obstructed the integration of a concept of motherly womanhood into her total self-concept.

These brief references to her childhood cast light on her willingness to marry a man with a "paranoid condition." Her husband was the son of a business tycoon and had never worked, but had been able to increase his inheritance in the stock market. He managed his affairs from an office in his home. Suspicious of others and sometimes delusional, he amassed money defensively in order to feel secure. Although my patient's parents were well-to-do, the man she had married after an acquaintance that went back to their high school days was vastly richer. She had dated other young men without ever falling in love or becoming sexually involved. Since she felt that her role was to be adored by them, I suspect that in spite of her considerable beauty they found her rather boring in the long run. She was aware that she had chosen her husband largely because he could provide her with luxuries of all kinds, and access to the society of wealthy and important people. Her dreams of luxury had mostly come true, but he was not altogether generous; rather, as might have been expected, he was somewhat stingy.

She continued being an ornament, taking her stand at the center of any cocktail party in her striking clothes, attracting men as a flower attracts bees. Her purpose in life was to be admired above all others, and her recall of social events was limited to the memory of compliments she had received or failed to receive while attending them, and her *envy* of other women who had been in any way conspicuous. It seemed to me that the feeling of envy was perhaps the only human emotion she could maintain long enough to differentiate from other emotions, and name it. She never remembered any serious subjects that might have been introduced at a gathering.

Although her husband withheld any open adoration he was nevertheless the means of her obtaining adoration from others. Because of his personality make-up he exerted no pressure on her for intimacy, and because of her own nature she found this lack of pressure entirely acceptable. He often disappeared from parties to which he had taken her, returning only in time to pick her up. I suspect that this was further evidence of a "fit" between the two since her presence at parties without an escort enabled her to bask in the attention of many men. Her husband, in turn, might have been gratifying possible homosexual wishes by sharing her with them. Nevertheless, he was capable of great anger toward her when they did have differences.

At the outset of her analysis, before I had learned very much about her in the analytic setting, I had thought of her as having a hysterical personality. I felt that she dissociated the affects related to the incident at the shore. She was not able to describe exactly what had led to the frightening episode, but I got the vague impression that she had teased her husband by bypassing him for the attention of other men. I also thought initially that her fear of pregnancy centered around her perception that her father "took" something (a penis) away from pregnant women, that her display of "superlative" femininity on social occasions was a challenge to other women, and that because of the bad temper and frightening aspects of the father of her oedipal age she had further difficulties working through her oedipal problems. As the analysis opened she had little to say except expressions of jealousy over the successes of other women, often her married sister or her mother, who now lived elsewhere. On the couch she was a large doll waiting to be adored by me in the only relatedness she anticipated between us. She dressed elaborately for her sessions with me. No therapeutic alliance in the classical sense came about. It slowly became evident, as her analysis progressed and I gathered more information about her life, that she had a narcissistic personality organization.

In a few months she spoke of herself as being beneath a glass dome. This was a fantasy that existed prior to her analytic experience and of which she was aware in other life situations; for example, when she exposed herself to the adoration of others she felt separated from her admirers by a sheet of glass. I had already entertained this fantasy about her, but had never communicated it to her. She felt that my voice simply glanced off the surface of her glass enclosure without reaching her at all. She often asked me to repeat something I had said, and on the very few occasions on which I complied she "forgot" my remarks within a few minutes. The permeability of her glass enclosure was entirely under her control. Although I was aware of its having been erected to control the distances involved in her object relations, other symbolism connected with it also came to the surface. She spoke about her husband's dislike of sex, and how their infrequent sexual relations took place only in the daytime. Her husband was potent only after spanking her on the buttocks. Frigid, she complied, without gratifying herself with the fantasy that she was having sexual relations with any one of her many admirers. She then made the curious disclosure that she had gone to a gynecologist the day before her wedding and had him perforate her hymen surgically. She said her reason for this was that she did not want her husband to know that she was a virgin. Encouraged to associate to this behavior, she revealed oedipal elements that suggested a desire for her father's love, and a wish to be deflowered by the gynecologist/father before submitting herself to another man. Moreover, in a counterphobic gesture she was initiating penetration by the fearful gynecologist/father. The integument that surrounded her was, on one level, an externalization of her hymen, and having control over the penetrability of her glass dome was, I felt, like having control over her hymen. When I tried to explore the subject with her, however, my suggestions fell on deaf ears. The assumption that her fantasy of a glass enclosure contained any symbolism stemming from structural conflicts was lost in the dominant narcissistic associations that pointed to her being unable to tolerate the notion that her husband might imagine that she was not loved by all men of importance and that he was the first to claim her. The loss of her maidenhead in that fashion meant in a sense that she herself was the first to claim it.

In a dream that repeated itself a few times she saw a daisy lying on the bottom of a glass vase. She was quick to appreciate that she herself was the flower, and to intellectualize, without affect, a wish to regress to the womb.

My explorations with her were directed to the defensive-protective aspect of the fantasied glass shield—her feeling of being protected by it and the possibility of being frustrated again as she had been by her mother's coolness. On the rare occasions on which she expressed the wish to have at least one crack in her fantasied bubble, she would say that she sensed the need to face the rage—especially toward her mother—that she could not face as long as she stayed within her bubble. I explained to her the price she was paying for her unwillingness to face human emotion; for some time this made no sense to her, but slowly she began to exhibit curiosity about what personal relationships could be outside her narcissistic pattern. I used her dream of the flower enclosed in a vase to suggest that her glass enclosure was januslike inasmuch as although it excluded me and my words, it was sufficiently transparent for her to "see" me by noticing small changes in the environment such as my having different books on my desk, etc., and thus she was aware of my presence in spite of being unable to regard me from the couch. I confronted her with the proposition that in spite of her aloofness, which was coupled with a desire to have my total adoration, she was also interested in learning more about me in piecemeal fashion.

The flower, moreover, suggested to me something gentle and promising, something that could open into full bloom. She had permitted me to glimpse this. She then spoke about the dangers of the outside world—the temper tantrums her husband and her father had, her father's belligerence with a gun, and his involvement in the pain of womankind. I sensed that although she wanted me to adore her, she nevertheless had "paranoid" ideas about me and felt a need to remain within an enclosure lest I pounce on her and, worse, be cold toward her. It was about this time that she spoke of the memories of the black maid. She expected me to scorn her feeling so warmly toward a black woman only historically reported, and when I did not do so, her anticipation of the environment was modified. I began looking forward to my hours with her, although she still induced boredom in me at times, and continued to discount my very existence. I became alert, however, when in the middle of the second year of her analysis, she reported a dream with some excitement. It was again a dream of the flower and the vase, but this time the vase fell from the table, the glass broke, and the flower was exposed.

If I had expected the appearance of a transference neurosis in the classical sense at this point I was doomed to disappointment. Up to this time my patient lived all alone under her fantasied glass dome. The dome enclosed the couch as she lay on it, presenting herself for me to take care of without participation on her part, but feeling at times that I might fail to do so. It seemed possible that the dream in which the vase broke might indicate the breaking of her glass cage, and her liberation, but it was all too clear that she still lived within a glass enclosure although it was now enlarged to include an arena much larger than my couch. In this arena she now frantically pursued new activities directed toward the *solitary mastery* of her childhood conflicts. She resisted my attempts to explore aspects of her activity that might point to the possibility of a transference neurosis. I was still excluded from direct interaction with her, and felt that she required me to be a spectator of her exhibitionistic behavior. This new situation was on the one hand like what Kohut (1971) describes as a mirror transference—one in which the patient strives to become "the twinkle in the analyst's eye." On the other hand, the notion that her activities had a great deal to do with her relationship with me induced "paranoid" trends in her, as in her fear that I would not approve what she was doing, or would disrupt it.

Her new "program" began when she attended an auction at which her attention was caught by a scrawny, *ill-fed* horse. In time her analysis was to show that this ill-fed animal was a representation of her "hungry" self, the early self that was supported only by a defective holding environment against which a defensive narcissistic organization had established itself. She felt compelled to buy the horse and get it in shape. An old black woman worked where she stabled her new acquisition, and as the two women worked together on the horse my patient felt close to her, although she was careful for some time to keep these feelings from me, telling me nothing, in fact, about the woman's existence for a long time. I was the cold mother, and the black woman of the stable was the black maid of her childhood. Her rage toward the cold mother-father-analyst surfaced when I interpreted to her that she was reconstructing her childhood experience of tenderness toward the maid and the way in which her early mother representations were primitively split. Dismissing my interpretation, she reduced me once again to being a spectator of her activity. She gave up her glittering high-style dresses for riding togs, and spent most of her time around the stable. Her dreams included the horse she had purchased which, as the months went by, did credit to the care she gave it. Interpretation of her dreams of the horse's need for care and food slowly made her understand that the animal did represent her deprived self-concept against which a glorified one had been defensively erected. She came to know her gratitude to the black maid, as well as to the black woman at the stable. It was now necessary that she split off that life experience from that of a doll who existed to be adored by others.

Soon my patient's need to collect admiration lessened. Her mood became "solemn." I could now see an alliance developing between us, and a transference neurosis reflecting structural conflicts emerging. Her dreams about horses continued, but now the dominant symbolism of the horse referred to her penis. The horse was a penis between her thighs, and she often dreamed of putting him over jumps and having him "go up" with power. She became a tomboy and spent a great deal of time currying her horse and entering him in horse shows.

One day she reported a dream in which her horse fell as he jumped a fence, and bled from the neck. The idea of giving up her penis enraged her. A few weeks later she dreamed of a bag full of small animals, and her associations to this concerned pregnancy. She totally rejected the idea of ever becoming pregnant; in a return wave of narcissistic concern with her appearance, pregnancy meant nothing to her but a deformity of her beautiful body. The fantasy of the glass dome of her first analytic year had returned, but she dreamed again and again of the horse "between her thighs" and of blood, although she did not want to.

The owner of the stables, an elderly white man, became her friend and a "good" father in her eyes, just as the black woman was a "good" mother. He promised to have her called at any time, day or night, when a foal was expected. She had by then been going to the stables for a year. True to his promise, the stable owner called her when a foal began to come, and my patient rushed to be on hand although it was two o'clock in the morning. She was able to see the foal delivered, and on the following day she excitedly described during her hour with me what had happened. She had observed the extrusion of the birth sac and had thought, seeing one of the long, folded legs within it, that perhaps the mare was delivering a penis. She subsequently spent much of her time with the "new mother and her baby."

She seemed to be working through her fear of giving up her penis, of becoming pregnant and bearing a child. An affective closeness toward me surfaced dramatically in the third year of her analysis when she lay on the couch blushing and silent before gathering the courage to tell me that she had just begun her menses. Although she had never had menstrual difficulty or irregularity, on that occasion in my office she was experiencing her *very first menses,* as it were. In the home of her youth such intimate matters were never mentioned, and her confiding in me signalled the ripening of the classical—and exaggerated—transference neurosis. She demanded that I love her although, since she had fantasies about my wife, the situation represented a triangle. She defensively spoke of having a penis so that she had no need of me. Her interest in the activities of the stable waned, and the horse from which she could not separate herself a year earlier was sold. I sensed that she was beginning to feel some affection for her husband and was ceasing to regard him as little more than a means whereby she could attract adoring attention. He stopped spanking her before intercourse.

The couple bought a modest house after living for some time in rented quarters in a socially exclusive neighborhood. They had more friends than formerly, and she no longer felt jealous about the beauty of other women. Her feeling was now centered around competing with the women she fantasied I had, and she was no longer preoccupied with beauty and wealth but with the joy of becoming my life partner. She knew that I am Turkish, so she imagined being married to me and traveling on a magic carpet to Istanbul, where we would live together happily ever after. There was an Arabian Nights quality about this phase of her analysis, in which she envisioned the Prince and the Princess living in delight forever. Although the oedipal theme is clearly to be seen in this interaction, I recognized also something that Coppolillo (1967) has described. Referring to the findings of Boyer (1956) and Giovacchini (1964) that certain ego defects are directly traceable to massive maternal stimulation in childhood, Coppolillo described a patient with a specific symptom that seemed to arise from cultural deprivation. During this patient's childhood, at the time when he was accessible to the enchantment of fairy tales and other cultural expression, his mother had intruded, deflecting his attention to a vastly more compelling object—the mother herself. Copollilo's patient, although holding a master's degree, had great gaps in his knowledge of human expression, and remained culturally naive.

The Arabian Nights quality of my patient's fantasies not only served the oedipal factor in her transference neurosis but awakened her interest in the world at large, and its culture. Her interest in Istanbul led her to become inquiring about geography and history, areas in which, considering her social and educational background, she had surprising gaps. This awakening led her to an interest in the arts and she began to visit art galleries, developing a sound appreciation of the creative products of human experience. Coppolillo notes that, as Winnicott (1953, 1966) had suggested, "the cultural expressions of humanity make excellent transitional objects." For example, the fairy tales of one's childhood are laid aside and, being neither repressed nor externalized, become available for use again when needed.

I believe that maturational aspects of my patient's transitional object were reactivated in her analysis, and at this point she began to gain knowledge of the world. The black maid had given her songs and, perhaps, folklore, but once her very early childhood was over and she moved away from the actual care of the black woman and became her mother's "doll" this kind of cultural investment had to be dissociated. Her mother had impeded the child's cultural growth by overemphasizing her being "a doll." As she acquired new knowledge and concepts about life in general, and learned new functions with the help of her analysis, she even became competent in handling investments. The knowledge that she could take care of herself by using some of the skills her husband had used made her feel secure about surviving in the event of a separation from him.

She was no longer frightened by the thought of pregnancy, and demanded that I give her babies. I learned that her frigidity had disappeared—the erotic transference was extreme, to say the least. She declared that she was ready to leave her husband to marry me, and in an attempt to make me jealous she had an affair which lasted no longer than a week when its transference meaning

was analyzed. She began to pay more attention to her marriage
and to consider the realistic problem of staying with her husband
or leaving him. I continued interpreting her transference distortions and offered no opinion about what the outcome of her
indecision should be. Her husband had improved greatly in
therapy, and was, in fact, able to terminate it after his wife
terminated her analysis. Throughout my patient's analysis I felt
no need of consulting her husband's analyst, nor did my colleague
need consultation with me.

Carefully taking stock of her life with her husband, my patient
decided that in many ways she cared for him and that his
suspiciousness (now lessened) and the limitations of his lifestyle
(now more flexible) did not outweigh the comfort she found in
living with him. When she decided to continue her marriage she
talked about bearing his babies. With this decision we came to the
termination phase of the analysis, which we agreed should take
three months. A date for termination was set. On the following
day she came to my office with fresh daisies in her hair, looking
happy and womanly. It was only during her hour that she realized
that her flower-laden coiffure was a message to let me know that
the flower in the glass vase was out of its enclosure and blooming.
Nevertheless, as expected, oedipal wishes and defenses against
them returned for review in the termination phase. I must emphasize that the "glass dome" fantasy as activated in her daily life also
returned once again before final resolution.

A month before the analysis ended my patient re-resolved
under the eye of a well-developed observing and integrating ego
her desire to have me as her sexual partner. She then spoke of
buying a farm and living on it with her husband. She had long ago
given up wearing elaborate costumes and the riding togs that had
followed them. Now she felt very womanly and motherly, and
dressed accordingly. She had fantasies of raising many animals—
horses, sheep, dogs, cats, etc.—recalling her dream of the bag full

of animals. She no longer feared pregnancy but wanted to be a great mother—an earth-mother (idealized black maid). Such exaggeration was a remnant of her old narcissistic self-regard. In the past, she had been alone in her glorified self-concept, and had the illusion that she needed no one. While adhering to such a self-concept she denied warmth toward the black maid image, which was devalued. Now, however, this defensively erected self-concept was no longer needed, and her identification with the black maid image could surface. But when it did surface it was overvalued. She would be more realistic about herself if she could hold to the "gray area" between the "earth mother" and the "cold mother."

She began looking for a suitable farm, and found one that had something about it that fascinated her. She told me about this farm and began negotiations with the real estate people three weeks before the date set for the termination of her analysis. She could not, however, altogether understand the fascination the place held for her. When she visited it again she spontaneously realized the reason for its unique appeal; unlike most Virginia farmhouses, it was surrounded by *a stone wall* in the New England manner, and was the only one she had seen with a wall. She told me that she then realized that the wall represented to her her old invisible "glass enclosure" in which she had protected her grandiose self. Now she had an "earth mother" image to protect. This insight made her decide against buying the walled farm—her dependence on walls was gone. The analysis was terminated according to plan.

Fourteen months later she had an accident while riding, and came to the hospital where I have my office. She stopped by to talk, but there was no time to investigate the possibility that any psychological factors led to her accident. Nevertheless, she spoke of not doing any more hard riding because she could not afford any injury that would keep her from caring for her baby daughter, born nine months after her analysis ended. As she talked about her infant I felt that she wanted me to know her as a satisfactory mother. When she described her child as beautiful I felt that her emphasis reflected only a proud mother's love for her infant.

I had Christmas cards from her for a few years, but my second meeting took place by chance in the fifth year after termination. It took place in a grocery, where she was shopping with her two children, to whom she introduced me with evident pleasure. She was much involved in looking after them, and she was now motherly in appearance, a little stouter than she had been. The house she lives in now is in town on a lot surrounded by a little picket fence, and I think she has a dog. I feel sure that the fence is nothing more than a decoration. One can only conjecture whether or not it is tinged with her desire to protect her self-concept for psychological reasons, but I believe—at least I want to believe—that she could survive comfortably without it.

Discussion

The analysis of this woman pretty much followed Modell's (1976) basic movements through the three phases he described as typical in the analysis of the narcissistic personality. It is usual for such persons to show aloofness on the one hand and paranoid trends on the other at the outset of their analysis. I have no objection to including these paired manifestations in the first phase that Modell calls the "cocoon" transference. When the patient clings to his solitary but narcissistic grandiosity and has at the same time a feeling that the analyst is adoring him, he seems to be relating to the analyst. This belief is, nevertheless, evidence of unrelatedness in fact, since the analyst is not perceived in this situation as an altogether separate being but is included in the patient's concept of his grandiosity as a confirmer thereto. It is when the patient feels that his analyst is not adoring him that his condition may seem to be paranoid and/or he devalues the analyst to the point of denying his existence. I have concluded (Volkan 1975, 1976) in dealing with psychotic and borderline patients in analytic treatment, agreeing with Boyer (1967) and Kernberg (1975), that although the treatment of such patients does not start with a classical transference neurosis, an upward-evolving transference relationship toward a triangular oedipal situation occurs once the analysis helps the patient to develop object relations of advancing maturity. A similar statement can be made about the process involved in the analysis of narcissistic personalities; narcissistic transference gives way to transference neurosis. Modell's (1976) description of the three phases confirms this. I would like, however, to suggest a slight modification to his schema; I believe that in high-level narcissistic patients elements of the transference neurosis can coexist with the cocoon transference from the beginning of the analysis, although they do not get "hot," as it were, and the patient may use them defensively to cover up the narcissistic transference. I hold that they cannot be effectively analyzed until the analysis of the narcissistic transference is sufficiently advanced.

The case I describe here, like the analysis of the patient in an iron ball (Volkan 1977), gives me further indication of the need to analyze the fantasied "wall" erected to protect the grandiose self, before attempting to complete the analysis of the grandiose self. Once the patient's fantasy of a protective integument—whether he calls it a wall, a bubble, or pillows around him—is observed and analyzed, the patient may use his analyst as a transitional object and, through the progressive side of this phenomenon, enlarge his knowledge of the world and his ability to test reality.

Modell views the reappearance of the cocoon transference in the second and third phases as unavoidable regressive movements, and this is often the case. However, I believe that after a therapeutic alliance and a movement into the oedipal realm develop, aspects of the cocoon transference naturally remain among the shadows of the transference neurosis and occasionally emerge quite clearly. Moreover, I expect it to return for a final resolution during the termination phase, as was clearly demonstrated by the patient I have described, who wanted a farmhouse with a wall around it. My remarks here about the fate of the bubble fantasy that dominates the patient's daily life are like those I made (Volkan 1976) about mending the primitive splitting of contradictory self- and object representations of borderline patients. From the treatment of borderline patients I have demonstrated, with detailed clinical examples, how, after mending their opposing "all good" and "all bad" units, they develop transference neurosis, in spite of which the background situation, until recently so turbulent, must have attention *throughout* the analysis. I also showed the reappearance of primitive splitting for review at the termination phase (Volkan 1975, 1976). Likewise, I believe that the appearance of the "bubble" fantasy in the termination phase of the analysis of a narcissistic patient is analogous to the expected appearance in the neurotic patient of neurotic conflicts already dealt with by analytic working-through.

Modell states that the vicissitudes of the oedipus complex are unmistakably present in the third phase, although they may not emerge as completely as in a "classical" case. I would like to add my observation about certain peculiarities of the aspects of oedipal elements in this phase; I suggest that they are very often tinged with narcissistic glorification as the patient regards himself as "Number One" and thus behaves as though he or she is the only oedipal child in the whole world. One senses that the struggle between the oedipal father and the oedipal son is a struggle between giants. The symbol of the penis is not a snake, but the lofty thrust of the Washington Monument. The narcissistic woman patient does not simply utter her dearest wish when she speaks of bearing her analyst's baby—she is giving a queenly order that this come about, as the patient described here used to do.

I am aware that such an observation may evoke the thought that something went wrong in the two earlier phases, and that elements of the patient's as yet unanalyzed narcissistic orientation remain into the third phase, but I cannot agree with this. The fact is that aspects of narcissistic manifestations persist throughout the analysis. When the patient enters a "triangular" relationship in his analysis, he or she goes through a "glorified" version of it, the resolution of which, after working it through, is similar to what one expects from a "classical" analytic case in which the vicissitudes of the oedipal realm in analysis are not glorified.

Summary

Patients with narcissistic personality organization often report a fantasy of being enclosed within a "glass bubble." During analysis they may behave as though the fantasy has been actualized to control psychological distance, interposing an "invisible wall" between patient and analyst.

This paper follows the entire analysis of such a patient and indicates the fate of her fantasy. It is suggested that the cover of the bubble, the main function of which is to protect the cohesiveness of the patient's grandiose self, needs to be analyzed before the analysis of its contents—the grandiose self—is attempted. Although the analysis of the narcissistic patient goes through phases with an upward-evolving transference toward the oedipal realm, it is recommended that the narcissistic type of object relations manifested by the patient in the "glass bubble" fantasy be examined throughout the course of the analysis.

References
Boyer, L.B. (1956). On maternal overstimulation and ego defects. *Psychoanalytic Study of the Child* 11:236–256.

——— (1967). Office treatment of schizophrenic patients: the use of psychoanalytic therapy with few parameters. In *Psychoanalytic Treatment of Characterological and Schizophrenic Disorders,* eds. L.B. Boyer and P. Giovacchini, pp. 143–188. New York: Jason Aronson.

Cambor, C.G. (1969). Preoedipal factors in superego development—the influence of multiple mothers. *Psychoanalytic Quarterly* 38:81–96.

Coppolillo, H.P. (1967). Maturational aspects of the transitional phenomenon. *International Journal of Psycho-Analysis* 48:237–246.

Giovacchini, P. (1964). The submerged ego. *Journal of American Childhood Psychiatry* 3:430–432.

Greenacre, P. (1969). The fetish and the transitional object. *Psychoanalytic Study of the Child* 24:144–164.

Guntrip, H. (1968). *Schizoid Phenomena, Object Relations, and the Self.* New York: International Universities Press.

Kernberg, O.F. (1967). Borderline personality organization, *Journal of the American Psychoanalytic Association* 15:641–685.

——— (1970). Factors in the psychoanalytic treatment of narcissistic personalities. *Journal of the American Psychoanalytic Association* 18:51–85.

——— (1974). Further contributions to the treatment of narcissistic personality. *International Journal of Psycho-Analysis* 55:215–240.

——— (1975). *Borderline Conditions and Pathological Narcissism,* chapter ten. New York: Jason Aronson.

Kohut, H. (1971). *The Analysis of the Self.* New York: International Universities Press.

Kramer, P. (1955). On discovering one's identity. *Psychoanalytic Study of the Child* 10:47–74.

Modell, A.H. (1968). *Object Love and Reality.* New York: International Universities Press.

———— (1970). The transitional objects and the creative art. *Psychoanalytic Quarterly* 39:240–250.

———— (1976). 'The holding environment' and the therapeutic action of psychoanalysis. *Journal of the American Psychoanalytic Association* 24:285–307.

Niederland, W.G. (1956). Clinical observations on the 'little man' phenomenon. *Psychoanalytic Study of the Child* 11:381–395.

Smith, L. (1949). *Killers of the Dream*. New York: W.W. Norton.

Volkan, V.D. (1965). The observation of the 'little man' phenomenon in a case of anorexia nervosa. *British Journal of Medical Psychology* 38:299–311.

———— (1973). Transitional fantasies in the analysis of a narcissistic personality. *Journal of the American Psychoanalytic Association* 21:351–376.

———— (1975). Cosmic laughter: a study of primitive splitting. In *Tactics and Techniques in Psychoanalytic Psychotherapy,* vol 2, eds. P. Giovacchini, A. Flarsheim, and L.B. Boyer, pp. 425–440, New York: Jason Aronson.

———— (1976). *Primitive Internalized Object Relations.* New York: International Unversities Press.

———— (1977) 'Immortal' Atatürk: narcissism and creativity in a revolutionary leader. In *Psychoanalytic Study of Society,* vol. 9 (in press).

Winnicott, D.W. (1953). Transitional objects and transitional phenomena. *International Journal of Psycho-Analysis* 34:89–97.

———— (1966). The location of cultural experience. *International Journal of Psycho-Analysis* 48:368–372.

———— (1969). The use of an object and relating through identifications. In *Playing and Reality,* pp. 86–94. New York: Basic Books, 1971.

Chapter 11

The Psychotherapeutic
Approach to Aloneness
in Borderline Patients

Gerald Adler, M.D. and Dan H. Buie, Jr., M.D.

Through our clinical experiences in the psychotherapy of borderline patients, all of us have learned techniques that often prove effective. We also try to relate what we have struggled to learn in our clinical work with these patients to a theoretical model that makes sense and supports what we think we do. Not only does our theoretical framework give us emotional and intellectual support in our sessions with these difficult patients, but it can also help us expand our understanding of them and add to our increasing psychotherapeutic skills and knowledge. In this paper we shall continue the endeavor to describe clinical experiences and relate them to possibly useful ways of formulating borderline pathology.

In our treatment of borderline patients we have found the contributions of many workers helpful in ways we shall define. However, Winnicott's (1953, 1960a, 1960b) concepts of the holding environment, good enough mothering, and the transitional object have been especially useful early in the therapeutic work with these patients. In applying these concepts, we are aware that the therapist plays a major role in the establishment of this necessary holding environment; countertransference issues may seriously impede the clinical understanding and therapeutic work that can lead to its development. We have seen repeatedly that borderline patients are exquisitely vulnerable and can quickly lose the sense of our support in psychotherapeutic work with them. We also know how readily a tentative working alliance can disappear, especially when hungry incorporative and/or destructive feelings or fantasies emerge.

In our attempts to understand aspects of establishing working relationships with borderline patients in a framework of psychoanalytic psychotherapy we have recently been defining some issues which we feel are at the core of borderline psychopathology and which must be addressed in any psychotherapeutic approach with these patients (Adler and Buie 1976). In particular, we have stressed the borderline's experience with aloneness which can appear as part of his important dyadic relationships and of course, in psychotherapy. By aloneness, we mean an experience of isolation and emptiness, occasionally turning into panic and desperation. The type of aloneness that borderlines often describe, is frequently accompanied by a sense that there is no one there in reality as well as an incapacity to summon a fantasy of any positive sustaining relationship. Sometimes the aloneness may be experienced with frightening negative images or fantasies of important people; this may alternate with a fantasyless state. We contrast this aloneness with the capacity to be alone, that is, to be by oneself and to feel whole and separate with a sense of intactness and relatedness to past and present important people even though they are not present.

The variety of aloneness we are discussing is common in overt or latent form in most borderlines. One patient often felt that he stomped his therapist to death in his thoughts when he was angry. He was then left with a sense that there were no people in his world; there were no images or fantasies of anyone, except for dim, gray shadows. He related these experiences to similar feelings which occurred during stressful times in his life as far back as he could remember; ultimately they were traced to a screen memory at nineteen months of age. At that time his parents had suddenly left for several weeks because of a family emergency and he was placed in the care of an emotionally unavailable aunt. He always remembered the scene in which he was in a playpen in a gray dim room in which he could not see anyone but could hear distant voices talking.

We felt that the exploration of issues of aloneness can add clarity to an important aspect of borderline psychopathology and assist in our clinical interventions with borderline patients. Our study of aloneness in these patients has led us to examine the nature of their vulnerabilities and the conditions under which these vulnerabilities are activated. We have also explored the possible relationship of these vulnerabilities to certain aspects of the child development literature and certain specific developmental defects that seem to lie at the core of borderline disorders. In this paper we shall summarize some of these aspects of borderline patients and stress the clinical applications which result from studying the borderline's struggles with his desperate aloneness.

Utilizing the contributions of Kernberg, Grinker, Frosch, Chase, Winnicott, and Guntrip, we define borderlines as people with a relatively stable personality organization who tend to use primitive defenses of splitting, projection, projective identification, and primitive idealization, and whose vulnerabilities tend to become most manifest as they become involved in dyadic relationships. Intense longings to be held, touched, soothed, and nurtured, begin to emerge within these relationships, sometimes with frightening rapidity. Obviously, disappointments must necessarily occur because of their idealizations of the object and the enormity of their demands; their use of primitive defenses sometimes can also contribute in that they lead to misperceptions of the sources of their negative impulses and wishes. As the patient experiences disappointments, he usually becomes increasingly angry. This anger may be consciously experienced; or it may be experienced as a generalized upset, or as a feeling of increasing worthlessness or badness. We have felt that the anger precipitated by disappointment in a dyadic relationship is often the trigger that activates this major vulnerability of borderline patients, that is, the sense of aloneness with an inability to maintain images, fantasies, or memories of positive experiences with important people, including the current dyadic relationship.

These intense dyadic experiences, with resultant anger and an aloneness which may be manifest by the loss of sustaining fantasies of important relationships, are an inevitable experience in definitive exploratory psychotherapy of most, if not all borderline patients, but especially for those who fall into the more primitive sector of the borderline spectrum as defined by Grinker (1968). In our attempts to understand this experience of aloneness we have been impressed with the possible relationship of certain aspects of the child development literature to the regressive experiences that accompany borderline aloneness and which may occur during psychotherapeutic work with them.

Selma Fraiberg (1969) has utilized Piaget's (1937) studies of the infant's and small child's development of an object concept to define two kinds of memory of objects: recognition memory and evocative memory. She equates recognition memory with Piaget's stages IV and V of sensorimotor development. These stages involve the infant's transient capacity to remember an object for a few moments when it is removed from his field of vision; however, the infant cannot remember and pursue it when it is moved from one hiding place to another, even when moved in full view of him. During these stages, which occur prior to eighteen months of age, the infant requires the presence of the object in order to recognize its existence. Without seeing the object, he can maintain only a very transient capacity to remember it. Only after eighteen months does a child achieve an evocative memory capacity, that is, the ability to know that an object has continued independent existence even when outside his visual field. This achievement is designated as stage VI by Piaget and is demonstrated through the child's capacity to pursue an object that is hidden and moved from one place to another by sleight of hand. In order to accomplish this, the child must have a capacity to evoke an image unaided by outside cues.

Before the child has developed a firm evocative memory capacity, he often utilizes a transitional object, such as his blanket, to help evoke, for example, the sense of the presence of mother's soothing comfort. Observations of small children have shown that transitional objects are first actively used by the infant at about six months of age and are relinquished at about two years of age. Interestingly, this transitional object use coincides with the beginning of recognition memory capacity and ends when evocative memory is firmly established. That is, transitional objects are no longer necessary when the child is autonomously able to evoke the memory of soothing interactions with important people.

We emphasize this recognition memory–evocative memory line of development because we believe that the adult borderline patient has specific latent vulnerabilities within this developmental line. Our clinical observations convince us that adult borderline patients, when under stress, can lose evocative memory capacity for important libidinally invested objects and regress to recognition memory capacity or even earlier in relation to them. During these stressful periods they may attempt to depend on transitional objects, but often with very limited success.

The stress that often exposes this developmental vulnerability is the emerging anger that appears as unrealistic demands and longings are not met in dyadic relationships. The devouring hunger that is part of the incorporative urge mobilized in dyadic relationships, one that destroys the object in fantasy, may also impinge on the borderline's tenuous evocative memory capacity. We feel that this borderline rage can be divided into two categories: (1) recognition memory rage, and (2) diffuse primitive rage. Recognition memory rage is a state which occurs when the developmental regression mobilized by the borderline's rage stops at a point where recognition memory remains intact. Clinically this means that the patient can still recognize and experience the presence of the important person, for example, his therapist, when he is in his presence, but he cannot remember the therapist outside his office, that is, between appointments. The state of diffuse primitive rage occurs when the regression continues to a point prior to recognition memory. Clinically at such a time the borderline patient is usually in a state of panic, rage, despair, and some disorganization, and he is unable to recognize the presence of his therapist *affectively* even when in the office with him. We wish to emphasize that this affective nonrecognition prevails even though the patient may be able to perceive intellectually that the therapist is in the same room with him.

We want to relate these formulations briefly to Mahler's (1971, 1975) work, which Masterson (1976) has already ably utilized. We feel that the adult borderline's vulnerabilities to recognition memory rage and diffuse primitive rage can derive from failure of good enough mothering at probably all early levels of development, but most significantly at the rapprochement subphase from fifteen to twenty-five months. At that age, which coincides with the solidification of evocative memory and the giving up of the transitional object, the alternately clinging and independent behavior of the child requires extreme sensitivity and responsiveness by the mother. Our work with the adult borderline has given us the impression that both historically through his life and in the clinical situation the problems met with in the rapprochement subphase are relived. The developmental regression we have described as occurring during the treatment may be primarily related to the difficulties posed for the patient's development by maternal failures during this subphase. Because of the consequent retardation in the developmental line of recognition and evocative memory, working through of this subphase is both perilous and painful.

Clinical Implications

The decision to accept a borderline patient for intensive individual psychotherapy (more than once weekly) implies an agreement, tacit or explicit, to allow areas of the patient's vulnerabilities to emerge in the treatment setting. We feel that these areas often involve the vulnerabilities in the developmental line of recognition and evocative memory function, accompanied by the experience of aloneness that we have described.

The borderline patient who is vulnerable to a regression to recognition memory or earlier states will, at the same time, be someone who can only tenuously maintain a therapeutic alliance with the therapist. A solid capacity to form a therapeutic alliance grows in small increments from a series of settled developmental tasks from earliest childhood on, beginning with basic trust issues. As issues of trust, separation, individuation, and triadic conflicts are resolved, the successfully developing child has an increasing capacity to relate with confidence and a sense of separateness. This capacity also includes a potential for collaboration and self-observation. The borderline patient with his unsettled separation-individuation issues and his regression under stress to basic trust issues is left with a tenuous capacity to work consistently with his therapist. The loss of sustaining introjects, memories, and fantasies that occurs with the recognition

memory–evocative memory developmental line regression contributes to the regression and to the feeling that he is totally alone.

When the borderline does have higher level strengths that
contribute to alliance formation, he may feel that he is complying
and functioning as a "false self" (Winnicott 1960b) when the
therapist appeals to these ego strengths, especially when the
patient is under stress. Winnicott's discussion of the false self
aspects of primitive patients is particularly applicable to borderlines and helps explain their fury when they are supported to
use some of their strengths. To these patients, many of these
strengths, from which therapeutic alliance formation capacities
ultimately derive, are bound together with their sense that these
abilities are or have been required of them to maintain a conform-
ing, well-behaving false self.

The regression that occurs in the borderline under stress brings
him back to the basic trust issues which are related in Winnicott's framework to issues of the holding environment and good
enough mothering. Only after this holding environment is established over time in therapy can the borderline return to some of
his basic borderline issues: his sense of aloneness which goes with
his tenuous evocative memory capacity and his false self feelings
about his previous, more adequate functioning.

In the psychotherapy of adult borderline patients, their regressive vulnerabilities can quickly be mobilized, resulting in their
returning to feelings of distrust associated with a sense of nonsup-
port from their therapist. Concomitant can be a regression along
the recognition memory–evocative memory developmental line
that follows the emerging disappointments and rage in therapy.
This regression can lead to the panic of aloneness with loss of
affective cognitive capacities, that is, loss of sustaining fantasies
and images, as well as an ultimate breakdown of other cognitive
capacities necessary for alliance formation: self-observation and
capacities for delay of impulse gratification.

The goal of helping a borderline patient develop a more firmly established sense of trust and support in the therapeutic setting can seem in conflict with the necessity of allowing experiences in therapy of increasing anger with its regressive potential which can disrupt the alliance. Yet, this anger, with its relevance to the recognition memory–evocative memory vulnerabilities may be a critical area for the patient to experience in order ultimately to establish a stable evocative memory capacity. Many workers (e.g., Frosch 1970, Winnicott 1969, Adler 1975) have described the developmental issues involved in the child and/or adult patient learning that the object can survive his murderous or devouring rage without being destroyed or without retaliating. The result of this process is progress towards the capacity of the person to be alone in the positive sense, complete the stages of separation-individuation as defined by Mahler, and continue on to triadic and later developmental issues. Yet the experiences of this rage during therapy are often disruptive, with patients experiencing desperate aloneness, panic, and disorganization; in addition, these patients can be serious suicidal risks at such times.

The task of establishing a holding environment while gradually allowing the disappointments and rage to emerge is a major clinical task in the treatment of borderlines, and often requires all the skill, empathy, and capacity to tolerate rage, confusion, and disappointment that the therapist can muster. It is through addressing the issues of emerging aloneness in therapy that the therapist has the greatest opportunity to help the patient work through the issue of distrust in his holding environment as well as his related experiences of emptiness, panic, desperation, and rage that may accompany his aloneness in its most intense forms.

Most therapists begin working with their patients by assuming a position of a neutral, noncritical person who attempts to understand the patient's life story, conflicts, and dilemmas. For healthier patients who have largely resolved issues of distrust and separation-individuation, this may be what they most need in order to allow the emergence of the usual neurotic transferences. Narcissistic characters, too, can permit the mirror and idealizing transferences (Kohut 1971) to develop in such an environment. For these patients, the therapist's neutral, noncritical yet interested responses can establish rather readily a holding environment which these patients can utilize in working with their higher level conflicts as they appear. However, the borderline patient's distrust, primitive defenses, intense guilt, and worthlessness (often projected as the expectation of severe disapproval) often render the usual noncritical empathic responses inadequate for supportive holding. In addition, the aloneness issues may emerge too soon and in a disruptive fashion. If the aloneness issues appear more slowly, their first manifestations are often a sense of emptiness, boredom, and dissatisfaction on weekends, a time when the patient is separated from the therapist. The patient may become upset, or feel anger or rage at the therapist as increasing needs and wishes are experienced which cannot be met by the therapist. The painful feeling of aloneness that appears as part of the recognition memory–evocative memory regression often carries with it an appeal, usually unconscious, to the therapist to care, hold, soothe, and nurture.

The therapist who empathically assesses (1) where the patient is on the recognition memory–evocative memory developmental line continuum, (2) what issues in the transference or in the patient's daily life precipitated the current regression, and (3) how much of these feelings would it be bearable and useful for the patient to experience at that particular moment, is in a position to offer the appropriate caring, nurturing support that the patient requires at that point. Correct therapist responses are obviously as variable as the issues; the variation is further broadened by specific qualities in the patient as well as the particular personality and therapeutic style of the therapist. For example, empathic clarification that the patient has been experiencing periods of aloneness during weekends that are related to the long gap between sessions can be supportive for a specific patient. But to clarify further that the aloneness is related to longings for the therapist and a wish to be held by him, may at that time terrify the patient and be disruptive. When made too early, such a statement may plunge him into fears of engulfment before he is comfortable in acknowledging how important the therapist is to him and how much he longs for him. The correct empathic assessment and response supports the patient; it communicates to him the therapist's capacity not only to understand, but also to recognize and respect the current limited state of the patient's tenuous autonomy which is being strained by his desires for intense closeness.

The therapist's evaluation of the patient's current capacity to acknowledge and tolerate his anger with the therapist is also important. Will the therapist's attempts to help the patient admit that he is angry at the therapist be seen as an intrusive, destructive statement that the patient is a murderously bad person? Or will it help the patient acknowledge and discuss his anger and feel that it is acceptable? Most borderlines are terrified of their anger, which they feel is murderous and for which they expect destructive retaliation; too early exploration of the quality and quantity of their anger can lead to a breakdown of any alliance. However, it may be possible to help them acknowledge relatively early that anger is a problem for them and frightens them. This approach helps them gain some distance from the feeling; it puts a label on it and imposes some ego structure between the impulse and its expression. Often it is many months before a borderline patient can accept that there are rageful feelings within him without his primitive superego and projective defenses leading to a frightened, self-destructive and self-punitive response.

As more intense feelings of aloneness appear and are accompanied by increasing loss of evocative memory capacities, new questions are posed about the ways in which the therapist responds. The regression to recognition memory requires the therapist's expression of empathic understanding of how empty, alone, helpless, and frightened the patient feels when not in the presence of the therapist. This can lead to a mutual acknowledgement and discussion of these feelings and experiences which can partially alleviate the intensity of the aloneness by establishing and supporting the collaborative nature of the therapeutic work; this can be a step in the reestablishment and/or further development of a therapeutic alliance. The therapist also must decide whether exploration of genetic material at this point is useful; if so, he can offer the patient a framework that supports understanding and intellectual adaptive mechanisms. However, if ill-timed, this effort will be viewed by the patient as a noncaring groping for irrelevant explanations which simply leaves him more alone and expects him to reestablish a false self while he feels himself drowning in increasing desperation.

The empty aloneness that accompanies regression to recognition memory capacity and which may be part of or follow intermittent episodes of recognition memory rage must also be addressed by therapist and patient in other ways when the aloneness feelings become intolerable. As we have stated, the aloneness is usually experienced while away from the therapist when the longings, disappointments, and rage become major issues in the therapy. The problem for therapy involves finding ways to help the patient reestablish and maintain his tenuous evocative memory capacity between sessions. The therapist can find ways to help the patient remember that the therapist exists, and that the patient and therapist will be together again at the next session. These include ways of supporting the patient to remember aspects of their sessions and the material being explored (Fleming 1975). During longer separations because of vacations, some patients may spontaneously keep a journal to evoke the memory of the therapist and their interaction with him; the therapist may suggest this or similar ways to other patients; for example, talking into a tape recorder at times of intense aloneness may be effective for some patients. At certain points in therapy, it may be most useful for the patient to be able to phone the therapist in order to hear his voice, especially when evocative memory capacity fails more frequently or more completely. When he makes such offers, the therapist must carefully evaluate countertransference issues, the correct assessment of the patient's needs, and his own realistic personal limits. Use of the telephone is not abused by most patients when the offer is made after correct evaluation. If, however, the calls and demands escalate to unrealistic levels, it is usually evidence that the patient requires hospitalization, something which patient and therapist need to evaluate together.

Thus far we have not discussed an important clinical intervention that derives specifically from our theoretical framework: use of a transitional object. In psychotherapeutic work, a transitional object can consist of concrete objects that come from the therapist and are utilized by the patient to evoke the soothing aspects of the therapist and the therapist-patient interaction. Examples are a tape recording of a session which a patient may request, a postcard from the therapist when he is on vacation, or a prescription from the therapist which the patient may carry without filling. These transitional objects may help maintain a patient's tenuous evocative memory capacity through periods of therapeutic disruption either because of emerging intense feelings or therapist absences. When use of these transitional objects along with the other measures fails, hospitalization may also be indicated.

Diffuse primitive rage, the most primitive form of disorganizing rage, with its loss of the capacity to recognize the therapist affectively even in his presence, usually requires active intervention by the therapist. In addition to the measures described, active confrontation (Buie and Adler 1972) with the therapist's concerns about the patient, firm definition of the overwhelming affects and issues in a framework that the patient is most likely to hear, and an attempt to share responsibility for helping the patient to weather the experience may avoid hospitalization. However, hospitalizations are not unexpected in the intensive psychotherapy of the more severe borderline patients who have the greatest vulnerabilities in the recognition memory–evocative memory developmental line. Rather than a disastrous negative experience, it can be felt by these patients as a caring, protective, holding event that may consolidate much of the previous therapy. In addition it may continue to provide the holding environment that makes the exploration of the associated difficult affective issues possible in a safe setting.

Our experiences in working with patients on these defects in the recognition memory–evocative memory developmental line have taught us that patients do eventually grow and progress, with inevitable ups and downs, so that evocative memory capacity is finally established as a permanent achievement. When this occurs, the patient is no longer borderline. He then presents us with the issues that neurotic patients must resolve.

For the therapist this arduous long-term work with borderline patients provides the intellectual and emotional satisfaction of participating in the achievement of a major developmental milestone. It also presents the challenge of further defining these developmental defects in borderlines and increasing our understanding of relevant techniques that may facilitate treatment even more effectively.

References
Adler, G. (1975). The usefulness of the "borderline" concept in

psychotherapy. In *Borderline States in Psychiatry,* ed. J.E. Mack, pp. 29–40. New York: Grune and Stratton.

Adler, G. and Buie, D.H., Jr. (1976). Aloneness and borderline psychopathology: the possible relevance of child development issues. *International Journal of Psycho-Analysis* (in press, 1979).

Buie, D.H., Jr. and Adler, G. (1972). The uses of confrontation with borderline patients. *International Journal of Psychoanalytic Psychotherapy* 1:90–108.

Chase, L.S. and Hire, A.W. (1966). Countertransference in the analysis of borderlines. Paper read before the Boston Psychoanalytic Society and Institute, March 23, 1966.

Fleming, J. (1975). Some observations on object constancy in the psychoanalysis of adults. *Journal of the American Psychoanalytic Association* 23:743–760.

Fraiberg, S. (1969). Libidinal object constancy and mental representation. *Psychoanalytic Study of the Child* 24:9–47.

Frosch, J. (1970). Psychoanalytic considerations of the psychotic character. *Journal of the American Psychoanalytic Association* 18:24–50.

Grinker, R.A., Sr., Werble, B. and Drye, R.C. (1968). *The Borderline Syndrome.* New York: Basic Books.

Kernberg, O. (1966). Structural derivatives of object relationships. *International Journal of Psycho-Analysis* 47:236–253.

Kohut, H. (1971). *The Analysis of the Self.* New York: International Universities Press.

Mahler, M.S. (1971). A study of the separation-individuation process: and its possible application to borderline phenomena in the psychoanalytic situation. *Psychoanalytic Study of the Child* 26:403–424.

Mahler, M.S., Pine, F., and Bergman, A. (1975). *The Psychological Birth of the Human Infant.* New York: Basic Books.

Masterson, J.F. (1976). *Psychotherapy of the Borderline Adult.* New York: Brunner/Mazel.

Piaget, J. (1937). *The Construction of Reality in the Child.* New York: Basic Books, 1954.

Winnicott, D.W. (1953). Transitional objects and transitional phenomena. In *Collected Papers.* London: Tavistock, 1958.

—— (1960a). The theory of the parent-infant relationship. In *The Maturational Process and the Facilitating Environment,* pp. 37–55. New York: International Universities Press, 1965.

—— (1960b). Ego distortion in terms of the true and false self. In *The Maturational Process and the Facilitating Environment,* pp. 140–152. New York: International Universities Press, 1965.

—— (1969). The use of an object. *International Journal of Psycho-Analysis* 50:711–716.

Chapter 12

Schizoid Phenomena in the Borderline

J. H. Rey, M.D.

The Schizoid Mode of Being

The period that followed the second world war revealed a remarkable change in the kind of patients seen by, or referred to, the psychotherapist and the psychoanalyst. The bulk of patients seemed to consist of a certain kind of personality disorder which defied classification into the two great divisions of neurosis and psychosis. We now know them as borderline, narcissistic, or schizoid personality organization. This simplification is the result of a long process of attempts at classification of all kinds.

An attempt has been made in this essay to extract aspects of human behavior and mental processes that seem to constitute the core of what we now know as schizoid or borderline personality organization. It can be found not only in those people with such a personality as will be described but also in people who may break down into schizophrenia, depression or mania, or as the underlying core of personality in people with hysterical or obsessional personality. By studying the "schizoid" traits in these various states I hope to be able to define the schizoid personality and the schizoid mode of being in its more or less pure form and distinguish it from the other states of which it may form part. It seems that those people represent a group of persons who have achieved a kind of stability of personality organization in which they live a most limited and abnormal emotional life which is neither neurotic nor psychotic but a sort of frontier state.

Schizoid and / or borderline patients when seen by the psychiatrist are usually in their early twenties. They complain of an inability to make contact with others and find it impossible to maintain any warm and steady relationship. If they actually manage to enter into a relationship it rapidly becomes intensely dependent and results in disorders of identity. They rapidly and transiently form identification with their objects, experience a loss of their sense of identity with accompanying intense anxiety, fear of fragmentation or dissolution of the self. They seldom establish a firm sexual identity and vacillate in their experience of maleness and femaleness. They are not homosexuals but have fears that they may be and their choice of love object, or attempts at choice of love object, is just as vacillating. They are demanding, controlling, manipulating, threatening, and devaluing towards others. They accuse society and others for their ills and are easily persecuted. This may be associated with grandiose ideas about themselves. In fact, their feelings are dominated by fantasies of relative smallness and bigness. When threatened by feeling small and unprotected and in danger they may defend themselves by uncontrollable rages and various forms of impulsive behavior. Other aspects of their abnormal affectivity are reflected in the sense of futility they complain of and which is characteristic of them. This is reflected as well in the special kind of depression from which they suffer, a form of depersonalized depression, that is, boredom, uselessness, lack of interest, etc., but with a marked deadening of the pain aspect of true depression. Together with this deadness there is a search for stimulants and production of sensory experience by means of alcohol, drugs, hashish, cutting themselves, perversions, promiscuity, etc. They often complain of various abnormal sensations, body image disturbance of various kinds as well as depersonalization and derealization experiences. Their body ego is no more structured and stable than their personality, ego or self. Their underlying state of perplexity and confusion is frequently apparent.

Their work performance varies a great deal. Often when they come to treatment they have given up their studies or their work or they are doing some form of manual or low level occupation although they may have achieved university standards. However, their working capacity may be preserved if they work in a structured situation.

There is one difference in my personal experience in the way the two sexes present themselves, with many more men responding to the description I have given than women. In the case of women, hysterical manifestations, that is, hysterical mechanisms of defense mark the underlying personality structures and they show more often than men histrionic behavior, acting out, hysterical fits, and overtly the claustro-agoraphobic syndrome.

The claustro-agoraphobic syndrome, however, is basic to both sexes; only certain manifestations of it are different. As Guntrip (1968) has so clearly described, the schizoid person is a prisoner. He craves love but is prevented from loving because he is afraid of the destructive force of his love so far as his object is concerned. He dares not love for fear that he will destroy. He finds himself enclosed in a dilemma, enclosed in a limited space and with limited objects and limited relationships.

It is the mechanisms at work in this "limitation state" that I intend to describe. Kindness and support in the transference situation is not enough to treat these patients. A thorough knowledge of their mental processes, fantasies, and underlying structures subtending their behavior is essential in combination with affective understanding.

I will begin with internal part objects and their language, projective identification, because we must begin somewhere in this Tower of Babel which makes up the schizoid structure. I mean this expression literally because these part objects whose structure we need to understand, speak to each other and speak to us in a confusion of languages which demand special interpretation.

In normal interpersonal relationships one or another aspect of the whole ego corresponds with one or another aspect of the ego of the other person. It is a relationship at the level of the integrated ego. Moreover, in normal conduct, apart from certain aspects of love and hate, when we tend to be concrete, the ego makes use of conventional signs which are conscious and of symbols which may be conscious or unconscious, both however, existing at a representational level. Schizoid communication by contrast often takes place at a level of "merchandise," a sort of barter agreement in which the subject feels himself to be given "things," made to accept "things," where "things" are done to him, etc.

Thus, after weeks or even months of refusing to speak of her intimate feelings a patient said: "You don't understand. If I speak to you I hit you, I poison you with the rotting and mouldy things which I am full of." She had previously simulated a suicide attempt in order to get her stomach washed out, to clean out some of these contents. Another patient said: "When you speak to me and ask me questions you bite me and tear out a piece of my flesh. I won't speak any more, I won't listen." It is a well accepted fact by psycholinguists that at first the utterances of the mother are considered to be experienced by the child as perceptual parts of mother like any other parts.

Moreover, more or less normal people think in terms of

persons, not objects placed somewhere in a container. But in contrast, this is just how schizoid thought functions. Thoughts are material objects contained somewhere and expelled into something or other; even the containing object is itself contained somewhere. It is thus that the schizophrenic is the patient who most concretely shows the true problem of claustrophobia and agoraphobia. In the consulting room he sits near the door or the window even if this can't be opened sufficiently for him to escape. He feels himself to be engulfed, immured in one object or another, and feels that he does the same thing with the objects which are inside him.

A schizophrenic patient illustrated this by explaining why he was frightened to lie on the couch. He was afraid of becoming engulfed in it and being so tall that his feet overlapped the couch; he feared that his father would see his legs poking out and cut them off. He could not distinguish between the couch and his mother in his unconscious fantasy and felt himself caught inside his mother with only his feet showing. This is concrete thinking where the idea is equivalent to the object and where these idea-objects are always contained or containing.

We must now consider the characteristics of these objects and their fate when they are displaced. This will lead us to examine the notion of partial objects and of splitting and denial. It is remarkable that these ideas which took on an increasing importance in Freud's thought remained unused, or almost so, by the adherents of classical psychoanalysis. To quote Laplanche and Pontalis (1967): "It is of some interest to note that it was in the field of psychosis—the very area where Bleuler too, from a different theoretical standpoint speaks of *Spaltung*—that Freud felt the need to develop a certain conception of the splitting of the ego. It seemed to us worth outlining this conception here even though few psycho-analysts have adopted it; it has the merit of emphasizing a typical phenomenon despite the fact that it does not provide

,n entirely satisfactory explanation of it" (p. 429). Similar comments could be applied to the concept of partial objects and of denial since these concepts are interdependent. I think it is necessary to make an important distinction between a pathological part object and a normal part object which is only partial in the sense that it forms one of the parts of an object which is capable of being assembled into a whole. Thus the maternal breast is a part object only by comparison with the whole mother formed by the integration of her various parts, and functions in an infant's fantasy like an object endowed with capacity for action, love, and hate.

Splitting plays a part in normal development also, for example, splitting of good and bad aspects of the object as well as of the subject and also the splitting of one object from others. But the schizophrenic behaves differently. Under the sway of persecutory anxiety and the fear of catastrophic dissolution of the ego, primitive and elemental anxieties which arise from the beginning of life, he proceeds to use splitting repetitively and intensively to get rid of bad parts of himself which leads to a fragmentation of the object and of the ego. The fragmented parts of the ego as well as fragmented parts of internal objects with the impulses and anxieties belonging to these fragments are projected into his objects which acquire by projective identification these split-off aspects of the self, now projected and denied. These objects become persecutors, and are introjected, but cannot be assimilated and are in turn projected into an external object (or even into an internal object in an intrapsychic relation) and the vicious circle continues. These objects, some of which Bion has called bizarre objects, are important as elements in the thinking not only of the schizophrenic but also of the schizoid patient. These processes do not only apply to bad aspects of the object or of the self. From fear of destruction, the good parts of the object or the ego are also split off and projected in the same manner into objects which are expected to look after them while they contain them, preserving and protecting them.

In the course of psychotherapy the schizoid, having projected his good parts into the therapist in order to preserve them, as if depositing them in a bank, becomes frantic if he cannot find his therapist because the loss of the therapist means also the loss of elements of the self and of his objects. Moreover, since the reparative activity of the schizoid is based on concrete reparation, as if he were rebuilding a house with its bricks, the loss of the bricks contained in the therapist makes reconstruction impossible. This, in my opinion, is one of the fundamental reasons for the schizoid's refusal to form an ordinary transference relationship with the therapist. Unless one can interpret this mistrust, which is fundamentally justified and which the therapist needs to understand, it is extremely difficult to ever obtain the confidence of the schizoid patient. Concurrently with these internal splits, the therapist, too, is split into good and bad objects and the transference relationship changes constantly and remains unstable and fragmented for a long time, changing not only from day to day but from minute to minute during the session.

Thus, a young schizophrenic whom I treated in hospital perceived me either as an object whom she could not do without, from whom she could not separate, and to whom she wanted perpetually to adhere, or within an instant as an object which she attacked so vigorously that I had to defend myself from her by force. One day she illustrated the change from a neurotic transference to a psychotic transference in a remarkable way: she spoke to me about her life at home in a reasonable manner and in contact with reality, and then all of a sudden, with astonishing rapidity, she went to the door and with piercing eyes and voice trembling with emotion she said: "Get down here in front of me, obey. You know how for years you have mistreated my mother and me, the cruelties and the torture that you have done. When you came to my room at three A.M. in the morning, etc., etc."

External reality had disappeared and only psychic reality remained. The image of the father and of me had become one. By projective identification I had become her father with his characteristics partly real and partly attributed to him by the patient by that same process of projective identification. At the end of five minutes, which seemed as long as five centuries, when I wondered what was going to happen, she became calm and resumed a more or less normal conversation. But she remained mistrustful, close to the door as if she might await the return of the "feared ones" which she called "they" and which would come to take her away to a hellish fate. She could not be friends with me because "they" became angry and punished her. It was best to be on good terms with "they." She asked if she could kill me to convince "they" that she did not love me. On the other hand, the idea of losing me was intolerable; after she let down the tires of my car so that I would be killed in an accident, she hid herself to watch me and ran after me to warn me that if I went in the car I was in great danger, without telling me why.

The fear of separation from the object and the desire to penetrate into it and fuse with it into a primal unity can be so intense that it surpasses human understanding.

Thus, a paranoid and persecuted patient complained ceaselessly with years of virulent reproaches full of rage and despair because I did not love her, after having seduced her by my interpretations and having led her to believe that she was loved. She found proof of my wish to torture her in the fact that I did not let her penetrate into me physically and fuse with me. On this subject she lost all contact with reality and insisted that such a fusion was possible. One proof of my refusal which made the analysis almost impossible consisted in reproaching me as often as she could that I was not in agreement with what she was saying. This produced two people, not one person, and I became a monster which, at least at that moment, she hated.

It is clear from what I have just said that the question of his identity is a major problem for the schizoid. The enormous difficulty of acquiring a stable ego is the result of faulty introjective identification, made very difficult by persecutory feelings and a fear of the object created by the projection of destructive, envious, and insatiable impulses which can become incredibly violent. They are neither heterosexual nor homosexual, not even bisexual. This arises from the fact that their identifications depend both on an internal object which is not assimilated and on a containing external object in which they live, and hence this identity depends on the state of the object and varies with it, with its identity and its actions. They have an external shell or carapace but no vertebral column. They live as parasites in the shell which they seem to have borrowed or stolen and this creates a feeling of insecurity.

Thus, an extremely schizoid young man, who during his treatment went through a breakdown diagnosed by all the psychiatrists except me as totally schizophrenic, would dress himself at night in clothes typical of a London businessman. He would enter his parents' bedroom at three o'clock in the morning, wake them and say to his father: "Am I now the person you wanted me to be?" Previously he had dressed himself in his mother's clothes for a number of years. Under the pressure of the psychotherapeutic group where he received treatment, which attempted to confront him with his lack of initiative and his failure to leave home and go to work, he decided to become a man.

One day some workmen happened to be working on road works in front of his house; he urinated in a bottle which he put at the front door as a gesture of contempt; he looked at himself in a mirror, brushed his hair in the style of Wellington and in a military manner marched around the courtyard, took some of his neighbor's washing which was drying on the hedge between their houses and threw it into her garden. He invited the workers to tell him who gave them permission to be there and then returned to his house. Since it was the first of May, a special day for workers, he sang a patriotic anticommunist song. Then he convinced himself that he was in danger because the workers were Communists and would attack him. Moreover, the BBC would begin to talk about him and the Irish rebels would come to get him. He had become important, but persecuted, and his homosexual passivity and his feminine identification entered into the conflict as a passive defense. Finally, to separate himself, to undo the identification with his parents, he became irritable, oppositional, and aggressive. They could no longer look after him and he was admitted to the hospital as an inpatient.

During individual sessions with me he sat on the floor to look up at me from a lower position as a sign of respect, like a baby. Then he said that if he lay down, or sat down, etc., he would, like a baby, fail to orient himself in relation to the things around him. Later he became preoccupied with multiple aspects of his personality: he no longer knew which parts of his parents he was made of, and each piece had a nationality: his father was English, his mother German/Polish, who now lives in England. Each "piece" had a special and separate characteristic. His father is a professor, but in addition was a military man through family tradition, but at the same time a pacifist; he is upper and lower class, conservative and socialist, etc. He began to believe that his mother was Jewish. He gave a nationality to each of these "pieces": one "piece" of him was Prussian, and very rigid, one "piece" English, one "piece" Polish, etc. Then he wanted to become a Jew and soon after he no longer wanted to. First he admired them, then he criticized them. Finally he explained to me why he wanted to become Jewish: it was because the Jews were fragmented, dispersed, persecuted, and dispossessed, living in a Tower of Babel of languages and of different nationalities and yet found their unity and their own identity by the fact that they were Jewish and this fact could transcend and unite all these fragments into an integrated whole.

What a marvellous unconscious description of the integrative functions of the object! He had to have this schizoid regression, this dissociation of parts which had been assembled in a faulty way in order to separate out the elements and to reconstruct the edifice. This example illustrates clearly the problem which integration of the ego poses for the schizophrenic or schizoid person.

Schizophrenic Breakdown

I have had the occasion to treat a young schizophrenic who had an attitude resembling catatonia and very interesting rituals in which a gesture of her limbs or her face was always annulled by an opposing gesture controlling and undoing the preceding gesture. I eventually understood that these gestures were either sexual or aggressive and needed to be controlled. After the death of her father she adopted typically catatonic postures and said that she could not move because she would come into collision with her father who was enclosed inside her.

Later, with other patients, I came to understand that the opposite of immobility could be seen in paroxysmal movements such as those of an epileptic fit, which by contrast results in the projection of internal contents outside where they can be attacked and destroyed. Then I came to understand the extreme mental rigidity of the schizoid who has to control all his objects, both internal and external. The anxiety of his sexual persecutory and destructive impulses is so great that no autonomy can be allowed to his objects. The fear of fragmentation is catastrophic.

Thus a schizoid man could alter nothing of his life or his attitudes and he said that he could never live anywhere else than at his home because if he moved he would have to take with him his room with all his furniture and things as they were without changing anything.

Transformation, Representation, and Symbolization

The second fact to consider with the schizoid is the mental apparatus necessary for the transformation of sensory or sensorimotor experience into representations, into images, into symbols and signs, and into memories, such transformations being essential both for the maintenance of ordinary human relationships and for the construction of a normal mental apparatus for thinking.

We have seen that the elements of thought in the schizoid have a concrete character which Freud himself described as one of the essential qualities of the system unconscious, namely, the representation of things instead of the representation of words. This defect in the function of transformation seems to be a basic defect in the schizoid. But at the same time we know that the schizoid is in many cases capable of great intelligence even though he treats people as things, and in this way removes the affectivity which for him is dangerous and persecuting. The coexistence of a schizoid type of personal relationship and of a highly developed intelligence can only be explained by a split in the ego which results in a partial ego, which is intellectual and highly developed such as Piaget or Hartmann would describe, and another part of the ego in which the development has been arrested at the schizoid stage and where the depressive position has not been worked through.

During psychotherapy with the schizoid, progress in treatment depends on the possibility of undoing this schizoid structure and of allowing normal symbolization of bizarre objects and of sensory experiences to occur, that is to say, make other modes of communication possible. It is sometimes possible to achieve this end without a catastrophic reaction, that is to say, without the coherent parts of the ego disintegrating. In other cases this is impossible and the patient needs to go through a frankly schizophrenic episode. For some this is a good thing, because it is the only way of returning to the point of bifurcation between normal and abnormal development where the growth of a paralyzed affectivity, previously enslaved and rigidly controlled, may be resumed. No one, I believe, can predict if this happens whether the patient will become a chronic schizophrenic or will progress towards new horizons.

The same situation applies to the schizophrenic in a clinically obvious schizophrenic state: does he have the potential to resume his development or not? This chiefly depends on the capacity of his mental apparatus for symbolic transformation and on the stage he has reached in relation to the depressive position. Indeed, there is a group of patients for whom the schizoid state is a regression and constitutes a defense against the suffering and pain of the depressive state; these patients have a better outlook than those who are true schizophrenics, that is to say, who have never reached the depressive state. A "schizoaffective" state where clinically the patient oscillates between a state of schizophrenia and depression is also well known and these cases again have a more favorable outcome with psychotherapy. We also know of cases who, without treatment, change from schizophrenia to depression or vice versa in the course of time.

Among those who have studied the function of transformation and representation in the mental apparatus, the work of Bion (1965) stands out as especially significant. I would like to give an example of defective transformation. Bion says, "In psychoanalytic theories statements by patients or by analysts are representations of an emotional experience. If we can understand the process of representation this will help us to understand the representation and that which is represented."

A patient told me the following dream:

I am dining with friends and get up from the table. I am thirsty and I start to drink. I realize that the bottle in my mouth has a neck shaped like a feeding bottle; there is no teat, but I think I can feel the flange which normally holds the teat in place. While I think of this I begin to see the bottle more clearly. I hold it in front of my face and see that it has the shape of a feeding bottle. In the bottle I see water. The level of the water falls and bubbles of air mount through the liquid, and because of this I am aware that some of the water has become part of me; but I cannot feel this thing that becomes part of me. I am anxious because I can neither understand nor feel the water passing from a state separate from me to become an intimate part of me. While I am thinking thus, the bottle becomes bigger. I see at that moment that on the inside of the bottle facing me, words are engraved on the surface in raised letters which give instructions on how to wean an infant.

In this dream the subject failed to transform the experience of the movement of water from the exterior to the interior of his body into a good experience in the form of a representation and a memory. He did not participate in the experience. He did not understand what happened; he tells us that he lacks the experience of the change. This can only be the experience in the mouth where the presence of water produces a sensation, a sensation which is needed to make the work of transformation possible. One part of the experience is lacking: it is as if he had been fed through a tube. But he tells us what was lacking, it was the teat and it was the experience of weaning, and of suckling from a mother. He took the bottle himself and gave himself a drink. The teat no doubt represents a maternal breast and a mother whose presence and whose bodily contact is absolutely necessary for the awareness and recording of the experience. It seems that in the absence of the good object, part of the work of assimilation did not take place.

Reparation

In addition to structural mechanisms of the schizoid phase and its mechanisms of defense I would like to consider a fundamental aspect of schizoid mentality. This is the law of the talion and the absence of the capacity for reparation which governs the whole behavior of the schizoid. It is this law of vengeance which is responsible through its incredible power in the schizoid not only for the stunted mental structure, but also for its lack of humanity. By the law of the talion I mean: "An eye for an eye and a tooth for a tooth"; "Let the punishment fit the crime"; "If I have stolen my hand will be cut off, if I have transgressed I will be punished, you have stolen and I will cut off your hands," etc. There is no forgiveness, no compassion, no reparation. There is only the terrible vengeance and anger of Jehovah preached by the prophets of the Old Testament.

Reparation in the schizoid state also obeys the law of the inverse talion. Like everything I have already described, it has to be concrete. I call this *repair* to distinguish it from reparation. We could perhaps call it recontruction in contrast to reparation. This reconstruction has some things in common with the restitution with which Freud was concerned. Reparation, on the other hand, is a notion unknown to Freud, and plays a fundamental role in the work of Melanie Klein. Even Freud's ideas on restitution remained sketchy and far from complete, as were his ideas on splitting and denial. Almost all analysts have rejected the fundamentally new theme which appears in his work after 1920 in which the life instinct as a constructive force was contrasted with the death instinct as an instinct of disintegration. People have quarrelled about words and have forgotten that analysis is rooted on observation. The study of the schizoid personality structure has led us back to the observations of a master on splitting, projection, and denial which his ultraconservative disciples had well buried. In reconstruction or repair, infantile omnipotence is retained and an attempt is made to reconstruct the damaged one. Reparation, by contrast, is not and cannot be an omnipotent act.

The Manic Defense

We will now consider the role of the manic state. On the one hand its role is a defense against the anxiety of disintegration and of schizoid persecution, and on the other hand a defense against the pain of the depressive state. One can observe this from the point of view of psychiatry in the clinical syndrome of hypomania, but also as a potential psychodynamic state during psychotherapy. We must not forget that the manic state can represent an exaggeration of a normal phase of maturation and of reparation. In manic states or in the manic defense we are no longer concerned with the maternal breast but with the penis. I believe that in all depressive states the object with which the subject has a relationship is, contains, or symbolically represents the maternal breast which as a partial object represents the mother who is destroyed, emptied, poisoned and thus in a depressed state; the subject feels this is his fault and becomes identified with this depressed object and, consequently, depressed himself.

The object of the manic state is the penis which is needed by the subject for the task of reparation: through it he can regain the destroyed object either as a direct substitute by identification or by recreating the contents of the mother, that is to say, by making her pregnant by filling her empty breasts, etc. The more the maternal object is destroyed by the subject's attacks, the more must the penis become omnipotent and the subject by identification becomes omnipotent also. In this manner the destroyed state of the object is denied. There is no reparation proper and after the manic phase the patient returns to his depression or his schizoaffective state at the level of maturation which he had previously reached.

A very schizoid patient dreamed that on his nose he was balancing a long pole which reached right to the sky with a baby balanced on the end. As he awakened he said to himself: "This fucking penis is good for nothing, it is so big that it is useless." On the couch, the patient of whom I have already spoken had identified his whole body with a phallus and he felt himself enlarge physically and be invaded by delusions of grandeur.

In the manic state we have a pseudo penis which repairs nothing; it serves to deny the reality of destroyed objects and presents itself as the universal substitute, which leads to the formation of a false self. Meanwhile, the aggressive impulses continue to destroy the object.

Manic reactions can actually represent a pathological deviation of a normal phase of development. I believe that when the separated fragments of the ego reunite, whether in a mosaic or in a fusion, it is done with the help of the fantasied action of the phallus. This is achieved on the one hand by an identification with the penis, adopting its characteristics and functions and, on the other hand, because, although a partial object it usually functions, as we have explained, as a representation of the whole object, the father, and enters into the relationship with the maternal breast, the partial object representing the mother. We have here the prototypes of the sexual identity of the two sexes and the prototype of the relationship between them. The role of the penis as a creator integrating and repairing through reproduction becomes clear in this model.

On the other hand, in the manic state there is a partial identification with the immeasurably grandiose aspect of the erect penis. The manifestations of this aspect are omnipotent, contemptuous, and persecutory as well. It is always present in a latent form in the schizoid and, when seen clinically as delusions of grandeur in paranoid states or as a feature of the depression of the manic depressive, illustrates the role of the phallus in the grandiosity seen in these conditions.

The patient referred to earlier, who felt himself to vary in size both physically and mentally, explained that he felt he had a permanent personality for the first time when he experienced the presence inside him of a hard column extending from his anus to his mouth which could resist all attacks. Later in his grandiose state he identified with Jesus Christ, grew a beard and became a carpenter, designed religious motifs and wanted to preach in church.

The Depressive Position

It will not be possible to go into the mechanism by which a depressive state develops even though this forms an essential phase in treatment. This is work about which much has been written and I want to concentrate on schizoid states. Suffice that we remember that in this process destructive impulses lose their intensity and loving impulses play a fundamental role. The good and the bad parts of the ego and also of the object unite gradually into a whole and the law of the talion loses its virulence. Primitive compassion begins to take over from the total egocentricity characteristic of the beginnings of life. The object achieves a life of its own and the subject becomes an object related to like any other object.

The Change From Schizoid States to Schizophrenia

These phases of development belong to the preverbal period. Instead of the biphasic development Freud proposed we have here to understand a triphasic evolution: first an archaic preverbal phase and an archaic verbal phase where the distinction can be thought of as an example of ontogeny repeating phylogeny, and, then, after the age of six, seven, or eight, a phase in which external reality dominates. I take the view that nonverbal schemata give a structure to verbal thought which in turn influences the preexisting nonverbal schemata. This reciprocal relationship sheds light on the disorders of verbal thought which are seen when a schizoid individual becomes schizophrenic. The task of defining what happens when this change from a schizoid to a schizophrenic state occurs is not easy. The more I understand the language and structure of the schizoid the more I find the distinction difficult.

From the point of view of classical psychiatry it is quite simple: are there delusions or hallucinations? If there are, it is schizophrenia, if not, it isn't. But in fact, when one works not only longitudinally but simultaneously in depth as the psychoanalyst does, the situation is quite different. We can see this if we compare material from schizoid patients with the delusional ideas of someone floridly schizophrenic.

Let us take an extreme case, a patient who had four schizophrenic breakdowns, each presenting a different clinical picture. In his hebephrenic-catatonic state, which began with an intense interest in the universe and the stars, he felt himself to be communicating with an extraterrestrial universe. As proof he took out of his briefcase some little oval and circular shaped pieces of ivory colored paper and assured me that their extraterrestrial origin was obvious. Much later he admitted that although at first he had firmly believed this, he later came to realize that he himself had simply collected these pieces of paper from somewhere.

We see here the interplay of a number of schizoid mechanisms. First of all the wish to be omnipotent to participate in the universe, which he held very strongly. To achieve this wish without becoming mad he had to avoid destroying external reality and instead tried to transform it. With the external physical proof he could thus reinforce the internal psychic reality of his wish. For this he had through the fantasy of projective identification transformed the pieces of paper and obtained in this way a formal proof of his experience. He had thus decided not to completely abandon external reality, but to grossly transform it by a process of splitting, by omnipotent wishing and by projective creation.

Some schizoid patients are past masters at the art of choosing objects which are precisely appropriate for their projections, that is, which have characteristics so similar to their projection that it becomes very difficult to make a distinction between the object and the projected fantasy.

It seems to me then that the schizophrenic goes further and does not concern himself with the existence of external reality but declares and delusionally believes whatever he wishes, having made a regression to a very primitive, infantile, stage where the distinction between psychic reality and external reality is almost nonexistent and hardly concerns him. There is only one reality, the reality of the internal fantasy world. In the schizoid world we find various gradations of abnormality in the type of morbid processes I have just described.

The Space-Time Continuum and Displacement in the Borderline

An attempt will be made now to examine the clinical observations previously described, in terms of the organization of space and time as in any other branch of knowledge. Piagetian observations, ideas and constructs have been extensively used both explicitly and implicitly but by no means exclusively. The main source for this work is clinical observation during treatment and psychoanalytical psychotherapy supervisions and interpretations of data. I have made use of Piaget only for the reason that psychoanalysis has never studied the structure of external reality, of space, displacement and time as have he and his pupils.

During the treatment of patients, especially of claustrophobic and agoraphobic patients, it appeared more and more evident to me that a fundamental organization of objects in space (including the patient himself) was underlying the mode of behavior observed. All sorts of physical and mental situations which claustrophobic and agoraphobic patients experience are very likely to refer to a primary situation which all the other secondary situations are substitutes for and symbolic of.

Claustrophobic persons are afraid to be in an enclosed situation, they develop extreme anxiety or panic and want to get out. The "situation" may be a room, a traffic jam, a marriage. When they are not contained they become agoraphobic and develop anxiety or panic. Thus they may be housebound, or may only travel so far alone from the place of safety and no further, or have to be accompanied. The manifestations of those conditions are well known. However, it was when I made the observation that this condition is really a basic one in schizoid states and schizophrenia that I realized it had a very important meaning. By a basic condition I mean that whenever schizoid and schizophrenic patients are seen in the context of dynamic treatment they reveal claustro-agoraphobic basic fears not in the least evident when their behavior is assessed from a purely phenomenological psychiatric approach. The mental and emotional disturbances of the schizoid state are disturbances in the early, primitive, and basic organization of the human being, ontogenetically speaking. It is the importance that Piaget gives to the early structuralization of space that led me to attempt the explanation of the way of life of the schizoid in terms of the early organization of space, movement, and time.

Spatial Development of the Infant and His World

The fetus is at first contained within the uterus which is itself contained inside the mother. It is relatively deprived of freedom of movement and displacement, although a certain degree of movement is possible. On the other hand it moves with the mother in the mother's external space. After birth one could say that the mother through her care, feeding, warmth, support, etc., recreates partially this uterine state for the baby. Although restricted still, the baby's personal space allows him more freedom than in the womb. It could be called the marsupial space. The baby now moves in the mother's space but only in that portion of her space which is his personal space. As he grows up his personal space increases until it has coincided with the maternal space and, if the mother is normal, for instance, not claustro-agoraphobic, that space will coincide with general space where the subject will be an object amongst objects. Simultaneously with this process a space internal to the subject is formed where psychic internal objects live in intrapsychic relationships. They are experienced very concretely at first, for example, as sensations or elaborated perceptions and even more elaborated later as representations of a very complex nature.

It would seem that everybody has an external personal space of some kind which persists, somewhat like the notion of territory in ethology and in which our object relations are somewhat different from those in the universal space. However, as Piaget has pointed out and described so clearly, space is not a Newtonian absolute space, neither is time absolute time; they are both constructs. The infant and the child have to construct their objects and their space, space being the relative positioning of objects as in the Einsteinian model.

The idea then would be to look at some aspects and stages of those early constructions and how they appear either unevolved or distorted as structures underlying the schizoid mode of being. The pure Piagetian approach is unsatisfactory, for although emotions, affects, and drives are accepted as intrinsic parts of the cognitive structures, they are not referred to as such. I will therefore present my own psychoanalytical and Piagetian-inspired elaborations.

Objects that are familiarly looked upon and treated as individual wholes by adults are certainly not experienced as such for the infant, and the child has to "construct" them, linking parts by action schemas as described by Piaget, that is, by interiorized actions of the subject on the object. Piaget says the child coordinates "the actions among themselves in the form of practical schemas, a sort of sensorimotor preconcept, characterized by the possibility of repeating the same action in the presence of the same objects or generalizing it in the presence of analogous others."

For Piaget more complex schemas are not just the association or synthesis of previously isolated elements. Thus, he writes of the sensorimotor schema that "it is a definite and closed system of movements and perceptions. The schema presents, in effect, the double characteristics of being structured (thus structuring itself the field of perception or of understanding) and of constituting itself beforehand as totality without resulting from an association or from a synthesis between the previously isolated elements" (Battro 1973). For Piaget the "sensorimotor schemas are not simply what we sometimes call patterns, that is to say they have further power to generalize and further power to assimilate" (Battro 1973).

As to schemas relative to persons, he says that "they are cognitive and affective simultaneously. The affective element is perhaps more important in the domain of persons and the cognitive element in the domain of things, but it is only a question of degree." Thus, he says that "an affective schema" means simply the affective aspect of schemas which are otherwise also intellectual.

So to summarize, for Piaget action is at the very beginning the source of all manifestations of life. It precedes thought, it controls perception and sensation, and it is by a process of combinations of actions of the subject on his object, followed by the internalization of these action schemas, that the precursors of thought are generated. Thus the infant puts his thumb in his mouth, then he extends this action to other objects than his thumb, then elaborates the action by using a rod or some such object to extend the reach of his arm to get to objects that he will take to his mouth or elsewhere.

I do not know if a study has been made of such a way of thinking in Freud's writings apart from the structural theory itself. But it is interesting to note that in the Rat Man, for instance, Freud makes constant references to psychical structures. In fact, Part II is entitled, "Some General Characteristics of Obsessional Structures" (Freud 1909). He says that "obsessional structures can correspond to every sort of psychical act" (p. 221). He says, "In this disorder (obsessional neurosis) repression is affected not by means of amnesia but by a severance of causal connections brought about by a withdrawal of affect. These repressed connections appear to persist in some kind of shadow form (which I have elsewhere compared to an endopsychic perception) and they are thus transferred, by a process of projection, into the external world, where they bear witness to what has been effaced from consciousness." This is as good a definition of mental structure as any structuralist could wish.

For the object relations psychoanalyst, therefore, there exists in the behavior of adults primitive object relationships or schemas, normal or pathological, which govern aspects of behavior. Some of these primitive internalized object relations may have remained unintegrated and function autonomously. Part-object psychology or the psychology of part object, part subject, part states, etc., relates to the study of the aspect of the genetic development of object relationships.

Starting with the need of the infant expressed as desire for gratification, there is little doubt that the infant wishes to make part of his endogenous space, that is, the precursor of the self, the gratifying objects he needs for survival and growth. His early discovery of the appearance and disappearance of the object in his space (i.e., early ego or self) will prompt him to desire the good objects as part of himself or of his good space in the only way he is capable, the concrete. The frustration of not being able to always keep the object in his spaces (i.e., internal space and personal space) will increase the desire for the object to be his possession. The growth of this desire and the need for securing such objects, if it reaches great intensity, will become greed. The frustration, anger, anxiety resulting from the nonpossession of the desired gratifying objects will lead to the desire to deprive of it the other space containing the desired objects, for the other space containing the objects is now in a state of no-pain or pleasure, a state previously experienced by the infant. The wish is not only to possess the object but to deprive the other space as he is deprived himself. This is envy.

Further, the infant left in his self-space whilst waiting for the gratifying object will have to substitute objects of his own self-space, for example, parts of his own body, or toys, etc. Thus in the place of the breast mother he will have thumb, excrements, or genitals as part of his space. They may prove helpful to wait for the appearance of the external breast-mother and thus temporarily relieve anxiety or frustration following nongratification. Nongratification may lead to punishing the nonself space by putting frustrating objects, say feces, into it, thus substituting for the good breast or transforming it into a bad object. However, those parts of the self-space put into the nonself-space are still considered to be somehow part of the self-space and a particular kind of bond is formed between self-space and nonself-space by displacement in or out of them, that is, by introjection and projection. This bond gives to early object relationship a quality of possessiveness and identification between objects which are at the roots of introjective and projective identification processes. This process is by no means abnormal when it is concerned with displacement of objects for need gratification and communication purposes.

Its persistence and distortions are, however, responsible for a large number of typical features of the schizoid way of experiencing. It creates the feeling of living in the object because part of oneself is in the object; it creates the need for never leaving the object out of control; it creates a sense of impending doom through the possible loss of part of the self if the object is lost. And it results in persecutory feelings if the projected or displaced part of the self is believed to have envious, greedy, and destructive impulses and accounts for innumerable other schizoid manifestations.

We must now proceed with the systematic examination of schizoid manifestations in terms of our space-time model and also illustrate with examples. First of all, I will try to show how one must extend the claustro-agoraphobic syndrome from a specific syndrome to a basic universal organization of the personality. A claustrophobic woman is seen for assessment for psychotherapy. She says she is afraid that something terrible will happen to her if she goes out. She insists she does not know what it is. I point out that there are only two possibilities, either it is something she will do to others or something others will do to her. She says after a lot of hesitation, "I'm afraid I'll do something mad." After more hesitation, she says, "I'll shout and people will think I'm mad." I say, "Shouting is something coming out of you, what else could come out of you?" She becomes extremely tense and nervous and after a while asks to be allowed to leave. I say that, of course, she can leave if she so desires, but on the other hand if she can have the courage to say what thought is making her so uncomfortable that she wants to leave, it might save her months of treatment and misery. She plucks up the courage and says "urine and feces." I will leave out the rest of the interview. This is a routine happening in various forms. What years of study of my own patients and patients treated by others has revealed I will put in schematic form.

It will be noticed that the patient wanted to remove herself from the space where she was in contact with what she felt as a threatening object. She wanted to leave the room. However, we also know that phobics avoid certain situations, for instance, eating in public; they will not go to a restaurant, or to the cinema, or to shops. They restrict their outside space until they are housebound. It is important to understand what the ultimate space into which they retire corresponds to in the unconscious.

The outside world or outside space is in such an instance transformed by projective identification into the body or internal space of the subject himself, identified with the internal space of the mother, and thus entering and coming out of a room is coming out of that which the room stands for—ultimately, the mother's body. A primitive imprinted state of birth experiences persists in the hierarchies of transformation and representation of that early experience. What is fixed in the mind is not necessarily the original experience of birth but one or another experience of a primitive similar state belonging to the hierarchy of space constructions, such as the marsupial space described previously. When something comes out of the body such as a shout, urine, feces, semen, saliva, vomit, it fires the system "coming out of" and produces the attached affect. The mechanism involved is the identification by projective identification of the subject with the contents of his own body and of his body identified with that of the mother. He thus experiences himself coming out of mother.

As I have said, the primitive emotional experience, the affect, has been dominant in the structurization of the self- and nonself-spaces. Displacement, then, of any kind of objects including the subject himself from self-space to nonself-space or vice versa is experienced in a primitive manner. Space in certain circumstances is experienced as it was once experienced in a part of the personality, split off from the rest and this way of experiencing space persists. The panic associated with that state and the bodily anguish and sensations are but persistence of the experience when the ego was mostly body ego. The coming into activity of that split-off archaic part of the adult self takes over and paralyzes the more adult ego, and thus, adult methods of coping with danger are not any longer available.

However, I realized the fundamental structure underlying it all when I came across the same experiences as a basic state with schizophrenics, for example, their difficulty lying on the couch from fear of merging and disappearing into it, and, out of the blue, expressing the same fear about mother; or their difficulty staying in the room with me unless they could be near the door or the window, even with bars; or the case of a person who has to be by the door of an airplane at 10,000 feet in the air to avoid panic. And, of course, as I have said, it is not only the mother but the early spatial structures constructed to replace the mother's internal space that are suffused with primitive emotional experiences.

As those spaces are structured by objects and their displacement, the objects in these spaces are gratifying or nongratifying, persecuting or protecting, good or bad. Here are two dreams from two very schizoid patients. One dreamt that he was quite happy inside mother. He then felt he wanted to find out about outside. He got out and started enjoying himself sexually and also doing aggressive things. Then he became anxious as he felt some people might be angry with him, and that he was outside in the open and unprotected. So he got back inside mother. Unfortunately, he realized that it was not much safer because he could do things to his mother from inside that would put him in danger just the same.

Another schizoid young man dreamt that he was living in a sort of tunnel-like building and he was moving about in the tunnel in a sort of trolley. At intervals there were openings from which he could see the outside world. Sometimes the trolley would stop and he would get out to mix in with this outside world, especially for sexual purposes. Then he would get back and resume the inside life. However, one day he was seized with a panic at the thought that the tunnel might close and he would be enclosed forever and he desperately wanted to get out. There is nowhere for the claustro-agoraphobic.

An example of coming out of a containing space and something coming out of the body and their linking together by a common experience is given by the following patient. He was the most severe claustro-agoraphobic I have come across. He dreamt that he had passed a stool several hundred feet long and it was still attached to his anus. It was unseparated from him. We proceeded with the session and when the end of the session approached he sat on the couch in a state of extreme terror saying, "Help me, help me, if I come out of the room outside I will only be a mass of liquified shit."

Here we can see that coming out of the room was associated with feces coming out of him and the identification with the feces was complete as he felt he would be nothing else than the feces. Further, he could not in the dream let the feces be separate from him. As he was himself identified with the feces he was afraid to be in an open space, unprotected after he left me. This patient could only go the lavatory to defecate if somebody knew he was in the toilet. He thus also demonstrates the fear of fragmentation if a part of him separates from the rest, and a fear of dissolution of self by identification with another object, e.g., the feces.

It is obvious that problems of identity, for example, being small or adult, being male or female, and so on, are understandable on the above basis of transient identification with objects. Demandingness, controlling impulses, possessiveness are all clearly connected with the fact that the parts of the self-space put into the nonself-space and vice versa cannot be allowed separateness and dictate such behavior to prevent catastrophic loss of parts of the self. To prevent loss of self, objects must be kept at a distance and vice versa. Thus a young schizoid man in an attempt to solve this problem would remain in his room and communicate with others by watching children play from his window and communicating with others at a distance by telephone. A woman attempted to live in my personal space by constantly walking near my residence or using the telephone to penetrate into my flat. When there was nobody there she would let the telephone ring and fall asleep being in my personal space. So the schizoid person, to prevent pain, anxiety, depression, etc., splits parts of himself, projects them and denies their existence. Immediately he experiences the opposite feelings: fear of loss, of fragmentation, attempts to remake contact, etc., and the vicious circle goes on.

Internal and personal spaces are not the same. Personal-space objects are transitional between universal space and internal space. There is a story about Voltaire, that he built himself a tomb half in the church and half outside to confound those who argued whether he was an atheist. The relative positioning of objects in space is astonishing at times. We know of the preoccupation of obsessionals not to let objects touch each other and the need for symmetry. But sometimes positioning is even more explicit. A very schizoid girl wondered if, when objects were on top of each other, for example, a bird flying over her head, it meant sexual intercourse. After the death of her father, she could not move because any movement would either hurt her father inside her or would have a sexual connotation. The relative positioning of objects was extremely meaningful to her. She would put her right foot on top of the left and do a short, quick tapping movement. This was sexual and was undone by putting the right foot from forward to backwards and instead of tapping she then did a larger and wider movement in the opposite direction.

I will now consider how immature "concepts" of time are involved in this way of being in the same way as those of space. A little autistic boy who wanted his sessions to be at the same time every day (and which I could not do) would take my watch and set it at the time he wanted. The time was the time indicated by the watch face, watches being very special spatial devices. We had to play a game of going from London to Brighton, and returning by train. We had to go from station to station and then return through each station in reverse order. Any fault on my part and everything had to be started all over again. He had seriated space as Piaget has demonstrated but could not decenter from it. He could pass from A to B to C to D, etc., but not from D to A to return to A. He had to move from each position to the next like Achilles and the tortoise, or like Zeno's arrow. These examples lead us to examine more closely the elements of displacement and movement and of time.

Piaget describes a simple experiment carried on with children of various ages. There are two tunnels, one visibly longer than the other. Two dolls, each on a separate track and moving at a fixed speed, are made to enter their respective tunnels at exactly the same time and to emerge at the distal end, also at exactly the same time. Children of a certain age repeatedly say the two dolls moved at the same speed although they agree that one tunnel is longer. The tunnels are removed and the experiment repeated. This time, the same children will say that the doll overtaking the other one goes faster. However, if the tunnels are put back again, they say that the dolls were going at the same speed. They are clearly basing their judgment on the relative positioning of the dolls irrespective of length and time. In that way and by combining a large number of delightfully simple experiments it is possible to reconstruct the stages through which the growing child passes as he constructs his adult ideas of space, speed, and time. At least these notions are involved in the notion of time: seriation or the ordering of events in time, e.g., B comes after A, C after B, etc., then class inclusion, e.g., if B comes after A and C after B, then $A—C$ is greater than $A—B$ or a whole class is greater than the subclass; finally, there is the measurement of time.

Similarly the notion of causality is developed in stages and depends on the emergence of other notions such as those of the permanent object, of space and of time leading to an objective view of causality instead of a magico-phenomenal one.

A woman, a very intelligent woman patient at that, said to me very seriously that she knows she will be married to me and live with me in my country of origin; that she will be married and live with her husband in England; and it will be the same with many other men—all simultaneously and without seeing any contradiction. In fact, she was angry by my suggesting there could be some difficulty in realizing this project.

Time past is time future which is time present, says T. S. Eliot. But this is obviously time inconsistent. Time as a seriation process makes it impossible to go back in time. To be in the same place years later is not the same as previously. But displacement and movement to the schizoid can be disastrous, as it may tear part of him away and leave him fragmented or empty or lost and it can do the same to his objects. Therefore, movements may be very slow or immobility may set in, as in the case of the girl with her father in her internal space. Movement brings about separation and loss, and if it comes fast, catastrophy. Rigidity, fixity, frigidity, impotence—are all defenses against that possibility.

A very severely ill woman one day revealed to her therapist that she could not leave the hospital immediately after her session.

This would be incompatible with her not collapsing. To take the bus and disappear quickly was dreadful. She wandered on the hospital ground first and then very slowly moved away, very gradually. The speed at which she moved from one place to another mattered very much. In depression, movements of the body and limbs become slower and slower until a state of depressive stupor is reached, and ultimate nonmovement is found in suicide. In mania, the contrary takes place, the speed of every movement including speech is increased and the patient cannot keep in one place. The sense of the passage of time is greatly altered in both states.

Piaget says, "Psychological time is the connection between work accomplished and activity (force and rapidity of action) or time is plastic; it expands according to the deceleration or contracts according to the acceleration of action . . . or time is conferred at its point of departure with the impression of psychological duration inherent in the attitudes of expectations, effort, and of satisfaction in brief in the activity of the subject." The schizoid patient, paralyzed in his activities, empty of actions with objects, can only experience duration in relationships in a completely abnormal way.

It is necessary at this point to return to the relationship between localization of object and the most important notion of permanence of subject. Piaget describes frequently a little experiment how in the first half year of mental life an infant who is about to grasp an object will stop his hands if the object is covered with a handkerchief. At a later stage, the baby will try to lift the handkerchief, to look for the object at the place *A* where it has just been covered. But Piaget then observes if the object placed at *A* is displaced to *B* in front of the child watching the displacement that he will often look for the object at *A*, where he had been successful in finding it in previous occasions. It is only towards the end of the first year that he looks unhesitatingly for the object at the place to which it has been displaced. Before this, he ignores series of displacements but is fixated on his own action on the object. Thus, object permanence, says Piaget, is closely linked with its localization in space.

It is absolutely vital here to differentiate between the concept of object in Piaget and the libidinal object of psychoanalysis. Piaget describes an object as a permanent object at the end of the sensorimotor stage, at about eighteen months. Where the subject himself is an object amongst objects this concept applies to all objects and in no way considers the question of libidinal investment which renders an object meaningful and unique to the infant. The libidinal object is meaningful long before the completion of the sensorimotor object. Of vital interest for understanding distortions of self and object of the schizoid person are the stages of object formation described by Piaget, especially because of the specific use of objects of the physical world for identification purposes in schizoid mechanisms of defense.

Since the individual has also to construct his own body image as that of other bodies in space and to gradually reach a sense of permanence of his identity, similar considerations apply here. As Marcel Proust has Swann say in *Swann's Way,* if one wakes up in the night in the dark, not knowing the time or where one is, then one does not know who one is. It is extremely interesting that Piaget has demonstrated by lovely, simple little experiments that the concept of identity of matter takes place in definite stages and that the concept of identity occurs, for instance, before the concept of conservation of quantity. Thus, by showing changing shapes of the same object, for instance, water, in differently shaped containers, it will take time before the child can say it is the same water. It will take more time before he is decentered from spatial ties such as believing there is more water in the tall thin tube than in the other. Only when able to coordinate two independent variables simultaneously, as width and height, will he achieve the right answer.

We now begin to understand the kind of level of organization of mental operations used by the schizoid patient when he feels instability, confusion of identity, disorder of body image, fears of impermanence, etc., since he is bound to experience himself differently in various localities, in various situations, with various objects.

The difficulty existing outside the space with which existence and permanence are so closely linked is enormous for the schizoid. Thus a young man only had a sense of existence when he drove his motor bike so long as there was a car in front of him or if his engine was going. If he passed the car or the engine stopped, he became depersonalized. A young woman who, although she had changed greatly in analysis, could only be the person she was in her mother's head. A young man who, often having lived alone for a considerable time in a room in a boarding house, made progress, started studying, but had to move out of his room to study, in order to have people about him, as he could not bear to be alone. So he sat in various public places like bars and cafes. Then he went through a phase when the place had to move with him and so he sat on buses and wandered everywhere whilst studying. Was he being carried by mother everywhere? In fact, after months of this behavior he had a dream that he was standing in a bus holding a baby, his baby, somewhat monstrous. Then the baby grew up and appeared normal but he lost him. In his association he said the baby was also himself. Some phobics, and perhaps most, will go nowhere unless accompanied, and this can reach amazing extremes with some patients.

For this paper I have attempted to introduce concepts of space, movement and time as the basic elements, the weft and warp of primitive human behavior. Primitive thought is centered on the first moves taken by the infant to structure space. This is done by the action of the subject on his objects and vice versa. Primitive notions of time then follow. Patterns of behavior belonging to any stage may persist and become active at any time later.

References

Battro, M. (1973). *Piaget Dictionary of Terms,* E. Ritschverimann and S.F. Campbell. Oxford: Pergamon.

Bion, W. (1965). *Transformations.* In *Seven Servants: Four Works by Wilfred Bion.* New York: Jason Aronson, 1977.

Freud, S. (1909). Notes upon a case of obsessional neurosis. In *Standard Edition* 10:153–310.

Guntrip, H. (1968). *Schizoid Phenomena, Object Relations and the Self.* London: Hogarth Press.

Laplanche, J. and Pontalis, J.B. (1967). *The Language of Psychoanalysis,* tr. Donald Nicholson-Smith. New York: W.W. Norton, 1973.

Chapter 13

Transference Psychosis in the Borderline Patient

Herbert Rosenfeld, M.D.

The development of a sudden eruption of a psychotic phenomena during the analysis of neurotic or borderline patients is a
very alarming experience for both patient and analyst. Very little
has been written on this subject, but even less is known about the
psychopathology and the significance of the "transient psychosis"
or "transference psychosis" in which the psychotic phenomena
generally only attach themselves to the transference and interfere
only very little with the patient's life situation outside the analysis.

Most transference psychoses clear up after a few days, weeks,
or perhaps months. Only on very rare occasions, particularly
when the patient breaks off the analysis during the transference
psychosis, will the delusions relating to the analyst persist for
many years. I have not had the opportunity to investigate these
unfortunate patients analytically, and will concentrate in this
paper on the significance of the eruption of a transient psychosis
or transference psychosis in neurotic and borderline patients
during analysis. My investigation is based on patients with whom
the transference psychosis could be thoroughly investigated in

analysis during and after the eruption of the transference psychosis.

I shall first discuss the origin of the term transference psychosis. I shall then describe the type of patient who may develop a transference psychosis during analysis. I shall consider whether there are any signs or symptoms during the analysis which indicate that an outbreak of a transference psychosis may be threatening. I shall also examine whether the transference psychosis should be considered a necessary event in the improvement of these patients, or an intrusion into or disruption of the therapeutic alliance, and as such to be removed as quickly as possible (Frosch 1967). If we conclude that the transference psychosis is a severe interference in the therapeutic process, it is absolutely essential to investigate the reasons for the severe threat to the analysis, so that therapeutic measures can be brought into action immediately. Finally I shall describe some typical transference psychotic states and the therapeutic measures which I have used in the treatment of them.

I first used the term transference psychosis (Rosenfeld 1954) to indicate that in treating psychotic patients by psychoanalysis, I found that the psychotic manifestations, object relations, and mechanisms attach themselves to the transference. This transference psychosis, similar to the transference neurosis in neurotic patients, forms the basis of the analytic work of interpretation and appears not to hinder but actually to further the analytic work with psychotic patients. Even when the transference psychosis emerged, the nonpsychotic part of the patient was generally still accessible and active, and only when the sane part of the patient was temporarily overwhelmed, and therefore completely dominated by the psychotic self, was there a danger that a delusional transference would become manifest in which the analyst was misperceived and the analytic work endangered.

Searles, as did I, used the term transference psychosis for

describing a variety of transferences in acute and chronic schizophrenic patients. Some confusion in the use of this term occurred when Reider in 1957 used the term transference psychosis for psychotic anxieties emerging in neurotic patients who apparently had no previous psychotic illness. He emphasized that "the transference psychosis should be differentiated from the psychotic transference in schizophrenic patients." Reider nevertheless seemed to be aware that some latent psychosis persisted in his patients, because the detailed scrutiny of these patients' pasts revealed brief childhood or adolescent psychotic episodes or identifications with a psychotic sibling. Following Reider, the term transference psychosis was used by Romm, Hammett, Holzman and Ekstein, Wallerstein, and eventually Kernberg to describe psychotic episodes lasting from a few hours to several months in patients suffering from a severe neurosis with regressive features or a borderline condition. In order to avoid confusion I shall use the term "transient psychosis" or "transference psychosis" to describe the sudden emergence of delusional misperceptions in the transference.

Diagnostic Criteria of Patients Liable to Form Delusional Transference Psychosis

In the first instance we have to inquire, as Reider and others have pointed out, whether the patient has suffered in childhood or later in his life from a psychotic episode or a severe infantile neurosis. In my experience, if the patient had psychotic disturbances in childhood or later, they appear invariably in the analysis, but they can often be worked through by the patient with the help of an analyst who is familiar with psychotic anxieties and mechanisms, without the eruption of an acute psychosis or transient psychosis. These patients often form some therapeutic alliance with the analyst, even with the psychotic part of their personality, while simultaneously retaining the therapeutic alliance with the nonpsychotic parts of themselves, diminishing the danger of delusional, transient psychotic episodes manifesting themselves in these patients.

Sudden delusional episodes or transient psychoses are, however, often encountered in the treatment of patients with *encapsulated or hidden psychotic states,* which erupt with great force and often temporarily overwhelm the patient's perceptive function, which creates delusional misperception of the analyst. Frequently the analyst is misperceived in the transference psychosis as an omnipotent, sadistic superego, but the erotic form of the transference psychosis in which the patient believes that the analyst is in love with him or her may also dominate the analytic situation for a time.

I have observed a woman patient who first formed a transference psychosis in which the male analyst was misperceived as an omnipotent, sadistic superego, which after some lapse of time changed into a delusional, erotic transference psychosis where the patient believed that the analyst was in love with her. The severely traumatized borderline patient is particularly liable to form a long-lasting transference psychosis, because the analysis destroys the very precarious defensive system of the patient, and exposes very primitive psychotic anxieties and guilt feelings, which remained unmodified through lack of the early holding environment combined with long-lasting separations from the parents.

Signs and Symptoms Indicating the Danger of a Threatening Transference Psychosis

It is of course important to examine whether there are any signs or symptoms which indicate the danger of a threatening transference psychosis. Unfortunately it is not possible to predict the occurrence of a transient psychosis with any certainty. One generally can diagnose a psychotic character (Frosch) and severe psychotic anxieties in neurotic or borderline patients. But many severely ill patients can work through their psychotic anxieties without the emergence of any "transference psychosis" which is characterized by the patient's loss of sense of reality leading to the delusional distortion of the image of the therapist.

I have, however, noticed in some patients that psychotic, extremely ego-alien dreams occurred more than two years before the eruption of a transference psychosis. The patients were generally unable to give any associations to these bizarre dreams. In one of the patients, after several bizarre dreams, an ego-alien but otherwise fairly harmless-looking dream eventually introduced the transference psychosis, in which the dream became complete reality in the session where it was reported.

In his summing up of the papers read at the Symposium on Severe Regressive States during Analysis, Frosch pointed out that many disruptive breaks (transient psychoses) were ushered in by dreams. For example, one analyst had reported that a severe, transient regressive state was triggered off by an overtly homosexual dream clearly related to the transference. The relationship of dreams to ongoing psychotic phenomena was also reported by some analysts. The dreams frequently revealed the patient's fear of disintegration.

I myself found that the patient's attitude to the dreams reported during the transference psychosis was particularly significant. For example, these patients often do not give any associations to their dreams but react to the analyst's tentative interpretation of a dream with violent hostility and feelings of persecution. In addition, such patients often use the dreams to justify their suspicion of the analyst, whose detrimental attitude they claim is illustrated in the dream. Some patients become very silent or hesitant before a transference psychosis. They seem unable to think and find it difficult to talk. This hesitation is occasionally related to overwhelming persecutory fears related to the analyst. But it also may indicate an accumulation of confused thoughts and ideas which the patients are afraid to allow to appear on the surface. Any pressure by the analyst to obtain more information during this period increases the danger of transference delusions being formed.

The Function of the Transference Psychosis

Whether the transference psychosis should be regarded as a setback or disruption of the analytic process or an ego-syntonic, necessary event is not always easy to decide. In some cases where the patient had a strong therapeutic alliance and felt well contained in the analytic situation, it seemed clear that the eruption of overwhelming psychotic anxiety in the transference situation was definitely progress, an attempt to bring into the analysis material which the patient had never been able to reveal. However, certain transference psychoses, which are expressions of strongly repressed, negative transferences denied for many years, have to begin with a definitely disruptive effect on the analysis, particularly when they last for many months and threaten to bring the analysis to an impasse. In these cases the patient stored up his criticism of the analyst, which then became confused with critical observations of past objects. The patient feels convinced of the correctness of his perception of the analyst who is accused of being constantly critical of the patient, and this delusional experience provokes in the patient violent critical attacks against the analyst. The patient feels fully justified in his attacks because he believes he is only defending his own self against the analyst's constant critical accusations. (Kernberg has made similar observations of some patients during their transference psychosis.)

Even in patients who form a severe transference psychosis it is essential to understand that the patient may find it necessary to express his intense positive and negative emotions in the form of a transference psychosis. The patient is particularly sensitive to the analyst's reaction during this period, and when he feels that the analyst can both cope with the situation without being over- whelmed by it and additionally can throw some light on the meaning of the patient's psychotic behavior, the transient psycho- sis can have a positive influence on the progress of the analysis.

Behavior of the Patient and Treatment During the Transference Psychosis

When a transference psychosis becomes manifest, the patient suddenly fails to cooperate in the analysis. He generally rejects all interpretations, or starts arguing about everything the analyst says, distorts the meaning of the interpretations, and very soon the distorted delusional image of the analyst is being described by the patient quite clearly. If the analyst tries to deal with the situation by more detailed or precise interpretation, the distor- tion generally gets worse. It is typical for most transient psychoses that the patient becomes very critical of the analyst, and often the transference distortion attaches itself to a slightly wrong inter- pretation or emphasis on the part of the analyst, which implies that the criticisms and accusations are related to some situations which the patient rightly or wrongly believes have been created by the analyst.

If the analyst becomes defensive and repeats what he has been interpreting before in an attempt to get through to the patient, the difficulty gets worse and the analysis may come to an impasse. It is generally very difficult to trace the origin of a transference psychosis which seems to come out of the blue, but if the analyst can trace this acute problem to a specific mistake on the part of the analyst or to some misunderstanding, he is in a much better position to understand and help the patient to clarify what is going on.

Often the analyst fails to remember clearly the issue which precipitated the situation. The patient himself may use this for increasing his attacks by insisting that the analyst should know exactly what has been going on, and the patient himself refuses to cooperate in clarifying the issue. I have often been consulted by colleagues for help in problems of this kind. The analyst is generally acutely distressed and feels paralyzed by the impenetrable wall which the patient's attitude creates. He also feels guilty, and this guilt is often stirred up and kept going by the patient's critical and sometimes belittling attacks.

Even if the impasse has been going on for several months it can often be cut short by a simple device. The analyst is encouraged to interpret only very little, and to listen very carefully to the patient's complaints which are often quite repetitive. It is particularly important to avoid interpretations of projection or projective identification in the transference, even if massive projective identification is evident in the patient's material. When the patient becomes provocative, it is essential for the analyst to avoid defensive behavior, because this is generally evidence for the patient of the analyst's weakness and inability to cope. When the patient realizes that the analyst is listening and trying to understand, it is generally not disturbing for the patient if the analyst asks for some simple clarification or elucidation of some points which have been made.

Occasionally the patient wants to sit up himself and talk to the analyst face to face. I would think that during an acute, long-lasting transference psychosis this is often even advisable. In some cases there is then distinct improvement of the acute condition after a few days, but occasionally it takes much longer.

Some Observations on the Psychopathology of the Transference Psychosis

It is important to remember that during the transference psychosis the patient is generally entirely preoccupied with the analyst whom he is watching all the time, but simultaneously the patient himself has almost completely lost his own capacity for self-observation, which is one of the reasons for his loss of insight. He is therefore unaware of his own projective processes, particularly the projection of unwanted parts of his self into the analyst.

Sometimes one can observe that the omnipotent part of the patient wants to see his own self and its relationship to objects in a way which satisfies both his ideal self, which is often grandiose, while he simultaneously demands from the analyst that he should be ideal in his capacity to understand. The omnipotent self of the patient insists, for example, that he has a right not to know, and so gets rid of any undesirable aspects of his self by projection into the analyst, and the projections of the patient are then delusionally perceived by the patient in the analyst. For this reason the patient expects that the analyst will retaliate and will misuse the analysis and his interpretations for projecting his own unwanted parts into the patient, a belief which is often quite openly expressed by the patient. This is one of the reasons why during the transference psychosis the interpretation of projective mechanisms increases the confusion and distortion of the image of the analyst.

So far I have only dealt very superficially with the issues which may cause the transference psychosis, and it is, of course, essential to trace and understand the deeper roots of the patient's behavior and thinking during the long-lasting forms of this problem. It has always been clear to me that problems relating to the development of the superego must play an important part in the development of these transient psychoses, and I believe I have found some answers to this problem.

Confusional states, in my experience, play an important part in the psychopathology of borderline patients and these confusions seem promoted by a primitive superego which itself has confusing and contradictory aspects. It is this superego which during the transference psychosis is projected into the analyst. So, when among other interpretations the analyst interprets destructive aspects of the patient which may clearly be shown in the patient's material, in dreams and in projections into other people, the patient is overwhelmed with anxiety, because he hears the analyst saying that he is one hundred percent bad, which threatens his whole self with death and disintegration or with madness as he will try to find omnipotent ways of escaping from this danger.

Since the patient in this state, as I described previously, is unable to think about his own problems and impulses, all his attention is focused on the analyst, who in the patient's perception sees him as extremely bad and destructive. To defend himself against this catastrophe, the patient becomes icily defensive. In addition he identifies himself with the primitive superego, and accuses the analyst in a very powerful manner. This problem seems to originate in the very early mother-infant relationship, is repeated in the transference and in the transference psychosis.

For example, the reason the analyst's interpretations have such a terrifying effect on the patient probably means that the analyst, like the mother in the past, has not been able to introject and contain the urgent needs of the patient to project this primitive, confused superego into him. The analyst is therefore perceived as rejecting the patient, and refusing to accept projections which for the patient is a vital necessity. In fact, the patient experiences the analyst as aggressively throwing his projections back at him. At that moment the process of projection gets out of hand, and the transference psychosis becomes manifest, with the patient misperceiving the analyst as his primitive, confusing, and sadistic superego. The patient then bombards the analyst violently with criticisms which seem to have the purpose of forcing the analyst to accept and introject the confused parts of the patient's self and superego which is a desperate attempt at reparation.

During this time the patient criticizes and accuses the analyst of not understanding what has been going on. Fundamentally, there are frequently some correct observations and criticisms of the analyst during the transference psychosis, because the analyst actually may not understand this basic problem, which is, of course, extremely important to take up and elaborate. This positive effort of the patient and the analyst to restore and re-create a functioning patient-analyst couple which represents a good mother-child union is interfered with by the patient, who still criticizes the analyst very violently even when he begins to understand, because through his identification with the confused, contradictory superego, the patient continues for some time to misperceive as criticism the analyst's positive and constructive understanding. Gradually balance and reparation can be achieved.

I believe that further progress in our understanding of the significance of the transference psychosis will depend on further detailed psychoanalytic investigation of patients who develop delusional transference episodes where the perception of the analyst is severely distorted for short or relatively longer periods.

Description of Clinical Case Material

I shall first report a transference psychosis which I would regard as a necessary and therapeutically important break-through of deeply repressed and split-off psychotic aspects of the patient's personality which erupted as a transference psychosis. Mrs. H. developed a transference psychosis lasting for about three to four days during the third year of her analysis. In this case the transference psychosis occurred at a time in the analysis when the patient felt more secure and understood. This apparently enabled her to bring some completely split-off or walled-off psychotic aspects of herself into the analysis.

She was one of those patients who had several psychotic, ego-alien dreams, followed by a short, transient psychotic episode. It erupted during and after a session where she reported a dream which became delusionally real in the transference situation. The patient never had a psychotic episode in childhood or later on, and there was also no history of a severe infantile neurosis. However, she had eczema and asthma in early and later childhood. The analysis revealed that there existed a split-off, psychotic part of the self which I recently described as a "psychotic island." This consisted of intense, aggressive, self-destructive, and deadly impulses combined with persecutory and damaged internal object relations.

The patient came into analysis because she was deeply depressed after several miscarriages. In addition, she had recently given birth to a premature baby who died after a short time. The analysis revealed intense feelings of disappointment with her parents at the height of the oedipus complex when a brother was born. She experienced during the early part of her analysis the violent rage that she had not been given by her father the baby she had intensely longed for. After this experience had been worked through in the analysis she felt much better and more hopeful, but she then found that she had developed a new symptom: the inability to conceive. Gynecological examination revealed atrophy of the uterine mucosa. Hormonal treatment was started, but there was no improvement for more than a year.

The patient was intelligent and very active. She also was very cooperative in the treatment, never late and only when she had an extremely ego-alien dream did she fail to give dream associations.

In one of those dreams, very early in the analysis, she observed a man who was swimming in a lake, fully dressed, with a bottle in his hand. Suddenly he started to drink from the bottle and she became aware that he wanted to drown himself. She shouted to him that she was going to help him, but he just looked triumphantly at her and continued drinking, and then he sank under the water. She tried to reach the rescue service through a telephone nearby, but she found that all the telephone wires had been cut. In spite of all the difficulties she managed to rescue him. There were no associations to the dream, and I had difficulty in accepting that this exceedingly lively and generally very positive patient could have dreams which were so powerfully self-destructive.

A second dream, which appeared about a year afterwards, had certain similarities with the dream of the drowning man, but was more focused and more clearly related to her uterus and to the fears that she could not have a baby. In the dream there was a baby who was born so ill that he could not be cared for properly and did not develop normally, so that he eventually had to be sent to a mental hospital in her home country where he received electric shock treatment. In the dream the reason given for the baby's illness was his having bent his legs in the womb. Again she had no associations in spite of the obvious implications that she had deflected her fear of having an incurable depressive illness onto the baby she might conceive. So her fear of a psychotic illness was more localized in the uterus like the baby who by bending his legs seemed to refuse to be born.

About a year later the patient reported a dream that she was staying in bed in the morning and her mother-in-law had to do all the housework. The patient felt guilty about being in bed so long. So she got up at about noon and attempted to assist her mother-in-law. Her mother-in-law, however, informed her angrily that she was tired and was going away for a holiday. Again there were no associations to this dream, and in addition she remained completely silent throughout the session, which she had never done before. I realized that the dream brought an important factor into the analysis, a factor which had been almost entirely absent so far, namely a rebellious, provocative attitude directed against the mother-in-law standing for the analyst. When the patient continued to be silent I realized that the silence was a clue to the meaning of the dream. I said to the patient that she had never behaved in the analysis as she did in the dream, and the only way we could relate the feelings of the dream to the analysis was her persistent silence in the session today where she behaved completely differently from other days by being uncooperative as she was in the dream with her mother-in-law. I also said that she apparently was afraid that at the moment when she showed any sign of not being a good patient I would get very angry and would threaten to leave her. I almost had to force myself to make my interpretation because, again, the dream had a strong ego-alien feeling. I also thought that the dream had a deeper meaning, and I related the dream to her fear of my not being able to cope with her and help her, and suggested that she had identified her uterus with the tired mother who could not hold her baby.

In the next session the patient was a few minutes late and said she had only come by chance because she had decided that she would not come. I had behaved in the last session in an incredibly clumsy way and she found this extremely infuriating. How could I as an experienced analyst so completely lose my temper with her. She did not sound anxious but extremely cold and furious. She obviously completely believed her perception, but would not elaborate on what had happened in the last session any further, and I realized that the dream about the tired, enraged mother-in-law had become completely real to her and had created a transference psychosis.

I knew from previous experience that the very worst thing I

could say was that she had projected her angry feelings into me, so that I seemed the person who was violently angry with her; this would have made her still more angry. In actual fact I pointed out to her that I was not aware of any of the feelings which she had perceived in me, but at that moment she was obviously convinced that she was right and that I was wrong. I added that it might take some time to sort out what had actually happened in this session. She agreed with this, but the anger and suspicion continued for three to four days. After that she sounded less hostile and admitted that she had probably made a mistake, but it was only after more than six months that she added some factors which made this dream more understandable.

In the dream the bedclothes were rather strongly tightened round her so that she actually felt tied into her bed as if the bed represented the womb. She also explained that she felt rather withdrawn on that day and had not wanted to talk, and she also had not wanted me to disturb her. So in the session where she had presented the dream, my talking was strongly resented because she experienced me as intruding into her withdrawn state. Both the dream and my interpretation had apparently helped to bring the withdrawn, split-off psychotic state right to the surface. Retrospectively it seemed to me that in the dream of the tired mother-in-law, the problem of the patient's own mother's incapacity to contain her was of central importance. The transference psychosis showed that she was helped to admit her intense rage and resentment against me relating to her parents, because she had always felt that she had had to please them, and had been afraid of the violent rage of her mother if she, the patient, expected to be looked after and contained by her when the mother felt unable to do so. I also thought that there were anxieties in her from a deeper source which were overwhelming, because tied up in the womb she kept her intensely destructive feelings which nobody could cope with and therefore she had to keep them locked up. With my "clumsy" interpretation about the womb I had intruded into this dangerous area. She feared that I would open up this area, and she was sure I could not cope with this because her feelings were too deadly and terrible. After the transference psychosis it became clear that her expression of intense fury and resentment had relieved her, she felt less blocked and was able to talk more freely and express some angry feelings.

Several months later she told me a dream which had been rather disturbing to her. In the dream there was a carpet which had a very thick pile and a horrid creature was embedded in it. It was so horrid that she did not dare look at it, but she knew it had a kind of greenish, deathly look. Again she could not say very much about this dream, but I felt that she was informing me that her uterus had recovered, that she was ready to have a baby, and, in fact, a pregnancy test arranged after a few weeks revealed that she was pregnant. This time she succeeded in giving birth to a healthy child.

For more than three years after the transference psychosis the patient acted out and expressed her deadly, negative behavior in the analysis. Only once again was there the danger that she could develop another transference psychosis, when she tried to provoke me to make interpretations about projecting negative, destructive, and self-destructive attitudes which she was constantly observing in other people. But soon she decided to cooperate and face up to the feelings which she wanted to deny.

It is interesting that the appearance of the transference psychosis had a distinct therapeutic effect, namely, the release of the psychotic island from its walled-in position in the uterus. It was clear to me that the patient had all her life succeeded in hiding her strongly destructive and self-destructive feelings, and they had probably never been conscious as part of her anger during the oedipal period. So we may have to assume that the transference psychosis revealed very walled-off feelings which the patient had resolved never to let out. The task of the analysis after the transference psychosis was to help the patient to integrate the feelings which had never been accepted by her or her parents. This implies that the psychoanalytic working through of the transference psychosis in the analysis is a vital process necessary for the therapeutic success of the analysis.

Significance of Long-lasting Transference Psychotic States

Any long-lasting transference psychosis is a severe threat to the analysis, disrupts the therapeutic alliance, and may lead to a complete impasse in the analysis. However we have here again to examine carefully to what extent mistakes of the analyst in understanding the patient contribute to the transference psychosis, and how much of the transient psychosis is created by early psychotic anxieties appearing in the analysis. We have to ask ourselves whether the long-lasting or severe transference psychosis in borderline states is inevitable, and whether the analytic approach to this problem contributes to a better understanding and to the therapeutic success in these patients. I believe that the analyst's misunderstanding of the patient can contribute a great deal to increasing the severity of the transference psychosis. Better understanding of the problems appearing during the acute flare-up certainly diminishes the danger of an impasse.

I also found that it is particularly important to realize that there are some strongly positive factors related to the transference psychosis which may easily be misinterpreted by the analyst, because these positive, reparative factors appear occasionally so violently in the analysis that it is difficult to recognize them as a desperate attempt at reparation, for example, to force the analyst to take notice of something which he had missed. I think that the technique of deflecting the negative transference in the transference psychosis to objects in the outside world is a desperate attempt of the analyst to save the treatment, but it prevents a better analytical understanding of the problem which seems to me essential.

Case Material Illustrating the Development and Treatment of a Long-lasting Transference Psychosis in a Traumatized Borderline Patient

The severe anxieties of traumatized borderline patients and the defenses against them are generally repeated in the transference situation, but this alone does not necessarily produce a transference psychosis. The traumatized patient is so sensitive that he is very easily disturbed by some slight interference in the analytic situation. So we often find that some slight mistake, or some collusion of patient and analyst combined with a slightly critical attitude of the analyst, may become superimposed on the transference situation. The analyst's remarks then become vastly exaggerated and distorted, and suddenly a distorted image of the analyst becomes completely real to the patient. The most common distortion is the delusional perception of the analyst as a very omnipotent, sadistic superego figure.

I shall now describe the development of a transference psychosis in a severely traumatized borderline patient. The patient's relationship with his mother was disturbed probably from the very beginning of life. There were early feeding difficulties, because the mother had been advised to breastfeed the child only for five minutes at a time. So the baby sucked greedily and held on to the nipple which soon became sore. This complicated the feeding situation which became still more painful for both mother and child. There were also periods of several weeks when the baby cried most of the time until the father found out that the baby was undernourished. As soon as the additional feeding was introduced the crying stopped. The mother was a very anxious and tense person, and she never seemed to be comfortable and confident about looking after her child.

In the analysis I became certain that the child never had a satisfactory holding relationship with the mother, because this problem became the most central preoccupation of the patient during the analysis. In addition there were many long-lasting separations from the mother, as the child was sent to a boarding school early in his life. The patient was very intelligent and was held in high regard for his achievements by his colleagues and teachers, but when he started analysis with me he immediately regressed and projected overwhelming anxieties into me. For example, he had great difficulty in talking clearly to me, but expected me to understand exactly what was going on in him and what he was feeling. There were many contradictory emotions which were difficult to disentangle.

He seemed to have intense idealization of me related to his expectancy that I would quickly lift the burden of his overwhelming anxiety, but this soon met with disappointment. He deeply resented that I expected him to talk and did not treat him from the first session as a newborn baby who would be completely safe and cared for in his mother's arms. This fantasy was only revealed to me in words many years later when we were working through the violent criticisms which had appeared in the transference psychosis. For a reason which I will discuss later, the nonverbal projections of that patient were sometimes misunderstood by me. One of the reasons for this problem was apparently related to the patient's intense projection of his mother's anxieties and guilt feelings into me. After two and a half years of analysis, the patient who had been outwardly very friendly became increasingly hostile and critical. He attacked not only what I had said in the past particularly during the first week of treatment, but he criticized my tone of voice and my bodily movements which seemed to give him more information about myself than my words. He said I often raised my voice which terrified him, and this disturbed him to such an extent that he could not think. Many of my remarks were remembered and quoted back to me out of context, and they always sounded to me extremely critical. I felt that he experienced my words as a statement that he was bad and unacceptable and nothing could be done for him.

During this period of the analysis the patient's criticisms and accusations gradually became more violent, and while he accused me of being critical of him as soon as I opened my mouth, he himself was so violently and repetitively critical that I felt in the countertransference situation like a small child battered into helpless rage and despair by his relentless accusations. After struggling for several months we reached an impasse in the analysis where he decided to end the analysis in a fortnight's time. I then asked the patient to sit up and encouraged him to go over all the criticisms and grudges which he had stored up against me. He was still critical and sullen, but he explained to me in greater detail many of the problems which we had been experiencing during the analysis. During these exploratory discussions I did not give any interpretations and adopted an entirely receptive and passive listening attitude to him. I also examined as much as possible my countertransference, as he constantly complained of tension in me which disturbed him. I noted that I was not so much disturbed by my failure, but I felt guilty and sorry for the patient who had not been able to receive from me what he had expected. I felt that parting would be painful, but on the last day before he was due to leave he told me that he would stay in treatment, and a very pleasant warm smile changed his sullen face completely.

It seemed to me from this experience that the patient had not only projected his own feelings and impulses but also the perception of his internal image of his mother who could not contain him into me, and it is this which changed me into a severe superego. The patient constantly complained and criticized me for not responding to him in the way he wanted to be understood, and again and again he made clear that he wanted me to become the empathetic, holding mother instead of the rejecting, critical one, and I had no doubt that he was convinced that I was like his mother but not identical with her. It seemed clear to me that the transference psychosis of this patient was primarily caused by his severe, primitive superego, and the analysis of this patient gave me the opportunity to examine the origins of this primitive superego in some detail, as from time to time he became paralyzed by his guilt feelings.

For two years after the first transference psychosis the patient cooperated very well. He seemed to be stronger and felt more comfortable in the analysis. He had been living in very restricted circumstances, and decided to expand his life by having better living conditions. But now he became increasingly anxious and felt attacked by severe guilt feelings which confused him and prevented him from making any decisions, because he criticized and questioned any decision he tried to make. He then had a series of dreams which he felt were a cry for help, and then felt again severely let down by me and was convinced that I had failed him again.

In one of the dreams there were four bandits who had been caught. The patient himself spat at them; they tried to defend themselves by saying that they did not deny that they had killed, but they had been forced to kill because they had been starving. When I questioned the patient about the bandits and his spitting at them, he said that he only spat at them because I hated the bandits. He stressed they were not as bad as I believed them to be, and he could not bear my violent attacks when I saw him only as a bandit and not as an angry crying baby who was trying to get help and was screaming in helpless rage. He felt my speaking at all simply as severe criticism, and he complained that he could not stand it; it killed him.

He said later that in all these dreams there was a positive factor which I had missed. This created a terrible feeling in his head, so that he could not think and he felt himself getting into a violent, disturbing rage in which he forcibly wanted to change my mind. However, his criticism of me was only partially justified. For example, in one dream he was a member of a bicycle racing team and he needed the support of the leader of the racing team to go ahead, but he feared that the other members of the team were envious of him and would not support him. The dream is very clear indeed. Outwardly it looked as if there was a problem of envy and jealousy involved. I thought that his desire to go ahead, which had recently been so undermined by his overwhelming guilt feelings, could be admitted in the dream, but I noticed that he had avoided giving name to his desire to go ahead. I felt I had to take the risk of another violent attack by naming this impulse. I pointed out to him that he seemed afraid to appear ambitious by admitting in the dream that he was part of a racing team which was obviously competing with other teams. He felt immediately violently criticized by me, as though he experienced me as trying to stop him from making any progress. As the patient had been feeling paralyzed in making any move ahead, my interpretation had been a positive attempt on my part to help him to recognize his wish to go ahead in life. He again insisted that I missed all the positive factors in this dream which he had asserted before.

When the patient is under the domination of the primitive, confusing, contradictory superego which is generally rapidly reprojected into the analyst, the patient is unable to recognize any interpretation or acknowledgement by the analyst of any positive aspects in the patient's own personality. In other words, the confusing superego seems to have the power to turn good impulses or feelings in the patient into bad ones. This situation makes any attempt at experiencing and using positive feelings quite impossible. When I began to understand the confusional element in the patient's material better, I became more able to analyze the confusional state which was related to the confusing and contradictory superego. I restricted my interpretations mainly to pointing out contradictions and confusions in the patient's material, and this gradually diminished the patient's delusional conviction that I was always insisting that I was a hundred percent right and he was a hundred percent wrong.

In my paper "Notes on the Psychopathology and Psycho-Analytic Treatment of Some Borderline Patients" (1978) I described in some detail the importance of confusional states for the understanding of the psychopathology of borderline patients, including their primitive superego. Even after the transference psychosis of this traumatized borderline patient had improved and he had become more cooperative, his intense feelings of persecutory guilt seemed to prevent him from making contact with people. He tended to withdraw into isolation and toward inanimate objects, the rocks which in his childhood had played an important role in his attempts to escape from the vulnerability of his mother which had been too painful for him to bear. I gradually found out that the patient had from very early on in his life a capacity for very detailed empathy and observation of his mother which was sometimes reenacted with me. He seemed to have an intense desire to repair and help his anxious mother who seemed frightened and defensive, and he wanted to be close to her.

When I succeeded in showing the patient that I understood his concern about me and his wish to help me and to be close to me, and we were able to understand that when his positive, reparative feelings were not recognized by me, he quickly attacked and evacuated them and this created intense feelings of emptiness, incapacity to think, and giddiness. In addition, his positive feelings were replaced by an overwhelming sense of guilt. When the patient realized that I understood this problem a very marked change took place in him. His feelings of guilt diminished, and he became more able to express his creative thoughts and feelings as he felt I better understood and accepted him.

Conclusions

In my research into the origin of the primitive superego of some very gifted borderline patients, I often found that the mother had difficulties in perceiving and responding to the primitive communications of the infant, which are conveyed by projective identification (Bion 1959). The inability of the mother to respond to the infant's projections is not only experienced by the infant as rejection, but creates some intense, primitive guilt because the child needs some space in the mother's mind to feel fully recognized by her and to experience interest in life. The sensitive, perceptive infant tends to feel responsible for creating a burden for the mother who cannot provide what is needed by the child. Under these circumstances, the early perceptive capacities of the infant related to some primitive feelings of concern are in danger of being destroyed and evacuated. This situation increases the infant's helpless rage instead of providing a possibility for the development of the primitive feelings of concern and reparation based on the experience of the mother's intuitive feelings.

Aggressive feelings tend to fill the empty space in the infant's mind, creating confusion of love and hate. It is the lack of response, the lack of space in the mother's mind which seem to create the primitive guilt and the early feelings of confusion which are reinforced by later experiences.

I believe that the better understanding of the confusing, primitive superego conflicts of the borderline patient will help the analyst to gradually analyze more successfully the severe transference psychosis in the borderline patient which is so often the cause of a long-lasting impasse or breaking off the analysis. The chance of the appearance of a transference psychosis is, of course, very much increased by lack of understanding or insensitivity of the analyst, who repeats the early misunderstanding of the infant-mother relationship. Many transference psychoses can probably be avoided by careful, sensitive understanding by the analyst. I believe, however, that the knowledge of the primitive, confusing superego which is bound to create misunderstanding between analyst and patient is necessary for working through the severe transference psychosis in analysis.

References

Bion, W.R. (1959). Attacks on linking. In *Second Thoughts*. New York: Jason Aronson, 1967.

Frosch, J. (1967). Introduction and summary of the symposium on severe regressive states during analysis. *Journal of the American Psychoanalytic Association* 15:491–507, 606–625.

——— (1970). Psychoanalytic consideration of the psychotic character. *Journal of the American Psychoanalytic Association* 18:24–50.

Kernberg, O. (1968). The treatment of patients with borderline personality organization. *International Journal of Psycho-Analysis* 49:600–619.

——— (1976). Technical consideration in the treatment of borderline organization. *Journal of the American Psychoanalytic Association* 24:795–829. This volume, chapter 7.

Hammett, V.P.O. (1961). Delusional transference. *American Journal of Psychotherapy* 15:574–581.

Holzman, P.S. and Ekstein, R. (1959). Repetition functions of transitory regressive thinking. *Psychoanalytic Quarterly* 28:228–235

Reider, N. (1957). Transference psychosis. *Journal of the Hillside Hospital.* 6:131–149.

Romm, M. (1957). Transient psychotic episodes during psychoanalysis. *Journal of the American Psychoanalytic Association* 5:325–341.
Rosenfeld, H. (1954). Considerations regarding the
psychoanalytic approach to acute and chronic schizophrenia. *International Journal of Psycho-Analysis*
35:135–140.
——— (1978). Notes on the psychopathology and psychoanalytic
treatment of some borderline patients. *International Journal
of Psycho-Analysis* 59:215–221.
Wallerstein, R. (1967). Reconstruction and mastery in the transference psychosis. Paper in the Symposium on Severe Regressive States during Analysis. *Journal of the American
Psychoanalytic Association* 15:551–583.

Contributors

GERALD ADLER, M.D. is Professor of Psychiatry and Director of Training in Adult Psychiatry at Tufts University School of Medicine in Boston. He is a faculty member of the Boston Psychoanalytic Society and Institute, and conducts a private practice in psychoanalysis.

Dr. Adler is coeditor of *Confrontation in Psychotherapy* and has published many papers on psychotherapy and the inpatient treatment of borderline patients.

DAN H. BUIE, JR., M.D. is Associate Professor of Psychiatry at Tufts University School of Medicine and a member of the Boston Psychoanalytic Institute.

ATTILIO CAPPONI, PH.D., received his analytic training at the Advanced Institute for Analytic Psychotherapy where he is now a Supervisor and member of the faculty and is also an Associate in Psychology at the Adelphi University Institute of Advanced Psychological Studies in Garden City.

Dr. Capponi is engaged in private practice in the borough of Queens, New York.

PETER L. GIOVACCHINI, M.D. is Clinical Professor of Psychiatry at the University of Illinois College of Medicine.

He is the author of *Psychoanalysis of Character Disorders* and of *Psychoanalysis of Primitive Mental States,* coauthor of *Psychoanalytic Treatment of Schizophrenic and Characterological Disorders,* editor of *Tactics and Techniques of Psychoanalytic Treatment,* and coeditor of *Adolescent Psychiatry,* Annals of the American Society of Adolescent Psychiatry.

Dr. Giovacchini is a member of the Chicago Institute for Psychoanalysis and the American Psychoanalytic Association, and is in private psychoanalytic practice in Chicago.

JAMES S. GROTSTEIN, M.D. is Director of the Interdisciplinary Center for Advanced Studies in Schizophrenia, Borderline and Narcissistic Conditions and is a Training Analyst at the Los Angeles Psychoanalytic Institute.

He is the author of *Splitting and Projective Identification* (in press), of *Freud and Klein: Divergencies Within a Continuum* (in press), and of a number of articles on the psychoanalytic treatment of schizophrenia and borderline disorders.

Dr. Grotstein is engaged in the practice of psychoanalysis in Los Angeles.

OTTO KERNBERG, M.D. is currently Medical Director of New York Hospital–Cornell Medical Center, Westchester Division, and is Professor of Psychiatry at Cornell University Medical College. Dr. Kernberg has been Director of the General Clinical Service of the New York State Psychiatric Institute, and Professor of Clinical Psychiatry at the College of Physicians and Surgeons of Columbia University. He served as Director of the C. F. Menninger Memorial Hospital in Topeka, Kansas.

Dr. Kernberg is Training and Supervising Analyst at the Columbia University Center for Psychoanalytic Training and Research.

He is the author of *Borderline Conditions and Pathological Narcissism, Object Relations Theory and Clinical Psychoanalysis,* and of numerous papers on the borderline condition.

Dr. Kernberg is engaged in the practice of psychoanalysis in the New York area.

JOSEPH LEBOIT is Dean of Training at the Advanced Institute of Analytic Psychotherapy, and has been Director of the Advanced Center for Psychotherapy for over twenty years.

He is editor of *Treatment Monographs in Analytic Psychotherapy* and the author of a number of papers on psychoanalytic psychotherapy.

Joseph LeBoit is a certified psychologist in New York State, and is engaged in private practice in Long Island.

J. H. REY, M.D., after several years at Maudsley Hospital, qualified in psychiatry and became senior lecturer in psychophysical relationships in the Institute of Psychiatry in London. He was engaged in research on the biochemistry, endocrinology, and neurophysiology of mental illness, with special interest in longitudinal studies of recurrent syndromes.

Dr. Rey was senior member of the Psychotherapy Department at Maudsley Hospital.

Because of his long attachment to a mental hospital, he became interested in the psychoanalysis of psychoses and borderline cases. He has had a lifelong interest in the psychology of Jean Piaget and in the relation of psycholinguistics to psychoanalysis. He is the author of a number of psychoanalytic papers and has lectured in various countries.

Dr. Rey is a member of the British Psycho-Analytical Society and is now engaged in private practice in Paris.

HERBERT ROSENFELD, M.D. settled in England after emigrating from Germany. He worked at Maudsley and Littlemore Hospitals and trained in psychotherapy at the Tavistock Clinic.

Since 1936 he has concentrated his efforts on the psychoanalytic approach to psychotic patients. He is an exponent of Melanie Klein's work and its applicability to his own analysis of transference in the treatment of schizophrenic patients.

Dr. Rosenfeld is the author of *Psychotic States: A Psychoanalytic Approach* and of numerous papers on schizophrenia and the borderline condition. He is member of the British Psycho-Analytical Society, practices psychoanalysis in London, and is engaged in teaching, in training analysts, and supervising a number of analysts from other countries.

HAROLD F. SEARLES, M.D. worked at Chestnut Lodge Sanitarium in Rockville, Maryland, for fifteen years, and during the last of those years was Senior Psychiatrist there. He is a Clinical Professor of Psychiatry on the visiting faculty of Georgetown University School of Medicine in Washington, D.C., and a Consultant in Psychiatry at the National Institute of Mental Health. He is Supervising and Training Analyst at the Washington Psychoanalytic Institute and has been President of the Washington Psychoanalytic Society of which he is a member.

Dr. Searles is author of the *Nonhuman Environment in Normal Development and in Schizophrenia, Collected Papers on Schizophrenia and Related Subjects,* and *Countertransference and Related Subjects* (in press), and of numerous papers on schizophrenia and the borderline condition.

Dr. Searles is in full-time private practice of psychoanalysis and psychotherapy in Washington, D.C.

HYMAN SPOTNITZ, M.D. is Honorary President of the Manhattan Center for Advanced Psychoanalytic Studies, the Philadelphia

School of Psychoanalysis, and the Center for Modern Psycho-analytic Studies in Boston.

Dr. Spotnitz is the author of *Modern Psychoanalysis of the Schizophrenic Patient, The Couch and the Circle, Psychotherapy of Preoedipal Conditions,* and coauthor of *Treatment of the Narcissistic Neuroses.* He has written extensively on analytic psychotherapy in the severe psychiatric disorders and on neu-rophysiology.

Dr. Spotnitz is engaged in the private practice of psychoanaly-tic psychiatry (individual and group) in New York City.

VAMIK D. VOLKAN, M.D., after graduating from the University of Ankara (Turkey) School of Medicine, received his psychoanaly-tic training at the Washington Psychoanalytic Institute where he is now on the faculty. Dr. Volkan is Professor and Acting Chairman of the Department of Psychiatry, School of Medicine of the University of Virginia in Charlottesville.

He is the author of *Primitive Internalized Object Relations: A Clinical Study of Schizophrenic, Borderline and Narcissistic Patients,* and of *Cyprus, War and Adaptation: A Psychoanalytic History of Two Ethnic Groups in Conflict,* and has published extensively in psychiatric and psychoanalytic journals.

Dr. Volkan is a founding member and present secretary of the Virginia Psychoanalytic Society and is engaged in private prac-tice of psychoanalysis in Charlottesville, Virginia.

Index